THE

DOROTHY DUNNETT

COMPANION

THE
DOROTHY DUNNETT
COMPANION

ELSPETH MORRISON

FOREWORD BY DOROTHY DUNNETT

VINTAGE BOOKS

A DIVISION OF RANDOM HOUSE, INC.

NEW YORK

FIRST VINTAGE BOOKS EDITION, JULY 2001

Library of Congress Cataloging-in-Publication Data
Morrison, Elspeth.
The Dorothy Dunnett companion/Elspeth Morrison;
foreword by Dorothy Dunnett.
p. cm.
Originally published: London: Michael Joseph, 1994.
ISBN 0-375-72587-3
1. Dunnett, Dorothy—Dictionaries.   2. Vander Poele, Nicholas (Fictitious character)—
Dictionaries.   3. Crawford, Francis (Fictitious character)—Dictionaries.
4. Civilization, Medieval, in literature—Dictionaries.
5. Soldiers of fortune in literature—Dictionaries.
6. Historical fiction, Scottish—Dictionaries.
7. Adventure stories, Scottish—Dictionaries.
8. Renaissance in literature—Dictionaries.
9. Businessmen in literature—Dictionaries.
10. Scots in literature—Dictionaries.   I. Title.
PR6054.U56 Z78 2001
823'.914—dc21
00-067407

Maps and Illustrations by Peter McClure

www.vintagebooks.com

Printed in the United States of America
10 9 8 7 6 5 4 3

For Jessie

Scire tuum nihil est,

nisi te scire hoc,

sciat alter

Contents

FOREWORD

SOMETHING personal first. The initial notes for this multi-volumed story about two men—Lymond and Niccolò—were taken in 1956 in the Mitchell Library, Glasgow. The rest of the research for the first novel took place in the Central Library in Edinburgh, and the manuscript went off to its publisher in 1960, just after the birth of the first of my two sons.

He is now thirty-four. Since then, I have become a habituée of the National Library of Scotland and of the London Library and the British Library in London. I have trawled other libraries and museums and galleries and bookshops all over the world for the material I use in these books, and slowly have learned that I should be taking note, for future reference, of the sources I use.

This was not at all the case with the Lymond novels, and I can't say that I am being much more dutiful with the Niccolò series. Racing the clock, in the thick of invention, one seizes what comes to hand without taking time to clip its ear and paste its pedigree into a ledger. The sources for the people, the places, the history in the earlier books are therefore largely absent among my own papers. Worse, so are the sources for the quotations.

It was my intention, in creating Francis Crawford of Lymond, and later Nicholas, to present the kind of man who remembers everything he has ever read. Lymond uses his learning as a weapon, and also as a defence. Nicholas begins by concealing what he knows but he lives in the same literate, articulate world, a hundred years earlier. The novels are full of allusions—to classical and Renaissance prose writing, to poetry, to songs, to liturgy, to folk verse and ballads and plays, to proverbs and jokes, some of them not entirely delicate. They appear in a number of languages. They were and are the plums in the pudding.

I didn't note where I got them. Only when the first twelve, the first fifty, the first hundred readers' letters began to arrive asking for the source, the second verse, the translation, did I realise what a hole I was in. I have stayed in a hole for thirty-four years.

Until now. For this book, Elspeth Morrison has had to recreate the skills of one of our more illustrious Edinburgh shades, and turn detective. In doing so, she has laid open my own thinking of thirty years ago, recovering for me forgotten nuances and deep-laid plans and designs. Quoted by Lymond or Nicholas, the first line of a poem may seem to fit the situation very well; but it is often the rest of the poem, unspoken, which tells the truth, and gives meaning to the fragments of dialogue fitted round it. Elspeth has resurrected the complete songs, the complete poems, the unexpurgated allusions. So I have been allowed, in an unforeseen way, to view my work again in the light of the hidden agenda which I did not even realise I had lost.

A different pleasure, for me, has been the ability of this book to show how the doings of Lymond and Nicholas have been dovetailed into the calendar of real events. It is a fact well known to any historical novelist, and salutary for their spiritual well-being, that readers assume that all the best bits are invented. Elspeth's biographies show what the authentic historical personages were actually up to in France and England, Malta and Russia, Turkey and Cyprus, Scotland and Venice, Cairo and Florence and Timbuktu during the span of the novels, and give an idea of how many of the dramas were in fact real. In many cases, where she has found them, she has put my own original sources, rather than later or more standard works, so that the basis for my history can be recognised. Sometimes no source can be given because the material derives from my own research and has not been published in this form before. She has also selflessly omitted facts and dates which may foreshadow that part of the story still to come, and diminish its impact.

No one knew, when this started, what sort of handbook this was going to be. The idea came from the publisher, Michael Joseph, where Susan Watt, a dear friend of old, has long warded over the adventures of Nicholas and where Richenda Todd has tended his every word for many years. This was to be a companion to the novels as they have been written so far, but it was to be Elspeth's concoction: a cornucopia of things informative, funny and beautiful which derived from the books, but which would also expand and enhance them. We talked about it a lot, in London and here in Edinburgh, curled up in armchairs with the wine of the country in our glasses, and papers covered with poetry littering the floor. We laughed a great deal, and became extremely excited on occasion when a new discovery threw fresh light on a phrase or a passage. One of the more obscure Chaucerian quotes emerged intact fom the prodigious memory of my husband Alastair, who is, of course, the original Lymond. But the book, from beginning to end, represents Elspeth's choice and Elspeth's taste and Elspeth's hard work, and no one could have done it better. I hope it will give to others as much positive pleasure as it has brought me, both during its making and from reading the finished work.

And I shall try to note down my sources in future.

Dorothy Dunnett
Edinburgh, June 1994

AUTHOR'S NOTE

The Dorothy Dunnett Companion is a comprehensive guide to the characters, references, allusions and quotations in the *Lymond Chronicles* and the *House of Niccolò* series (volumes 1 to 5). Whenever possible, the original sources have been quoted, and are referenced with suggestions for further reading at the end of each entry, along with dates of publication where available.

For ease of reference, all entries are listed alphabetically. Quotations are generally listed under the first word of the quotation that appears in the text, even if it is an indefinite or definite article: e.g. **an angry piece of flesh and soon displeased** or *Le temps a laissé son manteau*. Those that are not obviously quotations are listed under a key word and cross-referenced. Again to ensure that the entries can be readily found, quotations are given exactly as they appear in the original text, even when that text is corrupted. The names of historical characters who appear within the text of the novels are capitalised to differentiate them from real persons who are only alluded to: e.g. **ADORNE, Anselm** appears in the novels, but **Avicenna** is only referred to. Titled characters are listed under the name they are usually referred to in the books, but are also cross referenced: e.g. **GREY of Wilton**. Rulers and monarchs are mostly to be found under their first name, rather than that of their dynastic house or family title: e.g. **HENRI II**. Characters such as the **DE GUISES** are listed under the name rather than the preposition.

Following the title of each entry comes the novel in which it is located. Because there have been numerous editions of the novels (particularly the *Lymond Chronicles*) over the years, I elected not to give a specific page reference for each, but instead the abbreviated title of the novel (for the list of abbreviations see page xiii), followed by the section of the book (where appropriate) in Roman numerals, and then the chapter number in Arabic numerals: e.g. **O row my lady in satin and silk**: KINGS, III, 3. This quote can be found in *The Game of Kings*, Part III: 'The Play for Samuel Harvey', Chapter 3: 'Mate for the Master'. Subdivisions within chapters are not given. Where the subject of an entry appears many times, as is the case with the historical characters, then the book reference only is given. Characters who feature in more than one book are referred to under the first in which they make their appearance. Cross references within the entries are emboldened.

Full versions and translations of many of the poems within the novels have also been included, in most cases retaining the original spelling. When it came to the translation of foreign words and phrases, the criterion for inclusion was straightforward: those whose meaning is clear from the context have been omitted. Those in languages which may be unfamiliar to the reader or which shed additional light on the depth and meaning of the passage have been included. The same can be said for the classical and mythological allusions, some of which are more obscure than others.

The brevity of some of the entries (particularly with reference to the *Niccolò* series) is deliberate. They do not go beyond the timescale of the novels already in print, nor do they give information which might appear in future books.

ACKNOWLEDGEMENTS

THANKS to Mum and Dad, Lynn, Helen and David, Richenda, Dorothy and particularly Dr John Stephens, whose help and encouragement over the last twelve months has been inestimable.

ELSPETH MORRISON
Edinburgh, July 1994

Abbreviations

b. born

d. died

c. circa

fl. *floruit,* flourished

The novels of Dorothy Dunnett are abbreviated thus in the A–Z. For publication dates see page 416.

CASTLE   *The Ringed Castle*

CHECKMATE   *Checkmate*

KINGS   *The Game of Kings*

KNIGHTS   *The Disorderly Knights*

PAWN   *Pawn in Frankincense*

QUEENS   *Queens' Play*

RAM   *The Spring of the Ram*

RISING   *Niccolò Rising*

SCALES   *Scales of Gold*

SCORPIONS   *Race of Scorpions*

UNICORN   *The Unicorn Hunt*

THE
DOROTHY DUNNETT
COMPANION

A fin, fin et demi: CHECKMATE, III, 4: 'Finish the job to the end and beyond'.

A fool though he live in the company of the wise, understands nothing of the true doctrine: QUEENS, I, 6: Proverb taken from the Buddhist scripture, the Dhammapada. (Samuel Beal, *Texts from the Buddhist Canon, The Dhammapada*, London, 1902.)

A garden enclosed is my sister, my spouse: UNICORN, 16: From the biblical Song of Solomon, 4, 12 15:

> A garden inclosed is my sister, my spouse; a spring shut up, a fountain sealed. Thy plants are an orchard of pomegranates, with pleasant fruits; camphire, with spikenard, Spikenard and saffron; calamus and cinnamon, with all trees of frankincense; myrrh and aloes, with all the chief spices: A fountain of gardens, a well of living waters, and streams from Lebanon.

A grey eye looks back towards Erin: QUEENS, III, 1: Traditional Irish song from St Columkille's Remembrance of Erin, lamenting his exile in Iona, with 'a grey eye full of tears'. (P.W. Joyce, *Social History of Ancient Ireland*.)

A hunter went killing sparrows: KNIGHTS, II, 9: A proverbial Arabic story and caveat. (H. Howarth & I. Shakrullah, *Images from the Arabic World*, London, 1944.)

A *la fontaine je voudrais*: QUEENS, I, 5; KNIGHTS, III, 13: Song by Jean-Antoine de Baïf:

> A la fontaine je voudrais
> Avec ma belle aller jouer.
> Là dedans l'eau nous irions tous deux rafraîchir
> Notre amour trop ardent.
>
> Mille douceurs, mille bons mots, mille plaisirs,
> Mille gentils amoureux jeux se feraient là,
> Mille baisers, mille doux embrassements là nous nous donn'rions.

A la fontaine je voudrais . . . (refrain)

Nous irions par le fleuri pré courir aux fleurs,
Cueillerions l'or fin et l'argent et le pourprin,
Chapelets ronds et bouquets, chaînes et tortils nous y li'rions.

A la fontaine je voudrais . . . (refrain)

Si le destin le nous permet que feignons-nous,
Que n'allons-nous jouir heureux de so beaux dons?
En le printemps nous y convie de notre âge la saison.

A la fontaine je voudrais . . . (refrain)

Pèse bien: Qu'est-ce du monde, ô mon amour doux?
Si l'amour manque et la plaisance, ce n'est rien:
Du désir donc et du plaisir recueillons, belle, le doux fruit.

A la fontaine je voudrais . . . (refrain)

There to the fountain I would take
My darling who makes sport with me
And in the cooling spray to slake
This love which burns so ardently
A thousand sweetnesses, soft words, disports,
A thousand loving pastimes we would share
A thousand kisses, sweet embraces there.

There to the fountain . . . (refrain)

Across the flowery meadows would we tread,
The gold and carmine would we gather, with the white
And wreathe them into chains for her delight.

There to the fountain . . . (refrain)

If destiny should give us fief of all these gifts
Should we do other than accept them with a will?
For spring is ours, whose age is springtime still.

There to the fountain . . . (refrain)

Think well: what is this world, my darling dear?
If love and pleasure fail, then nothing boots
So from this repast let us keep the fruits.

(Tr. D.D.)

A *Madame la Dauphine*: QUEENS, II, 3: Clément Marot on **Catherine de Médicis**:

> *A Madame la Dauphine*
> *Rien n'assigne*
> *Elle a ce qu'il faut avoir*
> *Mais je voudrais bien la voir*
> *En gésigne.*

> *With Madame la Dauphine*
> Nothing is amiss.
> She has everything she needs to have,
> But I'd rather like to see her
> Lying down.

A *mhic*: QUEENS, I, 2: 'My son'.

A *mhuire*: QUEENS, I, 2: 'Oh Mary'.

A *sangre! A fuego! A sacco!*: CHECKMATE, I, 6: Battle cry of Jean de Ligne, Baron de Barbançon, Comte d'Aremberg (d. 1568); 'To blood! To fire! To pillage!' (Abbé de Brantôme, *Les Vies des Grands Capitaines François*, Vol. IV.)

A silken tongue, a heart of cruelty: KINGS, I, 1: Taken from the Scots poem, 'The Paddock [puddock, or frog] and the Mouse', where the frog beguiles the mouse into believing it is safe to cross the deep river on his back, with the intention of drowning his passenger halfway across. They are both rewarded for their respective acts of attempted murder and stupidity by ending up as prey for the hawk. The frog's wanton act of cruelty is symbolic of man's flattery and treachery. See also **Cryand with many a piteous peep**. Extract:

> My brother, gif thou will take advertence [warning],
> By this fable, thou may perceive and see
> It passes for all kind of pestilence,
> Ane wicked mind with wordis fair and slee.
> Beware, therefore, with whom thou fellows thee:
> To thee were better bear the stane barrow,
> For all thy days to delve while thou may dree [endure],
> Than to be matchèd with ane wicked marrow [mate].

> A false intent under a fair presence,
> Has causèd many innocent for to dee;

> Great folly is to give ower soon credence,
> To all that speakis fairly unto thee.
> A silken tongue, a heart of cruelty,
> Smitis more sore than any shot of arrow.
> Brother if thou be wise, I reid [advise] thee flee,
> Than match thee with a thrawart feignèd marrow.

(J. Ross, *The Book of Scottish Poems*, Edinburgh, 1878.)

A stout stomach, pregnant-witted and of a most gentle nature: CASTLE, I, 7: **John Elder** commenting on **Philip II.** (Beatrice White, *Mary Tudor*, 1935.)

A thief in the night: KINGS, III, 3: A reference to the biblical Day of Judgement; see II Peter, 3, 10:

> But the day of the Lord will come as a thief in the night, in the which the heavens shall pass away with a great noise, and the elements shall melt with fervent heat, the earth also and the works that are therein shall be burned up.

A town of price like Paradise: CASTLE, II, 7: The words of Thomas Tusser (1524–1580), author of the sixteenth-century model guide to farming, *A Hundreth Good Pointes of Husbandrie*, subsequently enlarged to five hundred useful tips in rhyme. Tusser took to farming in Suffolk in his thirties when his career as Musician in Residence to Lord **Paget** of Beaudesert was curtailed by illness. It was for the sake of his first wife's health that the Tussers eventually moved to Ipswich. See **He pincheth and spareth and pineth his life.** (Michael Pafford, 'A Sixteenth Century Farmer's Year', *History Today*, June 1970.)

A whoremonger, a haunter of stews, a hypocrite, a wretch and a maker of strife: PAWN, 27: The description given of the character of Sir John, the parish priest in *John John the Husband*; one of the 'merry plays' of John Heywood (c. 1497–1578). (Karl J. Holzknecht, *Tudor and Stuart Plays in Outline*, London, 1963.)

Abature: QUEENS, IV, 4: The flattened areas of grass caused by a deer lying upon it.

Abraham: KINGS, I, 5: The worthy patriarch Abram of the Old Testament, called by God at the age of seventy-five. He was rewarded for his devotion with the promise that he would be the father of nations; a promise sealed with the covenant of circumcision. Abraham and his wife Sarah fed the angels of the Lord on hearth cakes, and it was then that God announced that Sarah was to give birth to their son Isaac. (Genesis, 12–25.)

The term Abram- or Abraham-man (CASTLE, III, 3) referred to an inmate of Bedlam (the London insane asylum) who was allowed out to seek alms. It is particularly used to denote a beggar who feigns madness.

ACCIAJUOLI, Family: RISING, RAM, 9: Little is known about Nicholai Giorgio de'Acciajuoli other than his name, which appears in the Register of the Great Seal of Scotland, and the fact that he did have a wooden leg. The family of Acciaiuoli (as it can also be spelled) originated in Brescia, founding a steel works in Florence in the twelfth century. By the fourteenth century a branch of the family had established itself in Greece, gaining land fiefs in return for rents. At this point the Acciaiuoli ranked amongst the major Florentine banking families such as the Bardi. The Florentine side of the family bank was forced to liquidate its assets in 1345 when Edward III of England could not repay his loans.

The Greek branch, Dukes of Athens by 1385, remained in control of that city until the mid-fifteenth century. Duke Nerio II, a weak and effeminate ruler, died in 1451, leaving his Venetian widow Chiara and their son Francesco to bribe the Turks and usurp the regency of Athens for the next five years. The visiting Venetian noble Bartolomeo Contarini fell passionately in love with Chiara, so he returned to Venice, poisoned his wife and married the Duchess.

Contarini and his stepson were summoned by **Suleiman** to Constantinople in 1456 to explain themselves. Franco Acciaiuoli (the only son of Duke Antonio II who was Nerio II's brother and predecessor) usurped the throne, imprisoned his aunt and murdered Contarini. Francesco vanished without trace. The indignant Sultan ordered Omar, governor of Thessaly, to march against Athens in June 1456. Franco fled to the Acropolis, where he remained for nearly two years. At the end of this time Franco was eventually obliged to relinquish power and forced to leave Athens, in return for which he was given control over Boetia and Thebes by the Ottoman Sultan, leaving other members of his family to remain in Turkish-occupied Greece, or return to Florence having lost their wealth. The fortunes of the Acciaiuoli improved in Florence in the fifteenth century as supporters of the **Medici** against the Albizzi faction. Amongst their other acquisitive skills, the Athenian branch were renowned for their horse-breeding talents. (Franz Babinger, *Mehmed the Conqueror*, Princeton, 1978.)

Acrostics: RAM, 18: In Greek liturgical services the canon, invented in the late seventh century, consisted of nine hymns or odes which contained an acrostic running through all the verses. This warned the singers when the original canon had been shortened. Each ode was prefaced by its mode, which gave the starting note.

Ad lucrandum vel perdendum: KNIGHTS, III, 16: 'With the purpose of winning or losing'.

Ad unum mollis opus: PAWN, 8: 'An easy task for one person'.

Adieu la Court: CHECKMATE, III, 5: The original poem by Clément Marot is the same as that given in the text, save for the last line; 'Puisqu'à l'église nous allons'. Marot's lyric bids farewell to the joys of court to attend war, not church. (A. Darmesteter & A. Hatzfeld, *Le Seizième Siècle en France*.)

ADORNE, Anselm: RISING: (b. 1424) A remarkable man—financier, diplomat, jouster, assiduous pilgrim, shrewd magistrate and man of strong beliefs—whose career, binding together Burgundy, Scotland and the Genoese Levant over a great part of the fifteenth century, has even yet only half emerged from the myriad records in which he appears.

Anselm Adorne was born into the wealthy Flemish branch of the crusading and merchant family of Adorno, which provided Genoa with several Doges. He was well educated in letters and was taught Latin and other languages as well as knightly accomplishments. In 1436, when he was twelve, a short uprising in **Bruges** in which his uncle was involved led to the Adorne family making a brief retreat into exile from which both his father and uncle returned unscathed to take up high public office. In due course Anselm followed their example and became in his turn a burgomaster of Bruges, occupying the Hôtel Jerusalem, the magnificent family mansion which was used to entertain many of the town's most eminent visitors.

As a small child, he laid the foundation stone of the **Jerusalemkirk**, the church which his father and uncle had determined should be built next to their home as a replica of the Holy Sepulchre Church in Jerusalem. Despite two trips by the founders to the Holy Land to check the exact measurements, the final church—unfinished when they died and altered by Anselm—shows only an approximation to the original building in its size, windows, and stairs, although the actual tomb is said to be an exact copy of the Holy Sepulchre. The family employed its own chaplain, who lived next door to the church and read Mass every day (and was known jokingly in the town as the Patriarch of Jerusalem). The church exists today, lovingly preserved, with the tombs of Adorne and his wife at its heart. Piety mixed with worldly wisdom and a degree of political fervour appeared to characterise the whole family.

From the age of twenty, Adorne distinguished himself in the annual jousts of the **White Bear Society,** which attracted to Bruges the élite of the Burgundian court. He won first prize there in 1447, and later bested Corneille, Bastard of Burgundy, as well as accounting for himself creditably in combat against the famous **Jacques de Lalaing** who had jousted in Scotland at the marriage of **James II** and Mary of Gueldres. Adorne first attained public office at twenty-four, and was in frequent touch with the Genoese merchants who had their *comptoirs* in Bruges. One of them, the powerful Paul Doria, stood as godfather at the birth of Adorne's first child Jan in 1444 after Anselm's marriage to the young orphan Margriet van der Banck. Margriet had inherited fine lands from her mother's family, who were especially powerful in Zeeland. In all, the couple were to have twelve or more children, of whom at least two daughters were placed in a convent and several sons entered the church. The extended family included several brothers and sisters of Adorne, one of the latter marrying into the distinguished family of Sersanders in Ghent and bearing a son also named Anselm who was to share a large part of Adorne's life. As happened with the Adornes, this family were also involved in an uprising in Ghent and Daniel Sersanders, Adorne's brother-in-law, was at one point banished for provoking unrest.

By 1468 Anselm, now a practised negotiator trusted by both the Duke of Burgundy and the people, was chosen to travel to Scotland to persuade King **James III** to rescind an edict forbidding his subjects to trade with Bruges and its ports. During this stay, and a second visit late in 1469, Adorne formed the basis of a friendship with the seventeen-year-old King. Adorne must already have met many of Scotland's merchants on visits to Bruges, for a large number of them were related by blood to their opposite numbers in Flanders. The King's churchmen and higher officials, many of whom had studied at the university of **Louvain**, would also have been well known to him. James himself, son of Mary of Gueldres, was kin to Duke **Philip the Good**, and his aunt Mary had been married into the noble house of Veere and had helped rear the King's younger brother, **Albany.**

It is likely that King James, appreciative of Burgundian gossip, was also attracted by what Adorne could tell him of his family's travels to the Holy Land, and of the Genoese interest in the eastern Mediterranean, in which the Adorne family had a share and which in the past had occasioned direct traffic between Genoa and Scotland. Before Adorne returned home in 1469 he had been appointed a counsellor to the King and received the Collar of the **Order of the Unicorn**, of which he is the only known recipient and which is carved on the effigy which lies on his tomb. He was also given a freeholding of lands which paid dues to the church of Brechin (closely associated with Mary of Gueldres). This gift endowed him with the title of Baron Cortachy, and was no doubt meant to encourage him to further the cause of Scotland in Bruges. Adorne continued to maintain his own arms, consisting of three bands of checkers on a field of gold, with the motto 'Para Tutum Deo', but added the badge of the unicorn to the decorations in his house. He returned to Bruges also with cause to thank the Bishop of St Andrews, nephew of Bishop **James Kennedy** (an old friend of Bruges), for his care of Adorne's young son Maarten.

With the death of Duke Philip and the accession of Duke **Charles the Bold** in 1467, Anselm's standing in Bruges had increased in authority, but also in danger. **Thomas Boyd**, a Scottish lord who had married the King's sister, had subsequently been arraigned as a traitor and the couple, fleeing Scotland, proposed to come for the birth of their child to Adorne's home in Bruges. At the same time, a series of reversals in the long battle for power taking place in England (the Wars of the Roses) meant that Burgundy was deeply unwilling to commit itself to supporting one faction against another, which in turn made interfering with Scottish affairs a delicate matter.

Through either policy or coincidence, the arrival of the Princess Mary and her husband the Earl of Arran at the Hôtel Jerusalem in Bruges in 1470 exactly coincided with Anselm Adorne's departure on a fourteen-month tour of the Holy Land. Leaving his wife to deal with the royal visitors, Adorne collected a small party of merchants and churchmen and departed on a tour of Italy, Barbary, Egypt, Syria and the islands of Cyprus and Rhodes, which certainly included all the usual places of pilgrimage, but equally placed him in talks with the major powers of the day, from Pope **Paul II** to the Duke of Milan, the Doge of Genoa and King **Ferrante of Naples**; from the Sultan **Qayt Bey** at Cairo to **Zacco of Cyprus** and the **Knights of St John** at Rhodes; from the Doge of **Venice** and the representatives of **Uzum Hasan**, ruler of Persia to **Sigismond, Count of the Tyrol** and the Archbishop of Cologne.

The report he brought back, written by his son Jan (and still in rough form extant) was ostensibly a worthy travelogue for the eyes of James III of Scotland, to whom it was dedicated. Indeed, Adorne on his travels had identified himself as a representative of the King of Scotland to some of his hosts; to others he had introduced himself as an envoy of Burgundy. His more interesting report, no doubt, was made direct to Duke Charles, and dealt both with matters of trade, and with the degrees of enthusiasm and resources which existed among the Mediterranean powers for any future assault against the Turks.

The dichotomy of patronage—between Scotland and Burgundy—was to shape the rest of Adorne's life, in which he needed all his brilliance to steer a safe course for himself and his family among all the political upheavals to come. What Adorne did, how he did it, and the influence he had on the course of history still perhaps cannot be fully appreciated. (*Messager des Sciences Historiques*, Vol. XLIX, Ghent, 1881; M. E. de la Cost, *Anselm Adorne*, 1885; Heers & Groer, eds, *Itinéraire d'Anselm Adorno en Terre Sainte*; Jozef Penninck, *De Jeruzalemkerk te Brugge*; *Bruges, Église de Jérusalem, Corpus Vitrearum Medii Aevi*, Vol. 2, 1968.)

Aeolian music: KINGS, II, 2: An Aeolian harp is a musical instrument which is sounded by the motion of the wind on its strings. Aeolus was king of the Aeolian islands. Zeus gave him command over the winds, which he kept shut up in a deep cave to be released at his pleasure, or at the command of the gods. (Harry Thurston Peck, ed., *Harper's Dictionary of Classical Literature and Antiquities*, NY, 1962.)

Africa: European Discoveries: SCALES: Under **Henry the Navigator**, the Portuguese were the first to capitalise on the sea routes to Guinea and West Africa in general. Early Portuguese merchants trading with Guinea were starting a lucrative monopoly in slaves and gold which could yield between fifty and eight hundred per cent profit margins. By 1448, one thousand slaves had already been exported from Barbary and Guinea to Portugal; Prince Henry himself taking an active third share in the first shipment. Despite the obsessive Portuguese attempts at secrecy, the Genoese and Castilians soon began to move in on this new monopoly, learning the secret trade routes from the imported slaves themselves, or from renegades and Andalusian pirates. By 1454 the Castilians were claiming possession of Guinea, building forts, factories, civil settlements and taking time to evangelise. The first legitimate Flemish journeys (other than earlier Flemings trading without a licence from Prince Henry or travelling under Portuguese captains) were helped by the Castilians.

The main exports of West Africa were slaves, gold, Malagueta pepper and ivory. The gold trade yielded the highest profit, closely followed by the sale of human beings. Slaves were not only taken by sea, but across the Sahara; a journey typified by brutality from the captors as well as the climate. One 'enterprising' measure used by native traders was to castrate the male slaves so their trade would not be destroyed by the natural increase of their commodity; an operation from which less than ten per cent are estimated to have survived.

It can be argued that the slave trade from West Africa actually declined in the later part of the fifteenth century: a matter of price rather than morality. In Arguim in 1455 one horse would purchase eighteen slaves; by 1500 it would only purchase twelve, with a similar change in the exchange rate near Senegal. But that price increase was not caused by a scarcity of the potential commodity; rather by the increase in the horse trade. The horses themselves were not now as valuable to the indigenous slave traders as they had been nearly half a century before.

The slave trade would not have ended, but it might have stabilised had it not been for the discovery of the New World, and its exploitation, which created a rapid expansion in the need for a new and cheap labour force. In 1510 the first batch of slaves destined for the West Indies was bought at Lisbon. By 1540, ten thousand slaves were exported annually from the west coast of Africa. (John W. Blake, *European Beginnings in West Africa*, London, 1937.)

Agere aprum: QUEENS, IV, 2: See *Animal gregale.*

AKIL: See **Timbuktu.**

Alas . . . if angels should sniff at his shroud?: PAWN, 19: The line refers to a problem the poet Bábá Fighání of Shiraz (d. 1519) might have had trying to enter Paradise; 'stained with wine he sank into the earth'; a state of crapulence unacceptable to either the Prophet or his heavenly assistants. (E.G. Brown, *Persian Poetry in Modern Times.*)

ALBANY, Alexander Stewart, Duke of: UNICORN (1454–1484). The second son of **James II** of Scotland and his Flemish queen, Mary of Gueldres, and ambitious younger brother of King **James III**. By 1455 he had been created Earl of March and Lord of Annandale, and by 1458 he was also Duke of Albany. Two months before his father's sudden death in 1460 Alexander, aged six, was sent in the care of Bishop **Kennedy** to stay at the court of his kinsmen in Flanders: his mother, who was to die before he returned home, was related to **Philip the Good of Burgundy** and his aunt Mary was married to the noble-man Wolfaert van Borselen of Veere, who had been given the title of Earl of Buchan. (While in **Bruges,** Alexander officially held the title of Admiral of Scotland, in parallel to the van Borselen family, who occupied the same role in Veere.) On his way home to Scotland at the age of ten, Alexander and his companions were captured by an English barge and held in England for over a year, possibly to encourage Scotland to abandon their support for the Lan-castrian King Henry VI; possibly to impress or size up the boy for the future. By the time Alexander was freed, his friend Bishop Kennedy had also died.

The differences that were to grow between Alexander and his older brother were not glaringly obvious in the first ten years or so after his return. He took only occasional part in public affairs, and acceded, although probably without much enthusiasm, to the proposal that he should marry Catherine, the eldest daughter of William, first Lord Sinclair, who had just obliged the Crown by giving up the Earldom of Orkney. The marriage was over by the time that, sundered from Scotland, he made the French marriage that produced John, Duke of Albany, future Protector and Governor of Scotland.

D'ALBON, Jacques: QUEENS: See **St André, Jacques d'Albon.**

Alcohol: The Prophet Mohammed called wine 'the mother of all vices', and the product of the grape, 'the red insane one', was strictly forbidden by the Muslim religion. The Ottoman Empire permitted taverns, but only for the infidels, not for the true believers. Believers caught in drunkenness during the holy month-long fast of Ramadan would be forced to drink hot lead for their crime.

Alconosts: CASTLE, II, 6: The birds with human heads who inhabit paradise are mentioned as a subject of Russian embroidery. The imagery is reminiscent of ancient Egyptian iconography of the soul's flight to the afterworld. (Tamara Talbot Rice, *Russian Art*.)

Aldebaran: CASTLE, II, 13: The star whose name in Arabic means the Follower, because its ascendance follows the Pleiades. Aldebaran forms the bull's eye in the constellation of Taurus. In Arab folklore the constellations are flocks of camels, called 'the daughters of the night', and the skies are their pasture. (Albin Michel, *La Vie du Chameau*, Paris, 1938.)

Alecto, Magaera and Tisiphone attend you: QUEENS, III, 4: The three Furies of Hell; avenging deities personifying the bad conscience and remorse which follow evil deeds, also called the Erinnyes. They were not just confined to Hades, but would pursue the living to avenge their crimes. They are portrayed as blackened winged creatures, with blood dripping from their eyes and snakes entwined in their hair. They appear as characters in the contemporary *Tragedy of Gorboduc*, the play by Thomas Norton (1532–1584) and Thomas Sackville (1536–1608), 'clad in black garments sprinkled with blood and flame, their heads covered with serpents'. (Karl J. Holzknecht, *Tudor and Stuart Plays in Outline*, London, 1963.)

Alexander the Great: KINGS, II, 1: (356–323 BC) Conqueror of the world and hero of many medieval legends. Alexander was the son of Philip II of Macedonia and Olympias, and educated by Aristotle; he became king at the age of twenty when his father was murdered. After suppressing rebellion in his own territories, he extended his total control over Greece, Persia, Phoenicia and then Egypt. By the age of thirty Alexander had completely conquered the whole of Asia. Legend has it that he wept at the thought of having no more countries left to subdue. He died from a fever at the age of thirty-two.

ALFONSO I, King of Naples: RISING: (1395–1458) Also King Alfonso V of Aragon from 1416, he annexed the kingdom of Naples in 1443, taking it from its titular head, **René of Anjou**. Alfonso was known as 'Alfonso the Magnanimous' more for his patronage of men of letters than for his lenient style of government. Intent on expanding his own territories, Alfonso capitalised on the weakness of Genoa, and his own power as an ally for the other Italian city-states. Naples was at odds with Genoa over the control of Corsica; Genoa was eventually obliged to place herself under the protection of France, thus bringing outside powers into the Italian wars. (Garrett Mattingly, *Renaissance Diplomacy*, London, 1955.)

Alfonso V of Aragon: RISING: See **Alfonso I, King of Naples.**

Alfonso the Wise: UNICORN, 25: (1221–1284) Author of the *Lapidario*, a treatise on the medieval lore of stones and jewels. Alfonso of Castile imposed an astrological scheme over the stones, so each mineral is associated with a star and gains or loses power depending on whether or not the star is in the ascendant; for example, Sagittarius is illustrated with an **alum** star in his shoulder.

Ali Nur al-Din and Miriam the girdle girl: QUEENS, I, 5: A tale by Hasan of Bassorah; the same basic story—'The History of Ganem, Slave of Love'—is related in *The Arabian Nights:*

> . . . one of my slaves gave me in my lemonade last night a drug of a certain nature to produce complete insensibility . . . This insensibility is sometimes so great, that for seven or eight hours nothing can dispel it. (E. S. Ellis, *Ancient Anodynes.*)

Alichino: UNICORN, 48: The Devil-Buffoon and one of **Dante's devils.** His name means 'wing drooped', and he is also called 'the allurer' in Dante's *Divine Comedy.* He is held to be the origin of the character of Harlequin from the Italian *Commedia del'Arte.*

Alkibiades: CHECKMATE, III, 1: (450–404 BC) The son of Clinias and Dinomaché of Athens, brought up by his relation Pericles. By all accounts, he was a beautiful person of transcendent abilities and extraordinary wealth. Despite the exhortations of his friend and mentor Socrates, Alkibiades chose to direct his talents towards debauchery and licentious behaviour. He rose to power as a politician and military leader, but was eventually assassinated in 404 BC, probably by the brother of a girl he had seduced. He left behind him a son, also called Alkibiades, who is memorable only in that he never distinguished himself. (Harry Thurston Peck ed., *Harper's Dictionary of Classical Literature and Antiquities*, NY, 1962.)

Alla sanguina: CHECKMATE, V, 1: A reference both to the Milanese process of tempering steel for swords, and the result of the sword's use. The steel is heated to a high degree and then cooled to retain the strength of the metal without increasing its brittle potential. Heat tempering gives the resultant weapon or armour a blueish hue. Weapons fashioned by this process will exhibit a blue-red shimmer when drawn from the flesh. (Edward, Second Duke of York, *The Master of Game*, 1413, tr. from Gaston III, 1904.)

Allez à l'idole de St Germain et vous trouverez ce qu'avez perdu: CHECKMATE III, 4: 'Go to the idol of St Germain and you will find what you have lost'.

Alterius non sit, qui suus esse potest: PAWN, 24: Latin proverb: 'Let him not be another's who may be his own man'.

Alum: RISING: Potash alum, potassium sulphate or ammonia sulphate. Alum was the principal fixative used in the dyeing industry of late medieval Europe. It also possessed certain medical properties. As the principal mordant in the dyeing of cloth, it prevented discoloration of the dyes used. It was also used in glassmaking, tanning, and in the textiles industry as a cleanser to remove grease and impurities from wool. In medical terms it is a particularly versatile compound: as an astringent when applied directly to wounds to stop profuse bleeding; as an emetic when taken internally; and as an abortifacient (more effective than vinegar and green apples: RISING, 34). In solution it can be used to treat mouth and throat conditions, and when applied externally can treat excessive perspiration.

The principal markets for alum were Flanders, **Venice** and England and, until the middle of the fifteenth century, the two main areas of supply were Karahissar, near Trebizond, and Phocaea, near Smyrna. The Phocaean deposits were a Genoese monopoly; limiting supplies below the level of demand, thus keeping prices high. They maintained their monopoly from 1275 until 1455 when they were eventually ousted by the occupying Turks. The Venetians then controlled the Phocaean monopoly, paying excessively high tribute for the privilege, until they too were expelled in the war against Sultan **Mehmet II** in 1463.

In 1460, rich deposits of alum were discovered at Tolfa, near Civitavecchia in the Papal States; by the spring of 1463, Tolfa had four mines and 8,000 workmen. The church thus gained instant control over the only Christian supply of high quality alum. Despite the fact that monopolies were against church law, this is exactly what the church created; instead of alum money funding the enlargement of Mehmet's empire, the revenues raised were to fund a crusade against the Turks as enemies of Christendom (and rivals in this lucrative trade). The importation of Turkish alum was punishable with the serious threat of excommunication.

By 1466, the **Medici** bank secured the right to become the exclusive dealers in papal alum; all sales were to pass through their branches in **Bruges** and London. The monopoly was not absolute; if the price was too high or the commodity too limited, Turkish alum would still supply an alternative. (Charles Singer, *The Early Chemical Industry*, London, 1948; Raymond De Roover, *The Rise and Decline of the Medici Bank*, Harvard, 1963; *Black's Medical Dictionary*.)

Amboise: QUEENS: When Charles VIII of France returned from his military campaign in Naples in 1495, he brought with him some of the finest Italian artists and craftsmen. He set them to work on his château of Amboise, with the desire that they bring the finest elements of Italian classicism to the huge building programme which was to turn it into a sumptuous palace. The Italianate influence was most definitely in the ascendant, along with all of its fashionable innovations. Whilst in Florence, Charles had seen a lion menagerie; on his return he founded his own zoo at Amboise. He had also seen an artificial egg incubator at Poggio Reale, which he copied for his new château. The Tour des Minimes, constructed from 1495 to 1496, provided a continuous circular ramp by which to ascend to the château from the town below (wide enough for a coach), as did the Tour Hurtault completed a few years later. Charles did not have long to enjoy his new château: he died in 1498 from a head wound sustained from having misjudged the height of one of its doorways.

Under **Francis I**, the influence of the Italian Renaissance on Amboise reached its zenith; in 1516 he invited Leonardo da Vinci (1452–1519) to settle at the manor of Cloux, near Amboise, where he remained in the service of the monarchy until his death.

In the French wars of religion (1562–1598) Amboise was officially in neutral territory, but was stormed by the Huguenots, hoping to control the town and ultimately the monarchy. When they failed, over 1,300 Huguenots were hanged from its balconies in retribution. (Marcus Binney, *Châteaux of the Loire*, London, 1992.)

Ambrose, St: CASTLE, II, 3: (339–397) Born at Trier, he was the son of the Praetorian Prefect of Gaul. In 374 the Catholic laity demanded that he become their bishop; he accepted the see and devoted the rest of his life to the study of theology. Knowledge of Greek enabled him to introduce much Eastern theology to the West. Ambrose is remembered as an upholder of orthodoxy and is considered one of the four traditional doctors of the Latin church. (F. L. Cross, ed., *The Oxford Dictionary of the Christian Church*, London, 1974.)

AMIROUTZES, George: RAM: (d. 1463) Philosopher, Great Chancellor, Treasurer and Protovestarios to the last Emperor of Trebizond. Reputedly handsome and a great scholar, Amiroutzes had an encyclopaedic knowledge of physics, maths, geometry, Greek philosophy, rhetoric and poetry.

He was first cousin to Mahmut Pasha, head of the Ottoman advance guard sent to attack **Trebizond** in 1461. He encouraged **David Comnenos** to surrender and made him believe Mahmud Pasha's promise that he would be as well treated as Demetrius **Paleologus** (Despot of the Morea) had been. Instead of remaining in Trebizond, he would be given new territories and a guaranteed income. Amiroutzes also helped his cousin by discouraging resistance to the Turk and paralysing the impetus to defend the city.

Alone of the court of Trebizond, Amiroutzes and his two sons Basil (Mehmet Bey) and Alexander (Skender) not only survived; they rose to positions of favour and praise in Sultan **Mehmet**'s court. His knowledge impressed the Sultan, as did his loyalty. After the fall of Trebizond, Amiroutzes intercepted a letter from **Uzum Hasan**'s wife, asking for either one of David's sons or his nephew to be sent to her. The letter was handed to Mehmet, who interpreted it as a marriage-building Comnenos plot, for which the former Emperor and his family suffered. Treachery, or adaptability, certainly paid off for the former treasurer; his son Basil helped his father translate Ptolemy for the Sultan (for which he was amply rewarded) and Alexander became Turkish Minister of Finance. Both were raised as good Muslims. Amiroutzes dropped dead in 1463 while playing dice; the dice box still in his hand. (William Miller, *Trebizond, the Last Greek Empire*, London, 1926; Franz Babinger, *Mehmet the Conqueror*, Princeton, 1978.)

Amor ordinem nescit: PAWN, 23: 'Love knows no reason'.

An angry piece of flesh and soon displeased: CASTLE, III, 10: The description given is for the character of Dame Coy in the anonymous children's interlude 'Jack Juggler' (c. 1553): 'A very cursed shrew, by the blessed Trinity, and a very devil. She is an angry piece of flesh, and soon displeased, quickly moved, but not lightly appeased'. (Karl J. Holzknecht, *Tudor and Stuart Plays in Outline*, London, 1963.)

And bathe my son in morning milk: KINGS, IV, 3: See **O row my lady in satin and silk.**

And from the hornes . . . of Unicornes: CHECKMATE, V, 10: See **And from the sword (Lord) save my soule.**

And from the sword (Lord) save my soule: CHECKMATE, II, 2, 7: Psalm 22; the version used is that of the Geneva Psalms, printed by John Crespin in 1569 (extract; vv 19–22):

> Therefore I pray thee be not farre
> From meat my great neede:
> But rather sith thou art my strength,
> To help me (Lord) make speede.
>
> And from the sword (Lord) save my soule
> By thy myght and power:
> And keepe my soule, thy darling deare,
> From dogs that would devour.
>
> And from the Lion's mouth that would
> Me all in sunder shiver:
> And from the hornes of Unicornes,
> Lord safely me deliver.
>
> And I shall to my brethren all,
> Thy majesty record:

And in thy church shall prayse thy name
Of thee the living Lord.

And he took out his little knife: KINGS, I, 5: From the poem 'The Jolly Beggar',
attributed to King James V of Scotland (1512–1542). A gentleman woos a
maid by disguising himself as a beggar (extract):

There was a jollie beggar,
And a beggin he was boun,
And he took up his quarters
Into a landart town [country farmhouse]:
He wadna lie into the barn,
Nor wad he in the byre,
But in ahint [behind] the ha' door,
Or else afore the fire.
And we'll go no more a roving,
A roving in the night,
We'll go no more a roving,
Let the moon shine e'er so bright.

The beggar's bed was made at e'en,
Wi' gude clean straw and hay,
And in ahint the ha' door
'Twas there the beggar lay.
Up gat the gudeman's [farmer's] daughter,
All for to bar the door,
And there she saw the beggar-man
Standing in the floor.
And we'll go no more a roving,
A roving in the night,
Though maids be e'er so loving,
And the moon shine e'er so bright.

He took the lassie in his arms,
Fast to the bed he ran—
O hoolie, hoolie [quietly] wi' me sir,
Ye'll waken our gudeman.
The beggar was a cunning loon [rascal],
And ne'er a word he spak—
But long afore the cock had crawn,
Thus he began to crack:
And we'll go no more a roving,

A roving in the night,
Save when the moon is moving,
And the stars are shining bright . . .

He took the lassie in his arms,
And gae her kisses three,
And four-and-twenty hunder merk
To pay the nurse's fee:
He took a wee horn frae his side,
And blew baith loud and shrill,
And four-and-twenty belted knights
Came skipping o'er the hill.
And we'll go no more a roving,
A roving in the night,
Nor sit a sweet maid loving
By coal or candlelight.

And he took out his little knife,
Loot [let] a' his duddies [rags) fa',
And he was the bravest gentleman
That was among them a'.
The beggar was a clever loon,
And he lap [leapt] shoulder height,
O ay [always] for sicken [such] quarters
As I got yesternight!
And we'll ay gang [go] a roving,
A roving in the night,
For then the maids are loving,
And stars are shining bright.

(J. Ross, ed., *The Book of Scottish Poems*, Edinburgh, 1878.)

And in the land of Ham for them, Most wondrous woorkes had done:
CHECKMATE, II, 7: Psalm 106; the version used is that of the Geneva Psalms,
printed by John Crespin in 1569 (extract; vv 22–23):

And in the land of Ham for them,
Most wondrous woorkes had done
And by the red sea dreadfull things
Performed long agone.
Therfore for theyr so shewing them,
Forgetfull and unkind,
To bring destruction on them all
He purposde in his minde.

And of ech thought a doubt doth grow: CHECKMATE, V, II: The couplet quoted within the text comes from the poem by Henry Howard, Earl of Surrey (c. 1517–1547), 'O Happy Dames' ('A Lady Complains of her Lover's Absence'), on the grief of the lady parted from her love, fearing he will never return.

> O happy dames, that may embrace
> The fruit of your delight,
> Help to bewail the woeful case
> And eke the heavy plight
> Of me, that wonted to rejoice
> The fortunes of my pleasant choice.
> Good ladies, help to fill my mourning voice.
>
> In ship freight with rememberance
> Of thoughts and pleasures past
> He sails, that hath in governance
> My life while it will last;
> With scalding sighs, for lack of gale,
> Furthering his hope, that is his sail,
> Toward me, the sweet port of his avail.
>
> Alas, how oft in dreams I see
> Those eyes that were my food,
> Which sometime so delighted me
> That yet they do me good:
> Wherewith I wake with his return
> Whose absent flame did make me burn:
> But when I find the lack, Lord how I mourn!
>
> When other lovers, in arms across,
> Rejoice their chief delight,
> Drownèd in tears, to mourn my loss,
> I stand the bitter night
> In my window, where I may see
> Before the winds how the clouds flee:
> Lo, what a mariner love hath made of me!
>
> And in green waves, when the salt flood
> Doth rise by rage of wind,
> A thousand fancies in that mood
> Assail my restless mind.
> Alas, now drencheth my sweet foe
> That with the spoil of my heart did go,
> And left me! But, alas, why did he so?

And when the seas wax calm again,
To chase fro me annoy,
My doubtful hope doth cause me plain:
So dread cuts off my joy.
Thus is my wealth mingled with woe,
And of each thought a doubt doth grow:
Now he comes! will he come? alas, no, no!

(Gerald Bullett, ed., *Silver Poets of the Sixteenth Century*, London 1970.)

And the shapes of the locusts were like unto horses: CASTLE, II, 13: The Book of Revelation, 9, 7.

And then Sir Gawaine wept, and King Arthur wept and then they swooned both: QUEENS, I, 6: From the *Morte d'Arthur* by Sir Thomas Malory (c. 1404–1471).

And whoso list to hunt, I know where is an hart: CHECKMATE, IV, 1: Sir **Thomas Wyatt's** sonnet, 'Whoso List to Hunt':

Whoso list to hunt, I know where is an hind,
But as for me, helas, I may no more.
The vain travail hath wearied me so sore,
I am of them that farthest come behind.
Yet may I by no means my wearied mind
Draw from the Deer, but as she fleeth afore
Fainting I follow. I leave off therefore,
Since in a net I seek to hold the wind.
Who list her hunt (I put him out of doubt)
As well as I may spend his time in vain.
And graven with diamonds in letters plain
There is written her fair neck about:
'Noli me tangere, for Caesar's I am,
And wild for to hold, though I seem tame'.

(Gerald Bullett, ed., *Silver Poets of the Sixteenth Century*, London, 1970.)

~ Spanish Carrack ~

~Flemish Carrack~

D'ANDELOT, Claude de Laval: CHECKMATE: Brother of Admiral **Coligny** and Colonel General of foot soldiers in the French army. As a rival of the **de Guise** family, the Duke and Cardinal of Lorraine had him arrested in 1558 on suspicion of participating in the meeting of the Paris Protestants. He was accused of heresy, and freely admitted his Reformed opinions. **Henri II** liked the captain and summoned d'Andelot to appear before him, having first warned him what questions he would be asked. A simple lie would have saved his life, but d'Andelot was determined not to compromise his zealous beliefs, telling the King he approved of Calvin's doctrines, and now considered the Mass to be 'a horrible profanity and an abominable invention of man'. Henri II was so incensed at such heresy that he lifted a basin and hurled it in the direction of his former friend. Unfortunately it missed its mark and hit the Dauphin instead. (René de Bouillé, *Histoire des Ducs de Guise*, 1849.)

Andrew, St, head of: RAM, 9, 23: See **Paleologus, Thomas.**

Anet: QUEENS: An ancient fortress on the banks of the River Eure, which had been in the Brézé family since 1444. In 1547, when **Henri II** became King, he rewarded his mistress **Diane de Poitiers** with **Chenonceau** and money enough to rebuild Anet, employing **Philibert Delorme** as chief architect and mason. Work began in 1548 on a new château in front of the old fortress. First came a wide deep moat, followed by a Courtyard of Honour. There were three courts, separated from each other by an arcade; in one court stood the fountain of Diana. A vast park lay beyond the moat with an Hôtel Dieu for Diane's 'poor' guests.

Worth noting within the château was the double clock, with astrolabe and planisphere markings, including a zodiac with the diurnal motion of the stars and planets. Every quarter of an hour, mechanical hounds bayed, and on the hour a deer would strike the time with its hoof. Also encompassing the link between Diana the huntress and Diane the mistress was a series of tapestries specially woven at **Fontainebleau** for Anet; the birth of Diana, Diana killing Orion, Diana saving Iphigenia and the death of Meleager. Over the entrance to the château was the Latin inscription '*Phoebe sacrata est alae domus ampla Dianae / Verum accepta cuicuncta Diana repest*': 'By Phoebus [Henri II] is the spirit of this home dedicated to the generous Diana: Diana returns to him all that she has received'. Only one wing of the château and the chapel still exist. (Vivian Rowe, *Royal Châteaux in Paris.*)

Ango, Jean: QUEENS, I, 2; CHECKMATE, III, 3: (d. 1551) Sixteenth-century banker of Dieppe and sponsor of French journeys to the New World during the reign of **Francis I**. Ango's goal was to find trade routes free of Spanish and Portuguese pirates. His house in Dieppe, La Pensée, was built in 1525 of sculpted and gilded oak on stone foundations; a magnificent example of the wealth and architectural preferences of its owner. It was embellished with bas reliefs of Norman deeds and contained many Mediterranean statues and fountains in its garden. The interior was also luxuriously furnished with tapestries, Florentine engraved silver and marble statuary. After his triumphal entry to Dieppe in 1534, Francis I stayed at La Pensée and subsequently appointed Ango as Governor of the Chateau of Dieppe. (René Herval, *Dieppe*.)

Angra-Mainyo: KINGS, Gambit: Or Ahriman, see **Zoroaster.**

ANGUS, Earl of: KINGS: See **Douglas, Archibald.**

Animal gregale: QUEENS, IV, 2: The term used to describe a wild boar when not yet 'pigged with a full set of teeth' (PAWN, 1). The young boar will be referred to first as an *animal gregale*, and eventually becomes *solivagum*. For the first three years of its life the boar remains with its mother, and is known as a 'pig'. In the third year it gains its independence and wanders alone, hence *sengler*. An adult boar which has left its parent sow four or five years previously is referred to as a *sanglier*. The wild boar is a slow animal, so to make the pursuit and capture more exciting, the animal would be incited to wild frenzy, or *agere aprum*.

Anka: PAWN, 11: See **Chaos.**

Antabatae: CHECKMATE, I, 4: The name used for Roman gladiators obliged to fight wearing helmets without eye-slits. Individuals fighting blind, without any idea as to the location of the similarly handicapped enemy, seemingly appealed to the humour of the spectators. They are mentioned by Cicero, and pictures of them appear in the amphitheatre at Pompeii. The origin of their name perhaps comes from the Celtic for 'blind fighter'. (Harry Thurston Peck, ed., *Harper's Dictionary of Classical Literature and Antiquities*, NY, 1962.)

Anthony, St: KINGS, IV, 2; RISING, 4: St Anthony of Egypt (251–356); said to be the father of monasticism, not to be confused with St Anthony of Padua (1195–1231). Anthony of Egypt is the patron saint of hogs and swineherds (his profession prior to becoming an ascetic hermit). Later followers of his solitary religious life would wear a bell around their necks to warn people of their arrival. The smallest pig of a litter often kept as a pet was known as 'St Anthony's Pig', after one of the proctors of St Anthony's Hospital in the eleventh century who tied a bell around a pig's neck; after this, no one dared to harm it.

Antisthenes: CHECKMATE, II, 7: (b. 440 BC) Cynic philosopher; friend of **Socrates** and teacher of **Diogenes** who sold all his possessions and preached a doctrine of austerity. When asked by one of his pupils what philosophy had taught him, his answer was simple: 'to live with myself'. (Harry Thurston Peck, ed., *Harper's Dictionary of Classical Literature and Antiquities*, NY, 1962.)

Antique Triumph for the Heroes of Calais: CHECKMATE III, 2: See **Jodelle, Etienne.**

Ants, black: QUEENS, II, 1: Termites were used as ancient organic sutures, to clip together the lips of a wound. The body of the termite would then be cut off, leaving the jaws tightly attached to the flesh. (W.J. Bishop, *Early History of Surgery.*)

Anvari: PAWN, 13: See **Ottoman poetry.**

Aphrodite: SCORPIONS, 27: Greek goddess of love, beauty and fertility, comparable with the Roman deity Venus. Born of the sea, she is said to have landed on the shores of Cyprus (see **Fontana Amorosa; Kouklia**).

Apish toys of Antichrist: QUEENS, IV, 5: A sixteenth-century English Protestant comment on the Catholic practices of the church in Ireland. (A.G. Richey, *A Short History of the Irish People.*)

Apprentice bell: QUEENS, III, 5: The early church bell calling the apprentices to rise and be ready for work; the earliest work bell of the morning. Servants and apprentices in London would rise at five in the summer and at six in the winter. (Sir Walter Besant, *London in the Time of the Tudors.*)

Apollo, kissed in the woods like: CHECKMATE, IV, 3: The reference here, applied to **Nostradamus**, is to Branchus, a beautiful youth of Miletus, who was the beloved of Apollo. The Greek god endowed Branchus with the gift of prophecy by kissing him in the woods.

D'ARAMON, Gabriel de Luetz, Baron et Seigneur: PAWN: (c. 1490–c. 1554) French Ambassador to Turkey. One of the first biographical references to d'Aramon appears in 1537 when he took part in the French military campaign in Provence, and in the following year saw action in Piedmont. In 1539 he was forced into exile in Venice because of a dispute with the family of **Diane de Poitiers**, and was deprived of his lands and goods, later conferred on Diane by **Henri II.**

Whilst abroad, d'Aramon was employed by Pellicier, Bishop of Maguelonne and French Ambassador to Venice, who attempted to mediate and restore him to the favour of the King. He returned to France in 1541, but could not regain his property, and so left once again. By 1543, he was the resident French Ambassador at Constantinople; a position he held for ten years.

In 1551, d'Aramon intervened to help the **Knights of St John** at the Turkish siege of Tripoli. Through his influence with the Sultan **Suleiman** he managed to save the lives of the greater part of the garrison and its inhabitants, apart from those of Spanish birth. Initially the Ottoman commander Sinan Pasha only released the elderly and infirm amongst the Knights, but d'Aramon was reputedly worried at leaving the young French Knights as hostages to the Turks 'seasoned with luxuries and pleasures', so he ransomed them with his own money, and bartered thirty well-born Turkish prisoners he bought at Constantinople for the lives of the Spanish Knights; a generous gesture as France was still at war with the Empire. When he attempted to take the survivors back to the Order's headquarters on Malta, Grand Master **de Homedes** refused him admission, and spread rumours blaming him personally for the surrender of Tripoli.

D'Aramon was described as a generous host, especially to French visitors sent by the King. He ran an open house in Constantinople and would give money, horses and even clothes to any Frenchman struggling to return home. In 1553, he succumbed to fever and colic and retired from his post on grounds of ill health. He expected that after a decade of loyal service in the Levant he would regain his French goods and his lands, but his hopes were once more frustrated. In 1551 Henri II had made him a Gentleman of the Chamber and gave him a gift of two of the best-equipped galleys in Marseilles harbour; these at least he was allowed to keep. He retired to Provence, where he married for a second time, but died within two years of his retiral from ambassadorial service.

Archibishop of Pisa: QUEENS, II, 1: Francesco Salviati, Archbishop-designate of Pisa, was hanged for his part in the Pazzi plot of 1478 against the **Medici** family. Legend has it that as he was falling, to avoid the drop, he sank his teeth into the body hanging at the next gibbet. (Sieur de Varillas, *Secret History of the House of Medici*, tr. Ferrand Spence, 1685; Judith Hook, *Lorenzo de' Medici*.)

Archbishop's conscience: KINGS, III, 2: See **Clatter like the Archbishop's conscience.**

Archers: QUEENS: See **Scottish Archers.**

Arion: KINGS, I, 6: (b. 625 BC) Poet and musician from the Greek island of Lesbos. When he was returning by boat from his travels in Italy and Sicily, a group of Corinthian sailors resolved to murder him and divide his possessions between them. His last request before they flung him overboard was a chance to sing for the last time his best songs. At the sound of his voice a school of dolphins came close to the boat; one of which carried him safely to Taenarum on the southernmost tip of the Greek mainland. An ancient bronze statue of a man on a dolphin at Taenarum is said to be his offering of thanks to Poseidon, god of the sea.

Armour: See **Guns; Milanese armour.**

ARRAN, James Hamilton, Earl of: KINGS: (d. 1575) Governor of Scotland and Duke of Châtelherault in France, Arran had been **Mary de Guise**'s predecessor as Regent of Scotland. He was ousted from the position in 1554 when Mary de Guise took the position for herself, pensioning Arran off. A man of great wealth and refinement, Arran's genial and tolerant temperament earned him his nickname as 'the Temporiser'.

In public affairs he had showed himself to be most unsuitable as leader of the country; indolent and vacillating to the point of earning the hatred of both the Catholics and their Reformed rivals. He had initially shown sympathy towards the Protestants and Henry VIII of England had offered the hand of Princess **Elizabeth** to his son, although in 1548 he was drawn away from his English sympathies by a large amount of gold and the duchy of Châtelherault. He later hoped that his son would marry **Mary Queen of Scots**, but again he was frustrated in his ambitious dynastic plans and Hamilton junior was instead made a captain of the Scots Guard in France. See **Scottish Archers.**

Ars sine scientia nihil est: PAWN, 28: 'Art without science is nothing'.

As a skin bottel in the smoke So are you parcht and dride: CHECKMATE, II, 1: Psalm 119; the version used is that of the Geneva Psalms, printed by John Crespin in 1569 (extract, vv 83–4):

> As a skin bottel in the smoke,
> So am I parcht and dride:
> Yet will I not out of my hart,
> Let thy commaundement slide.
> Alas how long shall I yet lyve,
> Before I see the howre:
> That on my foes which me torment,
> Thy vengeaunce thou wilt power?

As hound that hath his keeper lost: CHECKMATE: IV, 1: From the lyric by **Sir Thomas Wyatt:**

> For what I will in woe I plain,
> Under colour of soberness;
> Renewing with my suit my pain,
> My wanhope with your steadfastness.

Awake therefore of gentleness:
Regard, at length, I you require,
The swelting pains of my desire.

Betimes who giveth willingly,
Redoubled thanks aye doth deserve;
And I, that sue unfeignedly
In fruitless hope, alas, do sterve.
How great my cause is for to swerve,
And yet how steadfast is my suit,
Lo, here ye see: where is the fruit?

As hound that hath his keeper lost,
Seek I your presence to obtain,
In which my heart delighteth most,
And shall delight though I be slain.
You may release my band of pain;
Loose then the care that makes me cry
For want of help, or else I die.

I die, though not incontinent,
By process yet consumingly
As waste of fire which doth relent,
If you as wilful will deny.
Wherefore cease of such cruelty,
And take me wholly in your grace,
Which lacketh will to change his place.

(Gerald Bullett, ed., *Silver Poets of the Sixteenth Century*, London, 1970.)

As snailes do wast within the shel: CHECKMATE, I, 6: Psalm 58, 8; calling for God's vengeance on corrupt rulers. The version used is that of the Geneva Psalms, printed by John Crespin in 1569.

ASCHAM, Roger: CASTLE: (1515–1568) Educated at Cambridge and appointed reader in Greek in about 1538. Ascham left Cambridge in 1548 to become tutor to the fifteen-year-old Princess **Elizabeth**. A quarrel in the household led him to resign in 1550 and return to Cambridge. His opinion of court life was less than flattering: 'To laugh, to lie, to flatter, to face, / Four ways in court to win men's grace'. Later that year he became secretary to Sir Richard Morison, the English Ambassador to the Court of **Charles V** at Augsburg. On his return to England in 1553 his academic prowess led to his appointment as Latin secretary to **Mary Tudor**, a position which gave him a secured salary of forty pounds per annum. Ascham, however, held strong Protestant views and under Edward's reign had referred to the Catholic church as 'the Roman beast and its dogmatic filth', a dangerous statement to have made when orthodox Catholicism was being restored by his new employer.

The following year, Elizabeth was briefly brought to court, which gave the two of them the chance to resume their studies of six years before. Queen Mary had attempted to restrict Ascham from regular visits to Elizabeth, but in 1558, with Elizabeth's accession, he was appointed as her private tutor. Only one work was published by Ascham during his lifetime: *Toxophilus*, a treatise in English on archery, stressing the importance of physical training in exercise. The parallels between Ascham's extensive library and that of the fictional Lymond are particularly striking.

In 1554, Ascham married Margaret Howe, his 'sweet Mag'; he was thirty-eight, she was nineteen. The marriage lasted until his death, but it was not without early problems caused by her attempted abduction by a rival lover. (Lawrence V. Ryan, *Roger Ascham*.)

Ask thyself, cries Maimuma from the grave: KNIGHTS, II, 4: The gravestone in question and its fear of judgement dates from the Arab occupation of Gozo (870–1090) and is the last resting place of a young Arab girl. (Sir Harry Luke, *Malta*, 1938.)

Asmodeus: KINGS, IV, 1: The Destroyer; the wicked angel who appears in the Book of Tobit in the Apocrypha. Asmodeus fell in love with Sara, daughter of Raguel. To ensure that she would not place her affections elsewhere, he murdered Sara's husband on her wedding night. He subsequently caused the death of seven of her husbands before Tobit intervened. Tobit successfully married Sara and drove Asmodeus into Egypt, exorcising him with a charm made from the liver and heart of a burnt fish.

Assai sa, chi nulla sa, se tacer' sa: PAWN, 11: Italian proverb; 'He who knows nothing, knows enough if he knows how to keep quiet'. It expresses the same level of diplomatic silence as that necessary for the perfect secretary, who should learn how to hold his pen, his liquor and his tongue.

At Martinmas I kill my swine: KNIGHTS, III, 16: From the traditional rhyme which gives a guide to the farming year from January to December:

> (Jan) By this fire I warm my hands
> (Feb) And with this spade I delve my lands
> (Mar) Here I set my things to spring
> (Apr) And here I hear the fowlis sing
> (May) I am as light as bird in bough
> (June) And I weed my corn well I-now
> (Jul) With my scythe my mead I mow

(Aug) And here I shear my corn full low
(Sept) With my flail I earn my bread
(Oct) And here I sow my wheat so red
(Nov) At Martinmas I kill my swine
(Dec) And at Christmas I drink red wine.

At the end of life, parent and kinsman are as a blind man: CHECKMATE V, 8: From the Dhammapada, the Buddhist scriptures (extract):

Men concern themselves about the matters of wife and child; they perceive not the inevitable law of disease (and death), and the end of life which quickly comes, as a bursting torrent (sweeping all before it) in a moment. Then neither father nor mother can save one; what hope, then, can be placed in all one's relatives? At the end of life, parent and kinsman are as a blind man set to look after a burning lamp. A wise man understanding this should carefully practise himself in the Rules of Religion.

(Samuel Beal, *Texts from the Buddhist Canon, the Dhammapada*, London, 1902.)

Atant la gent Camile apele: CHECKMATE, I, 5: This verse and the subsequent verses quoted throughout the rest of the chapter come from the twelfth-century epic, *Le Roman d'Énéas* and relate the burial of **Camilla the Volscian**. Only those verses quoted within the text have been translated; all tense changes are in the original quoted version:

At that Camille calls the people [together]
        He summoned the damsels,
        He revealed their Lady to them,
        She was all covered in blood . . .
        They washed her in rose water,
        And cut her fine locks,
        And then they perfumed her:
        There is balm and there was plenty of myrrh,
        They adorned her body well within it . . .

        In a silken sheet from Almeria
        Was the maiden buried,
        And then they placed her in a bier
        Which was rich and expensive.
        . . . The bed was covered with cotton
        And above it was placed a tapestry
        Which covered all the bedding . . .

They dress Camilla in a shift,
Made of a fine tunic of Baghdad silk;
She had a crown on her head of fine gold,
And held the sceptre in her right hand,
And had her left hand on her breast.
In the middle of the vault was set
The tomb where Camilla was placed . . .

A golden inscription was on the tomb,
Letters of black were on it,
Her epitaph was written there.
The letters read, the verse says:
'Here lies Camilla the damsel,
Who was most brave and most beautiful
And who greatly loved chivalry
And upheld it all her life. . . .'

(André Mary, ed., *La Fleur de la Poésie Française*, Paris, 1951.)

Athens, Duchess of: RAM, 9: See **Acciajuoli Family.**

Athos: CASTLE, II, 5: One of the greatest mountains in Macedonia, 150 miles in circumference, projecting into the Aegean Sea, most famous for its rigorous exclusion of all females. Even cows were forbidden at one time. It was suggested to **Alexander the Great** by the sculptor Dinocrales that the mountain could be sculpted into the likeness of the King. The sculpture's left hand would hold a great city, and his right would encompass a great lake. Alexander was no doubt attracted by the thought of such an egotistical monument, but the plan was rejected as the area would not have been fertile enough to support a great city. Since the middle ages, Mount Athos has been home to various monastic communities and is also known as the 'Holy Mountain'. Like **St Catherine**'s it was once a treasure house for icons. (J. Lempriere, *A Classical Dictionary*, London, 1815.)

Atlantis: CASTLE, II, 6: The legendary sunken kingdom in the Western ocean, between the Pillars of Hercules. It is described in Plato's dialogue 'Timaeus' as a beautiful and prosperous island, but it sank into the sea due to the impious behaviour of its inhabitants.

Atropos: QUEENS, IV, 5: One of the three Greek goddesses known as the Fates; daughters of Zeus and Themis. They give good and bad fates to mortal man: Clotho is the Spinner, who spins the thread of life; her sister Lachesis, Disposer of Lots, determines its length; and finally Atropos, the Inflexible or Inevitable, cuts the thread. Clotho is portrayed with a spindle; Lachesis with a scroll or globe; and Atropos with a pair of shears or a pair of scales. (Harry Thurston Peck, ed., *Harper's Dictionary of Classical Literature and Antiquities*, NY, 1962.)

Attic: KINGS, Gambit; SCORPIONS, 28: The title given to a restrained, dignified and severe form of oratory or behaviour, that makes only sparing use of oral or visual elaboration. The twelve independent states of Attica were united by the legendary Theseus into one political body, with Athens as the capital.

Attila: KINGS, I, 1: (d. 453) The bravest warrior and sole leader of the Huns after AD 444. His army of seven hundred thousand men was the terror of all civilised nations in Europe and Asia; Attila was the self-styled 'Scourge of God' for the chastisement of the human race. His reign of terror ended on the evening of his marriage to the beautiful virgin Hilda. During the celebratory nuptials, he burst a blood vessel and suffocated to death. (Harry Thurston Peck, ed., *Harper's Dictionary of Classical Literature and Antiquities*, NY, 1962.)

Au bout de la trace on trouve toujours ou le chameau ou le propriétaire du chameau: PAWN, 10: 'At the end of the route, one will always find either the camel or the camel driver'. (Albin Michel, *La Vie du Chameau*, Paris, 1938.)

Au travail, on fait ce qu'on peut, mais à table, on se force: CHECKMATE, I, 4: 'At work one does what one can, but at table one makes a real effort'.

D'AUBIGNY, John Stewart: QUEENS: (d. by 1579) The fifth seigneur d'Aubigny, and youngest son of John Stewart, third Earl of Lennox. Given the perfidious behaviour of his brother **Matthew Lennox**, it would not be surprising if d'Aubigny had been involved in the **Poison Plot** against the young **Mary Queen of Scots**, even though he was not directly implicated. Very little biographical information exists about the French side of the Stewart family; John and his wife had one son, Esmé (1542–1583), probably a playmate of the Queen of Scots, and later a great army leader. John d'Aubigny's widow, Anne de la Queulle, remained a gentlewoman in ordinary at the French court after her husband's death.

Aucassin and Nicolette: QUEENS, III, 3: A thirteenth-century legend of Provence. In verse and song it tells of the romantic adventures of a young man and his love for the captive Nicolette. See below.

Aucassins, damoisiax, sire!: CHECKMATE, V, 8: From the songs of **Aucassin and Nicolette**, the same sections of verse as in QUEENS, III, 3 are partially quoted again:

Aucassins, damoisiax, sire!
Ja suis jou li vostre amie!
Et vos ne me haés mie!

Por vos sui en prison misse,
En ceste cambre vautie
U je trai molt male vie.
Mais, par diu le fil Marie,———
Longement ne serai prise
Se jel puis mie . . .

Douce suer, com me plairoit
Se monter povie droit,
Que que fust à recaoir,
Que fuisse lassus o toi!
Je te baiseroie estroit!
Se j'estoie fix a roi,
S'afferriés vos bien a moi
Suer, douce amie.

Aucassin, young man, sir!
I am indeed your beloved!
And you do not hate me!

For you I have been put in prison,
In this vaulted room
Where I lead a most dismal life.
But, by God, son of Mary,
I shall not be held for long
If I can yet . . .

Sweet sister, how it would please me
If I could rise directly,
Whatever falling back would mean,
If I could be up there with you!
I would kiss you warmly!
If I were a king's son,
You would indeed have dealings with me,
Sweet sister, friend, beloved . . .

D'AUMALE, Duke of: CHECKMATE: See **De Guise, Claude.**

Aunque manso tu sabuesso, no le muerdas en el beco: KINGS, I, 5: 'Although your bloodhound is tame, don't bite it on the nose'.

Aussi Dieu aide aux fols et aux enfants: PAWN, 20: 'God also helps fools and children'; said of **Brusquet, Henri II**'s fool. In 1559, Brusquet accompanied **Charles de Guise**, the Cardinal of Lorraine, to Brussels for peace talks with the Duke of Alva. At the feast celebrating the conclusion of the talks, Brusquet rolled himself in the table cloth (cutlery, plates and all) and staggered from the hall without so much as a scratch. (Brantôme, *Les Vies des Grands Capitaines François*, Vol. IV.)

Aussi tost veu, aussi tost pleust: CHECKMATE, V, 5: 'No sooner seen than loved'. Specifically, said of **Claude de Guise** by Louis XII of France.

Aut bibat, aut abeat: CHECKMATE, II, 9: 'Drink or get out'. A command also popular at the ancient festivals of the Greeks.

Aut Caesar, aut nihil: CASTLE, II, 9: Latin proverb; 'Either the top job or nothing'.

Aut nulla Ebrietas, aut tanta sit ut sibi curat: CHECKMATE, I, 3: 'Either no drunkenness, or let there be so much [of it] that it cures him'.

Avicenna: KINGS, IV, 3; PAWN, 2: (980–1037) Abou ibn Sina, Arabian physician and philosopher, composer of a treatise on logic, and another on metaphysics; called both the Hippocrates and the Aristotle of the Arabs. He is said to have memorised the Koran by the age of ten, and was known in the Arab-speaking world as 'the Prince of Physicians'.

Ay ay dios. Y cuando: KINGS, I, 5: 'O God. And when . . .'.

Bacchantes: QUEENS, II, 1: Title given to the followers of **Dionysus**, more often referring to women than men. Gathering on mountains, they would celebrate the spring festival of the god dressed in fawn skins and wreathed in vines and ivy, drinking and dancing themselves into a frenzy. The zealous and liberally erotic nature of these ancient revels led to moral and judicial censure from the Greek authorities, lest the devout should be further encouraged to constantly recurring acts of licentiousness. (Harry Thurston Peck, ed., *Harper's Dictionary of Classical Literature and Antiquities*, NY, 1962.)

Baden: PAWN, 1: Aargau, Switzerland. In the fifteenth century Baden was the most famous and popular spa north of the Alps. Around the main square were thirty different hostelries, each with its own bath house. Poggio Bracciolini, papal secretary, visited Baden in 1418, leaving a detailed account of the promiscuous single and mixed bathing arrangements. He also noted the fact that there were public galleries above the baths, where gentlemen gathered to watch the ladies swimming below, flinging silver coins or garlands of flowers to them. It has been suggested that one reason why the baths were considered a cure for barrenness in women is the opportunity they would have to cuckold their sterile husbands, whilst 'taking the cure' in an atmosphere of such apparent moral laxity. Swiss and German wives often included in their marriage contracts the right to take the waters every two years.

The baths of Baden produced water 'so hot they would scald the hair off a hogg', according to Fynes Moryson, an early-seventeenth-century traveller. Men, women, monks and nuns would all sit in the waters together, separated by partitions with windows through which the clients could converse, hold hands or kiss. The sulphurous waters of Baden were described as clear; the only objects noted as floating in them were the small tables for cards, chess or food. (E.S. Turner, *Taking the Cure*; Fynes Moryson, Gent., *An Itinerary*, 1617.)

Baldachin: SCORPIONS, 15: From the Italian *baldacco*, meaning Baghdad; where the cloth originated. It later came to describe a silk canopy over a throne or altar, supported by pillars or fastened to the wall, and in the Roman Catholic church the canopy held over the priest at the procession of the Host.

Baldwin, William: CASTLE, III, 9: Co-author of the sixteenth-century play *The Mirror for Magistrates*, written for Henry VIII, and author of *Love and Life*, which was in fact written, although perhaps only the cast list remained extant in the Hall of Revels.

Banachadee: QUEENS, I, 2: See the second line of verse quoted under **O Dermyne, O Donnall, O Dochardy droch.**

Bandinello's Hercules: QUEENS, I, 3: The statue of Hercules and Cacas by Baccio Bandinelli (1488–1560) in the Piazza della Signoria in Florence. **Benvenuto Cellini** and Bandinelli were great rivals; when they differed in opinion over the relative merits of a classical statue of Ganymede, Cellini chose to inform his enemy of the scurrilous verses which accompanied the exhibition of the Hercules in 1534:

> Well then, this virtuous school says that if one were to shave the hair of your Hercules, there would not be skull enough to hold his brain; it says that it is impossible to distinguish whether his features are those of a man or of something between a lion and an ox . . . his sprawling shoulders are like the two pommels of an ass's pack saddle; his breasts and all the muscles of the body are not portrayed from a man, but from a big sack full of melons set upright against a wall . . .

Bandinelli retaliated by calling Cellini a sodomite. The merits of this artistic debate in front of **Cosimo de' Medici** were recalled in Cellini's memoirs. (Benvenuto Cellini, *Autobiography*, edited & abridged by Charles Hope from the translation by John Addington Symonds, Oxford, 1983.)

Barbarossa: KNIGHTS, II, 2: The name given to two renegade Greek brothers on account of their red beards: Horuc (1475–1519); and Kheir-ed-Din (c. 1475–1546), Bey of Algiers. Kheir-ed-Din was the commander of Sultan **Sulieman's** fleet, and conquered Tunis from Sultan Muley-Hassan who had usurped the throne by murdering thirty-three of his brothers. The Bey was an ally of **Francis I** of France; in 1534 a Turkish embassy to Francis brought lions (one of which was tame) and tigers for his menagerie from Sultan Kheireddin Barberousse. (Andrew Haggard, *Two Great Rivals*; G. Loisel, *Histoire des Ménageries de l'Antiquité à Nos Jours*, Paris, 1912.)

Barillo: SCORPIONS, 29: Or barilla, a carbonate produced by burning certain sea plants, and essential to the production of both glass and soap.

Bascinet: SCORPIONS, 43: Helmet which covers the whole head, including the ears and back of the neck, providing lightweight all-round protection from glancing or direct blows.

Bastard sword: QUEENS, IV, 3: Short thick sword, favoured by the Swiss mercenaries, also acceptable as a weapon in public duelling. (George H. Powell, *Duelling Stories of the Sixteenth Century*, tr. from Brantôme.)

Bastinado: KNIGHTS, II, 7: Beating inflicted with a long, thin stick from the soles of the feet to the stomach; a Turkish torture adapted by the **Knights of St John.** It generally causes death by internal haemorrhaging. Thirty or forty harshly dealt blows will disable the victim for months.

Be not so rude and ignorant, As is the horse and mule: CHECKMATE, V, 7: Psalm 32, 9; the version used is that of the Geneva Psalms, printed by John Crespin in 1569 (extract; vv 7–10):

> When trouble and adversity,
> Do compasse me about:
> Thou art my refuge and my joy,
> And thou dost ryd me out.
> Come hither and I shall thee teach,
> How thou shalt walke a ryght
> And will thee guide, as I my selfe
> Have learnde by proofe and fight.

> Be not so rude and ignoraunt,
> As is the Horse and Mule:
> Whose mouth without a rayne or byt,
> From hame thou canst not rule.
> The wicked man shall manifold
> Sorowes and griefe sustayne:
> But unto him that trustes in God,
> His goodness shall remaine.

Bears have weakest heads, as Lions have strongest: CASTLE, II, 6: Referring to the Roman fascination for pitting men against ferocious animals in the arena: a blow to the right part of the skull can kill a bear outright, whereas lions are one of the hardest to defeat. The attraction of these wild animals in combat or on show continued to be fashionable for many years. Emperor **Charles V** had at least three lions in his menagerie in the 1530s, and kept them shorn in a style similar to his poodles; totally shaved apart from the ruff and the crupper. Bear baiting was particularly popular with the Elizabethans. (G. Loisel, *Histoire des Ménageries de l'Antiquité à Nos Jours*, Paris, 1912.)

Beaton, David, Cardinal: See **Wishart, George.**

BEATON, James, Archbishop of Glasgow: CHECKMATE: (1517–1603) One of the Scottish Councillors sent to negotiate the marriage of **Mary Queen of Scots** to **Francis II,** Dauphin of France. Beaton was a loyal friend to the Queen Dowager of Scotland, **Mary de Guise,** and a staunch opponent of religious reform in Scotland, maintaining his religious principles with an unblemished public and private reputation. At the age of fourteen he was sent to Paris by his father to study and at the age of twenty was employed by the French King on a mission to the Queen Dowager. He was consecrated Archbishop of Glasgow in 1552, and remained in his Scottish see until the Reformation. On the death of the Queen Dowager, Beaton and his allies went to France, taking with them the charters and treasures of his diocese, thus saving them from the destructive hands of the Reformers. He remained in Paris until his death, acting as Scots Ambassador to the French court. Throughout his life Beaton had been a great benefactor of the Scots college at Paris (founded in 1325), eventually bequeathing to the college his manuscripts and personal fortune.

BEATON, Janet: KINGS: (1515–1568) Wife of **Buccleuch,** her third husband. She came from an influential family whose kin included the Cardinal of St Andrews (murdered in 1546), and was a lady in waiting to **Mary Queen of Scots,** a mistress of **James V,** and a wet nurse to James VI. With Buccleuch, she had six children, three surviving to adulthood.

After the murder of her husband by the **Kerrs,** Janet Beaton gathered two hundred of the Scott family and hounded Lord Cranstoun, one of the supporters of the Kerrs. It is in this guise that she appears in Sir Walter Scott's *Lay of the Last Minstrel.* She later became the mistress of James Bothwell, murderer of Mary Queen of Scots' second husband Henry, Lord Darnley, and was publicly rumoured not only to be a witch, but also to have been involved in the murder plot itself. (David Steel, *Border Country.*)

Beggar's leprosy: QUEENS, IV, 5: Counterfeit illness achieved by painting the face with glue and wrapping a tight scarf around the neck to make the skin livid. An alternative was to paint oneself with calf's blood mixed with rye dough. (Stephen Paget, *Ambroise Paré and His Times.*)

Bektashi: PAWN: For full details of the religious order founded by Haji Bektash Veli (b. 1248), see John K. Birge, *The Bektashi Order of Dervishes,* London, 1937.

Bella gerant alii; tu, felix Scotia, nube: CHECKMATE, II, 5: 'Some wage war; thou, happy Scotland, give in marriage'.

Belle qui tiens ma vie Captive dans tes yeulx: CHECKMATE, V, 9: Sixteenth-century French song written by the Burgundian priest Jehan Tabouret

(1519–1595), under the pseudonym of Thoinot Arbeau. Both verses are fully quoted within the text:

> Fair maid, who hold'st my life
> Captive in thine eyes,
> Who has ravished my soul
> With a gracious smile,
> Come quickly to my aid
> Or else I needs must die.
>
> So come close, my fair one,
> Come close, my treasure,
> Rebel no more against me
> Since my heart is thine
> And to appease my ill
> Give to me a kiss.

(Tr. Frank Dobbins, and taken from the LP: The King's Singers, *A French Collection*, 1973, EMI, CSD 3740.)

Benedicta inter mulieres: CASTLE, I, 6: 'Blessed art thou among women, and blessed is the fruit of thy womb': Elisabeth's greeting to the Virgin Mary (Luke, 1, 42); also quoted by Cardinal **Pole** in his greeting to the ever-hopefully expectant **Mary Tudor.**

Berber slut: PAWN, 7: Thomas Coryates, an English traveller in the Levant and the Far East in 1612, described Bedouin women in the above manner, as wantons 'ringed under the nostrils and ringed on the right nostril unto the spoil of kissing'. (Samuel Purchas, *Purchas, His Pilgrimes*, 1905 edn of the Hakluytus Posthumus collection.)

Berla: QUEENS, II, 1: See **Carping tract of . . .**

Berwick: KINGS, UNICORN: Strategically very important town in the wars between Scotland and England. It was also a centre of commerce; its customs revenues accounting for nearly a quarter of the income from all the English ports. In the thirteenth century, it was described as 'a second Alexandria', but this period of prosperity ended when Edward I (1272–1307) reconquered the city for the English in 1296; putting to death over half of its 15,000 inhabitants and allowing the English burghers to massacre the colony of Flemish merchants and workmen imported by Alexander III of Scotland (1249–1286).

The town rapidly sank thereafter to the status of only a small seaport, but recovered its trading links over time. Berwick changed hands regularly between Scotland and England over the following generations, but has remained in English hands since 1482, although—because of its importance—not without regular attempts by the Scots to regain it.

In 1560 **Elizabeth** of England intervened in the Scottish Reformation; the Treaty of Berwick provided English assistance to help the Protestant Lords of the Congregation against a reimposition of Catholicism by the French. Peace between Scotland and England was maintained during the rest of her rule, but the castle at Berwick remained garrisoned until the Union of the Crowns in 1603.

Bessarion, Cardinal: RAM, 4: (1403–1472) The influential Greek scholar, churchman, humanist and collector of manuscripts. Born in **Trebizond**, Bessarion probably came from the artisan or merchant class of the city. He was christened John, but was renamed in honour of St Bessarion when he entered the Order of St Basil in 1425. Described as the most Latin of all the Greeks, Bessarion did his utmost to promote unity between the Latin church of the West and the Orthodox church of the East. In 1436 he became Metropolitan of Nicosia. Bessarion attempted to maintain the role of mediator between the papacy and the Byzantine Empire.

Intransigence, rigid dogma and fanaticism prevented union between the churches of East and West, but Bessarion did his best to meet both halfway. Whilst in Rome from 1439 to 1450, he learned fluent Latin, but kept his Greek costume and long beard, despite ridicule from the clean-shaven Latin and Frankish Catholics. Hopes of real union had faded by 1440, but Bessarion remained the agent of Byzantium, constantly appealing to the Pope for aid against the Turks. He was a candidate for the papacy itself in 1455, but was passed over in favour of the Spaniard, Alfonso Borgia, Bishop of Valencia (1378–1458) who became **Calixtus III.**

Bessarion became the supervisor of the papal **alum** works at Tolfa. Even after Trebizond fell to the Turk, he remained as a diplomatic link and matchmaker between the East and West, sponsoring the match between Zoë Paleologus and Tsar Ivan the Great. His home became a haven for all exiled Byzantine nobles, officials, humanists and academics. Bessarion's passion for collecting ancient manuscripts was famous. He sent agents to Greece, Germany and even England, copying what he could not purchase. He constructed one of the foremost libraries of his day, comprising 3,000 books and costing him 40,000 gold écus. After his death, it was gifted to Venice, later to become the starting point for the Marciana, the Library of St Mark.

Bien vienne la belle bergère: SCALES 42: Song mentioned by Olivier de la Marche. According to his memoirs, it formed part of the entertainment provided for the wedding feast in Bruges in July 1468 of **Charles, Duke of Burgundy** and the English princess Margaret of York. The singers included a golden lion, 'big as the largest war-horse in the world', and draped in a silk cover bearing the Burgundian arms. It sang the tenor part. On its back, dressed as a shepherdess in cloth of gold with basket and crook (and a dog on a lead) rode Madame de Beaugrant, the dwarf of the Duke of Burgundy's daughter, who sang the other part of the chanson. At the end of the song the shepherdess was lifted on to a table and offered to the new Duchess Margaret as a gift, 'which she received very humanely'.

Bien vienne la belle bergère:
De qui la beauté et manière
Nous rend soulas et esperance.
Bien vienne l'espoir et fiance
De ceste signeurie entière.
Bien devons celle tenir chère,
Qui nous est garand et frontière
Contre danger, et tant qui'il pense.
Bien vienne.

C'est la source, c'est la minière,
De nostre force grande et fière.
C'est nostre paix et asseurance.
Dieu louans de telle aliance,
Crions, chantons, à lie chère,
Bien vienne.

Be welcome, pretty shepherdess
Whose shining mien and comeliness
Sweet solace and fair promise yield.
And welcome, gracious hope and shield
Of all this land and its noblesse.

We owe a gage of tenderness
To thee, our bulwark measureless
Against dread dangers yet concealed—
Be welcome thou.

Lo, here the fount and genesis
Of this our pride and hardiness.
Lo, here our peace, our trust, our bield,
May God commend the knot thus sealed
Which, shouting, singing, we address—
Be welcome thou.

(Tr. D.D.)

Bilma: SCALES, 33: The largest of the camel trains, the *azalai*, set out each autumn from Air to fetch salt from Bilma. As late as 1908 it still comprised

20,000 camels. By a strange and inexplicable phenomenon, it is said that the mountain nearest to Bilma would 'sing', giving the inhabitants of the city at least two days warning of the *azalai's* approach. A similar experience has apparently been noted in the hills of Ross-shire: if the weather conditions are suitable, the mountains are said to 'roar' to each other. (E.W. Bovill, *The Golden Trade of the Moors*, London, 1958; Dr F. Fraser Darling, *A Herd of Red Deer*, London, 1937.)

Binche: CASTLE, II, 5: The home of Maria, Queen Dowager of Hungary and Regent of the Low Countries, sister of Emperor **Charles V**. The gardens at Binche were filled with artifice: white marble caves twenty-four feet high, a statue of Parnassus in mother of pearl, and the nine muses in white marble. There were flowers of embossed silver in marble rockeries alongside bushes carved from coral. Scented fountains showered spray over the visitors, who would also be suitably impressed by artificial rain, thunder and lightning. It was taken by the French in their war against the Emperor in 1554, and razed to the ground. (Jane de Iongh, *Mary of Hungary*.)

Blasius, St: PAWN, 22: An early-fourth-century Bishop of Sebaste in Armenia, also known as St Blaise, martyred under Licinius. He is said to have miraculously restored the life of a child who had choked to death on a fishbone, and is sought as an intercessor for the sick, especially those troubled with throat problems. He is also patron saint of woolcombers, as he was torn to pieces by combs of iron. (Simeon Metaphrastes, *Life of St Blaise*.)

Blessed Gerard: KNIGHTS, I, 2: Founder of the Order of the **Knights of St John** in 1023 as a hospital order for distressed and sick pilgrims, funded by the pious merchants of Amalfi. His successors eventually turned a small group of monks into a rich and powerful crusading order. (Edward J. King, *The Knights of St John in England*.)

Blessed shall ye be when men shall hate you: CHECKMATE, I, 3: Gospel according to Matthew, 5, 11.

Blois: QUEENS: Referred to by the chronicler Froissart (c. 1337–1410) as one of the finest châteaux of the kingdom. In 1498 on the death of Charles VIII at **Amboise**, the Count of Blois, Louis d'Orleans, became King of France. The royal court was installed at his family home. In 1515 the new King, **Francis I**, began a building programme at the château that was to take four years and totally rework the façade, including constructing the famous double helix octagonal staircase, perhaps designed, or at least inspired by Leonardo da Vinci. (Marcus Binney, *Châteaux of the Loire*, London, 1992.)

Bloodwite: KNIGHTS, III, 16: The legal jurisdiction concerning an assault with bloodshed; comparable to 'Blood Money'. It described money paid to the next of kin of a murder victim, to induce them to forgo their right to seek blood for blood. (*Selections from the Records of the Regality of Melrose*, Vol. III, 1547–1706.)

Blubbering Echo: QUEENS, I, 4: Mountain nymph; daughter of Aër and Gaea, attendant to Hera, or Juno. According to Ovid's *Metamorphoses*, she offended the goddess by talking too much and was deprived of the power of speech, leaving her only the ability to repeat the sounds she had heard. She fell in love with Narcissus, but it was not reciprocated, causing Echo to pine away until nothing remained but her voice. The lines quoted come from the anonymous Scottish poem, the 'Complaynt of Scotland', published in 1548. (Henry Craik, ed., *English Prose Selections*.)

Boat will sink that carries neither monk, nor student, nor whore, the: PAWN, 3: A sailor's saying concerning the crossing from Padua to Venice. It was presumably a fairly safe crossing, although one could not always be sure of the moral pedigree of one's fellow passengers. (Fynes Moryson, Gent., *An Itinerary*, 1617.)

Bob me on the noll: KINGS, IV, 1: From the poem by John Skelton (c. 1460–1529); 'The Bowge of Court' (1498), a satire on the Court of Henry VII, written in Skelton's favourite swift recurring rhymes (extract):

> Wolde to God it wolde please you some day
> A balade boke [ballad book] before me for to laye
> And lerne [teach] me for to synge re, me, fa, sol
> And when I fayle, bobbe [slap] me on the noll [head].

***Bochki* vaultings:** CASTLE, II, 7: Russian horseshoe arched roofs; *bochki* meaning barrel.

Boisterous gown of black velvet: CASTLE, II, 3: Anecdote related by George Cavendish (d. 1561) of a Venetian doctor called Augustine. When Augustine was taking dinner with Cardinal Wolsey, his gown accidentally knocked over the giant cross at the Cardinal's dinner table, injuring another of those present. This was taken to be a particularly bad omen for Augustine. (Henry Craik, ed., *English Prose Selections*, Vol. 1.)

BOLOGNA, Ludovico de Severi da: RISING: See **Ludovico de Severi da Bologna**.

***Bon regime* sanitatis:** UNICORN, 40: A satirical poem by Charles d'Orléans, the royal poet of the French court who was captured at the Battle of Agincourt in 1415 and spent twenty-five years as a prisoner of the English. The full text of the poem is available in *La Fleur de la Poésie Française* (ed. André Mary, Paris, 1951); its indelicacies are probably better left untranslated.

Bona, Queen of Lithuania: CASTLE, II, 5: Bona Sforza, mother of Sigismund Augustus (1548–1572), Grand Duke of Lithuania and King of Poland. The daughter of the Duke of Milan, she was famous for her beauty and haughty nature, whilst her court fostered an imported Italian taste for culture and luxury. (G. Vernadsky & M. Karpovich, *A History of Russia*, Vol. IV.)

BONHOMME, Macé: QUEENS: Sixteenth-century printer of Lyons, responsible for the printing of **Nostradamus's** *Centuries* in 1555.

BONKLE, Edward: UNICORN: (d. by 1496) First Provost of the Collegiate Church and Hospital in Edinburgh dedicated to the Holy Trinity and founded by Queen Mary of Gueldres in the lifetime of her husband, **James II** of Scotland (d. 1460). Bonkle is remembered now from his presence, wearing the robes of a canon, in the magnificent altarpiece painted by Hugo van der Goes for the College which now hangs in the National Gallery of Scotland.

Although the barony of Bonkle is in the south-east of Scotland and once belonged to the Stewarts, the best-known branch of the family were merchants who settled in Edinburgh and established a vigorous outpost in **Bruges** where they intermarried and became burgesses. Alexander Bonkle, a Bruges resident, was naturalised by 1469, in which year he joined **Anselm Adorne** in welcoming to Bruges the envoy of **James III**, come to settle a trade dispute. The following year Alexander acted as courier between the two countries, carrying letters from Duke **Charles the Bold** and from the town of Bruges to King James and to the nobles and towns of Scotland.

In Scotland, one or two of the family entered the church. William Bonkle became abbot of Arbroath. Edward appears first in a lay capacity, in an Edinburgh court writ of 1452 and then in 1459, when he was admitted as a **guild** brother of Edinburgh 'in return for his help and counsel'. From 1464 he was called 'Dominus', indicating perhaps that he had become a priest with only a bachelor degree. After 1459 he held a minor church office in Methlick, which he exchanged later to become rector of Crieff and canon of Dunkeld. By 1462 he had become involved with the building of Trinity College, and was first given the title of Provost in 1464.

Little is known of his private life. It is probable that he was the son of Robert Bonkle, an Edinburgh bailie, and had at least two brothers in public positions. He never married, but had an illegitimate son John (RISING), born almost certainly before he entered the priesthood. John Bonkle seems to have been a student at St Andrews in 1457–1458 and again in 1463, and from at least 1484 made his career in Scotland.

The choice of Edward Bonkle for Trinity Hospital probably reflects the close Flemish family connection appropriate to its founder Mary of Gueldres, who continued to hold the project dear to her heart all her life. The Flemish connection also explains the commissioning of Hugo van der Goes about 1473 to paint the Trinity panels, which give us a portrait of James II's son **James III** and his wife Margaret of Denmark, and their eldest son **James IV** as well as Edward Bonkle himself. It also includes, played by angels, a representation of the organ Edward bought for the College in 1466. It is not known whether Hugo van der Goes ever visited Scotland, but Andrew Haliburton, a well-known Scottish merchant of the day, was married to Cornelia, the daughter of one Catherine van der Goes and Sanders Bening, a friend of Hugo's in Ghent. (Colin Thompson & Lorne Campbell, *Hugo van der Goes and the Trinity Panel*; James D. Marwick, *The History of the Collegiate Church and Hospital of the Holy Trinity*; *Burlington Magazine*, May 1984.)

Boot, The: KINGS, I, 1: Also referred to as 'The Booties', the Boot was described as 'Four pieces of narrow boards nailed together of a competent length for the leg . . . which they wedge so tightly on all sides that not being able to bear the pain, they promise confession to be rid of it.' This method was similarly used to crush the hands in addition to the feet, and for additional torment, the French used a similar device to the boot with eight wedges instead of four. (Honoré de Balzac, *About Catherine de Medici*; *Morer's Short Account of Scotland*, 1679.)

BOUCCARD, Monsieur: QUEENS: Equerry to **Francis II**, when Dauphin of France. On one occasion, owing to bad weather, the Dauphin was obliged to practise his shooting skills indoors. He evidently needed more practice in the art, as he unfortunately missed the target and shot his equerry instead. Monsieur Bouccard lost the use of an eye. Bouccard perhaps got his revenge on the monarchy after he became head of the Protestant artillery in the religious wars which plagued France up until the end of the sixteenth century. (Abbé de Brantôme, *Les Vies des Grands Capitaines François*, Vol. III.)

BOUCHARD, Hélène: CHECKMATE: Dieppe draper and widow. The Bouchard household was home to a Protestant coven, and more than likely was the house where **John Knox** stayed *en route* to Scotland in 1557. In this year, the Protestants were meeting secretly at Madame Bouchard's house, and within three years were preaching openly in the town. (René Herval, *Dieppe*.)

Bouquet in one hand and a bell in the other, A: CHECKMATE, I, 6: Reference to the Brotherhood of St John the Evangelist, founded in 1401 as an association of scriveners, illuminators and binders of the printing trade in Lyons. The headquarters of the confraternity were in the church of St André des Arcs until 1582. Members were obliged to close their premises for their two saints' days. The day before each, a crier would announce the forthcoming festival, walking through the quarter with a bouquet in one hand and a bell in the other. (David T. Pottinger, *The French Book Trade in the Ancien Régime 1500–1791.*)

BOURBON, Louis de: QUEENS: See **Condé, Louis de Bourbon Prince of.**

Boute-feu: PAWN, 5: Firebrand.

Bows: PAWN, UNICORN: Large Ottoman bows of the fifteenth and sixteenth centuries were between four and six feet long, weighing just over twelve ounces and made of horn and sinew, softened into shape by heat. The archers carried twelve arrows at their belt, each of which was two feet long. The crossbow or arbaletre was more powerful, and required less skill to use than the longbow. They became obsolete as a weapon of war by the beginning of the seventeenth century, but were still popular in hunting.

BOYD: Thomas, Earl of Arran: UNICORN: (d. c. 1474) During the minority of **James III** of Scotland, the country was mainly governed by his mother, Mary of Gueldres (d. 1463) and **James Kennedy,** Bishop of St Andrews (d. 1465). In 1466, the Boyds of Kilmarnock seized control of the fourteen-year-old King, and effectively ran the country for the next three years. Robert Boyd was made governor of the King's person and keeper of the fortress of the kingdom; a position he intended to keep until the King was twenty-one. His son Thomas married the King's sister Mary and was created Earl of Arran. Robert Boyd had overseen the marriage treaty between Scotland and Denmark, by which Orkney and Shetland came under Scottish dominion.

Whilst Thomas was in Denmark concluding the negotiations, and his father was on a diplomatic mission to England, the family were overthrown by enemies who had successfully usurped the Boyds' position of favour with the King. In their absence they were attainted for treason, and condemned to die.

Break out in bolga: QUEENS, II, 2: See **Senchan Torpest.**

Bring the skin up over my ears, like the widow did to the Judge: QUEENS, I, 5: From a sermon of Hugh Latimer (c. 1485–1555), Bishop of Worcester and Reformed preacher. His preaching was notable for its use of graphic imagery:

> The greatest man in a realm can not so hurt a judge as the poor widow, such a shrewd turn she can do him . . . She can bring the judge's skin over his ears and never lay hands upon him.

(Henry Craik, ed., *English Prose,* Vol. 1.)

Brother, whi art thou so to me in ire?: From the medieval mystery play of *Cain and Abel;* these are Abel's words to Cain. (J.Q. Adams, *Chief Pre-Shakespearian Dramas,* Boston, 1924.)

Bruges: Already established by the seventh century, the town was named from the nearby bridge, a *brugge*, which appears on the earliest seals of the developing town. In 1200, Bruges was granted a charter by Baldwin IX of Constantinople, allowing it the right to hold a fair. The fair took place in May, coinciding with the Procession of the Holy Blood (established in 1303). By the fourteenth century the town had become a great trading centre, particularly in cloth of every variety. The city was at its commercial height in the fifteenth century when it is estimated that the population was between forty and fifty thousand. At this time, Spangnaerts Street, in the heart of the cloth dyeing area, was said to be such a busy thoroughfare that schoolboys would not walk along its cobbles but leapt from bale to bale of the cloth which filled the street from end to end. The carnival was also at its most popular and lucrative for the city then, especially the lottery, which took place at the same time and required a whole day to draw the winners. Residents assert that the concept of the lottery was invented in Bruges.

Trade and profit were not restricted solely to natives of Bruges. 'Merchant strangers' could deal freely with each other if they employed the services of a resident factor (for which they paid a tax). Cloth and trade went hand in hand with banking and investment, the staple profit industries of the Lombards, and the source of the city's rising prosperity. Foreign merchants flocked to Bruges, where they established consular houses. In the fifteenth century, nations represented by consuls in the city included the Austrians, Biscay merchants, Castilians, English, Florentines, French, Genoese, Germans, Irish, Lucca merchants, Portuguese, Scots, Smyrna merchants, Spaniards, Turks and Venetians.

Municipal freedom was granted but also controlled by the Dukes of Burgundy, who exhorted heavy taxes in return for trading privileges. When the city rebelled against Duke **Philip the Good** in 1438, it was ruthlessly crushed, but trade soon recovered. Even during plague and famine, the city continued to pursue its cloth and luxury trades. Tafur, a visiting Spanish nobleman, said of Bruges in this year:

> And without doubt the goddess of luxury has great power there, but it is not a place for poor men, who would be badly received. But any one who has money and wishes to spend it, will find in this town alone everything which the whole world produces . . . indeed there is no part of the world whose products are not found here at their best.

The harbour of Bruges was at Sluys, ten miles away from the prosperous city. Goods were unloaded from the merchant ships and carried by barges and lighters along the estuary of the Zwyn; first to Damme and on to Bruges. The lifeblood of the city was its connection to the sea, and its canals. The city went into decline when the estuary silted up in the later part of the fifteenth century and this connection was severed. (Wilfrid Robinson, *Bruges, an Histori-*

· FLANDERS ·

cal Sketch, Bruges, 1899; Malcolm Letts, *Bruges and its Past*, London, 1924; A.D. Duclos, *Bruges, Histoire et Souvenirs*, Bruges, 1910.)

Bruslez, noyez, pendez, ompellez: From *Pantagruel*; François Rabelais' (c. 1494–1533) list of potential tortures and forms of execution for the evil heretic's doctrinal misdemeanours, altered here as Lymond's threat against 'these wicked women'. The list quoted within the text includes burning, drowning, hanging, impaling, cutting up, mincing, crucifixion, boiling and barbecuing.

BRUSQUET: QUEENS: Henri II's court jester, and perpetual foil to **Piero Strozzi**'s chastening sense of humour. Brusquet first came to royal attention in 1536 at the French army's camp at Avignon where he set himself up as a doctor to the Swiss mercenaries and Landsknechts. Some he cured of their injuries by chance concoctions, many others he unfortunately did not. **Montmorency** promised to hang him, but Henri (then Dauphin) took a liking to the dangerous fool and interceded on Brusquet's behalf. Henri favoured Brusquet with several court appointments, making him Master of the Paris Post. Brusquet became incredibly wealthy from this preferment as he was in financial control of all post horses travelling to and from Paris.

He and Strozzi fought on every possible occasion. When Piero appeared before Henri dressed in a magnificent cloak of black velvet with elaborate silver embroidery on the cuffs, Brusquet jealously covered Strozzi's back with lardons (strips of bacon fat used for larding), then commented on the 'lovely gold aiguillettes' on his cloak. Strozzi, recognising the joke made at his expense, took off the cloak and insisted on presenting it to Brusquet as he had admired it so much.

The position of fool gave much licence, often at the expense of the employers: **Catherine de Médicis** had heard how ugly Brusquet's wife was, and asked that she be presented to her at the Louvre. Brusquet told his wife that the Queen was incredibly deaf, and that she must do her utmost to make herself heard. The semipolite shouting match that ensued could be heard all the way to the basse-court. After a later attack by Strozzi on the gullibility of Brusquet's wife, which deeply humiliated the jester, he retaliated by informing Pope **Paul IV** that Strozzi had taken two galleys from Marseilles and was on his way to 'take the turban' with **Dragut Rais** and pillage Civitavecchia en route.

Strozzi was in fact at Calais, and only laughed when he heard of the temporary confusion this had caused the Pope.

In later years, Brusquet sided with the Protestant faction (his son-in-law was amongst them), helping to 'lose' all of Henri's dispatches concerning the Huguenots. With the backlash against the Reformers after Henri's death, Brusquet's home was sacked, and he was forced to flee Paris and stay with **Diane de Poitiers**. He died shortly after writing to Strozzi's son, thanking him for his help in memory of his father. (Abbé de Brantôme, *Les Vies des Grands Capitaines François*, Vol. I.)

Buailim-scaith: QUEENS, IV, 5: Gaelic, 'I strike the shield'. Legend has it that when the King of Tara attacked Concobar, the moan of his shield when struck caused the shield of every Ulsterman to reverberate in sympathy, and so his chiefs knew he was in danger. (P.W. Joyce, *A Social History of Ancient Ireland*.)

BUCCLEUCH, Sir Walter Scott: KINGS: (c. 1490–1552) Buccleuch inherited his title and the barony of Branxholm from Sir Walter (1426–1469), first to take the title. Buccleuch rose to prominence and was knighted on the eve of Flodden in 1513, but he was imprisoned in Edinburgh Castle for opposing Margaret Tudor in 1524, and accused of fermenting disorder and misrule in the borders. In 1526, he once more came into royal favour as the young King **James V** requested his help in escaping from the power of the Douglas family. Sir Walter and his men were involved in a skirmish at Melrose when they tried to rescue the King, during which Sir Andrew Kerr of Cessford was killed by one of Buccleuch's servants. Despite the fact that Buccleuch was openly favoured by the King after the fall of the Douglases in 1528, the family feud between Sir Walter and the Kerrs continued and culminated in his murder, reported thus:

> In this zeir, all wes at guid rest, exceptand the lairds of Cesfurde and Fernyhirst with thair complices slew schir Walter Scott, laird of Balclewche, in Edinburgh, quha was ane valzeand guid knycht.

Buccleuch's body was brought back to Hawick and buried at the church of St Mary's. (*A Diurnal of Remarkable Occurents That Have Passed Within The Country of Scotland 1513–1575*, Edinburgh, 1833; William Fraser, *The Scotts of Buccleuch*, Edinburgh, 1878.)

BUCHANAN, George: CHECKMATE: (1506–1582) Scots historian and scholar, educated in France. He taught grammar at St Barbe, where he was tutor to **Cassilis**. In 1536 he returned to Scotland as tutor to one of the illegitimate sons of **James V**, but his Reformed opinions were out of sympathy with the prevailing religious climate. After satirising the Franciscans he was imprisoned in St Andrews. He escaped and returned to France in 1539, where he became tutor to Montaigne, amongst others. On the death of **Mary de Guise** he returned to Scotland, openly Protestant. His violent temper and religious opinions kept him in opposition to **Mary Queen of Scots** and after the murder of Lord Darnley it was Buchanan who asserted that the damning casket letters (implicating Mary in the plot) were in her handwriting. From 1570 to 1578 he was tutor to the young James VI of Scotland, and probably did more than any other individual to set him against restoring Mary to Scotland.

Budé, Guillaume: QUEENS, II, 6: (1486–1540) The foremost French humanist, jurist, mathematician, theologian, critic, archaeologist and Hellenist. Described by Erasmus as 'the French prodigy' and favoured by Louis XII of France and **Francis I**, who paid great attention to his opinions and ideas. He was responsible for the creation of the royal library at **Fontainebleau** and the Collège de France (College Royal), founded in 1530. Amongst the first professors of the college were Budé's disciples and followers: the mathematician Orontius Finaes (1494–1555); the encyclopaedist Guillaume Postel, (1510–1581); and the Greek scholar Jean Dorat (1508–1588).

Buke of the Howlat: KINGS, III, 2: or 'The Book of the Owl', the title given to the Scots poem of Richard Holland (d. 1482), written in a highly alliterative style. The owl catches sight of himself in a lake, and declares he is without doubt the ugliest of all creatures:

> Wa is me, wretche in this warld, wilsome of wane!
> [lonely in my habitat, or dreary of hope]
> With mair murnying in mynd than I meyne may
> [more mourning in mind than I may moan]
> Rolpit, reuthfully roch, in a rude rane
> [hoarsely cried out in a harsh repetitive rant].

He demands to know why his visage is so gruesome, and seeks an answer from the peacock, the Pope of all the birds:

> 'I come to speir [ask]', quod the spreit [ghastly
> creature] 'into special [particularly],
> Quhy I am formed so foule,
> Ay to yowt and to yowle,
> As ane horrible owle,
> Ugsum our all [loathsome over all].'

The peacock's solution is to make the owl more attractive by giving him a feather from the plumage of every other bird. However, the owl then becomes so arrogant and conceited that he is stripped of all his new finery, and ends right back where he started. (Priscilla Bawcutt & Felicity Riddy, eds, *Scottish Longer Poems 1375–1650*, Vol. I, Edinburgh, 1987.)

BURGUNDY Dukes of: See **Charles the Bold; Philip the Good.**

Buridan's Ass: KINGS, II, 2: A creature utterly lacking in the strength of mind to make a decision one way or the other, and from doing nothing, achieves nothing. From the sophism attributed to the French philosopher Buridan (d. c. 1360):

> If a hungry ass were placed exactly between two haystacks in every respect equal, it would starve to death, because there would be no motive why it should go to one rather than to the other.

Burnous: PAWN, 4: A practical white over-robe as worn by Maltese women and men, and described by several sixteenth-century visitors to the island. Still a common garment in Arabic countries.

Bury me at Leibethra, where the nightingale sings: KINGS, IV, 3: See **Orpheus.**

BUTLER, Thomas, Earl of Ormond: QUEENS: (1532–1614) 'Black Tom'; the handsome favourite of Queen **Elizabeth** of England. He became the tenth Earl of Ormond at the age of fourteen when his father was poisoned. Butler was brought up in England and showered with honours, thus alienating him from his Irish national sympathies. Knighted by King Edward in 1547, he became the first-ever Protestant in his family, later fighting in Ireland on the English side.

Buy a fit of mirth for a groat: QUEENS, II, 1: A reference to sixteenth-century broadsides and comic ballads, which sold at the price of three for a halfpenny, hence the potential for hysteria from the bulk purchase of a groat's worth.

Cache-cache: QUEENS, II, 2: The game of hide and seek.

Cacodemon: KINGS, II, 1: From the Greek, meaning 'evil spirit'. Also the name astrologers gave to the Twelfth House of Heaven, from which come only prognostications of an evil nature.

CA'DA MOSTO, Alvise: SCALES, 4: (c. 1432–1483) Venetian noble and trader, who left the first written accounts of the European discovery of Africa. Having sailed with the private and state galleys of Venice for eight years, Alvise sought a career in Portugal in 1453 when his father was exiled from the Republic of Venice. Prior to his African journey, Alvise had sailed to the Barbary coast, Candia and Flanders; not as a trained navigator but as a merchant, with the honorary title of 'noble bowman' on his Candia trip. In March 1455 he sailed from Cape St Vincent to the West Coast of Africa on a **caravel** owned by the Portuguese captain Vincente Dias. A second voyage followed in 1456, this time with the Genoese, also visiting the Cape Verde islands. There were no new discoveries made on either of these journeys, but what is significant about his account (written before 1460) is the information it gives about pre-colonial Africa.

After Africa he returned to Venice, still trading as a merchant, and was appointed by the Venetian state to various civic offices. (G. Crone, ed., *The Voyages of Cadamosto*, Hakluyt Society, 1937.)

Caelum, non animos mutant, qui trans mare currunt: CHECKMATE, III, 9: Latin proverb: 'Those who sail overseas change only their skies, not themselves'.

Cailleach-chearc: QUEENS, I, 2: Affectionate Gaelic term for an older woman.

Calamitosus est animus futuri anxius: PAWN, 4: 'A mind worried about the future is a destructive thing'.

CALIXTUS III: RAM, 4: Alfonso de Borgia (1378–1458), Pope from 1455 to 1458 and the candidate who was elected instead of **Bessarion**. Calixtus was a skilled diplomat who had taught canon law to the secretary of King **Alfonso V of Aragon.** He dreamed constantly of uniting the East and West in a new crusade against the Turk, rehabilitating Joan of Arc in his efforts to interest the French. His plans were never fulfilled. (See **Ludovico de Severi da Bologna.**) A dry, quiet Spanish legal scholar, he was despised and shunned by the Italian humanists. Calixtus countered by surrounding himself with countrymen and family; his nephew later became Pope Alexander VI in 1492. Alexander similarly advanced his own son, the infamous Cesare Borgia (c. 1475–1507).

Calvin, John: KNIGHTS, III, 8: (1509–1564) The formulator of the Reformed creed, who turned Luther's rebellion into a defined, circumscribed and severe religious faith. Calvin's father (d. 1531) had been attorney registrar to the diocesan court of Noyon, notary to the Chapter, and procurator fiscal to the episcopal county. His regular fights with the church culminated in his excommunication. John's elder brother, Charles, who took over from his father, was also excommunicated, which helps to explain why Calvin had little time or sympathy for the unreformed church of France. John was educated first at Noyon, then Paris and Orleans; graduating first with a law degree, then continuing to study the humanities. In 1536 he travelled to Geneva, which had adopted the Reformed Lutheran faith in the previous year. He lectured in theology and formulated the new creed, which spread rapidly. By 1558 there were estimated to be 400,000 Protestants in France, and by 1561 over 2,000 Reformed churches. Whilst in Geneva, Calvin tutored **John Knox,** who was to help bring the dogmatic religion back to Scotland.

Calypso: KINGS, I, 2: Greek goddess and queen of the isle of Ogygia (said to be Gozo). She rescued Odysseus, but detained him on her island for seven years before finally relenting and sending him home, having first shown him how to build a raft on which to escape. (Homer, *The Odyssey*, tr. Walter Shewring, Oxford, 1986.)

Camelopard: KINGS, II, 3: The giraffe, described by Bellon and Thevet in their early journeys in the Levant as a strange tall creature with the features of a camel, but spotted like a leopard. **Pierre Gilles** would travel miles to dissect one of these strange creatures. (Pierre Gilles, *De Topographia Constantinopoleos*, 1562.)

Camels: RAM, 31: Called by the Arabs *benat el leil*, the daughters of the night, camels provided the most suitable form of transport through the arid landscapes of the North African desert regions. In addition to its value as a beast of burden, the camel also provided food, drink, fuel and shelter. The camel's dung made excellent fuel, said to drive away demons and evil spirits. It was the

Bedouin's dream to die on his favourite camel's back and be buried in its skin. Camel hair and skin provided leather and rope, whilst its sturdy bones could be used to pitch a tent when wooden stakes were not available. To provide additional liquids on long journeys, a camel full of water could be muzzled to prevent it from ruminating and using up the supply. When necessary, the camel could be slit open. Drinking the sweet milk of the female camel meant the Bedouin was not so reliant upon water.

Racing camels were altogether different from the beasts of burden used on the desert caravan trains. A well-bred camel leaves lighter prints compared with a baggage camel and the thoroughbred has a smaller head, fine muzzle, long legs and an elegant well-muscled knee. The soles of its feet should be rounded; a little convex, with a cushion of fine shining hide. Colour was also important; brown or tawny camels were popular in the north, with grey or white varieties in mid-Arabia. The red camel was generally prized as the favourite, followed by the grey; its coat should be as silky as a jumping mouse (*jerboa*). The well-trained camel should be silent rising and kneeling, and a mark of a strong, vigorous animal is its ability to rise with a passenger already on its back.

Camels feature widely in the religion and mythology of the Arabs. Mohammed, son of a camel driver, confided the hundredth name of God to the camel which had saved his life; it appears as one of the few animals allowed into Paradise. An invisible caravan of camels called *khadra*, 'the green ones', transported the bodies of the faithful dead to Mecca. The stars were considered to be flocks of camels that pasture the skies (see **Aldebaran**); many of the stars, including Venus (Chala), were given camels' names. (Albin Michel, *La Vie du Chameau*, Paris, 1938; A.G. Leonard, *Camels*.)

Camilla the Volscian: CHECKMATE, I, 5; RAM, 42: Daughter of the tyrant king Metabus. Having been overthrown, her father fled and brought up his daughter in isolated woods, dedicating her to the service of the goddess Diana. Camilla was remarkable for her swiftness of foot and military prowess. Attended by a band of warriors, she led the Volscians in battle against Aeneas. She was killed in battle, but the goddess avenged her by intervening and slaying Camilla's attacker with one of her own arrows. The legend of Camilla within the text is taken from the twelfth-century classical French epic *Le*

Roman de Énéas (c. 1160), a liberal reworking of Ovid and Virgil which includes the death of the proto-Amazonian heroine. See *Atant la gent Camile apele*. (André Mary, ed., *La Fleur de la Poésie Francaise*, Paris, 1951.)

Campus Sceleratus: PAWN, 9: In Ancient Rome, the unchaste virgins of the temple of Vesta would be suitably punished for their infidelity to the goddess. They were taken in silence out of the city via the Gate of Salaria, then buried alive in the Campus Sceleratus; sealed in a cave with only a lighted candle, water and milk. (Fynes Morison, Gent., *An Itinerary*, 1617.)

CAMULIO, Prosper Schiaffino de' Medici: RISING, 33: (fl. 1450–1480) Although he occasionally used 'de' Medici' as part of his name, Prospero Camulio was a Genoese whose anxious career in public life was in many ways similar to that of **Tommaso Portinari**, although he seldom spent long in one place. The family home of the Schiaffini was the fishing village of Camogli, south of Genoa: a republic in a state of flux throughout Camulio's lifetime. In addition to the contending powers of France and Milan, Genoa was divided by the ambitions of its internal factions: the Adorno (kinsmen of **Anselm Adorne**) and the Fregoso.

While preferring the Adorno and Milanese as his rulers, 'Master Prosper' was willing latterly to go anywhere and do anything for anyone. In 1456 he became a member of the household of **Francesco Sforza**, Duke of Milan, at the salary of thirty florins a month. Sforza sent him far afield in Italy to persuade Genoese exiles (with limited success) to unite to expel the French from the city. Asked from 1457 to sort out an inheritance dispute in the Pallavicino family, Camulio was afterwards accused of having falsified the books, and never quite cleared his name. From 1460, however, his career prospects seemed promising: Sforza sent him as Milanese envoy to **Louis**, the expatriate Dauphin of France, to **Duke Philip of Burgundy** and to King **Edward IV** of England (who were mostly at odds with one another) to assure them all of the Duke of Milan's friendship. He was also to find out whether or not the English meant to attack France. (His dispatches from Ghent, Brussels, **Bruges**, Antwerp and St Omer—from where he reported on the ceremony of the **Order of the Golden Fleece**—have been preserved, as have the reports of Bishop Coppini, his fellow envoy.)

Camulio's personal credit with the Dauphin of France came to a sudden end due, he thought, to poisonous rumours spread by Burgundian enemies as well as the inexplicable silences from Milan, which hadn't paid him for months. Despite some support from Bishop Coppini, he was never again sent to France by the Duke. He was used, however, on short missions to Pope **Pius II** and to **Cosimo de' Medici** in Florence, but after 1462 served the Duke only as a secretary within the household. Even when King Louis XI of France offered Genoa to Sforza, no great position was offered Camulio as he hoped, although the Duke still assured him he was his chief adviser in Genoese affairs. This was probably unwise for, frustrated, Camulio began to regard himself as the future lord of Genoa, and in 1467 was thrown out of the Republic.

Having failed to win a post with **Piero de' Medici** in Florence, he tried to persuade Milan to reinstate him as secretary and pay him arrears of eleven years of salary, denying rumours (probably true) that he had been plotting with Genoese exiles against Duke Galeazzo Maria of Milan. For the next few years he made repeated vain appeals to Milan, but after taking holy orders he obtained a post in 1469 with the Emperor Frederick III as counsellor and envoy. Deeply unhappy with 'barbarous Germany', he again bombarded Milan with demands, sending his brother with the gift of two Turkish horses to Galeazzo Maria. Then in the 1470s he passed (at last) to the service of Pope **Sixtus IV** (elected in 1471) whose family by great good fortune came from the Savona area, just west of Genoa.

It should be noted that, despite his quarrelsome nature, his blunt language and what has been described as 'his quick but disorganised mind, full of plans and ideas', Camulio was a man of some learning, personally interested in humanism and astrology and a collector of books. In 1468 the famous maker of African maps, Gratiosa Benincasa, was corresponding with the 'magnificent gentleman Prospero Camulio, *medico Genuensi'*. The latter reference is presumably a misinterpretation of Camulio's full name. One Niccolò de Medicis de Camulio in 1348 held the position of Genoese notary on the affairs of **Chios**, the Genoese-controlled island which dealt with Turkish **alum** and where members of the Adorno, Medici and Camogli families traditionally had an interest. Little is known of Camulio's own family, apart from the fact that he had one son, Antonio, who was in the service of King **Ferrante** of Naples, a brother Liberio, and a sister married to Pier Candido Decembrio, the humanist.

Candidior candidis: KNIGHTS, III, 7: 'Whiter than white'.

Candles: CHECKMATE, II, 7: To sell by inch of candle means to sell at auction. Beeswax candles were extremely expensive compared with tallow. Imports were always healthy before the Reformation to meet the requirements for church candles. In non-Catholic countries, the demand was kept almost as high by the need for chancery seals.

The promise in UNICORN, 2, to offer candles was made by devout sailors, such as Luca di Maso degli Albizzi, travelling with the Florentine galleys (1429–1430). Luca had vowed to offer candles in no less than five separate churches if he survived the return journey to Leghorn.

Cannibal rainbows: QUEENS, III, 6: Belief held by the ancient Zulus that rainbows devoured people and, when thirsty, descended to drink. (William Black, *Folk Medicine.*)

Cannibalism: CHECKMATE, II, 1: Although London is traditionally regarded as the home of Sweeney Todd, the Demon Barber of Fleet Street (who turned his customers into pies), there is a sixteenth-century French version of the same myth concerning a pâtissier of the Maison des Marmousets in Paris. The resultant pastries were particularly fine, because of his use of delicate human flesh as a filling. The Paris Parlement tried and punished the barber responsible and his accomplice the pâtissier, ordering that his house be razed to the ground. (De Breul, *Antiquité de Paris*, 1612.)

SCALES: Fifteenth-century Portuguese traders were often attacked in the Gambia by natives who believed that the white men only wanted to buy slaves with the intention of eating them.

Cannon: RISING, 1: Heavy artillery appears with increased frequency on the fifteenth-century battlefield; the development of field fortifications led to its use as an offensive weapon of attack rather than remaining on the defensive ramparts of a besieged town. Larger artillery was still best suited to siege warfare, because of the time and problems involved in dismantling and moving the weapons. Huge siege weapons, such as Mons Meg, were all named, and each had its own distinctive character; no two weapons being exactly the same. Because of their size and power, they became symbols of power rather than simply weapons.

Specially constructed wheeled carriages improved the mobility of the siege guns, although they were still very heavy and cumbersome to transport. Most armies used horses to pull the guns, although the papal armies preferred oxen. Where roads or weather conditions were bad, the transportation caused added problems. The heavy large-calibre guns fired stone balls, weighing 150 kg each; these balls were either transported with the weapons or cut on location by the army's own stonemasons. Added to this was the real danger of the temperamental weapon shattering or exploding, especially if it had been damaged or its casting was flawed, as **James II** found out to his cost at Roxburgh. See also **Guns.**

Canst thou bind the Unicorn with his band in the furrow?: UNICORN, 41: With reference to the unfathomable nature of God's plan to mere mortals who cannot compete on a level of omnipotence. The image of the unicorn is a prevalent one in the Bible; see for example Numbers 23, 22, 'God brought them out of Egypt; he hath as it were the strength of an unicorn'. The verse within the text comes from the Book of Job, 39, 9–11:

Will the unicorn be willing to serve thee, or abide by thy crib? Canst thou bind the unicorn with his band in the furrow? or will he harrow the valleys after thee? Wilt thou trust him, because his strength is great? or wilt thou leave thy labour to him?

Cape Gata: SCORPIONS, 9: Location of the Cypriot monstery of St Nicholas, founded in the fifth century by the first Christian Duke of Cyprus. The surrounding land was granted to the monks on the condition that they kept at least one hundred cats on the premises to keep the area free from snakes. As the cats could not live purely on the venomous serpents, the monks were to feed them every night and morning to supplement their natural hunting instinct, summoning them with a bell.

The monastery survived until the Ottoman invasion of Cyprus in 1571. It has since been rebuilt, set amongst pleasant gardens in which graceful young cats once more abound. (George Jeffrey, *A Description of the Historic Monuments of Cyprus*, London, 1983.)

Carai, Land of the: CASTLE, I, 6: A native tribe of North America, as encountered by the first travellers to the New World and noted by **Richard Eden** in his compilation of their travels. (Richard Eden, *The First Three English Books on America, 1511–1555.*)

Caravel: Modelled on the Arabic *dhow* of the Levant, the caravel was a small, shallow and easily manoeuvred boat greatly used by the Portuguese in their discovery of West Africa during the time of **Henry the Navigator.** They were between sixty and ninety feet long, twenty to thirty feet across the beam. Built of pine, they never weighed more than one hundred tons. The shallow bottom of the boat gave their captains greater confidence in sailing close to the uncharted African coast without beaching. A fifty-ton caravel would be able to

CARAVELS

sail up the River Gambia (the only fully navigable river in Africa), at a maximum speed of seven knots.

Another benefit of the caravel was the **lateen-rigged sails**, enabling the sailors to sail against the prevailing wind and improving their chances on the return voyage. The crew was also small; a fifty-ton caravel would carry only about twenty-six men in total. Where sickness or attack depleted the crew, it was possible to sail with only a fraction of this number: on one occasion some early explorers returned home with only five surviving members of the crew (none of whom were considered seasoned African discoverers or highly skilled navigators).

The routes, charts, instruments and even the new boat design of the Portuguese in the fifteenth century were kept from the outside world for as long as was humanly possible. It became a national obsession to preserve their new discoveries (and the financial benefits of exploitation) from their Genoese, Venetian and Castilian rivals. (G. Crone, ed., *The Voyages of Cadamosto*, Hakluyt Society, 1937.)

Carbines: PAWN, 4: See **Match-lock carbines; Wheel-lock carbines.**

Caritas generis humani: QUEENS, II, 4: 'Love of the human race'.

CARLOTTA, Queen of Cyprus: SCORPIONS: (c. 1437–1487) Daughter of the weak and effeminate King John II of Cyprus and his second wife Helen, daughter of Theodore II **Paleologus**, Despot of the Morea and Duke of Sparta. Helen was violently opposed to the Latin church of the West and vindictive to her personal rivals in the affection of the King; when the King's mistress Marietta provided John II with a son (and potential heir), Helen bit off her nose in retaliation; facial mutilation being a standard punishment for adultery. Helen virtually ruled Cyprus for sixteen years and was successfully made Regent of the kingdom whilst her weak and pliable husband was still alive. Carlotta was the only one of their three daughters to survive to adulthoood.

In 1458, both Carlotta's parents died, and she was crowned Queen of Cyprus. On returning from the coronation ceremony that October, her horse shied and Carlotta temporarily lost her balance and her crown. This was considered a particularly bad sign by her enemies and rivals. The following year, in an attempt to guarantee the legitimate succession of the Lusignan line, Carlotta married her first cousin Louis, Count of Geneva (d. 1482), son of the Duke of Savoy. They did not have long to establish their rule over Cyprus before the throne was usurped by Carlotta's illegitimate half-brother **Zacco**. She and her husband fled to Kyrenia.

Carlotta attempted to get help from Rhodes to regain her throne. To raise funds she sold most of her personal jewellery and pawned the property of the Dominican friars who had fled with her. She travelled widely in Europe in the following years, attempting to rally military and financial support. In October 1461 she had an audience in Rome with Pope **Pius II**, who gave her horses so she could collect troops in Piedmont and Savoy, touting her claim from Geneva to Aragon.

When Carlotta arrived in Savoy, she sought help from her mother-in-law the duchess and her aunt Anna. She was not favourably received; there were already too many Cypriot hangers-on at the court of Savoy to tolerate more expenditure on the island. She promised the Duke that if she and her husband should die without heirs, the crown and territories would revert to the Duchess of Savoy and her heirs; a territorial claim that was to pit Savoy against Venice when **Catherine Corner** later abdicated.

In 1462 she returned to Rhodes to continue the offensive against Zacco. Sultan **Mehmet II** had already favoured Zacco, but Carlotta sent an ambassador to the court of the Sultan in a vain attempt to get him to change his mind; the unfortunate envoy, James II de Flory, Count of Jaffa, was sawn in half by the Sultan.

After the fall of Famagusta, she continued at a distance to try and relieve Kyrenia until the autumn of 1464. The town was starving, reduced to eating horses, dogs, cats and mice. It eventually fell when Sor de Naves, Sicilian defender of the town, conceded victory to Zacco and the Mamelukes. Carlotta lived on charity under Pope Pius and then returned to Rhodes; hoping to pursue her claim once more when Zacco had died. Zacco left a widow and a legal claim which could not be pursued without the force of arms; the Order of **Knights of St John** at Rhodes declined to assist, and Carlotta once more sailed for Italy. In 1485 she ceded Cyprus to Savoy; giving away what was not in her possession and a claim to the throne not recognised by the Venetians. Two years later, having resigned herself to a life of good works and pious charity, she died. She and Louis had only one child, presumed stillborn.

Carmagnola, Francesco Bussone: RISING, 2: (c. 1385–1432) One of the finest and most successful mercenaries of the fifteenth century. He took control over the various campaigns to restore the territorial limits of Milan under the Visconti. In 1425 he entered Venetian service, where he used his mercenary army against his former employer. He was accused of treason by the Republic of Venice, the Signoria, for plotting with Visconti against Venice and was publicly executed in 1432.

Caro mio: PAWN, 9: 'My dear'.

Carping tract of sweet Berla-speech: QUEENS, II, 1: Concerning the ruling of the **Senchus Mor** on whether restitution should be made by the attacker after a period of time has elapsed from the original assault; particularly with reference to skull fractures. (See also **Bloodwite**.) Before the Senchus Mor, the law had already been partially formulated by a previous empirical ruling of the judge Berla:

> There is a year thrice
> For the full testing of the head
> As teaches concerning it
> A tract of the sweet Berla-speech;
> One year for the testing of the hand,
> After which there is no demand;
> There is said to be for the testing of the leg,
> A short period along with a year.

(*Ancient Laws and Institutions of Ireland.*)

Carrying hods in Egypt: KNIGHTS, III, 4: Meaning, 'arduous labour from which there is no respite'. An expression used by Sir Richard Morison (d. 1556), the English Ambassador to the court of **Charles V** at Augsburg (1550–1553). 'Merry Morysine' was reprimanded for the frivolous humour he included in his dispatches. (English Calendar of State Papers, Foreign; August, 1550.)

Carver, Robert: CASTLE, III, 3: (1487–c. 1546) Scots musician and composer, famous for his polyphonic motets and hymns, amongst them 'O Bon Jesu', the nineteen-part motet which is the most famous of his extant works (surviving in manuscript form in Scone, Scotland). He was the foremost composer of contrapuntal music in the sixteenth century, particularly gifted in his sensitivity to the emotional power of large choral works. (CD: Taverner Choir, *Taverner, Browne, Carver: Masterworks from Late-Medieval England and Scotland,* 1989, EMI CDC7 496612.)

Caryatid: CASTLE, II, 6; SCALES, 14: Female figure in architecture that supports a burden; often used as pillar ornamentation. Named after the women of Caryae in Laconia who were reduced to a state of abject slavery by the Greeks as punishment for conspiring with the invading Persians. (Harry Thurston Peck, ed., *Harper's Dictionary of Classical Literature and Antiquities*, NY, 1962.)

CASSILIS, Gilbert Kennedy, Earl of: CHECKMATE: (c. 1517–1558) Protestant Reformer and Councillor of Scotland at the wedding of **Mary Queen of Scots** and the Dauphin of France, **Francis II**. In 1530 he was sent to Paris to study under **George Buchanan.** He and Buchanan returned to Scotland in 1535. In 1542 Cassilis was captured by the English after the Scots' defeat at the battle of Solway Moss. He was imprisoned in the Tower of London, and later released under the supervision of Thomas Cranmer, Henry VIII's Archbishop of Canterbury. It is under the influence of Buchanan and Cranmer that Cassilis adopted the Protestant religion, and as such was an early supporter of **George Wishart.**

He returned to Scotland after signing the Treaty of Greenwich, promising to advance the marriage alliance between the young Scots queen and **Edward VI.** Even when the marriage plans fell through, Cassilis maintained his good relationship with England; the only one amongst the nobles sent north to return to England and pay off his ransom. In 1554 he helped the Queen Dowager **Mary de Guise** take the regency from the Earl of **Arran,** and was appointed Lord High Treasurer as his reward. His Reformed religious beliefs and favour for England led him to refuse to aid the Queen Dowager in a planned invasion of England in 1557; a war which could have united Scotland against the English, when public opinion increasingly perceived the French control of Scotland to be a greater threat to personal liberty and national importance than the political aspirations of the Reformers.

He died in France in 1558, having succumbed to the 'poison' affecting several of the councillors on their attempted return to Scotland. He died at the end of November, having had time to make his will, and his body was brought back to Scotland where it was buried in the Collegiate Church of Maybole.

Catechumen: RAM, 39: Student or recent convert; particularly with reference to a pupil learning the doctrine and beliefs of the church prior to baptism.

Catherine, St, Monastery of: UNICORN, 40: Home of a community of monks from the fourth century, tending what is believed to be the Burning Bush of Moses. Originally from Cyprus, the virgin saint in question was martyred in Alexandria when she had defended her chosen faith against the Emperor Maximinus's philosophers. Having won her point of disputation, she was martyred on a wheel (hence the firework known as a Catherine wheel and her status as patron saint of wheelwrights). It is said that when the wheel turned, her bonds were miraculously cut, and so the heathens were obliged to behead her. After her death, her body was flown by angels to Mount Catherine (Djebel Katrin), where it was discovered by the holy men. In the tenth century her remains were removed from their mountain chapel and placed in the fortified monastery within the church dating from the sixth century. In 1063, a military order called the Order of St Catherine was established at **Mount Sinai** to preserve the remains of the saint and to protect Christian pilgrims. It adhered to the strict rule of St Basil, the monastic rule prevalent in the Orthodox church of Greece and Russia.

Today the monastery retains only the skull and one hand of the saint. With the schism that split the Christian church of the East and West in 1054, St Catherine's remained in communion with Rome. To raise funds for the monastery and their order, six monks were sent to France to collect revenues and to sell relics, which explains why Rouen Cathedral now has more of St

Catherine than the monastery itself. The monastery became greatly influenced by the Byzantine church (especially in terms of the art and icons it collected), but never completely severed its links with the West. The monastery provided a meeting place for three antagonistic cultures, as Christians, Jews and Muslims all respected the sanctity of the place. There has been a mosque inside the heavily fortified walls of the monastery since the twelfth century, protecting it ultimately from Saracen despoilation.

The site of the Burning Bush is now encompassed by a chapel; the bush itself is said to have been uprooted for relics before 1216 by the Christians. Some things do not change: the monks resident at the monastery still make their own bread, sifting the wheat by hand to ensure that none of the local teeth-breaking granite remains. Amongst the icons and devotionary gifts, the chalice from Charles VI of France gifted in 1411 still remains at St Catherine's. (John Galey, *Sinai and the Monastery of St Catherine*, Massada, 1979.)

Catusaye, three thousand monkeys of: QUEENS, II, 1: Father Odoric of Pordenone travelling through India and China in 1318 wrote of visiting a Buddhist temple at 'Catusaye' where the monkeys came to be fed by hand at the sound of a bell. (G. Loisel, *Histoire des Ménageries de l'Antiquité à Nos Jours*, Paris, 1912.)

Caxton, William: KINGS: (1422–1491) The source of the quotes at the beginning of each chapter is Caxton's *The Game and Playe of the Chesse*, dating from 1474. Its second edition (1477) was the first book ever to be printed in England. The first edition dates from Caxton's residence in Bruges, and probably comes from the press of **Colard Mansion.** Caxton translated the *Game* from a fourteenth-century version by Ferron and de Vignay, based on the late thirteenth-century Latin original by Jacques de Cessoles, a Dominican brother at Rheims. The game is seen as an instructive handbook; not on the rules of the game, but on life. It is an ethical discourse on how to lead a sober life and fulfil one's moral duties.

Caxton was brought up in Kent, of a family which probably originally came from Norfolk. He was enrolled by his father in the Mercers' company in 1438, under Robert Large, later to become Lord Mayor of London. On Large's death in 1441 Caxton's apprenticeship was broken and he subsequently went to Bruges. In 1453 he returned to London to be formally inducted as a member of the Mercers' company. He became Governor of the English Nation of Merchant Adventurers in Bruges, loyally serving his country over a long period. After the marriage of **Edward IV's** sister Margaret of York to Duke **Charles the Bold,** Caxton entered the service of the new Burgundian Duchess, who shared his literary tastes. At her request he translated the *Recuyell des Histoires de Troyes* of Raoul Le Fevre.

The subsequent demand for handwritten copies wore him out, and so he considered turning to printing. He spent the summer and winter of 1471 in

Caxton's Mark

Cologne, a centre of the relatively new trade, and returned to Bruges in 1472, where he formed a partnership with Colard Mansion. Together they published the *Game and Playe of Chesse*.

Having won the favour of both Edward IV and his sister, Caxton returned to London in 1476, establishing his printing press in Westminster. In all, Caxton and his press were responsible for ninety-nine distinct productions, including many translations. (William Caxton, *The Game and Playe of the Chesse*, 1474, reprinted facsimile edn, London, 1883; Geoffrey Hindley, *England in the Age of Caxton*, London, 1979.)

Ce Christ empistolé: CHECKMATE, II, 2:

> This Christ with pistols, all blackened with smoke,
> Who like a demon moves, holding in his hand
> A huge cutlass, red with human blood.

Ce Lyon qui ne mord point; Lyon plus doux que cent pucelles: CHECKMATE, I, 2: 'This Lion which does not bite; Lion more gentle than a hundred maidens'. Clément Marot referring to the town of Lyons.

Ce n'est rien: c'est une femme qui se noie: KINGS, II, 3: 'It's nothing, just a drowning woman'.

Ce petit homme tant jolly: CHECKMATE, IV, 2: A popular lampoon against Louis de Bourbon, Prince of **Condé**:

> This pretty little man
> Always chatting and laughing
> Always kissing his sweetheart.
> God protect the little man.

Condé liked to laugh and was not averse to making fun of himself; the lampoon extends to sixteen verses, and is in the style of a vaudeville (i.e., a popular song interspersed with topical allusions). (Brantôme, *Les Vies des Grands Capitaines François*, Vol. IV.)

Ce que Dieu garde est bien gardé: CHECKMATE, V, 3: 'That which God protects is well protected'.

C'est du vin de Montmartre Qui en boit pinte, en pisse quarte: CHECKMATE, II, 1: Traditional French proverb, saying a great deal about Montmartre wine and its uriniparous qualities.

C'est ne pas tout de boire; il faut sortir d'ici: KINGS, I, 7: 'Drinking is not the be all and end all; let's get out of here'.

C'est tout de même que de manger la poule et puis son poulet?: CHECKMATE, IV, 3: 'Is it not the same if you eat the hen and then its chick?'. A proverb roughly similar in sentiment to 'You might as well be hanged for a sheep as a lamb', but in this context the sexual *double entendre* relating to both mother and daughter is deliberate and refers to a fictional twist in the story. It also touches on the supposed historical scandal of **Condé**, and his involvement with **St André**'s wife and daughter.

C'est Vertu, la nymph éternelle: PAWN, 15: It is Virtue, the eternal nymph'.

Cellini, Benvenuto: PAWN, 6; CHECKMATE, V, 2: (1500–1571) The foremost Florentine goldsmith of the sixteenth century. Cellini was apprenticed at the age of thirteen to a goldsmith, but was also an accomplished musician, artist and sculptor. He was in Rome from 1519 to 1540 where he was patronised by Pope **Clement VII**. From 1540 to 1545, he worked for **Francis I** of France, creating for him the magnificent salt cellar which is one of Cellini's few surviving works.

In 1545 he returned to Florence, and was patronised by Duke **Cosimo de' Medici**. His statue of Perseus is displayed in the Piazza della Signoria, alongside **Donatello**'s Judith and Holofernes and Michelangelo's David. Cellini's memoirs, dictated in 1558, are an excellent insight into the character of the man: from his artistic intentions to the arrogant egotism that always gives him the last and best word in any argument. (See **Bandinello's Hercules**.) (Benvenuto Cellini, *Autobiography*, edited and abridged by Charles Hope from the translation by John Addington Symonds, Oxford, 1983.)

Cerbottana: QUEENS, I, 3: As described by Cellini: short hollow wooden sticks, through which pellets of earth are blown. The weapon was used to kill birds. (Benvenuto Cellini, *Autobiography*, edited and abridged by Charles Hope from the translation by John Addington Symonds, Oxford, 1983.)

Certon, Pierre: QUEENS, I, 6: (c. 1500–1572) A musical colleague of Claude de Sermisy and composer of courtly *chansons*. Certon was in minor clerical orders, and earned his fame as a singer at Notre Dame in Paris from 1529. In 1532 he sang at the royal chapel. Amongst his surviving works are several on the perennial theme of cuckoldry, including 'La, la, la, je ne l'ose dire', published in 1538. (Record: The Purcell Consort of Voices, *Doulce Memoire*, 1972, Decca, ZRG 667; The Kings Singers, *A French Collection*, 1973, EMI, CSD 3740.)

Ceuta: SCALES, 8: The first Portuguese foothold in North Africa in the fifteenth century; captured by **Henry the Navigator** in 1415. It was the first European base to be established on the African continent. Ceuta was a trading colony for the ancient Romans, built like Rome on seven hills, hence its original name *Septem Fratres*, Seven Brothers, and its Arab name Sebta. It was a commercial and industrial trading centre for carpets, ceramics, ivory, gold and slaves; caravans would come from the interior to trade with Ceuta; local Arab exports included brassware, coral jewellery and tuna fish. When the Portuguese occupied Ceuta, trade with the Arab enemy ceased, but the colony retained its strategic importance. As Prince Henry himself said:

> Africa is the gateway to the empire of the world! Ceuta is nothing by itself—but once the whole coastline is ours, we shall have a second Portugal!

Ceuta provided the springboard from which the Portuguese discovered and colonised West Africa in the rest of the century. The discoveries that followed were thus motivated by the territorial and economic power they gave to Henry's homeland. Ceuta was a base the Portuguese were loath to lose. (Ernle Bradford, *Southward the Caravels: The Story of Henry the Navigator*, London, 1961.)

Chacque automne autre fois oubliait en Ferrare: CASTLE, II, 4: A reference to Pope **Leo X** and his passion for hunting, showing how a good hunting fowl can salve the problems of a mind overloaded with higher things:

Each autumn, once more, he forgot in Ferrara
Thanks to a few birds the weight of his tiara.
(Lady Apsley, *Bridleways Through History*, 1936.)

Chacun son tour: CHECKMATE, III, 2: 'Each in his own turn'; not the same as *chacun à sa marotte*; 'Each to his own', or 'Everyone has their own hobby'.

Chambord: QUEENS: The central portion of the château is a feudal castle, rebuilt extensively by **Francis I** in 1519, similar in style to Vincennes. It was originally the King's hunting lodge, built on a grand scale. Its pure Italianate concept and design are attributed to Leonardo da Vinci, who worked for Francis from 1516 until his death three years later (See **Amboise**). It embodied the spirit of Francis more than any of his other buildings. As his sister Margaret of Navarre wrote:

To see your building without you, is to see a corpse. To look at it without hearing your intentions is like reading in Hebrew.

Building work continued after Francis's death in 1547, although the outer wings were never completed. The capitals of the façade still carry his heraldic emblem of the salamander. Henry VIII of England was jealous of the magnificent lodge, and built his own palace of Nonesuch in the woods to the south of Hampton Court as a fractionally larger rival to Chambord. (Marcus Binney, *Châteaux of the Loire*, London, 1992.)

CHANCELLOR, Diccon: CASTLE: (d. 1556) Richard (or Diccon) was employed by the Muscovy Company on both their first and second journeys to Russia. He and **Sir Hugh Willoughby** were entrusted with the furtherance of navigational discoveries in the north, and hoped to find the elusive north-eastern passage to India. The first journey in 1553 took Chancellor safely to Muscovy and back, although the less experienced Willoughby and the crew of the *Bona Esperanza* did not survive. Chancellor returned to England from this first voyage in the summer of 1554, and undertook a second voyage to the White Sea in the summer of the following year, although he and most of the crew drowned when the ship broke up near Pitsligo in Aberdeenshire.

Chancellor had been recommended to the Muscovy Company by **Sir Henry Sidney**, who described him as 'a man of great estimation for many good parts of wit'. The recommendation was a very personal one; Sidney had tutored and encouraged the pilot in his navigational studies. He was also deeply admired by his other colleagues, amongst them his friend **John Dee** who made mention of 'the incomparable Richard Chancellor'.

According to **Richard Eden**, Chancellor was born in Bristol and had already accompanied the great English barque, the *Aucher*, on its journey to Chios and back in 1550. Those who sailed and trained with him in his journeys to Muscovy were excellent mariners by the time he had taught them; many were able to take their own commands within five years. In addition to his skills as a pilot, Chancellor was also a skilled mathematician, on a level with Dee. They worked together on a new table of Ephemerides (an astronomical almanac) in 1553 and Chancellor was able to use his skills to make and improve the precise instruments necessary for their safe navigation through uncharted northern waters.

Details of his family are largely unknown, save for the fact that in 1553 he had two sons and that he dedicated his book on his Russian discoveries to his uncle, Christopher Fotheringham. (E.G.R. Taylor, *Tudor Geography: 1485–1583*.)

Changeons propos, c'est trop chanté d'amours: KINGS, I, 1: 'That's enough of love; let's change the subject'.

Chaos: KNIGHTS, I, 1: A yawning unfathomable pit from which rose the first of all things: Uranus (the heavens) and **Gaea** (earth). From the marriage of heaven and earth came all other gods and elements. Another version claims the firstborn of Chaos were Gaea, Tartarus (Hell) and Eros (Love). According to the Bektashi dervishes, Anka was described as a mythical bird with a name but no body (PAWN, 11), chaotic because it was a shapeless mass and existed only in the mind. (John K. Birge, *The Bektashi Order of Dervishes*, 1937.)

Chargé d'ans et pleurant son antique provesse: KINGS, III, 2: 'Weighed down by years and weeping for his former glory'.

CHARLES V, Emperor of the Holy Roman Empire: CHECKMATE: (1500–1558) Charles's grandfather the Emperor Maximilian had married Mary of Burgundy, daughter of **Charles the Bold**. Through Mary he inherited Burgundy and Flanders. His father (Archduke Philip the Fair) had married Joanna the Mad, daughter of Ferdinand, King of Aragon and Isabella, Queen of Castile. Through them, Charles inherited both Spain and Naples. His territorial dominions have only since been rivalled by the conquests of Napoleon.

Of medium height and fair complexion, Charles was not considered handsome, although he was accredited with an air of dignity and distinction. Determined and resolute to the point of ruthlessness, he did at least have a sense of humour (lacking in his son, heir to the throne of Spain, **Philip II**). In 1519, with the death of the Emperor Maximilian, Charles was elected to the throne of the Roman Empire, defeating **Francis I** of France in a contest where the largest bribe shared between the hereditary electors secured the throne. He then abolished the elective principle of the Imperial throne, meaning the French monarchy would never get a second chance to bid for the coveted title and territories. Charles and Francis were enemies for life, as the sixteenth-century wars show; their battlefields extended from the French borders to the Italian states. The emnity was maintained by their sons, **Henri II** and Philip II.

Charles was a great military campaigner, used to spending twenty-four hours a day in the saddle, in full armour. He undertook forty expeditions in war and peace. His great victory at the age of thirty-two was to defeat **Suleiman** and drive the Sultan's corsairs from Tunis.

He was also a heavy drinker and like so many of his contemporaries was crippled with gout. His one respite from the encroaching infirmity of old age was his passion for clocks. When suffering from insomnia, Charles used to summon his servants; together they would disassemble a clock and lovingly put the artifice back together. Nothing seemed to please him as much as the intricacies of a new timepiece, other than disappointing his enemies by remaining alive. As Charles told the French Ambassador to Augsburg in 1551, 'I find no physic that doth me more good than my desire to disappoint others that so fain would have me gone'. The gout, haemorrhoids and fits of melancholy increasingly plagued his last years, leading him to remark bitterly: 'Fortune is a woman . . . she does not love old men'.

He eventually abdicated in 1556 and retired to a villa next to the remote Castilian monastery of Yuste where he died in 1558. The Imperial crown went to his brother Ferdinand, whilst Spain and most of the Spanish and Castilian possessions in the New World went to Philip II.

CHARLES VII, King of France: RISING: (1403–1461) Reigned from the age of nineteen and with the aid of Joan of Arc (c. 1412–1431) successfully won the Hundred Years War between France and England. He was anointed as king at Orléans in 1429 by Joan of Arc. War ended in 1453 with the French victory at Castillon. That decisive victory saw the beginning of France's development as a cohesive national state; unified in its patriotism and fervour for St Joan.

Charles's later reign was typified by the problems he encountered enforcing his overlordship of the Duchy of Burgundy, and his turbulent and antagonistic relationship with his son, **Louis XI**. Feudal overlordship had technically ended, but Charles did his best to undermine the independence of the state of Burgundy; attempting for example to wrestle the Duchy of Luxembourg from the control of the Duke. He pursued **Philip the Good** with petty harassments and major conflicts. War between them seemed inevitable by 1461.

The troublesome relationship between Charles and Philip was worsened by the latter's obsequious servitude to the troublesome Dauphin, a fugitive in Brabant since 1456. The close relationship between Louis and Duke Philip intensified Charles's hatred and mistrust of the Duke; especially when Philip expressly refused to send Louis back to France. The deterioration of relations between France and Burgundy crushed all possible hopes for a joint crusade; the armies were deployed on home ground instead.

Whilst at Genappe, Louis was overjoyed to hear of his father's final illness. He constantly employed astrologers to calculate the exact hour of Charles's death. It is said that not only was he happy to hear of his father's demise, he had actively been praying for it. (Richard Vaughan, *Philip the Good: The Apogee of Burgundy*, London, 1970.)

CHARLES THE BOLD, Duke of Burgundy: RISING; SCALES: (b. 1433) Also known as 'Charles the Rash' owing to the aggressive and authoritarian bearing he had displayed ever since he was a youth. Charles was the only legitimate son of Duke **Philip the Good**, but for much of his childhood, Charles and his father were not on the best of terms. The young Count of Charolais was principally jealous of his father's close relationship with the Dauphin of France, **Louis XI**, and the personal advancement of his enemies the Croy family in the Burgundian court. Under Charles's grandfather, John the Fearless, the Croy family had risen to a position of power and authority and represented a challenge to Charles's own hereditary title and accession. The situation was finally resolved in 1464 when Charles managed to oust the Croys and was subsequently reconciled to his father, mostly thanks to the intercessions of his mother, Isabelle of Portugal.

Charles received the Dukedom in 1467 on the death of his father and reigned for the next ten years. In July 1468 he married his third and final wife, Margaret of York, sister of **Edward IV**. Their royal entry to **Bruges** in 1468 is well chronicled (including the downpour which ruined the clothing of the dignitaries and the plague which brought a premature close to the nine days of celebrations). The marriage brought Burgundy and England together against the French. When the exiled Edward IV stayed in Flanders from 1470 to 1471, Charles greeted his brother-in-law with a certain degree of coldness. However, hatred for Louis XI of France overcame his personal ambition for the English throne, added to which Edward was clearly popular in Bruges and a potentially valuable ally. Charles was the sworn enemy of Louis XI, and Burgundy remained at loggerheads (and outright war) with France throughout the following decade. On his death Charles left vast debts, but only one legitimate heir. Mary of Burgundy was the daughter of his second marriage to Isabelle de Bourbon (d. 1465). She was to marry Archduke Maximilian, grandfather of Emperor **Charles V**. (Richard Vaughan, *Philip the Good: The Apogee of Burgundy*, London, 1970; Malcolm Letts, *Bruges and its Past*, London, 1924.)

Charon: CHECKMATE, IV, 8: Boatman of the River Styx, and conductor of the souls of the dead to the afterworld. The dead would pay Charon with an *obolus* (small coin) placed under the tongue. Those who had not been buried with the correct funeral rites and those who could not pay the ferryman would be condemned to wander the shores as restless spirits. Charon could not accept any living passengers into his barque unless they had obtained a golden bough from the Cumaean sibyl. For transporting Heracles across the river without a passport, Charon was imprisoned by the gods for a year; thus he was unlikely to make the same mistake twice. See also *J'irai donc maugré toy*.

CHARTRES, François de Vendôme, Vidame de: QUEENS: Regarded as a somewhat frivolous diplomat and courtier of France, Chartres spent six pleasurable months in England as a hostage for French payments to England. In March 1550, the French agreed to pay 200,000 crowns for Boulogne, and send three hostages to England until payment of the next instalment of the same amount. Whilst in England, the Vidame was often entertained in leading the young King **Edward VI** from his studies, saying, 'What needs your majesty for so many books?' The Vidame was far happier devising masques and court entertainments than expanding his education through literary study. He and fifteen other nobles once performed a masque for the King with the Duke of Suffolk dressed as a nun. The spectacle (including games and fireworks) and the elaborate banquet which followed were estimated as costing the Vidame nearly four thousand crowns.

He refused an offer of marriage from the second daughter of the Duke **de Guise**, thus winning the approval of **Catherine de Médicis**. After **Henri II**'s death, she and the Vidame conspired together against the de Guise family.

Charybdis: KINGS, Gambit: **Scylla** and Charybdis are the two rocks between Italy and Sicily. Charybdis was the lower of the two, nearer to Sicily. On the rock was a giant fig tree, under which dwelt Charybdis, daughter of Poseidon and **Gaea**, described as a voracious woman who had stolen oxen from Heracles. Three times every day she would swallow down the waters of the sea, and vomit the waves back up, causing a terrible whirlpool. (Homer, *The Odyssey*, tr. Walter Shewring, Oxford, 1986.)

Chasse à cor et à cris: CASTLE, III, 7: 'Hunt with hue and cry'.

Châteaubriant: QUEENS, IV, 3: The original sixteenth-century owner of the château, Jean de Laval (1487–1543), was suspected of embezzlement and murder, having apparently slit his wife's wrists. He was not charged, however, for he promised to give **Montmorency** one third of all his immovable goods, comprising all the family's estates and titles. This deprived his own heirs, one of whom was the Princess de la Roche-sur-Yon (QUEENS, IV, 4). When Laval died, his three heirs took Montmorency to court claiming that their father had been insane to offer such a bribe to the Constable. The matter dragged on until 1604, when the Parlement of Paris finally confirmed Montmorency's title. (G.G. Toudouze, *Françoise de Châteaubriant*; Abbé de Brantôme: *Les Vies des Grands Capitaines François*, Vol. IV.)

Chaunticleer: KINGS, II, 2: The proud and stupid cockerel from the 'Nun's Priest's Tale'. (Geoffrey Chaucer, *Canterbury Tales*.)

Cheke, Sir John: CASTLE, III, 1: (1514–1557) Born and educated at Cambridge, he rose to become the university's professor of Greek (1540–1547). He also served as tutor to **Edward VI** and **Elizabeth** in their childhood but briefly left court in 1549 because his wife had offended Protector **Somerset**'s wife.

Cheke was a great patron of religious and learned men, and considered one of the foremost authorities in Greek for his time. In 1552 he received his knighthood, but fell from grace shortly thereafter. As one of Lady Jane Grey's supporters, he was placed in the Tower of London and charged with treason. He was pardoned and released in 1554, and given a full licence to travel abroad, but in 1556 was brought back to London and again placed in the Tower, this time for his heretical Protestant religious beliefs. Cardinal **Pole** succeeded in making Cheke recant completely. After a brief penitential and a public confessional discourse Cheke was freed, but died shortly thereafter.

Chenonceau: QUEENS: Built on the site of a fifteenth-century water mill, the château and its bridged arcade span the breadth of the River Cher. The estate was purchased in 1513 by the financier Thomas Bohier, Receiver General of the Finances of Normandy, who began to build the new château two years later. Bohier was forced to cede the estate to **Francis I** in 1535, having been implicated in a series of financial scandals. **Henri II** presented it to **Diane de Poitiers** in 1547. Under her control the new and elaborate gardens were laid out (with the importation of specialised fruit trees). She also employed **Delorme** to construct the bridge across the river. After the death of Henri II, **Catherine de Médicis** forced Diane to swap Chenonceau for Chaumont. Catherine maintained the estate as a place of luxuriant pleasure, but it became a mirthless retreat in 1590 for Louise de Lorraine, widow of the murdered King Henri III. (Marcus Binney, *Châteaux of the Loire*, London, 1992.)

Chi asini caccia e donne mena, Non è mai senza guai e pena: PAWN, 4: Italian proverb; 'He who drives an ass and leads a lady, is asking for labour and grief'.

Chi Asino va a Roma, Asino se ne torna: CHECKMATE, IV, 9: 'He who goes to Rome an ass, will return an ass'.

Chi beve bianco: CASTLE, III, 7: Partially quoted within the text, the reference is to Neapolitan wine: *'Chi beve bianco, piscia bianco, a chi beve rosso, avanza il colore';* 'He who drinks white wine, will urinate white, and he who drinks red, will produce colour'.

Chi fida in Grego, sara intrego: CASTLE, III, 7: Proverb on the traditional perfidious nature of the Greeks; 'He who trusts a Greek, will be cheated'.

Chi mi! Qu'io no pensara di partime!: CHECKMATE, V, 1: 'Who me? I'm not thinking of leaving'.

Chi scrire a chi non responde o egli e matto, o egli ha di bisogno: CASTLE, III, 10: 'Who writes to one who does not reply, is either a fool or in need'.

Chi te carezza piu che far' no 'suede, [suole], O che gabbato t'ha, O che gabbar' te vuole: CASTLE, III, 7: 'He who is being unusually amiable, has either deceived you, or is about to'.

Chiausi: PAWN, 23: Or Chauci, one of the tribes of Germany inhabiting the north-west part between the Ems and the Elbe; never subdued by the Romans. (Harry Thurston Peck, ed., *Harper's Dictionary of Classical Literature and Antiquities*, NY, 1962.)

Chimera: CHECKMATE, I, 5: Or Chimaera, a fire-breathing monster of Lycia. Its front part was a lion, its middle was a goat, and the hindquarters were serpentine, with the tail ending in the head of a snake. For good measure the creature also vomited flames. It was brought up by King Amisodarus as a plague to men, but was finally conquered by Bellerophon with the aid of the winged horse Pegasus. The quixotic nature of the chimera was said to represent the volcanic nature of Lycian soil.

Chios: PAWN, 19: Described as 'The Great Turk's Garden', rich in figs, almonds, oranges, lemons, grapes and olives. What tantalised European visitors to the island were the richly dressed and apparently sexually liberated womenfolk. It is said that the women could choose to sleep with any man they wanted, with their husbands acting as intermediaries. The price for such company (including supper) was one Venetian zecchino, at the time equal to nine English shillings. **Nicolas de Nicolay** also visited the island, noting the exceptional beauty of its women and their 'amorous courtesy'. Chios was also the only producer of gum mastic, and the island was vital to the Genoese as an outpost and depot for Phocaean **alum**. (Stanley Mayes, *An Organ for the Sultan*, London, 1956.)

Chrisom child: QUEENS, III, 6: With reference to the christening robe worn by a child newly anointed with chrism (holy oil) at baptism as a symbol of the cleansing of original sin. If the child died within a month of its baptism, the robe would be used as a shroud; hence chrisom or 'chrysom-child'.

Chronos: KINGS, IV, 2; SCALES, 8: Cronus was originally the Greek god of the harvest, who became synonymous with *chronos*; time. Husband of Rhea, who was the daughter of **Gaea**, Cronus feared that his children would grow to be more powerful than he and reject his authority. To avoid this, he devoured each of his children as soon as they were born, much to the distaste of his partner. Zeus was the only child not to be swallowed, and he later supplanted his father and became the national god of the Greeks. Chronos is represented as an old man with a hooded mantle, carrying the familiar sickle or scythe.

Chrysippu: PAWN, 5: Stoic philosopher of Tarsus, author of over three hundred treatises. Some of his theories were somewhat bizarre; such as his approbation of parents marrying their children, and the notion that human corpses should be eaten rather than buried (see **Mummification**). He died either from an excess of wine; or from laughing too much on seeing an ass eating figs from a silver plate. (J. Lempriere, *A Classical Dictionary*, London, 1815.)

Chrysostom: CASTLE, III, 14. (c. 347–407) Meaning 'Golden-Mouthed', the title given to St John Chrysostom, Bishop of Constantinople and Doctor of the Church. He was Deacon of Antioch in 381, and ordained as priest in 386 with special responsibility for preaching. For the next ten years, his oratory was at its most powerful, and he was made Patriarch of Constantinople in 398. However, his moral crusade to reform the corruption of court, clergy and commons made for powerful enemies such as the Empress Eudoxia of Constantinople. He was removed from his see in 403 and shortly afterwards exiled and harried from Antioch to Pontus. Enforced travel in harsh winter conditions eventually killed him.

The monastery of St Chrysostom on Cyprus was founded in the fifth century. A young princess of Cyprus developed an ulcer or leprous condition, and Bishop Chrysostom recommended that she should retire to the mountain north-east of Nicosia to improve her health. When she bathed in the waters of the natural fountain, her affliction was cured and so she built the original convent, dedicating it to the saint; hence 'restored like Chrysostom'. (William Holden Hutton, *Constantinople*; Rupert Gunnis, *Historic Cyprus*, Cyprus, 1936.)

Cittern: KNIGHTS, III, 3: Wire- (not gut-) strung instrument of the Renaissance, with a flat, pear-shaped body. (CD Set: Musica Reservata, *The Instruments of the Middle Ages and Renaissance*, 1993, Vanguard Classics, 08 9060 72.)

Clarion: QUEENS, IV, 3: A trumpet particularly noted for the clear and shrill notes it can produce; which make it most suitable as a field trumpet; from Latin *clarus*, meaning clear.

Clatter like the Archbishop's conscience: KINGS, III, 2: The Earl of Angus, **Archibald Douglas**, and the Earl of **Arran** were sworn enemies and rivals. In 1520, Arran was determined to expel Angus and his supporters from Edinburgh. Angus promised to leave if his safety could be assured. His uncle Gavin Douglas attempted to get Cardinal Beaton, Archbishop of St Andrews and Chancellor of Scotland, to mediate on his behalf. Beaton, who was on Arran's side, claimed to know nothing about Arran's planned attack on the Earl and protested on his conscience that he knew nothing of the matter, striking his hand on his chest. As he did so, Gavin Douglas heard the rattling of the Cardinal's armour, worn under his church robes. Gavin's retort became a proverb: 'My Lord, I perceive your conscience clatters'. Neither the prelate nor Arran could be trusted and attempts at mediation were abandoned. There followed the battle called 'Cleanse the Causeway' which left seventy-two bloody corpses in Edinburgh's High Street.

Clearing nut: KINGS, IV, 3: Seeds which, when rubbed on the inside of a vessel, would clear water standing in that vessel.

CLEMENT VII: (1478–1534) Giulio de' Medici; relation of **Catherine de Médicis**, patron and friend to **Filippo Strozzi**. He was elected a cardinal by his powerful cousin, Pope **Leo X**, in 1512 and combined his role of papal adviser with traditional Medici control over his home town of Florence. In 1523 he was elected Pope, and sought to prevent foreign powers from gaining any further foothold in the political arena of Italy. Perceiving the Empire of **Charles V** presented the greatest threat to Italian liberty, Clement dragged Rome into the league against the Empire in 1526; a decision which led to the sack of Rome in the following year, and the Pope's imprisonment in the Castel San Angelo. He managed to escape, but was forced to flee Rome until 1528, when he eventually made peace with the Empire.

Clepsydra: QUEENS, II, 2: Water clock. The first clock with rotating wheels and a statue pointing to the hour was invented by Ctesibius in 135 BC. Water clocks were first used to measure time in the Athenian courts of justice.

Clothing: Throughout history, the style and quality of clothing have been an excellent indicator of the wealth and status of the wearer. Sumptuary laws were enacted all over Europe to prevent those of inferior social standing from aping their superiors in terms of dress by a provocative show of wealth. The style of clothing also delineated one's chosen career; the gowns and robes of the legal, academic and clerical professions are still relevant today. These sumptuary laws also provided a moral safeguard for the urban populace; an outrageously licentious display of breasts or boastful padding of genitalia was generally forbidden, with prostitutes easily recognised from their high heels, red caps or bells. In terms of public display, Venice was most strict on the clothing of its patriciate; modest black gowns and cloaks were worn in public, although the richest of fabrics and jewellery could lie beneath. With reference to what lay well underneath the clothing of both sexes, there are interestingly enough no documented examples of *mutande* (underpants) for women in fifteenth-century Italy.

By the sixteenth century, sumptuary laws were either loosening up, or being ignored, especially when recognition at court or elegant society was reliant upon staying one jump ahead of one's fashionable rivals. During the reign of **Henri II** of France, ordinary dress for court could be expected to last for less than three months. A stylish woman's dress would need ten ells (one ell equalling 1¼ yards) of material for a standard size, and up to sixteen ells of fabric for the larger figure. Artifice, from cosmetics to high shoes, was always a popular enhancement of reality, although it seems one could go too far. Sixteenth-century Venetian women were described as '*Grande de legni, grosse de straci, rosse di bettito, bianche di calcina*' (PAWN, 15), 'Tall with wood, fat with rags, red with painting, white with chalk'. (Jacqueline Herald, *Renaissance Dress in Italy: 1400–1500*, London, 1981.)

Clotho: QUEENS, I, 2: One of the three Fates, and spinner of the thread of destiny. See **Atropos.**

Cluricaun: QUEENS, III, 2: In Irish folklore, a malicious elf who appears in the form of an old man and is knowledgeable about hidden treasures.

Coal: UNICORN: Coal has been mined in Scotland since at least the early thirteenth century, pioneered by the Cistercian monks of Newbattle. The earliest known seams of coal appeared as outcrops on the ground surface, dug in the same way as turf and peat. The burning properties of the mineral were apparently first discovered by shepherds lighting a fire over the black deposits. They saw that the stones themselves were burning, not just the firewood they had kindled. As surface supplies of the sulphurous mineral dwindled, the early miners began to follow the seams underground. Pope **Pius II** during his visit to the Lothians in 1435 noted that Scotland's poor were given the black stones to burn instead of wood. The church kept its monopoly over coal production until the beginning of the fifteenth century, when lay landlords began to develop the coal deposits on their own land.

Mostly, the poorer quality dross coal was used in the forges of blacksmiths and for the growing salt industry. It was believed for a long time that the noxious fumes emitted from the burning stones were damaging to health. The higher-grade mineral, often called 'great coal', from the area around the Firth of Forth was more popular, even with Scotland's monarchy and nobility; although it burned more rapidly, it did not produce such a quantity of sulphurous fumes.

By the sixteenth century, as the price of timber increased, the mining of coal for domestic and exported fuel (hence 'sea coal') had become one of Scotland's fast-growing and lucrative industries.

Cock fighting: CHECKMATE, I, 1: From the days of the ancient Greeks right up to the sixteenth century and beyond, this was an extremely popular sport. Once a year in Athens there were cock fights at public expense; the champions having been reared and trained with great care over the previous year. Rhodes and Delos had the reputation of producing many of the best champion birds. Their legs would be armed with brass spurs, and the birds made eager and more aggressive for the fight by being fed with garlic beforehand; hence the expression 'like garlic to a gamecock'.

Coffee: PAWN, 2: See Qahveh.

Coinage: A detailed assessment of coinage is outwith the scope of this work, other than to make the point that the real worth of fifteenth- and sixteenth-century coinage is not always related to its face value. This is certainly the case with Scottish coinage in the sixteenth century, where the values of coins were altered to meet monetary crises. Scottish coinage was a mixture of domestic and foreign; French money was often used to pay the imported troops. A shortage of Scottish bullion meant that with consecutive devaluations of the coins of the realm, bad money began to drive out the good. Coinage was debased, and barter often replaced financial transactions. The Scots diplomat Maitland of Lethington (1528–1573) attempted to deal with the bullion crisis in Scotland, as did **Mary de Guise**, by exploring the possibility of mining the Scottish gold seam at Crawfordmuir, but their efforts were not successful. The lack of available bullion perhaps helps explain the popularity of alchemy in its attempts to produce gold easily.

The problems in sixteenth-century Russia were very similar, especially with regard to the lack of gold. Russian subjects were advised to barter with foreign traders, to avoid gold ultimately leaving the country; most of the available money (if it had not been coined by the Moscow goldsmiths) was Hungarian or Rhenish in origin. (S.G.E. Lythe, *The Economy of Scotland*.)

COLIGNY, Gaspard, Admiral de: QUEENS: (d. 1572) Brother of *d'Andelot* and nephew of **Montmorency**. Both Coligny and his brother were staunch Protestants; Coligny became head of the French Reformers in 1569 and was considered a solid and dignified leader. He became a favourite of Charles IX of France, but the **de Guise** family despised the growing power of the admiral and attempted to assassinate him. The attempt failed, as Coligny was saved by the famous court surgeon Ambroise Paré. In the following year, still recovering from the murder attempt, he was accused by the de Guise family of conspiring against the King. Their second attempt on his life in 1572 was successful.

Collier à toutes bêtes: QUEENS, I, 4: An irreverent reference to the chivalric collar of the **Order of St Michael** as a halter for any beast.

Colonna, Vittoria: QUEENS, IV, 4: (1490–1547) The foremost female poet of the sixteenth century. Her neo-platonic sonnets are mostly on the subject of love, religion and loss. She was attracted to the Reformed church, but owing to her friendship with Cardinal **Pole** remained a Roman Catholic and later restored Michelangelo's faith in the church. She appears on the ceiling of Michelangelo's Sistine Chapel as Our Lady, whilst Pole is Ezekiel.

Colossus: KINGS, III, 4: According to Pliny, the most impressive of all larger-than-life statues was the bronze Colossus of Rhodes, one of the seven wonders of the ancient world. It was created by Chares of Lindus, a pupil of Lysippus. The statue took twelve years to cast (from 294 to 282 BC) and stood between ninety and a hundred and twenty feet high. It was placed at the harbour entrance for fifty-six years, until destroyed by an earthquake. The ruins of the Colossus remained in the area until AD 653, when enterprising Arabs sold the remaining pieces as scrap to 'a Jew of Edessa'. (Harry Thurston Peck, ed., *Harper's Dictionary of Classical Literature and Antiquities*, NY, 1962.)

Com me plairoit, Se monter povie droit: CHECKMATE, V, 8: See *Aucassins, damoisiax, sire!*

Come my friend, my brother most enteere: KINGS, IV, 3. Conclusion of the John **Lydgate** (c. 1370–1451) poem, 'Testament' (extract):

> Tarry no longer, towards thy heritage
> Haste on thy way, and be of right good cheer.
> Go each day onward on thy pilgrimage,
> Think how short time thou shalt abide here.
> Thy place is built above the starres clear,
> None earthly place wrought so stately wise.
> Come on, my friend, my brother most enteere,
> For thee I offered my blood in sacrifice.

(H. Macaulay Fitzgibbon, ed., *Early English Poetry*.)

Comfits, white: RISING, 37: Comfits are simply sweetmeats, a combination of sugar and fruit. To make your own fifteenth-century pine nut comfits (with the benefit of a twentieth-century sugar thermometer), take 7 oz fine white sugar, 2 tbsp of clear honey, 4 fl oz of water, a heaped tablespoon of ground or finely chopped pine nut kernels, 3½ oz of fine soft white breadcrumbs (or similar) and a teaspoon of freshly ground ginger. Heat the sugar, honey and water in a deep pan and cook until it has reached a temperature of 110° C / 230° F.

Immediately turn the syrup into a bowl and beat the contents vigorously for two to three minutes. Add the remaining ingredients, mix well and pour the mixture into a shallow tin (wettened to avoid the mixture sticking). When it is cool, cut into small pieces to serve. (Maggie Black, *The Medieval Cookbook*, London, 1993.)

Comment le saluroye, quant point ne le cognais: KINGS, I, 3: 'How should I salute him, when I do not know him?'

Common woman, that dwells there to receive men to folly, a: KINGS, II, 1: A paraphrase from the Book of Proverbs, 9, 13–18:

> A foolish woman is clamorous: she is simple, and knoweth nothing. For she sitteth at the door of her house, on a seat in the high places of the city, to call passengers who go right on their ways: Whoso is simple, let him turn in hither: and as for him that wanteth understanding, she saith to him, 'Stolen waters are sweet, and bread eaten in secret is pleasant.' But he knoweth not that the dead are there; and that her guests are in the depths of hell.

Commutene: SCORPIONS: See **Zacco, King of Cyprus.**

COMNENOS, David, Emperor of Trebizond: RAM: (d. 1463) The weak, cowardly, proud, effeminate and inept twenty-first Emperor of the last outpost of the ancient Greek world, which fell to the Ottoman Empire in 1461. He was brother of Emperor John IV (d. 1458), but since John's son Alexios was only four years old when John died, David took the throne in his place, fully aware — after the fall of Constantinople in 1453 — that his Empire was open to attack. His Empire, partly due to the influence of **Amiroutzes**, was unprepared and incapable of sustaining the winter siege (by Mahmud Pasha and Sultan **Mehmet II**) until help from the West arrived. Instead of defending Trebizond and improving its fortifications, David attempted to create an alliance against the Turk, which was to include **Philip the Good, Uzum Hasan** of the White Sheep Tribe, the Prince of Georgia and as many Eastern Levantine princes as he could contact. Pope **Pius II** sent **Ludovico da Bologna** to help Trebizond by creating a Holy League of Princes against Mehmet's Muslim Empire. Although the promises of aid collected by Ludovico looked impressive, they could not act against the Sultan's inexorable progress.

David then attempted to ask for remission from his yearly tribute to the Sultan, requesting that **Uzum Hasan** negotiate on his behalf. Hasan's envoys enraged the Turk by asking also for the reinstatement of the yearly tribute that had been sent from the Sultan to Uzum's grandfather, in return for the continuing loyalty of the White Sheep. This undiplomatic demand provoked the Sultan into responding that he would come personally and give them everything they deserved; a thinly veiled threat that encouraged Uzum to back down. When Uzum made peace with the Sultan, David was left without his closest and strongest ally. It was only a matter of time before Mehmet began his rapid march across the mountains whilst his fleet besieged the city.

Mehmet promised that if David surrendered, he and his family would be well treated: resettled and given a sufficient income to rival their current standard of living and taste in expensive entertainments. The Empress Helen departed before the arrival of the Turk to visit her son-in-law in Georgia. David handed the city over to the Turkish forces without resisting. He and his family were resettled in Adrianople; territories guaranteed to yield an income of 300,000 silver pieces per annum. Despite his passivity, David remained a dangerous figurehead. When Uzum Hasan's wife (David's niece) requested that either David's nephew Alexios or one of his own sons be sent to her, the letter fell into the hands of the Sultan. David was accused of fomenting a treacherous plot to undermine the Turkish alliance with Uzum Hasan, and the entire Comnenos family were brought to Constantinople.

While in Constantinople, David was told that he and his family must convert to Islam or face the sword. Having given up his empire without a fight, David at least had the courage adamantly to refuse to give up the Orthodox religion. He, his seven sons (and perhaps his nephew) were beheaded; the eighth son, George (aged three) was made a Muslim. The surviving sixteen year-old daughter, Anna, is said to have been taken to the Sultan's harem and then forced to convert and marry Zagan, Governor of Lower Macedonia.

The corpses of the last of the Comneni were unceremoniously dumped outside the city walls. The Empress Helen was told that if she did not raise a ransom of 15,000 ducats for the corpses within three days, she too would die. The money was raised by her allies within the stipulated period and Helen was allowed to bury her family with her own bare hands. She soon shrank into obscurity, mourning her murdered family in sackcloth and ashes. (George Finlay, *A History of Greece*, Vol. IV, Oxford, 1877; William Miller, *Trebizond, The Last Greek Empire*, London, 1926.)

¿Como?: PAWN, 8: 'What?'

Comus: QUEENS, I, 6: God of festive mirth and joy; represented as a winged youth, often in a somewhat crapulous state, a torch slipping from his relaxed hand.

Con qué la lavaré, La tez de la mi cara?: QUEENS, II, 1: A Spanish song:

> *Con qué la lavaré*
> *la tez de la mi cara*
> *con qué la lavaré*
> *que vivo mal penada?*

> ... *Làvanse les galanas*
> *con agua de limones*
> *lávame yo, cuitada*
> *con ansias y pasiones.*

> With what shall I lave it
> The flesh that is burning
> With what shall I lave it
> That racks me with yearning?

> Your gallant will bathe him
> In lemon for fashion
> But I seek my balm
> In the fine springs of passion.

(Tr. D.D.)

CONDÉ, Louis de Bourbon, Prince of: QUEENS: (1530–1569) The fifth and youngest son of the Duke de Vendôme; hunchbacked brother of the King of Navarre (d. 1562) and Jean de Bourbon, Sieur d'Enghien. Condé was a Bourbon Prince of the Blood, a brilliant military leader and Protestant enemy of the all-powerful **de Guise** family. It is said that his passion for lovemaking and politics led him to convert to the Reformed religion out of revenge and spite rather than conviction.

In 1559 he was found guilty of heresy, treason and conspiracy, on the strength of his Reformed sympathies, but when Charles IX was crowned King (1560), **Catherine de Médicis** found she needed the support of the Bourbons against the powerful anti-Lutheran and anti-Bourbon triumvirate of **Montmorency, St André** and Francois de Guise. She adopted a conciliatory policy, releasing Condé and ensuring that François de Guise was driven from court. Condé led the Protestants in the religious wars which were to continue for the next three decades. He was eventually killed in 1569 at the battle of Jarnac in the third French civil war, attempting to lead a troop of 250 Protestants against an army of 2,500 Catholics. See also *C'est tout de même que de manger la poule ...* and *Ce petit homme tant jolly.*

Consuetudo, consuetudo, consuetudo: CASTLE, I, 2: A bad-tempered legal admonition. '*Consuetudo*' refers to case law, thought to be vastly more valuable than statute (written) law.

Contra Vitam Recti Moriemur: The fictional motto of the Culters: ambiguously meaning either 'Despite the (misleading) evidence of our lives, we die honest', or 'We die honest, despite Life's efforts to thwart us'.

Contre les loups, il se faut aider des chiens: CHECKMATE, II, 5: 'Against the wolves, we must seek help from dogs'; a comment from the Constable of France, **Montmorency,** on the necessity of tolerating the increasing number of French Lutherans to secure a unified front against the greater danger of the empire of **Charles V.**

Coo-clink: CHECKMATE, II, 1: Scots for a cowbell.

Coquetry: CASTLE, II, 6: See **The note called Coquetry and the note called True.**

CORNER, Andrea: SCORPIONS: (d. 1473) Venetian merchant, trader and ally of Queen **Carlotta** of Cyprus. He and his brother initially served under rivals; thus ensuring at least half of the family would profit. In 1468 King **Zacco** deprived Andrea of his lands and possessions; a move which slowed down the marriage negotiations of his niece, **Catherine Corner,** but with the assistance of his brother (see **Corner, Marco),** Andrea soon came back to serve the new King and his bride.

CORNER, Catherine, Queen of Cyprus: SCORPIONS: (1454–1510) Daughter of **Marco** and Fiorenza of Naxos. She was married by proxy to **Zacco** in 1468, arriving in Cyprus in the autumn of 1472. At the time of her betrothal she had been given the honorary title of 'Catherine, Daughter of Venice'. This would give the Signoria (rather than the Corner family) control over the kingdom, should she die without issue. After the death of her husband, she ruled Cyprus on her own, but was finally persuaded to abdicate in 1489 and give Venice complete control over the island. She spent the rest of her life in exile at Asolo, near Treviso, spending her last days at Murano and Venice. To compensate for the loss of her throne, she received the same dowry from Venice as she had received as a bride; an income sufficient to maintain a staff of eighty, a retinue befitting a former monarch. Her 'court' was a meeting place of artists, musicians and humanists; her portrait was painted by Gentile Bellini and Titian amongst others.

CORNER, Marco: SCORPIONS: Venetian merchant and citizen, father of **Catherine Corner,** Queen of Cyprus. He had a substantial interest in the **sugar** trade of Cyprus; he held the lucrative sugar plantations of Episkopi. Corner was an ally of **Zacco,** helping to fund his seizure of the throne and ensuring that he had a close working relationship with the Signoria of Venice. Despite this, Corner was later to suffer under the quixotic King; in 1468 the Venetian senate was forced to complain to Zacco that his officials had been diverting water from the Cornaro sugar fields to Kolossi. All the sugar cane perished, causing a loss of revenue estimated at 10,000 ducats. Venice was soon to get her money's worth out of Cyprus. The family was also strongly represented in **Bruges**, and had mining interests in the **Tyrol**.

Coronez est à tort: QUEENS, IV, 5: 'The crowning is wrong', from the twelfth-century gest *Li Coronemenz Loöis*.

Corsario a corsario, no ay que gañar los barilles d'agua: CHECKMATE, III, 5: Literally, 'Corsair to corsair, one shouldn't fight over barrels of water'. Meaning one crow shouldn't pick out the eyes of another.

Cosmetics: PAWN, 19: (See also **Hair dyes**.) The cosmetics of the seraglio and of the ancient world bear close relation to many of the traditional organic compounds still available today. Pliny and Ovid (first century AD) offered relatively easy face-pack recipes similar to this one. Firstly, take 2 lbs of husked barley, 2 lbs of bean flour and ten eggs. Dry and grind the flour and barley, adding 3 oz of hart's horn. Sieve the ingredients, adding 21 narcissus bulbs (pounded in a mortar). Finally add the eggs, 2 oz of balsam, 2 oz of Tuscan seed and 1 lb of honey. The recipe does not state how many faces this recipe should cover. The simplest recipe was simply cornflour or breadcrumbs soaked in asses' milk and made into a paste applied to the face and worn overnight.

The Arabs used to manufacture *kohl* by removing the inside of a lemon and filling the husk with plumbago and burnt copper. The mixture was heated on the fire until it carbonised, then powdered in a mortar with coral, sandalwood, pearls, ambergris, chameleon and bat's wing. The ingredients were then moistened with rose water. The compound not only heightened the beauty of the wearer, it was also said to protect against the danger of the 'evil eye'. (Ayton Ellis, *The Essence of Beauty*; Eugene Rimmel, *A Book of Perfumes*, 1867.)

Costive bowels: CHECKMATE, IV, 1: The English had a reputation for suffering from constipation, on account of their sixteenth-century eating habits, and according to Sir Thomas Elyot (c. 1499–1546), 'English bowels are oftwhiles costive'. The diet of the English peasantry included coarse black bread, milk, cheese, eggs, peas, beans and occasionally bacon or fowl. A winter diet of salted meat, bread and peas would in itself encourage scurvy. Vegetables were prominent, such as turnips, parsnips and carrots, but the nobility eschewed them. Green vegetables were seen to encourage wind and melancholy, although garlic and onions were popular. Fresh fruit was similarly avoided as it was believed to cause fever and diarrhoea. Prunes, raisins, olives and almonds were often eaten instead. Milk was similarly not recommended, other than for the young or very old, for which the services of a wet nurse were employed. (W.S.C. Copeman, *Doctors and Disease in Tudor Times*.)

Cotignac: See **Quince paste.**

Cotswold lions: CASTLE, I, 6: Sheep, so-called in the plays of John Heywood (c. 1497– c. 1578); as in the blustering boaster Thersites, 'now have at the lions of Cotswold', and Ralph Roister Doister, 'as fierce as a Cotswold lion'. The Gloucester hills were famous for their wool; one of England's greatest staple exports. (Karl J. Holzknecht, *Tudor and Stuart Plays in Outline*, London, 1963.)

Coup de Jarnac: QUEENS, IV, 3: A treacherous or unexpected blow. In 1547 **Henri II** of France approved a duel between two nobles: Guy Chabot, Sieur de Jarnac and Le Chataignerale. Jarnac had apparently cast aspersions on the latter's honour. King **Francis I** had expressly forbidden duelling, but the new King allowed the contest to proceed. With the first blow of his sword, Jarnac hamstrung his opponent, rendering him helpless. With the second, he slew him.

COURTENAY, Sir Edward: CASTLE: (1526–1556) Earl of Devonshire and potential suitor to **Elizabeth** because of his family's descent from the younger daughter of **Edward IV.** His father, the Marquis of Exeter, had been executed in 1539 for treason, and from the age of twelve, Edward spent the next fifteen years of his life in the Tower of London. He is described in contemporary accounts as handsome, well proportioned and well educated. He spoke several languages, but had spent so much of his life in confinement that he had neither the spirit nor experience for a position of power. He was released and restored to his earldom by **Mary Tudor,** but was again imprisoned because of his potential implication in the **Wyatt** rebellion of 1554 which sought to depose Mary and replace the Catholic monarch with Elizabeth and Courtenay as a Protestant couple. Wyatt at first confessed that this was the case, but retracted before he was executed.

Courtenay was released in 1554 due to the lack of evidence against him, and then travelled to Venice. According to **Peter Vannes,** the former English Ambassador to Venice, Courtenay tried to avoid arousing further suspicion by leading a more solitary life than he needed to, although rumours still abounded of further plots against Mary, with either himself or Elizabeth as the rallying point. The threat Courtenay posed to the Catholic succession eventually ceased with his unexpected demise. He died in September 1556 of a 'great hot ague', contracted as a result of being caught in a rainstorm and unable to find shelter. The chill developed into a full-blown fever when he travelled to Padua.

Vannes took care of his burial and personal possessions on Mary's behalf. Amongst Courtenay's correspondence was a letter from the retiring English Ambassador to France, Sir James Mason, dated July 1556. It affirmed that the

Queen had a good opinion of Courtenay, and that nothing was intended or believed against him or the Lady Elizabeth, 'for everybody thought them to be of too much wisdom, honour and truth to be parties to any such matter'. (*English Calendar of State Papers*, Foreign, 1556.)

Courts of Admiralty: See **Doctors' Commons.**

Cows, pigs, horses, sheep, goats: QUEENS, I, 4: Irish song, mostly quoted within the text; 'The Reason I Love Derry'. (P.W. Joyce, *Social History of Ancient Ireland.*)

Cradle between two coffins: QUEENS, II, 3: See **de Médicis, Catherine.**

Cramp rings: CASTLE, I, 8: Following a practice traditional since the days of Edward the Confessor, **Mary Tudor** blessed two large covered basins of these gold and silver rings, worn to prevent cramps and the 'falling sickness', each year in Passion Week. One was sent to her father-in-law, Emperor **Charles V.** His cynical response to another supposed miracle cure for his own infirmity was to hope 'that they would prove more effective than those of her predecessors'. (*Spanish Calendar of State Papers*, 1554.)

Crassus' Lamprey: CASTLE, II, 5: Crassus (c. 112–53 BC) was the third member of the first Roman triumvirate with Pompey and Caesar. Using his great wealth to indulge his taste for the exotic and eccentric, the Senator trained his favourite eel to feed from his hand when he called it. He decked it in earrings and pearl collars, and so adored his pet that when it died, he wept and wore mourning. (G. Loisel, *Histoire des Ménageries de l'Antiquité à Nos Jours*, Paris, 1912.)

Cremorne: CHECKMATE, V, 9: Also known as a crumhorn, it is a double-reeded Renaissance instrument; forerunner to the oboe and bassoon. So called because of its distinctive 'J' shape: *crum* meaning 'curve'. Each crumhorn normally has a limited range of an octave or ninth; thus several different sizes of instrument would be used at the same time to form an ensemble. (CD Set: Musica Reservata, *The Instruments of the Middle Ages and Renaissance*, 1993, Vanguard Classics, 08 9060 72.)

Cristallo: SCALES, 3: The name given to the clear, transparent glass which is easily worked in its molten stage. Venetian *cristallo* from the island of Murano could be delicately shaped and was the finest in the world, governing style and taste in glassware from the thirteenth to the eighteenth century. The drawback of the glass was its fragility; the more complex the design, the more brittle it became.

Crocodiles of Arsinoë: KINGS, I, 5: The crocodiles of the ancient Egyptian menagerie had collars around their necks and rings on their claws, and were trained to come and feed on cake when called. (G. Loisel, *Histoire des Ménageries de l'Antiquité à Nos Jours*, Paris, 1912.)

Croesus: RAM, 32: (560–546 BC) King of the Lydians, and reputed to be the wealthiest monarch ever, he was the first to introduce gold currency to the trading markets of the world. The first gold piece was not a coin, but an oblong ingot (the Greeks started to experiment with round embossed coins, but it was the Romans who introduced the serrated edge to prevent slivers from being shaved off the sides; see **Coinage**). Croesus was eventually overthrown by **Cyrus**.

Cropnose: SCORPIONS: See **Zacco, King of Cyprus**.

Crotel: QUEENS, II, 3: Hare excrement.

Crucifix marque-vin: CHECKMATE, III, 2: Bibulous parody of the name of the cross erected in Paris to commemorate the flood of the Seine in 1496, the Crucifix marque-eau, which was erected at the corner of the Rue de la Perle. (Henri Saural, *Historie et Recherches des Antiquités de la Ville de Paris*, Paris, 1724.)

Cry peip! where ever thou be!: KINGS, III, 4: From the poem by Robert Henryson (c. 1430–1506), 'The Upland Mouse and the Burgess Mouse' ('The Taill of the Uponlandis Mous and the Burges Mous', or 'The Twa Mice'). A town mouse visits her younger sister in the country and, finding her hungry and cold, takes her back to the luxury and plenty of the town. They feast together in the larder, but the country mouse is terrified by the appearance of the larder-keeper. The urban rodent scuttles to her mousehole, leaving her sister to her fate:

> But as God would, it fell a happy case,
> The spenser had nae leisure for to bide,
> Nouthir to seek nor search, to scare nor chase,
> But on he went, and left the door upwide.
> The bold burgess his passing weel has spied,
> Out of her hole she came, and cried on high,
> 'How, fair sister! cry peip, where'er ye be?'

After this scare, and a near-fatal game of cat and mouse, the younger sister decides that town life is not at all suited to her temperament, and joyfully leaves for the country. The moral, of course, is:

Blessèd be simple life, withouten dread;
Blessèd be sober feast in quietie;
Wha has enough, of no more has he need,
Though it be little into quantity.
Great abundance, and blind prosperity,
Oft-times makes ane evil conclusion;
The sweetest life, therefore, in this country,
Is of sickneress [security], with small possession.

See also **Of Cat, nor Fall, nor trap I haif nae Dreid.** (J. Ross, ed., *The Book of Scottish Poems*, Edinburgh, 1878; David Rintoul & J.B. Skinner, eds, *Poet's Quair*, Edinburgh, 1966.)

Cryand with many a piteous peep: KINGS: IV, I: From Robert Henryson's (c. 1430–1506) poem 'The Paddock [puddock or frog] and the Mouse', a retelling in Scots of the popular fable. See also **A silken tongue, a heart of cruelty.** Extract:

Upon a time, as Æsop could report,
A little mouse came till a river side;
She might not wade, her shankis were sae short;
She could not swim, she had nae horse to ride:
Of very force behovèd her to bide;
And to and fro beside that river deep
She ran, cryand with many piteous peep.

'Help oure [over], help oure,' this silly Mouse gan cry,
'For Goddis love, some body oure this bryme.'
With that a Paddock in the water by
Put up her head, and on the bank gan climb;
Which by nature could dook [dive], and gaily swim.
With voice full rauk [hoarse], she said on this manner:
'Good morn, Sir Mouse, what is your errand here?'

(J. Ross, ed., *The Book of Scottish Poems*, Edinburgh, 1878.)

Crying the coronoch on high: KINGS, I, 3: A Highland dirge and cry of great mourning. From the anonymous Scots poem describing the Scots defeat at the Battle of Harlaw in 1411 (extract):

Frae Dunidier as I came through,
Down by the hill of Banochie,
Alangst the lands of Garioch,
Great pity was to hear and see

The noise and dulesome harmonie,
(That ever that dreary day did daw [dawn]!)
Cryin' the coronach [dirge] on hie,
Alas, alas, for the Harlaw! . . .

There was not, since King Kenneth's days,
Sic strange intestine cruel strife
In Scotland seen, as ilk man says,
Where many likely lost their life;
Which made divorce 'tween man and wife,
And many children fatherless,
Which in this realm has been full rife;
Lord! help these lands, our wrongs redress!

In July, on Saint James his even,
That four-and-twenty dismal day,
Twelve hundred, ten score and eleven,
Of years since Christ, the sooth to say;
Men will remember as they may,
When thus the veritie they knaw;
And many a ane may mourn for aye
The grim battle of the Harlaw.

(J. Ross, ed., *The Book of Scottish Poems*, Edinburgh, 1878.)

Cuando amigo pide, no ay mañana: CHECKMATE, II, 7. 'When a friend asks, there is no tomorrow'.

Cullet: SCALES, 3: Broken scraps of glass which could then be melted down and reused.

Culverin: SCALES, 12: One of the earliest and heaviest forms of **cannon**, weighing eighteen hundredweight. A demi-culverin is half the size and weight. The name comes from the French *couleuvre*, meaning snake.

Cum duplicantur lateres qui venit: CHECKMATE, II, 2: Referring to Moses, 'he who appears with two tablets'.

Cum fueris alibi, vivito more loci: PAWN, 24: 'When you are abroad, live according to the custom of the place'.

Cum fueris Romae, Romano vivito more: PAWN, 24: 'When you are in Rome, do as the Romans do'.

Cy gist qui pen dant qu'il vivoit: CHECKMATE, V, 11: A double-edged Parisian epitaph, translated below:

> Here lies one who during his life
> Committed all forms of roguery
> He whispered, preached, versified
> And cultivated Philosophy . . .

(Henri Saural, *Histoire et Recherches des Antiquités de la Ville de Paris*, 1724.)

Cyclops: KINGS, I, 7: Homeric giant with one single large eye. Odysseus met Polyphemus, strongest of the Cyclops, after leaving the land of the **Lotophagi**. They are described as a rude and lawless race, not caring for agrarian pursuits such as planting and sowing crops; choosing to dwell individually rather than communally. (Homer, *The Odyssey*, tr. Walter Shewring, Oxford, 1986.)

Cypriot sheep: CASTLE, II, 5: The fleeces of Cypriot sheep were combed to collect a type of myrrh called Labdanum. The sheep collected the sticky gum on their coats from catching in the thickets of cistus, a variety of rock rose. (Aytoun Ellis, *The Essence of Beauty*.)

Cyprus: See **Carlotta, Queen of Cyprus; Kolossi; Nicosia; Zacco, King of Cyprus.**

Cyrus: KINGS, IV, 1: (d. 529) King of the world, friend to the conquered **Croesus**, and founder of the Persian empire. At the time of his death, most of the ancient world (excluding Egypt) was under his control. He was eventually conquered by Queen Tomyris of Scythia, who threw his head in a bowl of blood, saying '*Satia te sanguine quam sitisti*', 'Go and glut thyself with the blood of men'. The incident is referred to in Dante's *Purgatory*, Canto XII.

D

Dabit Deus his quoque finem: CHECKMATE, IV, 9: 'God will give an end to these miseries'.

Daedalus' honeycomb: CHECKMATE, I, 5: Rivalling the Cretan labyrinth he constructed for the Minotaur (the monster that was created as a result of Pasiphaë's carnal relationship with a bull), the legendary inventor, craftsman and artist Daedalus created a honeycomb of gold for Aphrodite's temple on Mount Eryx in Sicily.

Damascening: SCALES, 8: Originally cloth from Damascus, this refers to a pattern woven rather than printed; a cloth interlaced with gold or silver thread. Steel weaponry was damascened by the inlaying of other metals (often gold on steel or silver on iron).

Dammi con chi tu vivi, io saprò quel'che tu fai: PAWN, 18: More correctly *Dimmi con chi tu vivi . . .* ; 'Tell me with whom you live, and I will know what you are doing', or what you are 'up to'.

Damnum fatale: QUEENS, IV, 1: 'Inevitable misfortune'. Roman innkeepers were liable for the valuables of their guests except when lost through a *damnum fatale.*

Damoclean results: QUEENS, IV, 2: Damocles, one of the flatterers of the elder Dionysius (tyrant of Syracuse, 430–367 BC) was prone to overestimate the good fortune of his monarch. Dionysius invited him to be the guest of honour at a magnificent banquet, to experience the reality of the monarch's happiness. In the midst of the festivities, Damocles saw a sword suspended over his head, held by a single horsehair. This preternatural vision quickly dispelled any transitory feelings of happiness.

Dante's devils: KINGS, IV, 1; CASTLE, III, 1: Those who appear in Dante's *Divine Comedy* and are named within the text include Malacoda, the fiend who accompanies Dante as envoy to hell, **Alichino** 'the allurer or deceiver', Calcabrina 'the Grace scorner', Ciriatto Sannuto 'the tusked boar', Grafficane 'the doggish' and Rubicante, 'the red with rage'. (Dante Alighieri, *The Divine Comedy*, Cantos XXI & XXII.)

Darnley, Henry: CASTLE: See **Lennox, Margaret; Mary Queen of Scots.**

DAVID, Emperor of Trebizond: RAM: See **Comnenos, David, Emperor of Trebizond.**

Day of March: KNIGHTS, III, 10: Traditional Scottish and English border judicial meetings, often held at Hadden Stank. Their intention was to judge those who had broken the law on both or either side of the border and, if need be, hand them over for sentencing and punishment. Criminals were punished according to the laws of the country where the crime was committed rather than their original nationality. Wardens were appointed from both sides of the Scots-English border to enforce judgements, and make restitution to the injured parties. The meetings also served to crush cross-border and private feuds.

Before the meeting, injured parties would submit their bills of complaint to the appropriate warden, who would pass them to his colleague across the border. The accused would then be arrested, or summoned to attend the next March meeting. To prevent private grudges being intensified rather than alleviated by these meetings, **James III** of Scotland not only regulated the numbers of those attending, but weaponry for each man was limited to a knife or sword. Days of March were well attended: by the mid-sixteenth century commerce and entertainment drew the populace in addition to the judicial features. In times of war, the meetings would continue, although preceded by the **heralds** of both countries formally announcing a truce until sunrise the following day. (*County Histories of Roxburgh, Selkirk and Peebles*, 1899.)

De los álamos vengo: KINGS, Gambit: A song by Miguel de Fuenllana, musician at the court of **Philip II** of Spain:

> De los álamos vengo, madre,
> De ver como los menea el aire.
> De los álamos de Sevilla,
> De ver a mi linda amiga.
> De los álamos vengo, madre,
> De ver como los menea el aire.

> I come from the poplar trees, mother,
> Where I watched how they tossed in the wind.
> (From the poplars that grow in the city
> Where I watched the sweet charms of my pretty.)

I come from the poplar trees, mother,
Where I watched how they tossed in the wind.
(Tr. D.D. From the LP: Victoria de los Angeles & Ars Musicae, *Spanish Songs of the Renaissance*, EMI Records; ALP 1883.)

De par cinq cens mille millions de charretées de diables, le cancre vous est venu aux moustaches: QUEENS, III, 6: 'By five hundred thousand million cartloads of devils, the plague has got hold of your whiskers'.

De una mula que haze hin, y de un hijo que habla latin, liberanos, Domine!: QUEENS, I, 6: 'Deliver us, O Lord, from a mule that brays and a lad who speaks Latin'. The original reference in this quotation was to a 'daughter' who spoke Latin.

Dead man's pinches: QUEENS, III, 1: Small discolorations of the flesh, which have appeared overnight. (W. G. Black, *Folk Medicine*.)

DEE, John: CASTLE: (1527–1608) Pedagogue, mathematician, astrologer and alchemist of the Elizabethan court. He learned Latin in London and at Chelmsford before proceeding to St John's College, Cambridge, where it is said he was a model student, spending eighteen hours a day on his studies. After graduating, he travelled to Louvain and then Paris to lecture and further his studies. Dee was responsible for awakening **Elizabeth**'s lifelong interest in astronomy and astrology. Not only did he chart her horoscope, but those of Queen **Mary Tudor** and **Philip II**, which he showed to Elizabeth at a time when she was confined as a threat to her half-sister. Following this, Dee was arrested and charged with 'lewde and vain practises of calculating and conjuring'. His house in London was searched, his papers seized, and he was imprisoned. The Star Chamber acquitted him of treason, but he could still have suffered on a count of heresy: while in the Bishop of London's prison, he shared his cell with a heretic who was later burned. Dee was questioned on his religious beliefs, but was acquitted and released in 1555.

Dee was a close friend of Pedro Nunes, the great Portuguese mathematician, with whom he corresponded all his life. After his death, Nunes was his chosen literary executor. Dee also had a lifelong fascination for mechanics and mechanical toys. Amongst his most famous creations was the *scarabeus*; a winged mechanical beetle which flew up to the ceiling. He also created an owl, a jay and a raven, all four times life size. These clockwork models produced noise and had eyes that flashed. They were among the most costly of his projects, for which he had help from a Dutch horologist, a German instrument-maker and a Frenchman who specialised in making false eyes.

When Elizabeth acceded to the throne, she entrusted to the astrologer the task of choosing the most propitious date for her coronation. She further

favoured him with a series of ambassadorial appointments. He travelled widely in Europe; from the court of Emperor Maximilian II of Hungary to that of Emperor Rudolph II of Prague. He was the author of seventy-nine treatises on various subjects, and several important translations including Euclid. One of the more interesting writings is his 'Conversation with Angels', begun in 1581 and obsessing him for most of the rest of his life, in which Dee tried to obtain divine and prophetic revelation from certain spirits. It was alleged that Dee was conversing with satanic demons, not angels as he had hoped, and his reputation and financial status went into decline under James VI. (Wayne Schumaker, *Renaissance Curiosa*, NY, 1982; Peter French, *John Dee*, London, 1972.)

Defecto de boca ... quiere decir 'ideal': KINGS, I, 5: 'A defect of the mouth ... he means "ideal"'; a diplomatic way of explaining **Grey of Wilton**'s insults.

DEI, Benedetto: SCALES: (1418–1492) Florentine merchant and well-travelled representative of the **Portinari** managers of the Medici bank. His contemporary, Leonardo da Vinci, described Dei as a fabulist; in his own eyes, Dei was an invaluable asset to the Medici: as traveller, merchant, bank agent and spy for Florence. He was the arch-enemy of **Venice**, and supported the close relationship between Florence and the Sublime Porte from 1460 to 1472. Obviously he had the organised mind of a merchant: he is mentioned by **Marco Parenti**'s biographer as a compulsive list-maker, especially of the top political and mercantile families of Florence.

He travelled with the Florentine galleys to Constantinople in 1460, and by 1462 was trading in Trebizond and Caffa, bringing back two hundred Genoese refugees from **Chios**. In 1462 he was trading in Trebizond, followed by more galley journeys from 1463 to 1467, to Syria, Negroponte and Chios. In 1468–1469, Dei reported on the alum galley from Civitavecchia to Sluys, probably hired by the Medici and their associates in Naples via the Portinari.

Representing the Portinari and as an agent of the Medici, Dei established himself in **Timbuktu**, and by 1470 was doing good business in coarse cloth, serge and other Lombardy fabrics. By 1471 he claimed to have sold 7,500 pieces of Lombardy cloth in the East. His is the first recorded visit of a European to the trading city, but by this time his routes were not unusual; he may have been preceded by others. In 1469 he claimed to have already been there, describing it as being below the Kingdom of Barbary, in the dryest land on earth. (Mark Phillips, *The Memoir of Marco Parenti*, London, 1989; E.W. Bovill, *The Golden Trade of the Moors*, London, 1958.)

Déjà la nuit en son parc amasse un grand troupeau: KNIGHTS, II, 7: Joachim du Bellay (1522–1560):

> Déjà la nuit en son parc amassoit
> Un grand troupeau d'étoiles vagabondes,
> Et pour entrer aux cavernes profondes,
> Fuyant le jour, ses noirs chevaulx chassoit.

> Déjà le ciel aux Indes rougissoit,
> Et l'aulbe encor' de ses tresses tant blondes,
> Faisant gresler mille perlettes rondes
> De ses trésors les prez enrichissoit:

> Quand d'occident, comme une étoile vive,
> Je vy sortir dessus ta verde rive,
> O fleuve mien! une Nymphe en rient.

> Alors voyant cete nouvelle Aurore,
> Le jour honteux d'un double teint colore
> Et l'Angevin et l'Indique orient.

> Now shepherds Night his flock of straying stars
> And to his yawning caverns, fleeing day,
> Drives his black steeds.

The clouds already blush towards the East,
And dawn's bright tresses loose their dewy pearls
Upon the meads.

When from the West, a living star now stands
A smiling nymph upon thy bank, O Loire,
Among the reeds.

So Dawn, abashed before this second Sun
Tints twice the river and the glowing East
With colour fleet.

(Tr. D.D. A. Lagarde & L. Michard, eds, *Littérature Française, XVIe Siècle*, Vol. II, 1961.)

Della Robbia, Luca: KINGS, IV, 1; PAWN, 29: (1400–1482) Florentine sculptor, trained in the masonry workshop of Florence Cathedral. He began his artistic training as a goldsmith, but soon dedicated himself to sculpture. Amongst his works for the cathedral in Florence were a series of bas-reliefs in marble for the Cantoria, or Singers' Gallery, and a bronze door for the sacristy.

Della Robbia is best known for his technical innovation of vitreous glazes, allowing the finished sculpture, medallion or relief to be exhibited outdoors, impervious to the damp.

In 1529, **Francis I** visited the workshop of Luca's nephew, Girolamo della Robbia, at Suresnes, near Paris, and commissioned him to make medallions for the château de Madrid in the Bois de Boulogne.

Delorme, Philibert: QUEENS, II, 3: (1515–1570): Architect and brilliant mathematician and designer of the tomb of **Francis I** at St Denis. Born in the Lyons area, Delorme, the son of the city's Master of Works, was trained as a priest. He travelled extensively in Italy, and in 1548 was commissioned by **Diane de Poitiers** to build her new château at **Anet. Henri II** made him Counsellor and Architect to the King, Superintendent of Buildings, and Chaplain in Ordinary. He was given many archbishoprics and further rewarded by nomination as a canon of Paris. In 1464, **Catherine de Médicis** grew tired of her villa, Les Tournelles, and asked him to construct a palace for her at the Tuileries, but he died without completing the project. He was also the author of a seminal treatise on architecture. (Louis Battifol, *The Century of the Renaissance*, tr. E.F. Buckley, London, 1916.)

Demeter: KINGS, IV, 3: Goddess of agriculture and cultivation; her name signifies Mother Earth. She is the mother of Persephone by her brother Zeus. Her daughter's kidnapping by the king of the underworld, and the annual six months Persephone was forced to stay in Hades as his queen, caused Demeter to grieve so much that she neglected the earth, which then became barren; hence the explanation for the winter seasons. See also **Pelops.**

Demetrius: CHECKMATE, V, 1: (c. 4th century BC) Besieger of cities and restorer of Athenian liberty. He subdued **Cyrus** and advanced Greece against Egypt.

Deodands: PAWN, 15; CHECKMATE, V, 7: From the Latin *deo dandum,* 'something given to God'. In the cases of accidental death, the victim's goods and chattels would be sold, the profits going to the church to say Masses for the departed soul. Having died without opportunity for confession, repentance or indeed the Last Rites, these Masses would, it was hoped, serve to reduce the soul's term spent in Purgatory.

Despot of the Morea: RAM, 23: See **Paleologus, Thomas.**

Devshirmé: PAWN, 10: Instituted in the fourteenth century and known as the 'Tribute of Boys', this was a recruitment drive in the Ottoman Empire to secure a new, healthy and young group of recruits to the Sultan's army and administration. The enforced 'gift' of these Christian children to the Empire would occur at least every four years and represented a gathering of six to seven thousand boys at a time.

The brightest and most promising of the boys would be sent to the Sultan, to be educated and trained. The rest would be sent to farms in the country, to perform manual labour in the provinces of Anatolia and Greece. After six or seven years of work, these *Ajemoghláns,* 'recruits', would be sent to Constantinople to join the navy or army. After five years at least, the trained young men could become **Janissaries.**

The recruitment also had a missionary aspect in cutting them off from their Christian backgrounds; the youths would be educated and trained as Muslims. They tended to conform, at least outwardly, for no non-believer could become a Janissary.

For those who could not afford to pay the tax the Empire placed on its Christian subjects, the willing gift of a child could serve as payment. Some parents looked upon it as a privilege. They had no choice but to relinquish their children, but in doing so the most fortunate would not only receive military or administrative training, but could rise to a position of great wealth and power in the heart of the Empire.

Dhammapada: PAWN, 28: As used in the text, it refers to the collection of Chinese Buddhist scriptural texts, dating from the Wu dynasty, third century AD. The texts refer to incidents in the life of Buddha, his teachings and philosophy. (Samuel Beal, *Texts from the Buddhist Canon, The Dhammapada,* London, 1902.)

Diamond of Canada: KNIGHTS, III, 13: In 1541, a French expedition to Canada under Jacques Cartier brought back diamonds and gold, which turned out to be nothing more than pebbles and copper, hence the expression 'false as a diamond of Canada'. Ironically enough, diamonds have in fact recently been found in Canada. (Arthur Tilley, *Modern France.*)

DIANE DE POITIERS: QUEENS: (1499–1566) The mistress of **Francis I** of France, who afterwards became the mistress of **Henri II** when he was seventeen and she was thirty-seven. After the death of her first husband, Louis de Brezé, Count of Maulevrier and Lord High Seneschal of Normandy, Diane vowed only to wear black and white; the colours Henri adopted as his own. Considered to be the most powerful and intelligent of Henri's ministers, she chose many of his advisers for him. It was Diane who counselled Henri II on the Salt Tax, and he gave her the income from the tax on church bells, provoking Rabelais to comment, 'The King has hung the chimes of his kingdom on the neck of his mare'. (See *Marie sonne.*) Her house at **Chenonceau** was given to her by Henri II on his accession, to the disgust of his wife, **Catherine de Médicis**, who considered this to be bad management of state funds. Always at the forefront of fashion, Diane had 150 mulberry trees at Chenonceau for silkworm breeding; she wore nothing but silk, and encouraged both Henri and Catherine de Médicis to wear silk stockings from Italy. It is true that under Diane's tutelage, Henri gave away more in his first two years than his father had done in a reign of thirty-two years. Henri's affection for her was open; often they would spend eight hours a day together. Understandably, there was a great deal of rivalry and suspicion between the two women in Henri's life: Diane was warned by one of the King's Gentlemen of the Chamber (M. Andoins) that Catherine de Médicis had engaged an apothecary skilled in poisons. He also told her that the Duke of Nemours had suggested to Catherine that he should 'accidentally' throw acid over Diane to disfigure her face. Another supporter had promised to avenge Catherine by cutting off Diane's nose (the traditional punishment for adultery).

At the end of 1550, Diane's power was at its greatest. She had undermined **Montmorency** by favouring the **de Guises**; he had retaliated by promoting the King's affair with **Jenny Fleming**, hoping to discredit the planned marriage of Henri's eldest son **Francis II**, Dauphin of France, to the young **Mary Queen of Scots**, by casting aspersions on the morality of her governess. Diane herself chose to intervene in the education of the Scots Queen, and it was she who taught Mary etiquette and the manners of court. (See also **Fair Diana, the lantern at night,** and *Marie sonne.*) (Adrien Thierry, *Diane de Poitiers*; Grace Hart Seely, *Diane the Huntress.*)

Diet: See **Costive bowels.**

Digambaras: CHECKMATE, V, 13: A reference to the wealthy Hindu sect whose secular followers were required to practise the four virtues of liberality, gentleness, piety and penance. The sect contained two principal divisions: the S'wetâmbaras, and the Digambaras, who eschewed all material possessions, including clothes. Digambara means 'sky-clad', or naked, in Sanskrit.

Dio da i panni secondo i freddi: PAWN, 5: 'God gives clothing according to those who are cold'.

Diogenes: QUEENS, IV, 3: (b. 412 BC) Cynic philosopher and disciple of **Antisthenes.** He renounced ambition and was contemptuous of riches and honour. As a temporary protest of indignation against the luxuries of this life, he took up residence in a barrel. When **Alexander the Great** asked if he could do anything within his power to help him, Diogenes' simple request was to ask the conqueror to get out of his sunlight.

Dionysus: QUEENS, I, 5: The Greek god of luxuriant fertility and of wine; also called Bacchus (from *bacca*, berry). He is the god who first learned to cultivate the vine and extract its juice. He travelled the world on a chariot drawn by panthers and accompanied by a cortège of nymphs, maenads, satyrs, pans and centaurs. The spring festival celebrated in his honour was attended by the Bacchantes. (E. M. Berens, *Myths and Legends of Ancient Greece and Rome.*)

Dioscuri: CHECKMATE, V, 2: The twin sons of Zeus and Leda, Castor and Pollux. Castor was a charioteer and his brother a boxer. They represent the ideal types of bravery and dexterity in fighting, and are thus considered the gods of warlike youth. After their death, Zeus offered Pollux immortality, which he would only accept if he could share it with his brother. Thus the twins continued to live and die on alternate days, personified as stars.

Disfigurement: KINGS, SCORPIONS: Maiming was a particularly popular means of punishing minor crimes or infringements of the prevalent moral code; rather than kill the perpetrator, he or she is left with a visible indicator of their guilt. Two examples within the text are removal of the ears for 'coining' (counterfeiting money); and removal of the nose for adultery.

Divers: PAWN, 10: See **Pearl divers.**

Divinia proportio: QUEENS, I, 3: 'Divine symmetry'.

Dmitri Donskoi: CASTLE, 44: (1362–1389) Grand Prince of Moscow who continued the fight for Muscovite superiority, particularly in the struggle against Tver and Ryazan (supported by Lithuania). Under his leadership, Moscow eventually became predominant politically. Dmitri received his nickname after his first victory against the Tartars in 1380 at the River Don.

Do-to the book; quench the candle; ring the bell: KINGS, IV, 2: Referring to the ritual of excommunication according to the Roman Catholic church. After sentence has been pronounced on the victim, the priest closes the book of life, throws the candle to the ground, symbolising the soul being removed from the hope of seeing God, and then tolls the bell for the passing of the dead.

Do you melt it . . . or do you beat it: PAWN, 8: Ludovicus Vives, comparing the faith of Christians to the properties of gold; that it is a faith which holds its own under persecution and still gives witness to its purity. He also compares Islam to glass: 'Touch not glass, for though it be bright, yet it is brittle: it cannot endure the hammer'. (*Harleian Collection of Voyages*, Vol. I, 1745.)

Doctor's annuities: CASTLE, I, 8: Good Tudor doctors could charge extortionate consultancy fees; generally a gold coin on consultation was only the beginning, in addition came charges for the prescribed medicaments (whether helpful or not), and if the physician was successful in his diagnosis, the patient would be paying for the benefit for the rest of his life. Surgeons would charge a contingent annuity; due on the anniversary of the patient's operation. Over a number of years, the wealth of medical specialists would improve in direct proportion to the number of patients they had saved. (W.S.C. Copenham, *Doctors and Disease in Tudor Times.*)

Doctors' Commons: CASTLE, III, 2: The term refers to the common hall or dining table of the Society of Advocates in London, and used later to refer to the building in which they resided. The society dealt with cases outwith the ecclesiastical jurisdiction of the church courts. They thus presided over civil law cases concerning marriage, legitimacy and testaments of the deceased. In the fourteenth century the Court of Admiralty, a court created to try cases arising at sea, also came under their auspices; hence their jurisdiction over 'Wills, wives and wrecks'. With the English Reformation, membership of the ecclesiastical court was open to laymen, providing they were doctors in civil law. The term Doctors' Commons was first used in 1535. Their headquarters were at Paternoster Row, near Amen Corner, until 1568, when they moved to larger buildings. The body eventually became obsolete and was officially dissolved in 1857. (Leonard Digges, 'Doctors' Commons', *History Today*, June 1970.)

Dog stirrup: QUEENS, II, 1: A hoop, 7¼" by 5¼". Under English law, only dogs small enough to pass through this stirrup would be allowed to live in and near forests. A dog of this size would prove no threat to game reared in the area for lawful hunting. Previous to this legislation, larger dogs such as greyhounds owned by non-nobles would have to be 'lawed'. This involved cutting three claws from one forefoot, disabling the dog from being fast enough to catch deer. (Lady Apsley, *Bridleways Through History*, 1936.)

Domine Jesu Christi, qui es verus sponsus animae meae: CASTLE, I, 9: 'O Lord Jesus Christ, Thou who art the true bridegroom of my soul'.

Domine salve nos qui perimus: CHECKMATE, V, 7: 'God preserve us, we perish'.

DONATELLO: RISING; RAM: (1386–1466) Arguably the greatest sculptor of Renaissance Italy. Donato di Niccolò Betto Bardi was a student under Ghiberti and helped with the construction of the great bronze doors to the Baptistry of Florence (1404–1407). He rapidly rose to prominence for his own sculptures in marble, wood and bronze. Along with Brunelleschi and Masaccio, he was one of the first artists to embrace and develop the scientific theory of perspective.

Resident in Florence, Padua and Siena, he created some of the most dramatic sculptures of the fifteenth century, including the bronze statue of **Judith and Holofernes** in the Piazza della Signoria in Florence. His patron, **Lorenzo de' Medici,** constantly encouraged and commissioned the artist, keeping him busy well into old age. Most of the disturbing works created under Medici patronage were made for their own collection, not public exhibition. The Judith and Holofernes, for example, was originally designed as a fountain, and only placed in the Piazza after the downfall of the Medici in 1490. A public petition demanded its removal, claiming it was unseemly to display a statue of a woman murdering a man. Donatello's bronze naked David was also created for the private palace and personal pleasure of Lorenzo.

Despite his popularity and potential list of patrons, Donatello remained fiercely independent, and could only be wooed into completing a commission if it completely absorbed his imagination and skill. He left unfinished statues at Mantua and Ferrara, but in contrast produced a massive amount of work during the ten years spent in Padua (1444–1453), including the nearly life-size series of figures of saints and reliefs in the shrine of St Anthony, and the equestrian statue of the *condottiere* Erasmo da' Narni, the first of its kind since antiquity. He even stood his ground with the Medici; when Lorenzo gave him the gift of a scarlet cloak, Donatello refused to wear it, saying that as the son of a woolcomber he was not of the rank to wear a garment of the wealthy classes. He embodied the proud and haughty spirit of Florence in his *Marzocco*, the lion symbolic of the city (RAM, 6). (W. Janson, *The Sculpture of Donatello*, London, 1957.)

Donatiens, St: RISING: The collegiate church, situated on the Burg, was the centre of Bruges' religious life. It was originally founded as a chapel of the Virgin and rebuilt by Baldwin I in 865. By 961 it was a collegiate church, enlarged in 1080 and restored from 1345 to 1390. By 1560 it was the main cathedral of the city, but was demolished in 1799.

St Donatiens also provided a marketplace for the booksellers and illustrators of the city; their stalls were in the cloisters. **Colard Mansion** occupied a shop there from 1477 to 1484. The church was home to other traders; Turkish and Armenian merchants were specially privileged to sell their carpets and goods at its doors, and in 1468 there was also a seller of **spectacles** in its cloisters. (Malcolm Letts, *Bruges and its Past*, London, 1924; A.D. Duclos, *Bruges, Histoire et Souvenirs*, Bruges, 1910.)

Don't linger, I pray you cuckoo: KINGS, Gambit: From the verse of Alcuin of York (735–804), Abbot of Tours:

> *Carmina si curas, cuculus, citus ecce venito . . .*
> *Non tardare, precor, cuculus, dum currere possis.*

> If you love songs, cuckoo, then come again . . .
> Don't linger, I pray you cuckoo, while you may run away.

DORMER, Lady Jane, Duchess of Feria: CASTLE: (1538–1612) Daughter of Sir William Dormer and Lady Mary Sidney. Her paternal grandfather had been the treasurer of Henry VIII's army, but as a devout Roman Catholic, he was forced to leave court and retire to the country, where his home became a refuge for many other Catholics during the rule of **Edward VI.**

Jane's mother was the eldest daughter of Sir William Sidney, Governor and High Chamberlain to Edward VI. As a child, Jane was playmate to Edward although, unlike the new King and in keeping with her family, she developed into a devout Catholic: humble, obedient and holy. With the death of her mother in 1542, Jane was then cared for by her paternal grandmother. Her grandmother's family were similarly religiously motivated: one sister was an abbess, and two of her grandmother's brothers were **Knights of St John.** The family's faith was eventually rewarded when **Mary Tudor** came to the throne, and Jane and her grandmother were summoned to court. Jane was to stay with Mary Tudor for the whole of her reign, accompanying her monarch in the 'anonymous' distribution of alms to the poor.

She was described as tall, comely, lively and quick-witted. She was never short of suitors, even receiving an offer from **Courtenay**, which would have kept him away from the Princess **Elizabeth.** She would not accept any proposition without the direct sanction of Queen Mary however, and the Queen did not want to lose Jane's company. But Mary regretted her selfish impulse on her deathbed, saying that Jane would miss out on rich endowments if she remained single. Jane was eventually wooed by Don Gomez de Figuero y Cordova, Count of Feria, a pious Catholic, aged thirty-eight. Mary consented to their marriage, but would not have it solemnised until **Philip II** returned from Flanders. Jane and Don Gomez were married hastily in 1558 following the death of the Queen. Feria feared that Catholicism would not be in the ascendant in England for long. He left England immediately thereafter, taking with him many Spanish and English Catholics. Jane and her grandmother followed him in 1559.

The three travelled together until 1560, when her grandmother left them to settle at Louvain, where she remained until her death in 1571. Jane and her husband borrowed 50,000 ducats for the expense of their journey: more of a minor state progress than a protracted honeymoon, it included visits to the Duchess of Parma at Mechlin (where Jane gave birth to their first son, Lorenzo, in September 1559); the **Duke de Guise** in Paris; and **Francis II** at Amboise. While there Jane met **Mary Queen of Scots**, with whom she struck up an immediate friendship They continued to correspond until Mary's death.

Feria died in 1571, leaving debts totalling 300,000 ducats; which Jane had cleared completely by the time their son came of age. Jane Dormer remained devoutly religious for the rest of her life and took the habit of the third order of St Francis. She kept in touch with the Reformation politics of England and, like her father before her, turned her home into a haven for all exiled English Catholics. (Henry Clifford, *Jane Dormer, Duchess of Feria*.)

DOUGLAS, Archibald: KINGS: (c. 1489–1557) Sixth Earl of Angus. Married first to the daughter of Patrick Hepburn, first earl of Bothwell, Margaret, who died in 1513. His second marriage followed hard on the heels of this bereavement: in 1514 he married Margaret Tudor, the recent widow of **James IV** who had fallen at the battle of Flodden the previous year. This hasty marriage alienated Douglas from much of the Scottish nobility in general, and the Earl of **Arran** in particular. Margaret Tudor bore him one daughter: Margaret Douglas (later to become **Margaret Lennox**).

The marriage was far from happy. Margaret Tudor constantly tried to divorce him, succeeding without his approval when Douglas fled to England, accused of encouraging Border thieves and broken men (outlaws) to undermine the truce with England. By 1528 she was finally free of the husband she had nicknamed 'Anguish'.

After Margaret's death, Douglas married for a third time in 1543 (the same year as his Scottish estates were restored to him); yet another Margaret, this time the daughter of Robert, Lord Maxwell. Douglas decreed that all his land should pass to his male heirs from this marriage, bypassing his elder daughter Margaret by entail, and depriving her of what she would ever after see as her legal inheritance. His only son, James, died before him, so the battle over Tantallon and the family estates was fought out by Margaret Lennox, the Queen Dowager **Mary de Guise** and Douglas's nephew David.

Douglas's constant alliances with the English made him an object of suspicion in Scotland, first with Arran and later with the Queen Dowager. He played a double game in the Borders, changing sides depending on who appeared to be winning.

DOUGLAS, Sir George of Pittendriech: KINGS: (c. 1490–1552) Younger brother of the above and diplomatic leader of the English party in Scotland during the minorities of both **James V** and **Mary Queen of Scots.** He shared his brother's exile in England from 1528, and was an active supporter of the proposed marriage between Mary and **Edward VI.** He was regarded as a traitor by the Scots for sending plans to the English that guided them in their attacks on Scotland, although he did not take an active part in their border raids. He was the father of David, seventh Earl of Angus, who suceeded his uncle; and of James Douglas, Earl of Morton, Regent of Scotland during the minority of James VI.

The sister of George and Archibald was Janet Douglas, better known as Lady Glamis (d. 1537). When her brothers fell out of favour with James V, she was accused of murdering her husband John, sixth Lord of Glamis (d. 1528). Falsely accused of witchcraft and having conspired against the King, she was publicly burned alive on Edinburgh's Castle Hill.

DOUGLAS, Margaret: KINGS: See **Lennox, Margaret.**

Doux Nenny: QUEENS, II, 3: Clément Marot (1496–1544):

> *Un doulx Nenny avec un doulx soubrire*
> *Est tant honneste, il le vous fault apprendre:*
> *Quant est d'Ouy, si veniez à le dire,*
> *D'avoir trop dict je vouldroys vous reprendre*
> *Non que je soys ennuyé d'entreprendre*
> *D'avoir le fruict dont le désir me poinct:*
> *Mais je vouldroys qu'en le me laissant prendre*
> *Vous me disiez: 'Non, vous ne l'aurez point.'*

> A sweet refusal with a loving smile
> Would match a 'yes', were you of such a mind.
> Of cozening in truth I do not weary,
> But joy tastes best when seemingly denied.

(Tr. D.D.)

Dragoman: PAWN, 10: European corruption of the Arabic *terdji-man*, meaning 'interpreter'.

DRAGUT RAIS: KNIGHTS: (1485–1565) Governor of Tripoli and the most famous of the Anatolian corsairs, who had an unparalleled knowledge of the Levant. He was born of poor parents in the village of Charabalac. The Governor of Turkey was impressed with his intelligence as a child, and Dragut was brought to Egypt to be educated. He joined the military corps of the **Mamelukes** as a bombadier and became an expert in the field of artillery. He then turned his attention to the sea, starting as a gunner on the corsair ships and soon owning his own galliot at Alexandria. Dragut was joined by other corsairs, and before long the intrepid and cunning pirate was in control of his own squadron of ships under **Barbarossa**.

In 1540, he was captured off the Sardinian coast by Giannettino Doria, **Knight of St John** and nephew of Andrea Doria (1466–1560) the Genoese soldier and admiral. Dragut was forced to row as a common galley slave on Andrea's galleys. Barbarossa was furious at the capture of his favourite, and even more enraged when Doria refused to surrender his prize. Dragut was eventually freed four years later when Barbarossa threateningly appeared at the mouth of Genoa, complete with a hundred galleys. Dragut's brutal treatment as a galley slave only served to increase his hatred of all Christians in general, and the Genoese in particular. They in turn nicknamed him *chasse de diable*; 'the devil's own hunter'. Amongst his companions, Dragut was more diplomatically titled *Rais Draieco*, 'Dragon Captain'.

He held a particular grudge against Malta: between 1540 and 1565, he raided the archipelago six times. On the last occasion, his brutal treatment of the inhabitants of Gozo was in retaliation for the death of his brother in the raid of 1544. The Governor of Gozo had refused permission for Dragut to

GALLIOT

recover the body and give it a decent burial. He had a premonition about his brother's death at Malta, saying, 'I have felt in this island the shadow of the wing of death. One of these days it is written that I too shall die in the territory of the Knights'. (Ernle Bradford, *The Great Siege*, London, 1961; Henry Seddall, *Malta, Past and Present*.)

Drink, the cutthroat of so many men's lives: CHECKMATE, III, 2: Quoted from S.G.E. Lythe, *The Economy of Scotland 1550–1625*.

Dronken, dronken, y-dronken: KINGS, II, 1: Anon. 'Monologue of a Drunkard':

> Dronken, dronken, y-dronken —
> . . . dronken is tabart atte wyne.
> hay . . . suster, walter, peter
> ze dronke al depe [you have all drunk deep],
> ant ichulle eke [and I as well]!
> stondet alle stille [would that everything stood still] —
> stille, stille, stille —
> stondet alle stille —
> stille as any ston [still as any stone]
> trippe a lutel wit yi fot [trip a little with your foot],
> and let yi body go [and let your body go]!

Du fond de ma pensée: CHECKMATE, IV, 4: A song alluded to within the text, to which the first line is 'From the depths of my thoughts'.

Dudley, John: QUEENS: See **Warwick, John Dudley, Earl of.**

Dulcimer: QUEENS, IV, 1: Flat box-shaped wirestrung instrument. The strings are not plucked but struck with two light mallets held by the player.

Dunbar, on his heid-ake: CHECKMATE, III, 3: See **My heid did yak yester nicht.**

Dunnottar Castle: CASTLE, III, 3: This Scottish castle stands on an isolated rock jutting out from the sea about two miles south of Stonehaven. Once the site of a Pictish fort and then an early Christian church dedicated to St Ninian, it contained a castle, probably of wood by the twelfth century, and in 1297, when held by the English, was stormed by Sir William Wallace. By the end of the fourteenth century, Dunnottar was in the hands of Sir William Keith, Great Marischal of Scotland, who built on the rock a strong keep which remained for several hundred years the chief seat of the Marischals, increasing in magnificence especially under the fourth, fifth and sixth earls in the latter part of the sixteenth and first half of the seventeenth century. The site, now a substantial and spectacular ruin, is dominated by the great stone keep, once over fifty feet high, with a vaulted ground floor. The Great Hall, served by a spiral stair, is on the first floor and the Upper Hall is in the third storey. The chapel, which occupies one side of the quadrangle, has thirteenth-century windows, and is the oldest part of the remains. Towering dramatically above the stormy North Sea, the site is so extensive that it has been described as more reminiscent of a fortified town than a castle.

Duns Scotus: QUEENS, II, 3: (c. 1265–c. 1308): Franciscan scholar originally from Duns, in Scotland, an extreme philosophical realist who lectured in theology at Paris and Oxford. In the sixteenth century, his scholasticism was attacked first by the humanists and then by the Lutherans. Those who maintained and upheld his hairsplitting sophist philosophy, the Dunsmen, were accused of being opponents of progress and learning; hence the word 'dunce' to describe someone exhibiting slow-witted intransigence.

Durant les grandes chaleurs, on recherche les ombres des grandes arbres: CHECKMATE, IV, 3: 'In dreadful heat one seeks the shade of noble trees'.

E

Ecco il flagello de'i Principi: PAWN, 2: 'Behold the scourge of Princes', the nickname of Pietro Aretino (1492–1556), the Italian satirist, author of five comedies, a tragedy and many other scurrilous poems. His writings became very popular in Elizabethan England.

Echo: QUEENS, I, 4: See **Blubbering Echo.**

Eckhout: RISING: The abbey of **Bruges,** founded in 1050, took its name from the surrounding oak woods where it originally stood. The ancient abbey is now gone, but the memory of the abbey at least is preserved by the street name.

Écosse notre foi, la France notre coeur: CHECKMATE, II, 3: 'Scotland our faith, France our heart'.

Écumeur de mer: KNIGHTS, III, 7: Pirate, or buccaneer; literally, from the French *écumer* (v.t.), to skim the froth off or to scour; thus *écumer les mers* means 'to scour the seas'.

EDEN, Richard: CASTLE: (c. 1521–1576) Translator, born in Hereford. After studying at Queens' College, Cambridge, he was private secretary to Sir William Cecil, Lord Burleigh, in 1552, and in the following year translated and published Munster's *Cosmography.* In 1555 he published his most famous work, *The Decades of the Newe World,* or *West India,* a collection and translation of mainly foreign accounts. In this same year he was accused of heresy and retired from office, although he continued to write and be involved in the business of the Muscovy Company. At the time of his death, he was recognised as both a scholar and scientist by his peers.

EDWARD IV: RAM: (1442–1483) Son of Richard, Duke of York and Lieutenant-in-General in France under Henry VI, who was the last surviving male in the direct line of the House of Lancaster. Edward's father Richard had a good chance of gaining the throne for himself, and emerged as the foremost and vociferous critic of the ineffectual and mentally imbalanced King Henry

VI and his wife, Margaret of Anjou. York ruled as regent during the King's illness of 1453 to 1454, and was supported at this time by Richard Neville, Earl of Warwick, nicknamed 'the Kingmaker'.

The House of York rebelled against the King and his bride, and civil war resulted. The first major Yorkist victory came in 1460 with the capture of the King. Richard, Duke of York, was named next in succession when Henry was to die; a shortlived victory as Richard was killed by the royalists that same year. When Margaret of Anjou rescued the monarch in 1461, Edward claimed his father's heirdom and aspirations to the throne, but still had to crush his Lancastrian rivals. Henry, Margaret and their son Edward, Prince of Wales, fled to Scotland under the protection of **James Kennedy**, Archbishop of St Andrews. The Scots were encouraged to intervene on the Lancastrian side when Margaret handed **Berwick** over to them. Despite the intervention of the Scots, Edward maintained his control over England and thus, taking the title of Edward IV, began his first rule from 1461 to 1470.

Whilst Margaret attempted to court sympathy and support in France, Edward's sister Margaret married **Charles the Bold** in 1468, drawing Burgundy towards the Yorkist cause. When the Earl of Warwick rebelled against Edward, the Lancastrians once more came to power. Edward fled to the continent, seeking sanctuary in Bruges. He arrived in January 1471, already confident of his alliance with Burgundy, having been elected as a Knight of the eleventh chapter of the **Order of the Golden Fleece** in 1468.

Although Edward was popular in Bruges, he was not greatly supported by his brother-in-law the Duke of Burgundy. Charles was married to Edward's sister, but he initially sympathised with the Lancastrians. Whilst in Bruges, Edward took particular interest in the library and manuscripts of his host, **Louis de Gruuthuse**. Edward ultimately recovered the throne on his return in 1471, when both Warwick and the leading Lancastrians fell in battle against him.

EDWARD VI: QUEENS: (1537–1553) Came to the throne of England at the age of nine; Henry VIII's only male heir, and potential husband of **Mary Queen of Scots** according to the Treaty of Greenwich. In the six years of his reign, both his father's military and religious policies were pursued to their logical end by Protector **Somerset**, who ruled the nation during the King's minority. Somerset maintained Henry VIII's attempts to subdue the rebellious and uncooperative Scots; culminating in the Battle of Pinkie, a military catastrophe for Scotland that saw the young Queen of Scots taken first to the island of Inchmahome on the Lake of Menteith (KINGS, I, 3), and thence to France for safekeeping.

Edward, together with the support of Thomas Cranmer (1489–1556), the Anglican primate and Archbishop of Canterbury, finalised the break with the church of Rome, introducing the Book of Common Prayer and the Forty-Two Articles, the combined Lutheran and Calvinist confession of the Reformed church of England. The structure of the church was overthrown by **Mary Tudor** who executed many of the leading Protestants, including Cranmer, but the Reformed church was reinstated under **Elizabeth**.

Henry VIII's only son was described as handsome, affable, particularly polite, and advanced in the study of literature, sport and foreign languages for his age. He was also a generous patron; his courtiers flourished during his brief reign. Lord Burleigh, looking back on his career in 1584, said, 'In my whole time I have not for these twenty-six years been beneficed from Her Majesty [Elizabeth I] so much as I was within four years of King Edward'. Foreign visitors had a more cynical view of how best to please the King: the **Vidame de Chartres** led him from his studies to frivolous entertainments, thus proving that flattery worked anywhere, as long as one admired the monarch's interests (QUEENS, IV, 4): paraphrasing the words of Lysander, 'Deceive boys with toys, but men with oaths'.

Often in poor health, in 1552 the young King fell ill with measles and then smallpox, but recovered. By Christmas he had developed a racking cough, diagnosed as consumption; he died in the arms of **Sir Henry Sidney** on July 6, 1553. The rebellion that followed his death sought to put Lady Jane Grey (the Protestant great-granddaughter of Henry VII) on the throne. She was supported by **Warwick**, Earl Marshal of England, but her monarchy was to last only nine days. She was replaced by Edward's eldest half-sister, Mary Tudor.

Eh bien, dansez maintenant: KINGS, IV, 2: Cynical retort at the end of the fable about the grasshopper and the ant, retold by La Fontaine (1620–1695): 'Very well—dance now'.

Eine Deutscher bulet wie ein bawar: CHECKMATE, II, 5: The first line of a most unflattering characterisation of Germans: '*Eine Deutscher bulet wie ein bawar, füchst wie ein esel, und bezalt wie ein fürst*'; 'A German makes love like a clown, works like an ass and pays like a prince'. See also **National characteristics**. (Fynes Moryson, Gent., *An Itinerary*, 1617.)

ELBOEUF, Marquis of: CHECKMATE: See **De Guise, René**.

ELDER, John: CASTLE: (1506–1570) Originally from Caithness, Elder was a political priest, linguist and Latinist. A member of the collegiate church of Dumbarton, he fled south with **Matthew Lennox** in 1542 and remained with the Lennoxes to become tutor to their children. Whilst in England, Elder, who signed himself 'John Redshanks', wrote in favour of the supremacy of Henry VIII over the English church, and furthered English aspirations to an English-Scottish alliance. Then, on **Mary Tudor**'s accession, he proclaimed himself avowedly Catholic and, on the marriage of Philip and Mary, wrote with glowing hyperbole the Latin verses held by the two giants (See **Mind, voice, study** ... and **O noble prince** ...) at their royal entry to London. Elder was rival to **Ascham** in the quality of his penmanship. Above all, in educating the sons of **Margaret** and **Matthew Lennox**, Elder fervently hoped to advance the eldest, his precocious young pupil Henry Darnley (future husband of **Mary Queen of Scots**) and ensure that he would surpass all others with a claim to the throne.

Elephant hacked to death for refusing to bow: CHECKMATE, V, 3: An incident which occurred in the later years of the rule of Tsar **Ivan** the Terrible. As his mental instability increased, the Tsar would attack anyone that failed to agree with him; a paranoia that extended to the judgement and punishment of dumb animals. (Ronald Hingley, *The Tsars*.)

Elif: PAWN, 25: An Arabic letter which is a single straight line, hence 'slim and straight as an *elif*'.

Elijah: CASTLE, II, 13: The prophet of the Old Testament; the reference to the icon 'Elijah being fed to the ravens' is a typographical error; the allusion being to I Kings 17, 4–6 where Elijah retreated to the brook of Cherith, east of Jordan, and was fed by the ravens every morning and evening for the duration of the famine.

Élixir à successions: QUEENS, III, 2: The elixir of inheritance, or poison. Italy was supreme in the study and use of toxicology as a fine art, hence **Diane de Poitiers**' fear of being poisoned by **Catherine de Médicis**. One of the best cases of the above occurred in 1573, when Catherine's perfumer René was accused of 'doctoring' his wealthy uncles, a case which brought the accused and his victims a lot closer to Heavenly Judgement. (Honoré de Balzac, *About Catherine de Medici*.)

ELIZABETH I, Queen of England: CASTLE: (1533–1603) Daughter of Henry VIII and his second wife, Anne Boleyn. Elizabeth's mother was executed in 1536 and her daughter was later described by the Venetian Ambassador as the 'illegitimate child of a criminal who was punished as a public strumpet'. From the many portraits and contemporary accounts, Elizabeth was tall, attractive, had olive-coloured skin, and was most vain about the beauty of her hands. She had a queenly bearing and made the most of the physical resemblance to her father. She was a good scholar of Latin and Greek, and spoke Spanish, French and Italian.

With the accession of **Mary Tudor** in 1553, Elizabeth was placed under varying strictures of confinement. Like her father Henry VIII and her brother **Edward VI**, she followed the Reformed Protestant faith rather than the

Catholicism of Mary and **Philip II**. She became a focus for those who objected to the reinstatement of the old religion and were suffering under Mary's regime.

As long as Mary continued to rule without producing an heir, Elizabeth was a danger to the throne. Philip dissuaded Mary from declaring Elizabeth illegitimate and debarring her from the succession; to do so would have risked outright conflict with England's Reformed subjects. Other possible candidates for the English throne included **Mary Queen of Scots**, **Margaret Lennox's** family, and the daughters of the Duke and Duchess of Suffolk. In each case there was strife and potential instability; despite her continual plotting, Elizabeth was the most favoured in the eyes of the people.

During Mary's reign, Elizabeth behaved to all intents and purposes as the Catholic she was supposed to be; hearing Mass twice every day, once for the living and once for the dead. Upon examination as to the strength of her faith, she prayed to God that the earth might open and swallow her up alive if she were not a Roman Catholic. Her prayer does not seem to have been heard. She did however bear grudges; particularly against the religiously devout. She never forgave Cardinal **Pole** for burning one of her favourite servants who was a Protestant, and **John Knox** lost her as a potential ally by damning all female rulers in his treatise entitled 'A First Blast of the Trumpet against the Monstrous Regiment of Women'.

Elizabeth was on her knees in prayer when she was told of her half-sister Mary's death in 1558; to which she immediately responded in Latin, 'It is the Lord's day and it is marvellous in Our eyes'. Under Elizabeth, England was to become a Reformed, prosperous and militarily independent nation, poised between the Empires of France and Spain, but subject to neither. She reasserted royal supremacy over the church in England and, under her rule, England finally became a Protestant nation. Elizabeth became the focus and patron of the English Renaissance; the Gloriana of her age and the inspiration behind the flowering of the arts. (Penry Williams, *The Tudor Regime*, Oxford, 1979.)

Elysian Fields: QUEENS, III, 1: The abode of the blessed in the Greek afterworld, where they enjoyed all the pleasurable pursuits of life. Mortal relatives of the gods were transported directly to Elysium, where they could enjoy an immortality of bliss. Running through the beautiful meadows was the silent stream of Lethe, the waters of oblivion which cleansed the soul of distress and the memory of all former events.

Empedocles: QUEENS, III, 1: (fl. 450 BC) Sicilian philosopher, remembered as a poet, statesman and scholar of natural history and medicine. It is said that, wishing to be perceived as a god, Empedocles tried to conceal the nature of his death. He therefore climbed to the edge of the volcano Mount Etna, and threw himself into the abyss. His hopes were frustrated when the volcano regurgitated one of his sandals, proving to the world that he died by fire. (J. Lempriere, *A Classical Dictionary*, London, 1815.)

En défaut de mieux: UNICORN, 40: 'For lack of anyone better'.

En mai au douz tens nouvel: KINGS, I, 2: The first line of a song, quoted within the text:

> In May in the sweet new season
> When meadows grow green again,
> I heard beneath a bush
> A nightingale singing.
> Saderala don!
> It is so good
> To sleep beside the little bush.

En prison fut Sainct Jhan decapité, Pour avoir dict et presche verité: CHECK-MATE, V, 8: 'In prison St John was beheaded, For having told and preached the truth'. Verse appearing in the Cathedral of Amiens, referring to John the Baptist.

En un vergier lez une fontenele: PAWN, 29: The first verse of a poem:

> In an orchard next to a little spring
> Whose water runs clear and whose sand is white,
> A king's daughter sits, her chin in her hand,
> Sighing she remembers her sweet lover.

Epaminondas: KINGS, III, 3: Theban statesman and soldier. Due to his brilliant military tactics, the small Theban army at his command succeeded in completely overwhelming the Spartans in 371 BC. He concentrated all his army on one particular point, forced his way through the line of the Spartans and killed their King.

Epyaxa: UNICORN, 2: The wife of Syennesis, King of the Silicians. Cyrus, commander-in-chief of the Greek army against Artaxerxes, had not been able to pay his troops for over three months. Epyaxa arrived at the camp, giving Cyrus enough money to pay his troops four months' wages. According to **Xenophon**'s account, the commander and queen were also having an affair, which perhaps accounts for her generosity, although her munificence (or her physical appeal) saved the life of her husband when Cyrus later besieged their fortress. (Xenophon, *Anabasis: The March Up Country*, tr. W.D.H. Rouse.)

ERSKINE, John of Dun: CHECKMATE: (1509–1591) Very wealthy Scots Reformer, becoming the Laird of Dun early in life as his father, an uncle, grandfather and grand-uncle all died at the Battle of Flodden in 1513. He was a nephew of **Thomas Erskine**. In 1530 he accidentally caused the death of the priest Sir William Froster in the belltower at Montrose, so, diplomatically, he then went to France to further his education. He returned to Scotland bringing with him a French scholar whom he established at Montrose to teach Greek; the first time the language was available for tuition in Scotland. Amongst the first pupils was **George Wishart**, who thus learnt to understand and use his knowledge of the Scriptures in a manner which was to hasten the onset of the Reformation in Scotland. Erskine himself supported the Reformation, and was the host of **John Knox** when Knox briefly returned to Scotland in 1555.

Erskine was loyal and conciliatory to both the Queen Dowager **Mary de Guise** and her successor, but remained true to his religious convictions. Erskine was described by Knox in his (Erskine's) dealings with **Mary Queen of Scots** as 'a man most gentill of nature, and most addict to please hir in all things not repugnant to God'. Amongst other honours bestowed upon him by the Protestant Lords of the Congregation, Erskine was appointed as first Moderator of the Assembly of the Church of Scotland in 1561, a post he held for the next three years.

Erskine, Thomas: KINGS: (d. 1551) Master of Erskine and Commendator of Dryborough Abbey, a hereditary title also held by his father who had been sent to France with **Mary Queen of Scots.** Erskine junior was also Privy Councillor and Special Ambassador of the Queen Dowager, **Mary de Guise.** He was sent to Binche in 1550 to conclude Scotland's peace treaty with the Empire and then went to Brussels with the court, where it is said that no Scot was ever honoured more than he.

Chosen as a Scottish representative at the Treaty of Norham in 1551 (which concluded peace negotiations between Scotland and England), Erskine died after contracting the English 'sweating sickness'. (Teulet, *Pièces et Documents Inédits Relatifs à l'Histoire d'Écosse.*)

Estienne, Henri: CHECKMATE, II, 4: (d. 1598) Son of the famous French printer Robert Estienne, Henri edited works of ancient Latin and Greek authors and was compiler of a Greek dictionary; the prototype of all modern lexicons, the *Thesaurus Gracae Linguae*. His Latin–French dictionary was similarly the only one available for a considerable length of time. Estienne, his family and servants are said to have conversed only in the purest Latin.

Printers took an obsessive pride in the quality of their books; Estienne would exhibit the final proofs of his books in public, and offer a prize for anyone who could find a mistake in his work. Estienne and many other printers were amongst the first to come into contact with new and often heretical theology; the Reformed church found supporters and publicists amongst them.

On account of his sympathies with the Protestants, Estienne was forced to leave France and took residence in Geneva, but later returned to France under Henri III.

Estoilete, je te voi: CHECKMATE, II, 9: The first few lines of a verse or song:

> Little star, I see you
> That the moon draws to itself
> My beloved of the blonde hair . . .

Et chi est la fins dou Roumanch: CHECKMATE, I, 5: 'And here is the end of the Romance'; taken from the thirteenth-century Anglo-Norman romance of Guillame le Clerc. (Guillaume le Clerc, *Aventures de Fregus*, Abbotsford Club.)

Et tu ne vois pas au pied de ton rempart . . . Pour m'enlever mille barques descendre: PAWN, 3: 'And thou dost not see, at the foot of thy rampart, A thousand barges descend to carry me off'.

Etrurian mule who ate hemlock: CHECKMATE, III, 9. From a tale by Matteoli (1500–1577). Flaying alive was the method used to wake the hemlock-drugged mules; prevention rather than 'cure' would perhaps seem more efficacious. (E.S. Ellis, *Ancient Anodynes.*)

Eugenios, St: RAM, 33: Patron saint of Trebizond and local martyr. He was condemned to death during the persecution of Diocletian for having destroyed a statue of Mithras, a god greatly adored by the pagan Trapezuntines. King Alexios (1204–1222) erected a church and monastery in honour of Trebizond's first martyred saint, which was turned into a mosque by the invading Turks in the sixteenth century.

Eustochion, St: CASTLE, III, 7: Julia Eustochium (370–c. 419) was the first Roman lady of noble birth to take the vow of perpetual virginity. She and her mother **Paula** were converted by **St Jerome** who attempted to persuade them to lead the life of Egyptian hermits in the middle of Rome. An epistle Jerome sent to St Julia on the subject of virginity caused such hostility that she and her mother were forced to leave the city in 385. They settled in Bethlehem and founded a number of monasteries, controlled by St Julia after her mother's death.

Evil the drink and ill the resting place: CHECKMATE, III, 2: From the Holy Koran, as is the following half of the quotation referring to the rewards of Paradise rather than the torments of Hell:

These it is for whom are gardens of perpetuity beneath which rivers flow; ornaments shall be given to them therein of bracelets of gold, and they shall wear green robes of fine silk and thick silk brocade interwoven of gold, reclining therein on raised couches. Excellent the recompense and goodly the resting place.

Excellent the recompense and goodly the resting place: CASTLE, II, 6: See **Evil the drink and ill the resting place.**

Ezan: KNIGHTS, II, 6: The chant of the muezzin; calling the faithful to prayer by calling out the one-ness and omnipotence of Allah.

Castello da Mina

Fadeur exquise: CHECKMATE, II, 8: 'Exquisite indifference'.

Failnis: QUEENS, II, 2: The hound whelp of the Irish King of Iruaide; in legend, a dog 'more beauteous than the sun in his wheels of fire'. (Edmund Hogan, *The Irish Wolfdog.*)

Fair Diana, the lantern of night: QUEENS, III, 1: Referring within the text to Henri II's mistress, **Diane de Poitiers.** The original quote comes from the poem the 'Complaynt of Scotland' (1548). (Henry Craik, *English Prose Selections.*)

Faire d'une mouche un éléphant: CHECKMATE, V, 13: 'To make an elephant out of a fly', or in more recognisable terms, 'To make a mountain out of a molehill'.

Fairy Melusine: SCORPIONS, 9; 15: It was a legend of the ancient Poitou ancestors of the monarchy of Cyprus that their ancestor on the distaff side was capable of drastic transformation. The Countess Melusine was cursed because of a family argument: her father offended her mother, and their daughter, the Countess, intervened on her mother's behalf, imprisoning him in a mountain. In return, she was bewitched; every Saturday she would turn into a serpent from the waist down.

When she married Raymond, Count of **Lusignan,** she made him promise that he would never visit her at the weekend, but of course he did, and saw his wife as she should not have been seen. In despair, she quit her mortal husband and was fated to wander the earth as a condemned spirit. The transmogrification eventually became complete, and the Countess turned into a dragon. Whenever her descendants approached troubled times, the dragonlady would appear in the sky over the family home in a manner more terrifying to the eyes than the banshee was to the ears. A portrait of the winged Countess appears in the Book of Hours of the Duke de Berry. The confectioners of Poitou kept the legend alive, doing a roaring trade at the May fair producing *Melusines,* gingerbread women with a serpent's tail.

Faisons de fueille cortine et s'aimerons mignotement: CHECKMATE, II, 7: 'Let us make a curtain of leaves and make love with delight'. From a thirteenth-century *pastourelle*.

Famagusta: SCORPIONS: Said to have been founded in the third century, the town did not grow substantially until the fourteenth century after the fall of Acre in 1291. King Henry of Cyprus offered Famagusta to former traders of Acre as an asylum. It thus grew to be one of the main commercial and religious centres of the Levant, boasting a church for every day of the year. A fourteenth-century account relates the resultant wealth and ostentation of the **Lusignan** hierarchy and its obsession with hunting:

> In Cyprus, the princes, nobles, barons and knights are the richest in the world. For one who has a revenue of three thousand florins is no more accounted of there than if he had an income of three marbles. But they spend it all on the chase.

Famagusta remained under the control of the Genoese until it was successfully besieged by **Zacco**. After 1489, the Venetians made it the capital of the island, substantially remodelling the citadel. It remained under Venetian control until 1571, when finally it was taken by the Turks after a protracted and particularly brutal siege. The inhabitants were starved, and the few survivors treated particularly brutally.

The fourteenth-century cathedral of St Nicholas still stands, renamed Aya Sophia by the Turks and turned into a mosque. (Rupert Gunnis, *Historic Cyprus*, Cyprus, 1936.)

Fate plus mal que morte: KINGS, I, 1: 'Fate worse than death'.

Fattened like a thrush on flour balls and figs: QUEENS, II, 1: The ancient Roman diet for edible birds, plumped up with luxury foods. Normally the birds would grow adequately and remain healthy on a diet of millet and greens. (G. Loisel, *Histoire des Ménageries de l'Antiquité à Nos Jours*, Paris, 1912.)

Faustina: QUEENS, IV, 2: (d. AD 141) Wife of the Emperor Antoninus; she was famous for carnal debauchery. Her daughter, also Faustina (d. 176), married Marcus Aurelius. She similarly chose the paths of sensual pleasure, surpassing even her mother in the pursuit of excess. Their namesake became the third wife of **Heliogabalus** in the next century.

Faux conseils et mauvaises testes, M'ont fait bastir ces fenestres: CHECK-MATE, V, 7: 'Ill counsel and awkward fellows, Have built these windows for me', i.e. the speaker, a lawyer, has built his house from the profits.

Fed on recherché meats to sacred melodies: KNIGHTS, III, 9: A reference to the sacred lion of the Egyptian temple of Ammon Râ at Heliopolis. Sacred animal gods were kept in the sanctuary of their various temples behind veils of gold tissue. (G. Loisel, *Histoire des Ménageries de l'Antiquité à Nos Jours*, Paris, 1912.)

Feria, Count of: CASTLE: See **Dormer, Lady Jane.**

FERRANTE I, King of Naples: RISING: (1423–1494) Ferrante, or Ferdinand I, was the illegitimate son of **Alfonso V of Aragon**, who inherited his father's kingdom in 1458. At the beginning of his rule, he tried to reform the administration and financial institutions of Naples, but faced stiff opposition from the feudal barons, who called in John, Duke of Anjou and Calabria, son of King **René** in 1459. Ferrante finally repelled him in 1465 after a long struggle. His victory against the Duke at the battle of Troia in 1462 and the Angevin retreat from Manfredonia were commemorated more than ten years afterwards by the magnificent bronze doors of the Aragonese Arch in Naples. Ferrante, with only a sea channel separating his lands from those liable to be overrun by the Turk, kept on good terms, so long as he could, with Pope **Sixtus IV.** He continued to look to his claims in the Eastern Mediterranean, whether prosecuted in the form of a crusade attempt or by pressing his interest in Cyprus. He and his successors were harsh rulers, however, and Aragonese supremacy was to end in 1496.

Ferrante's first wife was Isabella, sister of the Prince of Taranto, and his second was Giovanna, sister of King Ferdinand of Aragon. Among the merchant colonies in Naples the **Strozzi** family prospered, becoming chief suppliers of wool and silk cloth to the King of Naples during their long exile from Florence, and advising on finance. One of the many humanists at the Neapolitan court was Pier Candido Decembrio, the brother-in-law of **Prosper Camulio**.

Fethy, John: CASTLE, III, 4: (fl. 1498–1531) Celebrated Scots organist and composer who introduced the Continental style of organ playing to Scotland from Flanders, which consisted of using all eight fingers and also both thumbs, an innovation at the time. Fethy taught at the Song School of Dundee in 1531, St Nicholas's in Aberdeen in 1544 and was principal fellow at the Edinburgh school in 1551. He received a payment of twenty shillings at his initial appointment in Edinburgh for 'tonying of the organis'. A composer of some renown, only one of his compositions survives: a setting of English words entitled 'O God Above', which was included in the Scottish Psaltery of the Reformed Church in 1566.

Ficino, Marsilio: RAM, 15: (1433–1499) Italian neo-platonic humanist and the star attraction of **Cosimo de' Medici's** Platonic Academy. Ficino translated all of Plato's dialogues for Cosimo, thus making the texts available to a wider audience than had ever previously been possible. (J.R. Hale, ed., *A Concise Encyclopedia of the Italian Renaissance*, London, 1981.)

Fide et diffide: KINGS, II, 2: 'Be careful whom you trust'.

Filles publiques: QUEENS, II, 1: The 'Ladies of Pleasure' of the French court and its liquor merchants were said to have uncanny knowledge of when the monarchy would next be on the move, probably because these two groups were most necessary to the needs of the extended court and would often receive the confidences of its nobles. **Francis I** never spent more than fifteen days in any one place, thus keeping the court and its hangers-on permanently on their toes.

Firbolg: QUEENS, I, 1: In ancient Ireland, there were two main races, with distinctive physical characteristics. The Milesians were tall, fair foreigners, whereas the Firbolg were the native small dark people. (A.G. Richey, *Short History of the Irish People*.)

Fire hoops: KNIGHTS, II, 3: An invention of **Parisot de La Valette**, of the **Knights of St John**. The light wooden hoops were dipped in brandy, then rubbed with oil and coated with cotton and wool which had been soaked in flammable liquid, saltpetre and gunpowder. When the enemy attacked, the hoops were lit and thrown with the use of tongs; a type of lethal frisbee which could entangle two or three soldiers' robes at a time. (Ernle Bradford, *The Great Siege*, London, 1961.)

First of ye chekker sall be mecioune maide: KINGS, Gambit: The chapter headings come from the first book to have been published in England, *The Game and Playe of the Chesse* by **William Caxton**, printed in London in 1477.

Flageolet: CHECKMATE, IV, 5: The more modern form of the old flute-à-bec, the simple form of straight flute. A complete range of flutes were in use in the Renaissance; they reached their height of popularity in the eighteenth century.

Flamens: KINGS, IV, 4: Roman priests who were not permitted to use knots in their dress. They were also forbidden to touch a dog, mount a horse, or leave the city by night.

Fleet, the: CASTLE, I, 8: Medieval London prison, named after the River Fleet, which joined with the Thames at Blackfriars Bridge. The Fleet was the prison used to incarcerate those to be questioned by the Star Chamber (the King's Court at the Palace of Westminster with jurisdiction over criminal proceedings). It later became a debtors' prison, and was destroyed in the Great Fire of London in 1666. (London Topographical Society, *The A to Z of Elizabethan London*.)

FLEMING, James: QUEENS: (c. 1534–1558) Fourth Baron Fleming and the son of **Jenny Fleming**. In 1548, he accompanied his mother to France in the retinue of the Scots Queen, and was in France again in 1549 with the Queen Dowager, **Mary de Guise**. In 1553 he was made Great Chamberlain for life, and Guardian of the East and Middle Marches. In 1557 he was elected as one of the Scots councillors to negotiate **Mary Queen of Scots'** marriage. He died in 1558 as a result of the 'poison' on the French ship taking them back to Scotland. He was one of the last to die, having returned to Paris in hope of a cure.

FLEMING, Jenny: QUEENS: Governess to **Mary Queen of Scots**, until replaced by Françoise d'Estamville, Madame de Paroy. The illegitimate daughter of **James IV** of Scotland and the Countess of Bothwell, Jenny was the widow of Lord Malcolm, third Baron Fleming, who was killed at the Battle of Pinkie in 1547. Her affair with **Henri II** earned her the hatred of **Diane de Poitiers**. Jenny Fleming was used by **Montmorency** as a pawn to drive a wedge between the King and his mistress. Fleming became pregnant by the

King, and was obliged to return to Scotland, loaded with presents and keepsakes from the fond-hearted monarch. Her son, Henry, remained in France and became famous as a poet and military captain, taking part in the massacre of the Paris Protestants on St Bartholomew's Day, 1572.

Jenny Fleming attempted to return to France in 1552 and rekindle the affair, very much against the wishes of the Queen Dowager, **Mary de Guise.** Fleming attempted to get **Arran** to help her, but Mary warned the Regent not to encourage or help her escape to France. The Dowager was loath to use force against Jenny Fleming and thus risk the anger of Henri II, but the entire de Guise family were worried that the interference of Fleming would create problems for them at court. One mistress was enough for the King; Diane would not willingly be supplanted, and **Catherine de Médicis** would not countenance a second rival without putting up a fight. Fleming was expressly forbidden from returning to France, and her daughter, Margaret Fleming, forced to promise that her mother would do as she was told, for once. (Baron Alphonse de Ruble, *La Première Jeunesse de Marie Stuart*, 1891.)

Flors de biauté: KINGS, I, 1: 'Flowers of beauty'.

Flowery Kingdom: PAWN, 9: The name for China, or *Chung-Hua*, so called because of its early cultivation of silk. The Emperor Foh-Hi ordered that the strings of his musical instruments be made from this new thread harvested from the bowels of the silkworm. Although export of the silkworm egg and seeds of the mulberry bushes was punishable by death, Chinese silkworms were introduced to Byzantium in the sixth century and their cultivation rapidly spread. (William Leggett, *The Story of Silk.*)

Fluctuat nec Mergitur: CHECKMATE, V, 6: The motto of Paris, 'Tossed but not Engulfed'; the crest of the city being a freighted vessel on a sea argent.

Fondaco: RAM, 17: From the Arabic *funduq*, meaning shop, the word has a variety of uses, depending on the context and location: 1) Store or private warehouse where goods of more than one merchant were stored and sold (Tuscany); 2) Public warehouse, usually in connection with a customs' house (South Italy and North Africa); 3) Private warehouse rented or leased for private storage (Pisa); 4) Public warehouse tax to be paid on all imported and exported goods (South Italy and Sicily); 5) Warehouse with living quarters attached, assigned to foreign merchants (Pisa, Venice, the Levant and North Africa, with more extensive living quarters in the last two locations); 6) Committee or Board in charge of the regulation of weights and measures (Lucca). (Florence Edler, *A Glossary of Medieval Terms of Business*, Massachusetts, 1934.)

Fontainebleau: CHECKMATE: Royal palace set within 42,000 acres of the second largest and most varied forest in the kingdom of France. Building began in 1528 under **Francis I** when the old pentagonal castle was destroyed and a new palace raised in its stead, decorated by Italian workmen including **Primaticcio** (1504–1570) and Il Rosso (1495–1540). They were amongst the group of Italian and French artists who worked in the French court from 1530 to 1560, transforming the former hunting lodge into the central collection point of the finest artists of the day. Their work and the influence it had on other artists earned them the title of 'The School of Fontainebleau', and put France on the map as a major centre of the arts.

The château was **Francis I**'s favourite home and included amongst its treasures sculptures by Cellini, Michelangelo and Tribulo; paintings by Jean and François Clouet, Leonardo da Vinci, Jean Cousins, Primaticcio, dell'Abbate, Raphael, Titian, Bronzino and del Sarto; and many other curios and objets d'art collected by Francis's agents from the length and breadth of Europe.

The gardens were equally ostentatious and reflected the height of courtly elegance under Francis I. The carp pond alone held over 1,500 fish. Also outdoors stood the entrance to the Grotte des Pins, a doorway of three arches supported by four virile Atlas figures. Francis I had Primaticcio paint the inside of the grotto with mythical frescoes. By tradition, women of the court used to bathe there, watched secretly by the men through a sunken mirror in the rock recess at the end of the grotto.

From 1544, Fontainebleau housed the Royal Library, founded by Francis I, later to become the Bibliothèque Nationale de France. Precious manuscripts were to be centrally collected at the château as a resource for any scholars wishing to consult them. Guillaume Postel and Guillaume Pellicier (French Ambassador to Venice) collected the manuscripts, which were catalogued and tended by **Budé**. His successor as librarian and collector was **Pierre Gilles**. (Louis Battifol, *The Century of the Renaissance*, tr. E.F. Buckley, London, 1916; Edmond Pillon, *Fontainebleau*.)

Fontana Amorosa: SCORPIONS, 32: The name given to a river which flows to the Mediterranean, six miles from the city of Polis (or Crusoccho) in Cyprus. Nearby is the spring which makes the imbiber fall hopelessly in love and the site of **Aphrodite**'s marriage to Acamas. Close at hand is said to be another spring which will allow the drinker to forget his passionate obsession. (Rupert Gunnis, *Historic Cyprus*, Cyprus, 1936.)

Food: See **Costive bowels.**

Forethocht felony: KNIGHTS, III, 10: Scots legal term for a premeditated crime; 'forethocht' meaning deliberately planned.

Formed so fowle, which is why I am: QUEENS, I, 5: See **Buke of the Howlat.**

Fortunae telum, non culpae: KINGS, I, 3: 'This dart pierced by mischance, not through anyone's fault'.

France, mère des arts, des armes et des lois: QUEENS, I, 3: Joachim du Bellay (1522–1560):

> France, mère des arts, des armes et des lois,
> Tu m'as nourri longtemps du lait de ta mamelle:
> Ores, comme un agneau qui sa nourrice appelle,
> Je remplis de ton nom les antres et les bois.
>
> Si tu m'as pour enfant avoué quelquefois,
> Que ne me réponds-tu maintenant, ô cruelle?
> France, France, réponds à ma triste querelle.
> Mais nul, sinon Écho, ne répond à ma voix.
>
> Entre les loups cruels j'erre parmi la plaine:
> Je sens venir l'hiver, de qui la froid haleine
> D'une tremblante horreur fait hérisser ma peau.
>
> Las! Tes autres agneaux n'ont faute de pâture,
> Ils ne craignent le loup, le vent, ni la froidure:
> Si ne suis-je pourtant le pire du troupeau.

> France, mother of Arts, of Arms, of Law,
> You have nourished me long at your breast.
> Now, like a suckling lamb calling,
> I fill the caves and the woods with your name.
>
> You claimed me once as your child.
> Why, O cruel one, don't you answer me now?
> France, France, reply to this my lament.
> But nothing answers save Echo.
>
> I wander the plain among wolves:
> I feel coming the chill breath of winter,
> Its trembling horror lifting the hair on my skin.
>
> Alas! Your other lambs lack no pasture,
> They have no fear of the wolf, or the wind, or the cold.
> Might it be
> Because I am the worst of the flock?

(Tr. D.D. A. Lagarde & L. Michard, eds, *Littérature Française, XVIe Siècle*, 1961.)

Francis I: QUEENS, I, 4: (1494–1547) King of France, acceded to the throne at the age of twenty in 1515; a frivolous, impudent, chivalrous and spendthrift monarch who led his country into nearly two generations of perpetual hostility towards the Empire of **Charles V** and England. Francis had the artistic taste of a connoisseur but exhibited the political sense of a lemming, his pursuit of venery taking precedence over all affairs of state, apart from war.

Francis sought election to the Imperial throne of Germany in 1519, but despite the French King's consistent bribes to the hereditary electors, **Charles V** won the contest, supported by Henry VIII of England. From that point onwards, the territorial rivals became the deadliest of enemies. Francis was captured by the forces of the Empire at the Battle of Pavia in 1525, and imprisoned in Italy, then Spain. On returning to France, he was forced to surrender Burgundy as a result of the subsequent treaty, and send his two sons to be hostages in Spain until the handover of the territories was complete. His son **Henri II** was only seven at the time, and was treated badly when his father broke the terms of the treaty. The two were only allowed to return to France in 1529 when the Peace of Cambrai was declared. His ordeal left the future King with an unequalled enmity of all things Spanish, especially the Emperor. (Louis Battifol, *The Century of the Renaissance*, tr. E.F. Buckley, London, 1916.)

FRANCIS II: QUEENS: (1544–1560) The adenoidal, sickly first husband of **Mary Queen of Scots**, and King of France from 1559 to 1560. The eldest son of **Henri II**, Francis was described as a surly, lazy youth, who took no part in the governance of his country when young. Although taciturn in nature, his affection for his chosen bride seemed clear; Mary was his elder by two years, but also his physical and intellectual superior. Having been together since the age of six and four respectively, Mary knew how to handle the young Dauphin. They were married in 1558, but the marriage was not to last for long.

In 1559, on the death of his father, Francis II became King, and his bride became Queen of France and Scotland, with a good claim to England also. His one enveloping passion was not an interest in affairs of state (still handled by his mother, **Catherine de Médicis**), but in hunting, taking after his grandfather. In November 1560, Francis returned from a day's hunt, complaining of violent earache. That evening he fainted, and succumbed to a high fever. The ear infection developed into an apparent abcess of the brain; there was little the physicians or his bride could do. Francis died less than a month later and was succeeded by his younger brother, Charles IX, with his mother ruling as regent. Mary and the **de Guise** family were finally supplanted at court.

The following year, she was obliged to return to Scotland. (Rosalind K. Marshall, *Mary Queen of Scots*, Edinburgh, 1986.)

Frankincense: PAWN, 27: See **Those who gather frankincense . . .**

Fraying post: PAWN, 12: Where the male deer rubs its new antlers to remove the velvet. A stag considered most worthy of hunting is one which has reached about six years of age, when the crown or *sur-royal* antlers begin to appear. At this age, the stag can correctly be called a 'hart'. Harts shed their horns in March; by June, the new horns have grown and are in velvet; and by July the antlers are generally fully grown. Then the hart will rub off the velvet to sharpen and burnish the antlers.

Discovery of a fraying post signifies that the hunting season can now begin in earnest. The man to bring the first fraying post of the season to King **Francis I** of France would receive a new coat as a reward, or if he were 'a gentleman of the venery', i.e. a member of the hunt, he would receive a new horse. (Edward, Second Duke of York, *The Master of Game*, 1413, tr. from Gaston III, 1904; Lady Apsley, *Bridleways Through History*, 1936.)

Funambulism: QUEENS, II, 3: The art of rope walking. An early European account describes an example during the reign of Charles VI of France in the fifteenth century. A rope was suspended from a high house on a bridge to the steeple of a church. The funambulist slid down the rope, holding a candle in each hand.

In 1546, in the court of **Edward VI** of England, rope dancing seemed once more in fashion; this time contemporary accounts tell of an acrobat sliding down the steep incline from the roof of St Paul's to the ground; head first. A popular special effect was a trail of smoke, caused by wearing a wooden breastplate grooved to adhere to the rope. The resultant friction would cause smoke to follow the funambulist on his descent. (Joseph Strutt, *Sports and Pastimes of the People of England*, London, 1801.)

GALLEASSE

Gabriel: KNIGHTS, II, 6: Sigad id Din, the Trusty Spirit, according to the **Bektashi.** He is chief of the four favoured angels, the spirit of truth, and also the archangel credited with leading Mohammed to heaven on his camel Alborak, and revealing the heavenly truths to the Prophet. According to the Yazidia text of the Koran, Gabriel was created on Thursday and made the sun, moon and stars. According to another legend, Gabriel taught the Prophet how to strengthen his muscles, enabling him to defeat forty men in battle.

Gaea: KNIGHTS, I, 1: The Greek goddess of the earth who came into being from **Chaos** and married Uranus, the heavens. Gaea is mother of all and nourishes every creature on the earth. She is also the goddess of death, summoning all earthly creations back to herself.

Gai comme un bonnet de nuit: CHECKMATE, V, 10: 'Merry as a nightcap'; a sardonic way of saying 'boring'. *'Triste comme un bonnet de nuit'*, means 'As dull as ditchwater'.

Galleasse: Or galliasse, a larger and broader ship than a galley; dependent mainly on sailpower, oars being used as auxiliary power in times of need. They could weigh over 1,000 tonnes, and in particular the oars tended to be longer and heavier than those of smaller galleys. A galleasse would have over fifty pairs of oars; each oar forty-eight feet long and rowed by nine men. An average galleasse would carry 270 soldiers, 130 sailors and 300 slaves. Because of their greater size and superior sailpower, galleasses were better in the open sea than galleys. Their greater stability and width meant they could also carry more broadside armaments than their counterparts. The galleasse, adopted by the English at the time of Henry VIII, was the first fighting entity in its own right, rather than merely a vehicle for the transportation of fighters. (*English Calendar of State Papers; Venetian Correspondence 1548–50;* E. Hamilton Currey, *Sea Wolves of the Mediterranean*, London, 1910.)

Galleys: Long ships, built especially for the transport of spices and precious wares. Galleys were long, narrow and equipped primarily with oars as their method of propulsion. Their speed also made them excellent warships. Standard galleys were triremes, with twenty-five or thirty benches each side of the main deck, arranged obliquely so each of the three men on the bench would row a separate oar. The oars themselves were between twenty-nine and thirty-two feet long, each weighing 120 pounds.

The Venetian trade galleys, known as great galleys, were in use from the late thirteenth century, These early galleys were built by the state in the Venetian arsenal and ensured that the city's supremacy as a world market and exporter for luxury goods was maintained. For their day, they were very large: 138 feet (41 metres) long and 23 feet (6 metres) across the beam, and drawing 9 feet (2.7 metres). The cargo below deck would weigh five to six hundred thousandweight (140 metric tonnes, with 30 tonnes cargo above deck). The Venetian trade galleys were used for light and precious cargoes, but still weighed in excess of 250 tonnes, because of the large numbers of crew and passengers on board. Even the galleys which visited **Bruges** would carry over 200 men as crew.

The great **Venetian galleys** of the late fifteenth century carried over 570 people in total, including 130 soldiers, 290 oarsmen, gunners, gunners' mates, personal assistants and servants to the commanding officer, his navigating officer and the patrician volunteers. To spread the esteem of **Venice** abroad, members of its top families accompanied the galleys; acting as mercantile ambassadors. It ensured the Venetian hierarchy were involved in both trade and the maintenance of the Republic's reputation. The regular galley sailings gave great maritime and mercantile experience to both the captain

GALLEY

and patrons. Both Venice and **Medici** Florence invested in state or communal galleys to increase their trading empires abroad. Heavy goods, such as English cloth, lead, tin or **alum** made excellent ballast.

It was the latter commodity that most interested the branch of the Medici bank in Bruges under **Tommaso Portinari**. In 1464, two great galleys, the *San Giorgio* and the *San Matteo*, were built under the instruction of **Philip the Good** at Pisa. They initially represented Philip's contribution to the prospective crusade planned by Pope **Pius II**. When the crusade did not take place, **Charles the Bold** leased them to Portinari. Because they were larger than usual galleys, they were particularly useful for trade; the *San Matteo* could hold 300 tonnes of alum alone. The galleys continued to fly the Burgundian flag, to indicate their sovereignty, and could still be taken back by the Duke if he needed them. This occurred in 1470 when Charles requisitioned them for his war against **Louis XI**. Portinari eventually lost complete control over the *San Matteo* (and its expensive cargo) in 1473.

The great galleys were no use for discoveries or long-haul journeys. They were too light and frail for prolonged ocean voyages, and so heavily manned for their size that they could not carry the massive amounts of provisions required for such journeys without having to put into port at least every seven days. Discoveries in uncharted waters were the province of **round ships** and the newly developing **caravel**.

The reliance upon oarsmen did act in their favour when the galleys were used as warships; it was the boast of the Levantine corsairs that they did not care how the wind blew, as they carried the winds in the sinews of their slaves. Weather would not stop the corsairs from plunder, but superstition would. The Arab corsairs would not set sail for the week before or after February 25, *Al-Aàsoom*. During these fifteen days, a galley of brass or iron was said to range the seas under the surface of the water ('The Turk's diabolical iron galley', CHECKMATE, V, 11). If this boat was met by chance, the unfortunate corsair and his ship would sink with all hands. If, however, the brass ship was seen by the real boat first, then the brass ship would disappear for ever. Few corsairs seemed likely to risk the lives of their crew on a gamble of their keensightedness, so for two weeks of the year, their slaves had a respite from rowing. (Frederic C. Lane, *Venice and History: Collected Papers*, Baltimore, 1966; *Venetian Ships and Shipbuilders of the Renaissance*, Baltimore, 1934; J. Morgan, *A History of Algiers*.)

Game and Playe of Chesse, The: KINGS: See **Caxton, William**.

Ganching: PAWN, 1: A brutal torture and slow death: the victim is tied by ropes fastened to the arms, then pulled up to a gibbet of hooks. The body is then dropped onto the hooks where it remains impaled. It was a standard punishment for common thieves found in Constantinople. Algiers had a special arrangement of hooks on the Beb-Azoun wall for the same purpose; criminals were forced to sit on the top of the wall with ropes around their necks. They would be pushed off onto the hooks below. A victim was noted as having survived for three days and two nights with the hooks through his ribs. (J. Morgan, A *History of Algiers*.)

Gare le chapeau!: QUEENS, II, 5: 'Watch out for the hat!'

Garlic and onions: PAWN, 20: An essential provision for those intending to cross the desert, because calves' heads, feet and tripe cannot be prepared without garlic. The Arabic legend recounting the origin of these essential plants blames Satan; when he was ejected from Paradise and stepped on the earth, garlic sprang from his left footprint and onions from his right. The amount of time that the devil spent on earth may perhaps account for the prevalence and popularity of the plants. (Alexander Pallis, *In the Days of the Janissaries*.)

Garlic to a gamecock: CASTLE, II, 6: See **Cock fighting**.

Gean-canach: QUEENS, IV, 4: Gaelic, meaning love talker.

Gehenna, lip of: KINGS, IV, 4: Jeremiah, 19, 6; the very edge of Hell itself and the place of eternal torment, where sacrifices to Baal and Moloch were offered, and named in the King James version of the Bible as 'the valley of slaughter'.

Gen-traige, Gol-traige, Suan-traige: QUEENS, II, 6: The three types of music according to ancient Irish tradition. The first, the *Gen-traige*, incites merriment. The second expresses sorrow and a period of mourning. The third type, the Suan-traige, are lighter lullabies and nursery songs. (P.W. Joyce, *Social History of Ancient Ireland*.)

Geomalers: PAWN, 10: A sixteenth-century religious cult of rich young men who travelled and studied the world as pilgrims. According to the travel notes of **Nicolas de Nicolay**, they called themselves 'Pilgrims of Love' or 'Men of the Religion of Love' because they liked to travel through the country at leisure, seducing both girls and boys. The Geomalers tended to wear knee-length purple tunics, with a leopard or lion skin around their shoulders, tied by its forelegs. They adorned themselves with silver earrings, bells and cymbals attached to the bottom of their tunics and round their knees. When they travelled in groups, the cymbals and bells would keep time with their singing. They never travelled without their books of Persian love sonnets, singing and reciting for food and gifts. (*Harleian Collection of Voyages*, Vol. I, 1745.)

Gerard: KNIGHTS, I, 2: See **Blessed Gerard.**

Germans woo like lions, Italians like foxes: CASTLE, III, 7: See **National characteristics.**

Gházel: See **Ottoman poetry.**

Ghíaur: KNIGHTS, II, 9: Arabic for an infidel or heathen; one who is not respected for his beliefs by the devout, but a despised non-Muslim.

Gib cat: KINGS, III, 4: In Scots this is the term usually used for a neutered domestic male cat, as opposed to a 'Tom cat'. It comes from the name Gilbert, although no firm evidence can be given as to why this name has come to represent emasculation. For 'Gib, our cat', see **The Frogge would a wooing ride.**

Gif thou should sing well ever in thy life: KINGS, I, 1: Quote taken from the Scots poem 'The Kingis Quair', or King's Book, the first Scots dream poem, reputedly written by James I (1394–1437) and heavily reliant upon the style and imagery of Chaucer. See **Hast thou no mind of love? Where is thy make?** for extract.

Giles, St: KNIGHTS, III, 17: (c. 8th century) Aegidius, the patron saint of Edinburgh. It is said that Giles was an Athenian who fled to France. He established himself as a hermit at the mouth of the Rhône, living on herbs and the milk of a white hind, his only companion. When Flavius Wamba, King of the Visigoths, was out hunting, he chased the hind to the hermit's abode. Wamba fired an arrow which missed the hind, and pierced Giles's leg. It is said that St Giles preferred to mortify the flesh rather than waste his prayers on a full physical recovery. Wamba was so impressed with the devout saint that he built him a monastery. A town grew up near his grave and became a famous place of pilgrimage. He is considered the patron of cripples and beggars.

In 1455, William Preston of Gordon acquired the armbone of St Giles from France, and presented it to the Edinburgh church which bore his name. Preston was honoured by having the right to carry the relic when it was borne through the church. A three-bay chapel was added to the church after 1455 to commemorate this gift, and still bears the name of its patron.

GILLES, Pierre d'Albi: PAWN: (1490–1555) Classical scholar and naturalist, traveller and librarian to **Francis I.** In 1544 he was sent by Francis to the Orient to hunt for ancient and obscure manuscripts to add to the King's library. He spent a great deal of time in Constantinople, and was fascinated by the animals of Sultan **Suleiman**'s menagerie. His travelling remit continued under **Henri II** and he travelled with **d'Aramon** throughout the Ottoman Empire. En route to Bitlis with the Turkish army, Gilles lost much of his baggage, books and research notes but was able to send some of his material home safely. From Alexandria, he wrote of sending skins of elephants (one of which he had successfully dissected at Aleppo), hippos, giraffes, a yak's tail and an ichneumon. Thanks to the support and protection of the French Ambassador, Gilles was able to carry out his archaeological study of ancient Constantinople (*De Topographia Constantinopoleos*). D'Aramon took Gilles back to France with him in 1550, but Gilles left for Rome soon after. He died suddenly in Rome five years later, still in the middle of his studies. His Latin study of Constantinople was published posthumously in 1562. (Jean Chesnau, *Le Voyage de M. d'Aramon.*)

Giotto's 'O': QUEENS, IV, 5: When the artist Giotto di Bondone (1267–1337) was asked if he was a capable artist, he proved his great skill by drawing a perfect 'O' with a single stroke of red paint.

Glaucus: KINGS, III, 4: Son of Minos and Pasiphaë who, as a child, fell into a vessel of honey while pursuing a mouse, and was smothered to death. He was restored to life by a 'dragon', or potion, given to him by Aesculapius.

Glengore: KNIGHTS, III, 6: The Pox. For further details of venereal disease, see **Syphilis.**

Glossa interlinearis: KINGS, IV, 2: Literally, a gloss between the lines of a text, generally found in sacred works, and most famously applied to the interlinear explanatory and theological writings attributed to Walafrid (Walafriedus) Strabo, or 'Squinting Wilfrid' (c. 808–849), considered as the author of the *Glossa Ordinaria*, for centuries the most widely used commentary on the Bible.

GNUMI MANSA: SCALES: Fifteenth-century tribal leader of the Gambia. When Gnumi Mansa met the Portuguese explorers under the captaincy of **Diogo Gomes**, he was quick to realise the potential benefit of making a link with this great Christian ambassador from the 'civilised' world. He asked Gomes to baptise him, but Gomes, being a layman, demurred, saying he would ask **Henry the Navigator** immediately to send him a priest qualified to do the job correctly. Gnumi Mansa then asked that if Henry was sending a priest, could he also send him a hunting falcon, for he was intrigued at the stories the Westerners had told him about Christians carrying a bird on their arm which would catch other birds. His shopping list then extended to two rams and sheep, ganders, geese, a pig, and architects who would design Western-type houses for him. Gnumi Mansa did adopt the name of Henry when Gomes was there, and promised that he would not kill any more Christian visitors to his province. The priest was sent to the African leader in 1458, but it is not recorded if Gnumi Mansa received the other rewards he desired as the price of conversion. (G.R. Crone, ed., *The Voyages of Cadamosto*, Hakluyt Society, London, 1937.)

Gobbam Saer: QUEENS, II, 3: Seventh-century legendary architect of Ireland. (P.W. Joyce, *Social History of Ireland*.)

God give me another lad like thee: KNIGHTS, III, 8: Prayer of mourning taken from the diary of Sir James Melville (1556–1601).

God hateth murder: CASTLE, II, 11: The eighth commandment that 'Thou shalt not kill', which Allah gave to Mohammed. It is acceptable verbally to revile your fellow Muslim, but never to raise a hand against him. Jews and Christians, as unbelievers, were not protected by this code, and could never justifiably strike back. Nonbelievers could not fight in the Holy Wars of the Ottoman Sultans; hence the wholescale conversion of the Janissaries and all foreign infidel slaves co-opted in the Ottoman military.

God hath a thousand handes to chastise: KINGS, Gambit: From the poem by John Lydgate (c. 1370–1451), 'God's Providence':

> God hath a thousand handēs to chastise:
> A thousand dartēs of punicion [punishment]:
> A thousand bōwes made in deverse wise:
> A thousand arlblasts [crossbows] in his dongeōn.

(Macaulay Fitzgibbon, *Early English Poetry*, London, n.d.)

Gods with feet of wool: KNIGHTS, III, 5; CHECKMATE, III, 7: Verse attributed to a 'Gentleman of Charrolois':

> *Jamais, jamais l'impieté*
> *Sans la vengeance n'a eté*
> *D'une, et d'une autre juste peine*
> *Cy haut, et là bas en enfer*
> *Si les Dieux ont les pieds de laine*
> *Aussi ont ils les bras de fer*

> Never, never blasphemy
> But vengeance follows privily

> Since righteous punishment may dwell
> Both here above and there in Hell.
> Though tread the Gods on fleece of gimmer [a young ewe]
> Their iron arms can crush a sinner.

(Tr. D.D.)

The 'righteous punishment' refers to the treatment meted out to the English captain of Ferniehurst when he was captured by the Scots and French in 1549. According to Sir Andrew Kerr of Ferniehurst, in the three months since the English captain had taken the castle, he had not omitted a single act of impiety they considered as worthy of the Moors of Africa; including raping all the young women within the castle, and torturing the old. When the English garrison was eventually forced to surrender, their captain came face to face with a Scot whose wife and daughter he had abused. The Scot cut off his enemy's head with such force that it bounced four paces from his corpse before stopping. This was greeted with loud applause and cheering from over a hundred other Scots soldiers observing the proceedings, who washed their hands in the blood. There followed an orgy of violent retribution from the Scots; to the extent of buying the remaining English captives from the French in order to torture them to death for their reprehensible conquering behaviour. (Ian de Beaugué, *Histoire de la Guerre D'Eccosse*, Maitland Club, 1556.)

Gold-wire dentistry: KINGS, III, 4: The art of using finely spun gold for fillings and oral embellishment has been practised since the days of the ancient Etruscans; no doubt in the case mentioned within the text, the dental work would serve to correct the pike-induced lisp of **Grey of Wilton**.

Golden Ass: KINGS, Gambit: From the Roman satire by Apuleius (b. c. AD 114), *Metamorphoses seu de Asino Aureo*, or 'The Golden Ass'. The story tells of Lucius, who swallows a magic potion by mistake and turns into an ass. The tale relates all the various adventures he undergoes until he eventually regains his human form.

GOMES, Diogo: SCALES: (b. c. 1420) Page to Prince **Henry the Navigator**, knighted in 1440 and made Magistrate of Sintra in 1446. Gomes travelled to Africa first in 1457 and again from 1459 to 1460; he is accredited with discovery of the Cape Verde islands and for purchasing the first slaves from this area. King Alfonso of Portugal granted him authority over the shores of the Senegambia and commissioned him to seize all ships in the area which were trading illegally and undermining the Portuguese monopoly in West African territory.

In the 1457 voyage, under his captain Gonzalo Alfonso, Gomes met

Gnumi Mansa and Bati Mansa, when the former converted to Christianity. In 1462, after his voyages and discoveries, he was made Warden of Sintra Castle. (G.R. Crone, ed., *The Voyages of Cadamosto*, Hakluyt Society, Second Series, No. 80, London, 1937.)

GRADO, Giammatteo Ferrari da: RISING: (d. 1472) Also known as Johannes Matheus de Ferrariis de Gradi, or Jean-Mathieu Ferrari da Grado. Born in Milan at the end of the fourteenth century, son of Jean Ferrari, a member of the college of physicians of Milan. An uncle of Jean-Mathieu was prior of the abbey of Miramondo and the brother of Jean-Mathieu, Beventinus, was notary to the Duke of Milan, and organised the 1450 donation of Filippe-Marie Visconti to **Francesco Sforza**. Jean-Mathieu's uncle Antoine was professor of the Faculty of Medicine at **Pavia** in 1387, and Jean-Mathieu's nephew Jean-Antoine was doctor to the Duchess Bona, wife of the Duke Galeazzo-Maria, and author of a work on fevers. Jean-Mathieu studied medicine at Pavia from 1425, and in 1432 became professor of logic at the university, where he stayed all his life. The Duke of Milan was the founder and protector of Pavia University and Jean-Mathieu became his physician, and also a member of the Duchess's special council when the Duke was away. Among his other famous patients were the Marquis of Mantua, Gaston IV de Foix, Prince of Navarre, Louis II of Gonzaga, and King **Louis XI** of France, whom he treated for piles (see **With Emeroides in the hinder parts**). The notes on his case histories are still extant. Jean-Mathieu died in 1472, leaving part of his fortune to his nephews and dividing his library between them and the hospital of Pavia. Although he married and had three children, none of them survived him.

Grand Joculator: CASTLE, III, 8: A reference to Berdic, the joculator, or court jester of William the Conqueror. (E.S. Turner, *The Court of St James's*.)

Greek fire: KINGS, IV, 1; SCORPIONS, 24: See **Naphtha**.

Greeks in bed, Italians at table, are most neat: CASTLE, III, 13: See **National characteristics**.

Gregale: QUEENS, IV, 2: See *Animal gregale*.

GREY of Wilton, Sir William: KINGS: (c. 1508–1562) Thirteenth Baron Grey of Wilton. He was made Governor of Boulogne in 1546, but returned to England to help Protector **Somerset** in his invasion of Scotland. It was in this year that he sustained the pike wound which was to leave him lisping for a considerable length of time; the pike broke one of his teeth, struck through his tongue and embedded itself in the roof of his mouth 'three fingers deep', as his son's biography gruesomely relates. He would have drowned in his own blood had not the Duke of Norfolk dismounted and come to his aid, lifting a firkin of ale to his mouth.

Grey's battle plans for the Protector's campaigns against Scotland were successful: as a reward he was given Hume Castle, and knighted at Berwick in September 1548. When he left control of the garrison at Haddington to **Sir Thomas Palmer,** his subordinate's rash actions lost most of Grey's troops and the ground they had won in Scotland. In 1551 when Protector Somerset fell from grace, Grey was dragged down with him and sent to the Tower of London, but later released and cleared of all charges. In compensation, he was given the Governorship of Guines, 'which office he kept till by the ears he was pulled out of the same', according to his son.

His brave defence of Guines is well portrayed by his son Arthur, who was with his father for the duration of the siege: Grey's heroic defence of the last English bastion in France was only undermined by the cowardly behaviour of the Spanish troops.

When captured after the fall of Guines, Grey was first made a hostage of **Piero Strozzi,** but sold on to Monsieur de Randan, and from him to his brother, the Count of Rochefoucault. His ransom was eventually set at 24,000 crowns. To raise the necessary cash, Grey was obliged to sell the family castle at Wilton on Wye. For his services to the crown, he was made a Knight of the **Order of the Garter** in 1557, elected by proxy as he was still a prisoner in France. On his return to England after a year as a hostage, he was made General of the English army and sent to help the Scottish Protestants against French attempts to annex their rebellious and heretical allies. Grey besieged Leith, and forced the French to leave. He died in 1562, leaving two sons (one of whom wrote his biography) and a daughter. (Arthur, Lord Grey of Wilton, *William, Lord Grey of Wilton, K.G.,* c. 1577.)

Gritti: PAWN, 15: A reference to the Venetian doge Andrea Gritti (1455–1538) who had an illegitimate son, Aloisio Gritti, who served the Turks. Aloisio was born in Constantinople to a Greek mother, when his father (then Venetian Bailiff) was a prisoner of the Turk. The son grew up to become a great military captain for the Ottoman empire, leading 1,000 **Janissaries** and 2,000 **Spahis** to Hungary. He was given the title of *Beyoglou,* 'Son of Prince', by the Turks.

GRUUTHUSE, Louis de Bruges: RISING: (c. 1423–1492) The family name of Gruuthuse comes from their control of the malt tax monopoly of **Bruges**, a lucrative income in an ale-drinking society. The noble Gruuthuse was a great jouster, who took part in the Bruges joust of 1443, where he won first prize, and jousted again at the marriage of **Philip the Good** in 1447 when the Duke married Isabelle of Portugal. In 1449, he was appointed cupbearer to the Duke, and in 1450 made his last appearance at the Bruges joust, although he later participated in the chivalric displays in 1454 at Lille, where the Feast of the Pheasant aimed to arouse interest in a new crusade to oust the Turk from Constantinople.

In 1452, as Governor of Bruges and Oudenarde, he defended the city from an attempt to embroil it in the Ghent rebellion against the Duke. In 1455 he married Marguerite van Borselen, daughter of Henry van Borselen, Admiral of Holland and Chevalier of the **Order of the Golden Fleece**, thus marrying into the upper nobility. His new brother-in-law, Wolfaert van Borselen, was the husband of Mary, Princess of Scotland and sister of **James II**. In 1461, he was also admitted to the Order of the Golden Fleece and was in the suite of Duke Philip himself. Duke **Charles** appointed Gruuthuse as head of the Burgundian army in 1468, and in 1470 he was appointed head of the Burgundian fleet.

Gruuthuse was a great collector of books and manuscripts, and patron of **Colard Mansion**. The family home, built of red brick, stood over one of Bruges' many canals, and housed his impressive library, equal in wealth and richness to that of **Louis XI** of France. Amongst its many works it included *The Penitence of Adam*, translated by Mansion. The collection held the attention of **Edward IV** during his stay in Bruges in 1471 when Gruuthuse acted as host. In thanks for his help and hospitality, Edward made him Earl of Winchester, a title he was eventually forced to relinquish by Henry VII.

Guilds: RISING, 2: As associations of workers within the same trade or occupation, caring for the physical and spiritual welfare of their members, guilds fulfilled several valuable functions for the town-dwelling craftsmen of medieval and early modern Europe. They provided a monopoly of trade, control of workers, and security of persons and goods; protected against poverty; and maintained the high reputation of their craftsmen by regulating the quality of goods produced as well as prices and hours worked by the members. The trade secrets of the guilds were closely guarded amongst their members; no outsiders could learn the secrets of the crafts—hence their other name of 'mysteries'. Admission to a trade guild was limited; for example, the Bruges fullers and dyers would admit only one apprentice at a time and training would take two to three years. After training, the apprentice became a journeyman, and perhaps eventually a master of his chosen trade. Women were not always excluded from membership; a widow could transfer her husband's guild membership to her next spouse, or become a guild-sister. Widows and orphans of deceased members would often receive help and financial support from the guild, as would those who had become bankrupt or impoverished (RISING, 37).

In addition to its role of self-regulation in terms of the quality of work produced, the guild was also a moral arbiter of conduct. No one could be admitted to membership of the Bruges guilds if they were living in adultery, or were known criminals. Spiritual welfare went hand in hand with trade solidarity. The religious confraternities or brotherhoods (especially in Venice) gave donations to charitable institutions, and had their own chapels of worship (UNICORN, 23).

By the beginning of the fourteenth century, there were fifty-two registered guilds in Bruges, each with its own charters and privileges and headed by its dean, elected by the members. By this time they had also begun to establish themselves in the government of the town; their largest visible presence being in the Procession of the Holy Blood at the time of the Bruges Fair. (Malcolm Letts, *Bruges and its Past*, London, 1924; Richard McKenney, *Tradesmen and Traders*, London, 1987.)

DE GUISE, Charles, Cardinal of Lorraine: QUEENS: (c. 1524–1563) Brother of **Mary de Guise**. Made Bishop of Rheims at the age of fourteen, Charles succeeded his uncle to the title of Cardinal. He was described as tall, fair, with a high brow and blue, cat-like eyes. His hair was grey by the time he was thirty, but his good looks remained. He was considered to have an avaricious nature, to be cautious rather than licentious, and a coward in battle, although vocal and aggressive when it came to verbal theological disputations. A good scholar and theologian with an extensive library, Charles was nicknamed 'The Transalpine Pope'. He was fluent in Greek, Latin, Spanish and Italian, but was vain about his own eloquence.

Charles and his elder brother **François**, known respectively as 'the lion and the fox', were in possession of all practical power in France. They advanced their own family to aspire to the thrones of three different countries and were foremost in ensuring that Scotland remained under French control for as long as possible. The harsh and autocratic Cardinal headed the oppressive regime against the Protestants during the reign of **Henri II**, but was generous to Catholics in exile. He entertained at his own expense over 2,000 English and Irish refugees in France, ensuring that the board and fees of any promising students amongst their number were paid.

DE GUISE, Claude, Duke d'Aumale: CHECKMATE: (1526–1573) Younger brother of **François, Charles**, and **Mary**. In 1546 he married Louise de Brézé, the eldest daughter of **Diane de Poitiers**. Like his brothers, he found favour at court, and was made Governor of Burgundy by **Henri II**. He proved himself a brave soldier. He was captured by the Emperor **Charles V**'s troops before the siege of Metz and his captors demanded a ransom of 100,000 écus, but, under pressure from the powerful de Guise family and the Duke's mother-in-law, the amount was eventually reduced to 60,000 écus, which they paid between them.

DE GUISE, Francis: KNIGHTS: (1535–1586) Another member of the de Guise family, he was Grand Prior of the **Knights of St John**, General of the Galleys and also Governor of Provence and Admiral of the Eastern Seas under **Henri II** and his successors.

DE GUISE, François, Duke: QUEENS: (1518–1563) Eldest brother of the family, and the same age as **Henri II**, he was known as the Duke d'Aumale until the death of his father in 1550 when he became Duke de Guise, and the title of Aumale passed to his brother **Claude**. His wisdom and prudence, in addition to his good reputation as a military commander, earned him the confidence of the King. He and his brother Charles, the Cardinal, were first to know of all internal affairs, either from their closeness to the King or via their network of spies.

In the war with England over Boulogne, François received a near-fatal injury. He always fought barefaced, and in 1543 a lance entered his face above the right eye, sloped through the nostril and exited at his left ear. The force of the weapon was such that the lance did not break until it was embedded more than six inches into his skull. He would have been left for dead had not the famous French physician, Ambroise Paré, after first asking permission from the Duke, put his foot on François's face to gain some purchase before pulling out the head of the lance. It was kept by his mother for the rest of her life as a keepsake and reminder that God was most definitely guarding the fortunes of the family. Thereafter François was referred to as Le Balafré, the 'Scarred One'.

The Duke received the credit for the taking of Calais in 1558 when he was Lieutenant-General-in-Chief of the French army, equal in rank to the family rival **Montmorency**. One criticism levelled against the great military leader was that in peacetime, he was prone to spend too much of his time sleeping. A string of mistresses kept him occupied for much of the time, but he was such a firm believer in hunting as a means of keeping fit for battle that his Protestant enemies were later to refer to his children as 'the falconer's sons'.

The family fell from their great position of power with the death of **Francis II** in 1560 when open conflict developed between the de Guises and their Bourbon rivals. The Reformed religion was gaining ground, but François maintained the family's obsessive hatred of Protestants until his assassination in 1563 by a hired assassin, paid by **Coligny**.

DE GUISE, Louis, Archbishop of Sens: CHECKMATE: (1527–1578) Became Cardinal of Lorraine after the assassination of his brother, **Charles**, in 1563. In his youth, he is said to have spent more time on pleasure than business, earning him the nickname of Cardinal des bouteilles ('Cardinal of the Bottles'), but adopted a more serious demeanour when he became older and more powerful.

DE GUISE, Mary: KINGS: (1515–1560) Queen Dowager of Scotland and mother of **Mary Queen of Scots**. The eldest child of Antoinette of Bourbon (sister to the Count of Vendôme) and Claude, Count of Guise. From about the age of ten, she was educated by her grandmother Philippa of Gueldres at the austere convent of Poor Clares, but at the age of fourteen was removed from the convent by her father's elder brother (Anthony, Duke of Lorraine), who took her to his home at Nancy. She made her début at court in 1531. In 1534 Mary was contracted to be married to Louis, Duke of Longueville, her dowry supplemented by **Francis I**. The next year, Mary gave birth to their first child, Francis, and in 1537 to Louis, her second. Her husband died in 1537 from a fever epidemic, and her second son also died, within four months of his birth.

Mary was given little time to grieve; **James V** of Scotland was also recently widowed. His marriage to Madeleine, the daughter of **Francis I**, had lasted only a matter of weeks until her tubercular disposition finally succumbed to the harsh Scottish climate. He sought the hand of Mary, eagerly supported by the French King. Mary was a wealthy and attractive widow, with more than one royal suitor. Henry VIII of England was also between wives after the death of Jane Seymour, and a French bride would have hindered the mechanics of the 'Auld Alliance' between Scotland and France. His interest gave more impetus for Francis to order Mary to consent to the marriage proposed by James V. The contract was signed in 1538, and she was married by proxy to her Scots husband at Châteaudun in the same year. She left her son Francis, Duke of Longueville, behind in France, cared for by her mother Antoinette. Mary's large family of eleven younger brothers and sisters (nine of whom survived to adulthood) meant that Francis would quite comfortably be brought up with aunts and uncles of his own age.

Arriving in Scotland, Mary quickly learned Scots so she could take an active part in the court and political life of her new homeland. She was crowned Queen of Scots early in 1540, when already pregnant; a double reason for celebration. The house of Stuart had chosen a queen who had already proved her ability to bear sons; a highly important factor in the dynastic struggles of both Scotland and England. In May 1540, Mary gave birth to James, heir to the throne. Within two months, she was pregnant again. Their second son, Robert, was born in April 1541. It was at this point that a twofold tragedy struck the family. The elder son James began to sicken, and finally died in April of 1541. His newly born brother died on the same day. This blow deprived Scotland of two potential heirs in a matter of hours and was seen as a particularly bad omen, taken exceedingly to heart by James V, who rapidly descended into a state of deep depression and paranoia.

By the spring of the following year, Mary was once more pregnant, but James was to have no time to devote to his French bride or prospective heir. In November of 1542, the Scots and English armies met at the climactic battle of Solway Moss. The Scots were thoroughly beaten by the English, and many hundreds of nobles were taken prisoner. James did not take part in the battle, but on hearing the outcome took to his bed, fevered and delirious. Mary went into labour, perhaps prematurely. On hearing that she had given birth to a daughter, James uttered his last coherent words, 'It cam' wi' a lass and it'll gang wi' a lass': prophetically reminding his hearers that the house of Stuart had begun with their royal marriage to the daughter of Robert the Bruce, and this sole surviving daughter would become the last of his Scots line of monarchs. He died shortly afterwards, and his young daughter **Mary** was crowned Queen of Scotland in September 1543.

After the death of the King, the Earl of **Arran** was made Governor of Scotland, and Cardinal David Beaton Chancellor. There seemed little room for the mother of Mary Queen of Scots in the political arena of the time. However, with the English encroaching farther into Scottish territory, the Dowager de Guise capitalised upon the French connection. Her family was increasingly powerful in the French court; a link utilised to its full extent with the alliance of 1548. The young Queen of Scots was taken to France for safety, and was to be married in time to the heir to the French throne; a familial alliance supplemented with military assistance to Scotland, which would create a united front against the English. This thwarted Henry VIII's plans of seizing the young queen as a bride for **Edward VI**.

Mary de Guise returned to France in 1550 and stayed for nearly a year. Her visit was not only a chance to visit her daughter, but an opportunity also to petition **Henri II** for more money and troops for Scotland. War against the English had united the nation to some extent, but the Reformed religion was gaining ground. Under **Edward VI** and later under **Elizabeth**, Scots dissenters found a religious ally in their traditional enemy over the border. To

keep control, Mary was forced to give the Protestants liberty of worship, despite her convictions to the contrary. In 1557 she wrote to her brother the Cardinal of Lorraine of the problems she was experiencing with her unruly nobles: 'They are more difficult to manage than ever . . . It is no small thing to bring a young nation to a state of perfection and to an unwarranted subservience to those who desire to see justice reign'.

She lived to witness her daughter marry the Dauphin of France and be crowned as Queen of France. Increasingly dogged by ill health and harried by the Protestants of Scotland and England, Mary died in the summer of 1560, besieged on all sides, and leaving behind her an aggressively independent Scotland, now ruled by its avowedly Protestant nobility. (Rosalind K. Marshall, *Mary of Guise*, London, 1977.)

DE GUISE, Réné, Marquis of Elboeuf: CHECKMATE: (1536–1566) Grand Prior of the **Knights of St John** after his brother Francis.

Gümush-arayân: PAWN, 13: Silver-searchers and employees of the Sultan **Suleiman's** Mint, primarily employed to detect counterfeit coins. They would travel round accompanied by ten **Janissaries** armed with cudgels, and had the authority to make people turn out their pockets in search of forged coins. If any were found, the offending counterfeiter would either have his hands removed—or his head. (Alexander Pallis, *In the Days of the Janissaries*.)

Guns: The development of hand-firearms changes the face of late medieval and early modern warfare. The earliest firearm was the *schioppetto*; three to four feet long, cumbersome and requiring a match to fire. It was in use in the fourteenth century, particularly in the defence of towns, but perhaps invented as early as the late thirteenth century. By the mid-1430s, companies of *schioppettieri* were apparent in field armies, specifically trained to use the unwieldy weapons. Because of the effective and brutal injuries they caused, they became increasingly popular as field weapons. In 1448, at the battle of Caravaggio, so many handgunners were on the field that the two opposing armies could no longer see each other for the amount of smoke they had generated. Handguns created fear and destruction, but by the late fifteenth century had not yet developed to the point where they would affect the outcome of a battle. Guns and ammunition became mass-produced for ever-hungry armies; they were cheaper to produce and more deadly than the crossbow, although they were not such beautifully hand-crafted weapons of destruction as their aesthetically appealing antecedent.

The *schioppetto* was superceded in the mid-fifteenth century with the development of the arquebus. It was heavier than its predecessor, but more practical; because it was fired using a trigger, one hand was theoretically free to steady the weapon. Fired from the shoulder, the arquebus could not, however, be loaded or shot when manœuvring.

The development of the handgun meant a consequent change in the types of armour worn on the field. As chain mail was incapable of deflecting the bolt from a crossbow, so too the light plate armour used by the cavalry was ill suited to protecting the wearer against speedily propelled hunks of lead. Field armour consequently became thicker and heavier to counteract the deadly arquebus, but inevitably became more cumbersome as firearms increased their range and accuracy. (Michael Mallett, *Mercenaries and their Masters*, London, 1974; J.R. Hale, *War and Society in Renaissance Europe: 1450–1620*, London, 1985.)

Gyges, ring of: QUEENS, III, 6: (c. 680 BC) Gyges the Lydian was originally a shepherd, but on descending into a chasm caused by a recent earthquake, he found a gold ring on the corpse of a buried giant. He removed the ring, and by experimentation discovered that if its bezel was turned inwards, he became invisible. By using the ring, he murdered the existing monarch, married his widow and ascended the throne of Lydia.

Hair dye: QUEENS, I, 6; RISING, 23: The recipe for chestnut hair is fairly simple: to colour blond hair or a beard chestnut within half an hour, add one part of lead calcined with sulphur to one pint of quicklime. Dilute with an unspecified amount of water, and spread over the hair. Leave for fifteen minutes, then rinse off. The longer the compound is left on the hair, the darker it will become, without colouring the scalp.

To colour black hair permanently chestnut, oil of vitriol is recommended (concentrated sulphuric acid), with the proviso that it should not touch the skin in the process. Another splendid organic way to achieve the colour necessary (either for vanity or deception) is to soak leeches in vinegar, and apply the contents direct to the scalp. (Sir Hugh Plat, *Delights For Ladies*, 1609; Aytoun Ellis, *Essence of Beauty*.)

Hâkim: KNIGHTS, II, 4: Arabic for 'Lord', or Colonial Governor of a province; a term of some esteem.

Hâmile: KNIGHTS, II, 7: Arabic for 'pregnant'.

Handball: KNIGHTS, III, 10: *Jeu de Paume*, or 'palm play'. Originally, as the name would suggest, a game in which the ball is driven back and forward between the players with the palm of the hand. It evolved from employing the naked hand, to the use of a glove, and gradually on to the use of a racket. Hand tennis, as it was also known, was particularly popular at the court of Emperor **Charles V.** Ladies of the court were particularly adept at the game, making full use of forearm and backhand strokes. (Joseph Strutt, *Pastimes of the People of England*, 1801.)

Handguns: See **Guns.**

Hanging: KNIGHTS, III, 17: Most popular form of execution for the common criminal of Edinburgh up to the present century. The last public hanging took place in the city in 1864, a tourist attraction in its own right. Members of the nobility could choose to die on the Edinburgh Maiden, particularly if condemned for treason. The Maiden is the genteel name given to the city's guillotine; 'once you had kissed her lips, you would lose your head for ever'.

By 1560, many outlaws in the Scottish borders were being drowned rather than hanged. This was primarily due to the amount of deforestation which had taken place. Before 1511, much of Scotland had been denuded of its best oak to build James IV's massive flagship the *Great Michael*. After Flodden (1513), most trees had been removed from the Selkirk area to provide land for the grazing of sheep, and in rural areas with a distinct lack of trees and halters, it made more sense to drown criminals than waste expensive resources such as wood on building scaffolds.

Hannibal: CHECKMATE, II, 7: (b. 247 BC) Son of Hamilcar Barca. At age nine, his father took him to Spain and made him swear that he would never be a friend to the Romans. In 221 BC, Hannibal had obtained undivided control over the army. He is most remembered for his expedition across the Alps using elephants.

Hanno: KINGS, IV, 1: (6th century BC) The commander sent by the Carthaginians on voyages of colonisation and discovery along the Atlantic coast of Africa. Pliny's *Natural History* notes that having been sent with his fleet to found colonies beyond the Pillars of Hercules, he continued south until he reached a river full of hippopotamuses and crocodiles, where the people spoke a language his interpreters could not fathom.

Beyond this, they discovered a fiery mountain which they called the Chariot of the Gods, and a strange land where the natives, both men and women, were covered in hair. On his return, he deposited an account of his voyages in the Temple of Moloch, and his exploits were recorded on a pillar at Carthage. (Harry Thurston Peck, ed., *Harper's Dictionary of Classical Literature and Antiquities*, NY, 1962.)

Happier than Augustus, better than Trajan: KINGS, I, 2: *Augusto Felicior, melior Trajiano:* the proverbial wish for each new Roman Emperor that in his reign he may have as many victories as Trajan, and a career as successful as the Emperor Augustus.

Happy are the cicadas' lives: KINGS, IV, 3: From Xenarchus: 'Happy are the cicadas' lives For they all have voiceless wives'.

Harpsichord: KINGS, IV, 2: Angel-wing shaped keyboard instrument, similar to the modern grand piano, but producing its notes by a plucking, rather than a striking action. A harpsichord has two or more sets of strings which can be used either together, or separately. (CD set: Musica Reservata of London, *The Instruments of the Middle Ages and the Renaissance*, 1993, Vanguard Classics, 08 9060 72.)

HARISON, Brice: QUEENS: (d. c. 1570) Burgher of Edinburgh and Scots trader with the Netherlands, Harison appeared on the side of the English when he supported the proposed marriage of **Edward VI** and **Mary Queen of Scots** after the disastrous Scots defeat at Pinkie in 1547. As a Reformed Protestant, Harison found support and patronage in London from Protector **Somerset**. When Somerset was replaced by the Earl of **Warwick**, Harison managed to ingratiate himself with his new English overlord by revealing the details of a suspected **Poison Plot** against the life of the young Scottish queen; revealed to him by the prospective perpetrator, one Robin or Robert Stuart.

Although initially imprisoned by the English for knowledge of the plot, Harison took the credit for its discovery, and on his release in 1551 was amply rewarded by the Scots. The Earl of **Arran**, then Governor of Scotland, gifted him £100, followed by a pension from the Queen Dowager **Mary de Guise** the following year. In 1554 he was made Conservator of the Low Countries. When the Protestants took control of Scotland in 1560, Harison was given merchant appointments in Edinburgh, now officially in favour as one of the religiously Reformed rather than saviour of the Queen. (Marcus Merriman, 'James Henrisoun and "Great Britain"', in Roger Mason, ed., *Scotland and England 1286–1815*, Edinburgh, 1987.)

Harquebuzier de ponant: CHECKMATE, IV, 1: Sodomite. See **St André**.

Hast thou no mind of love? Where is thy make?: PAWN, 29: From 'The Kingis Quair', probably written by James I of Scotland (1394–1437); the first Scottish dream poem. It concerns the King's imprisonment in England, and his romantic dream encounter with the heroine of the poem who was to become his wife, Lady Joan Beaufort. When the poet sees the love of his life, he chastises the nightingale for not singing to please her. See also **Gif thou should sing well ever in thy life** (extract):

> An other while the little nightingale,
> That sat upon the twiggis, would I chide,
> And say right thus, Where are thy notis smale,
> That thou of love has sung this morrow tide?
> Sees thou not her that sittis thee beside?
> For Venus' sake, the blissful goddess clear,
> Sing on again, and make my Lady cheer,
>
> And eke I pray, for all the paynes great,
> That for the love of Proigne, thy sister dear,
> Thou suffered whilom, when thy breastis wet
> Were with the teares of thine eyen clear
> All bloody ran, that pity was to hear

The cruelty of that unknightly deed,
Where was from thee bereft thy maidenhead.

Lift up thine heart, and sing with good intent,
And in thy notis sweet the treason tell,
That to thy sister true and innocent,
Was kythit [shown] by her husband false and fell,
For whois guilt, as it is worthy well,
Chide those husbands that are false, I say,
And bid them mend in the XX deuil [twentyfold] way.

O little wretch, alas! mayst thou not see
Who cometh yond? Is it now time to wring?
What sorry thought is fallen upon thee?
Open thy throat; has thou no list to sing?
Alas! sen thou of reason had feeling,
Now, sweet bird say once to me pepe [chirp],
I die for woe; me thinks thou gynis sleep.

Hast thou no mind of love!? where is thy make [mate]?
Or art thou sick, or smit with jealousy?
Or is she dead, or hath she thee forsake?
What is the cause of thy melancholy,
That thou no more list maken melody?
Sluggard, for shame! lo here thy golden hour,
That worth were hail [whole] all thy lyvis [life's] labour.

Gif thou should sing well ever in thy life,
Here is, in fay [faith], the time, and eke the space:
What wostow [knowest] than? Some bird may come and strive
In sing with thee, the mastery to purchase.
Should thou then cease, it were great shame, alas!
And here to win gree [victory] happily for ever;
Here is the time to sing, or ellis [else] never.

I thought eke thus, gif I my handis clap,
Or gif I cast, then will she flee away;
And, gif I hold my peace, then will she nap;
And, gif I cry, she wot not what I say:
Thus, what is best, wot I not by this day;
But blow wind, blow, and do the leavis shake,
That some twig may wag, and make her to wake.

(J. Ross, ed., *The Book of Scottish Poems*, Edinburgh, 1878.)

Haute à la main et un peu superbe: CHECKMATE, IV, 3: 'High-handed and a touch arrogant'.

Hawkwood: RISING, 12: Sir John Hawkwood (c. 1320–1394) was one of the finest foreign mercenaries to serve in Italy in the fourteenth century. Born in Essex, Hawkwood came to Italy in 1350, complete with his own company of soldiers, the **White Company**, and served in Piedmont and Italy. He fought for the papacy and the Visconti before ending up serving Florence, which granted him the right of citizenship and exempted him from tax. Even after his death he was treated as a state hero: he was given a public funeral at the city's expense, and his portrait was placed in the city's cathedral.

He and the King of Naverne Were fair feared in the fern: KINGS, III, 4: Popular song by Laurence Minot (c. 1300–1352); 'How Edward the King came in Brabant'. Minot was the author of a number of fourteenth-century English war songs, of which this is one (extract):

> Edward our comely king,
> In Brabant has his dwelling,
> With many comely knight:
> And in that land truly to tell
> Ordains he still for to dwell
> To time he thinks to fight . . .
>
> Thus in Brabant has he been
> Where he before was seldom seen,
> For to prove their japes:
> Now no longer will he spare,
> But unto France fast will he fare
> To comfort him with grapes.
>
> Forth he faréd into France,
> God save him from mischance,
> And all his noble company!
> The noble Duke of Braband
> With him went into that land,
> Ready to live or die . . .
>
> Our king and his men held the field
> Stalworthy with spear and shield,
> And thought to win his right,
> With lordés and with knightés keen,
> And with other doughty men bydene [besides]
> That were full frek [eager] to fight.

When Sir Philip of France heard tell,
That King Edward in field would dwell,
Then gainéd him no glee:
He tristed of no better boot,
But both on horse and on foot
He hasted him to flee . . .

The King of Berne has cares cold,
That was full hardy and bold,
A steed to bestride:
He and the King of Naverne
Were fair 'feared in the fern
Their headés for to hide . . .

(H. Macaulay Fitzgibbon, ed., *Early English Poetry, London*, n.d.)

He pincheth and spareth and pineth his life: CASTLE, III, 13: Taken from *A Hundreth Good Pointes of Husbandrie* (1557), the definitive sixteenth-century guide to successful farming by Thomas Tusser (1524–1580). Tusser's ideal farmer would utilise every product and side product of the agrarian year to increase the yield and cost-effective management of the farm. Although Tusser encouraged thrift, he satirised the miserly stinting that led to a life of penury rather than sensible money management. See **A town of price like Paradise.** (Michael Pafford, 'A Sixteenth-Century Farmer's Year', *History Today*, June 1970.)

He's crazy, the devil; he's crazy. He doesn't want to be a priest: QUEENS, II, 4: Pope **Clement VII** talking about Hippolito, Cardinal de' Medici. (Paul van Dyke, *Catherine de Medici*.)

He shall ben lyke the lytel bee: CHECKMATE, 2: Chaucer 'On the Primrose' (c. 1345–1400). (Geoffrey Chaucer, *The Complete Works*, ed. F.N. Robinson, Oxford, 1985.)

He sido mortificado, insultado — hombre — me hecho hazmerreír! — Mírame!: KINGS, I, 5: 'I have been humiliated, insulted man — made a laughing stock — Look at me!'

He wald upon his tais stand: CHECKMATE, VI, 13: William Dunbar (c. 1460–1520), 'Ane Littill Interlude of the Droichis [Dwarves'] Part of the Play', the last lyrical and touching stanza of a comic piece (extract):

My soir grandschir [great-grandfather], hecht[called] Fyn Mackcowll
[Finn Macoull],
That dang [struck] the Devill and gart him yowlll [made him yell],

The skyis raind quhen [when] he wald [would] yowll,
He·troublit all the air:

He gat my gudschir [grandfather] Gog Magog:
He, quehn he dansit, the warld wald shog [shake],
Ten thowsand ellis [ells] yeid in his frog
Off Heland plaidis [Highland plaid] an mair [more].

And yit [when] he wes [was] of tendir yewth [youth]:
Bot effir [ever] he grew mekle at fowth [massive],
Ellevin myle wyd mett [eleven miles wide made] wes his mouth,
His teith [teeth] wes ten myle squair [ten miles square].

He wald upoun his tais [toes] up stand
And tak the starnis [stars] doun with his hand
And sett thame in a gold garland
Aboif his wyvis hair.

He was the river, the barque and the oars: CHECKMATE, V, 7: From Olivier de Magny's Sonnet *'Magny and Caron'*. See *J'irai donc maugré toy.*

Heavenly Kasbah: PAWN, 27: From the Persian poem, the Gulistán of Sasdí: 'The Heavenly Kasbah . . . The Frequented House, daily visited by 70,000 angels'. (E.J.W. Gibb, *History of Ottoman Poetry*, Vol. II.)

Hecate's garden: CHECKMATE, II, 7: The underworld. Hecate was considered a triple divinity, with power over heaven, the night, and hell. She is invoked for all processes connected with witchcraft and the casting of spells. Popular sacrifices to Hecate included black lambs and young dogs. Offerings left to her were placed at crossroads on the last day of the month, and favourable gifts were eggs, fish, honey and onions.

Heels, breaking of: CASTLE, II, 1: A common Russian punishment for theft and a popular torture prior to the extraction of a full confession. The criminal would have his heels broken, and then be left alone for two or three days until the ankles began to swell, then the victim would be forced to walk.

Heliades: KINGS, III, 4: The daughters of Helios, the sun, and Clymene. They were so deeply affected by the death of their brother Phaëthon (who so recklessly borrowed his father's sun chariot for the day) that they were changed into poplar trees by the gods; their tears turned into the amber to be found on the banks of the River Po. Another legend names the Heliades as the seven daughters of Helios and the nymph Rhodus; the fabled first inhabitants of the island of Rhodes.

Heliogabalus: KINGS, Gambit: Varius Avitus Basanius (AD c. 205–222), high priest of the sun god Elagabalus or Heliogabalus, and known by the same name as his idol. In 218 he became Emperor of Rome, under the title Marcus Aurelius Antoninus. He was a host well versed in sadistic housekeeping: he kept tamed lions and leopards to frighten his dinner guests; when they were less than sober, he would lock them in their chambers and then loose the animals to scare them as they awoke. At banquets he inscribed on the spoons of his guests their destined lot for the evening (e.g. ten flies, ten pounds of gold or of lead, ten ostriches etc. [CASTLE, II, 6]). At one memorable feast he invited the principal men of Rome and smothered them to death under a deluge of roses. Other feminine touches included a senate of women, who had complete authority over important social issues such as dress, amusements and imperial visits. His horses were fed on Apamée grapes and his lions on pheasants and parrots. His short reign was the epitome of debauchery, extravagance and cruelty, which came to a swift climax with his murder in AD 222.

Help me to seek, for I lost it there: CHECKMATE, IV, 1: Another of the melancholy rondeaux of **Sir Thomas Wyatt:**

> Help me to seek, for I lost it there,
> And if that ye have found it, ye that be here,
> And seek to convey it secretly,
> Handle it soft and treat it tenderly,
> Or else it will plain and then appear:
>
> But rather restore it mannerly,
> Since that I do ask it thus honestly:
> For to lose it, it sitteth me too near.
> Help me to seek.
>
> Alas, and is there no remedy?
> But have I thus lost it wilfully?
> Iwis it was a thing all too dear
> To be bestowed and wist not where:
> It was my heart, I pray you heartily
> Help me to seek.

(Gerald Bullett, ed., *Silver Poets of the Sixteenth Century*, London, 1970)

Help us, Lord, upon this erde That there be spilt no blood Herein: UNICORN, 6: From the poem attributed to James I of Scotland (1394–1437) 'Peblis to the Play', about an expedition to enjoy the May festivities at Peebles in Scotland (extract):

> Then they to the tavern house
> With meikle oly prance [much jolly prancing];

One spoke with wordis wonder crouse [cheerfully],
A done with a mischance!
Braid up the board [fold up the leaves] (he hydis, tyt,) [he hastens to do it]
We are all in a trance,
See that our napery be white,
For will dine and dance,
Thereout,
Of Peblis to the play.

Aye as the goodwife brought in
One scored upon the wauch [wall].
One bade pay, another said nay,
Bide till we reckon our lauch [bill].
The goodwife said, have ye no dread,
Ye shall pay that ye aucht [owe].
A young man stert upon his feet,
And he began to lauche,
For heydin,
Of Peblis to the play.

He got a trencher [wooden plate] in his hand.
And he began to count:
Ilk [each] man twa and ane halfpenny,
To pay thus, we were wont [we were made to pay].
Another stert upon his feet,
And said, thou art ower blunt,
To take such office upon hand;
By G-d thou 'serves a dunt [deserves a blow]
Of me,
Of Peblis to the play.

A dunt! quoth he, what devil is that?
By G-d thou dare not do't,
He stert till ane broggit staff [pike staff],
Winchand [writhing] as he were wood [mad]:
All that house was in a reirde [uproar];
Once cried, Thy holy rood [cross]!
Help us, Lord, upon this erde [earth]
That there be spilt no blood,
Herein,
Of Peblis to the play.
(J. Ross, ed., *The Book of Scottish Poems*, Edinburgh, 1878.)

Henneberge, Countess of: PAWN, 9: In the legend to beat all fertility treatments, at the age of forty-two she is reputed to have had 365 children in one birth; naming all the boys John and the girls Elizabeth. (Fynes Moryson, Gent., *An Itinerary*, 1617.)

HENRI II: QUEENS: (1518–1559) King of France, who acceded to the throne at the age of twenty-nine, and was described as a sombre, taciturn, deeply religious young man, the opposite of his father **Francis I.** His childhood years spent as a prisoner of **Charles V** in Spain meant that he returned to France highly disturbed and aggressive (see **M. d'Orléans**).

He was described by his contemporaries as melancholy, with a dark almost Moorish complexion and dark hair, although he went grey around the age of thirty. Henri was a keen sportsman and hunter, not sharing his father's love of literature and learning, preferring soldiers to artists, and children to scholars. He knew little about music, but still attended the weekly concerts of his Queen **Catherine de Médicis.** His father had excluded Henri from his councils, so when he came to power, Henri relied greatly on the experience and advice of **Montmorency**, and of **Diane de Poitiers**, Henri's mistress since he was seventeen.

He was devoted to Diane, but it did not stop him from dalliances elsewhere. His affair with **Jenny Fleming**, the governess of his future daughter-in-law, was slightly different. Diane survived so long as mistress because of her discretion. Fleming, by comparison, was flamboyant, and openly boasted of her pregnancy by the King. This earned her the hatred of both Henri's wife and principal mistress. Above all things, Henri did not wish an open proclamation of his indiscretion, and Jenny Fleming was hastily sent home and replaced by a less attractive governess.

The scheming of the **de Guise** family ensured they gained a foothold in the King's confidence and the marital prospects of his children. This was especially true of **François**, later Duke de Guise. They were the same age and had grown up in the court together; it is said that the King had no secrets from him.

Henri was father to the last three Valois monarchs; **Francis II**, Charles IX and his brother Henri III. Their thinning bloodline was eventually succeeded by the line of the Bourbon princes of the blood. Henri's devout and sombre disposition led him—in partnership with the de Guises—to attempt to destroy the new Reformed religion, which was gaining ground in France. In 1549 he opened a special court in the Paris Parlement specifically for the prosecution of heretics, the *Chambre ardente*; or 'Burning Chamber'. Individuals accused of holding Lutheran ideas were condemned to death. War with **Charles V** in the 1550s meant the heretics had to be partially tolerated for a while, in the interest of internal peace. Hatred could be temporarily focused on the Emperor rather than the 'enemy' within.

Having successfully repelled the Empire's armies and driven the English out of Calais, Henri signed the Peace of Cateau-Cambrésis in 1559. In addition to making peace with the Empire, Henri finally withdrew from his involvement in the dynastic and territorial battles of Italy. He had little time to enjoy his peaceful (but increasingly Protestant) country. Following the treaty, Henri's daughter Elisabeth was betrothed to **Philip II** of Spain. To celebrate the wedding by proxy, a joust was held at the Rue St Antoine in Paris. The King was to run three courses, dressed in black and white, the colours of his mistress Diane. On the third course against Montgomery (son of Monsieur de Lorges, captain of the **Scottish Archers**), Montgomery's wooden lance shattered and the splinters lodged in the neck and face of the King. He was removed from the field, but never regained consciousness, dying of blood poisoning ten days later. He was succeeded by his insipid eldest son Francis II and his recent Scots bride. (Louis Batiffol, *The Century of the Renaissance*, tr. E.F. Buckley, London, 1916.)

Henry the Navigator: SCALES, 9: (1394–1460) Prince of Portugal, who established the first School of Navigation at **Sagres**, and inspired the Portuguese discovery and colonisation of **Africa**. Henry's motivation for the African voyages was severalfold: to combat Islam and the spread of the Ottoman Empire; to reconquer the Holy Land from the Turk, with the aid of **Prester John**; and to establish direct trading links with the slave and gold markets of Africa.

Henry was first inspired with the possibilities of Africa when he took part in the Portuguese capture of **Ceuta** in 1415. Whilst he was there, Henry heard tales from the Arabs about the gold and riches of **Timbuktu**. Henry was inspired, and under his leadership as navigator, crusader and commercial entrepreneur, the Portuguese discovery of West Africa gained momentum. What Henry wanted more than anything was a Portuguese sea route that gave direct access to the riches of the interior, presently in the hands of the infidel.

By 1419, the Portuguese **caravels** had discovered the Madeiras, followed by the Azores in 1431 and Cape Verde in 1445. Ideas and the journeys themselves advanced slowly at first, but when Antam Goncalves brought the first cargo of slaves and gold to Lisbon, both trade and discoveries sped up; commercial gain was a visible incentive. Henry retained the privilege by taking twenty per cent of each cargo brought from Guinea, and if he lent one of his own ships to the merchants, he took fifty per cent of the profits from the trip. The highest returns came in the years 1450 to 1458 when a dozen journeys were made per annum.

By 1460, the whole coast of Upper Guinea had been mapped and exploited by the Portuguese. After Henry's death, the voyages of discovery he inspired continued. The mouth of the Congo was found by the Portuguese in 1482, and the Cape of Good Hope was rounded by Bartholomew Diaz in 1487. By 1498, the long-dreamed-of sea route to India was finally completed by Vasco da Gama. (John Blake, *European Beginnings in West Africa: 1454–1578*, London, 1937; John Ure, *Prince Henry the Navigator*, London, 1977.)

Hephaestus: KINGS, III, 3: The Greek god of fire, and of all arts requiring fire for their execution; therefore also the god of smiths and smelters. Known to the Romans as Vulcan. Unlike most of his peers, Hephaestus was not physically perfect, but lame, following a dispute with Zeus when he was literally flung out of heaven by his father. Whilst on earth, he instructed mortals in all the arts of metalwork. Amongst the gods, he had the indispensable roles of smith, armourer and chariot-builder, and also supplied Zeus with thunderbolts.

Heralds: The duties and responsibilities of the medieval herald are those of proclaimer, messenger in times of war and of peace, and as the recognised expert in armorial bearings and pedigree. The art of heraldry began in the twelfth century, when hereditary devices were used in battle to identify individuals wearing full armour. The same devices, in times of illiteracy, served as signatures to transactions when appended as seals.

From as early as 1132, heraldic specialists, at first itinerant, made themselves particularly useful on the tournament circuit with their ability to remember and identify the great men of their time by their insignia. This gave them a military value, and soon every knight with a company of men was employing a herald. The information possessed by the heralds was gradually centralised to varying degrees. Scottish heralds are mentioned as early as 1364 and the Lord Lyon, whose court is pre-heraldic, holds the oldest heraldic office in Britain as one of the Sovereign's Great Officers of State. The most important and celebrated early Scottish record of arms was compiled in 1542 by **Sir David Lindsay.**

The use of heralds in tournaments was the most spectacular demonstration of their skills. The herald was entrusted with the duty of proclaiming the challenges, accompanying the combatants to the lists, and overseeing the resulting joust. They would keep score during the tournament, announce the victor and ensure that the rules of chivalry were followed. As the recognised experts in their field, they had powers of arbitration in all chivalric matters.

By the thirteenth century the official role of the herald encompassed more than these early duties as master of ceremonies and proclaimer. As diplomatic commissioners, the trust placed in them depended on how close they were to the confidences of their monarch or lord. In times of war and peace they were often used on diplomatic missions and regularly sent with letters and messages from one prince to another, often in the retinue of an ambassador. The herald's coat of arms was his passport of safe conduct; he could travel unquestioned and as a noncombatant could not be treated as the subject of an enemy power.

In times of war heralds would act as official messengers; delivering the summons to surrender to the captain of towns prior to a state of siege. They would arrange challenges of princes to pitched battles; obtain safe conducts for ambassadors through enemy territory; ensure the safety of soldiers wishing to parley or joust with the enemy; and help families negotiate the ransom of their captured relatives.

Their conduct was ordained to be of the highest and most impartial order; on no account would heralds spy on their enemy, nor would they reveal any military secrets which had been entrusted to them. To break these injunctions would contradict the chivalric notion of **war**, but unfortunately, in an imperfect world, this did sometimes happen. Abroad, the herald continued his ceremonial duties but gave way in everyday matters to the observant eye of the permanent ambassador. (Maurice Keen, *The Laws of War in the Late Middle Ages*, London, 1965; Sir Anthony Richard Wagner, *Heralds and Heraldry in the Middle Ages*, 2nd edn, Oxford, 1956; Sir Thomas Innes of Learney, *Scots Heraldry*.)

Herberstein, Sigismund von: CASTLE, II, 9: (1486–1566) German soldier and scholar, appointed Ambassador to Muscovy for the German Emperor Maximilian in 1517, a post he held until 1526. Herberstein spent sixteen months in Moscow from 1517 to 1518, returning to Russia again from 1526 to 1527, via Hungary and Poland. He left a written account of his travels and experiences of the unfamiliar customs of the natives, published in Latin in Vienna in 1549. This describes the Russians in less than glowing terms, 'Bloody, rude and blind as wild Irish'; a nation of wanton women and cunning men, with their 'Turkish Manners'.

His account notes the fact that women are given money by their husbands to paint their faces; some are so skilled in cosmetic deception that the paint and dyes cannot be seen. He also writes that the women behave like Muslim wives and only appear in public to attend church or weddings. He also comments on the extreme cold, to the point that corpses lie unburied all winter in their fir coffins because the earth is too hard to dig their graves. The plentiful supply of wood means that even the poor can afford coffins. Herberstein did not see any glass windows in the sixteenth-century houses, but slices of an opaque rock crystal called *sluda* provided a cheap alternative, cut very thinly and sewn with thread into window panes.

He considered Russia to be a savage place, there being no laws but the Tsar's will, answerable only to God not mortal man, hence all subjects lived in perpetual fear of the Tsar and his justice. (Sigismund von Herberstein, *Notes Upon Russia*, Vol. I, tr. R.H. Major, Hakluyt Society.)

Hercules ... 'Brûla son corps, pour se rendre immortel': KNIGHTS, II, 3: 'Hercules ... "burned his body to make himself immortal"'.

Here is non hoom. Here nis but wildernesse: CHECKMATE, IV, 2: From Chaucer's *'Balade de Bon Conseyl'* (or 'Truth'):

Flee fro the prees [throng of the court], and dwelle with sothfastnesse,
Suffyce unto thy good, though it be smal;
For hord [avarice] hath hate, and climbing tickelnesse [instability],
Prees hath envye, and wele [happiness] blent overal;
Savour no more than thee bihove [necessary] shal;
Reule wel thyself, that other folk canst rede;
And trouthe thee shal delivere, it is no drede.

Tempest thee noght al croked to redresse,
In trust of hir that turneth as a bal;
Gret reste stant [sticks fast] in litel besiness;
Be war also to sporne ayeyns an al;
Stryve not, as doth the crokke with the wal.
Daunte [tame] thyself, that dauntest others dede;
And trouthe thee shal delivere, it is no drede.

That thee is sent, receyve in buxemnesse;
The wrastling for this world axeth a fal.
Her is non hoom, her nis but wildernesse:
Forth, pilgrim, forth! Forth, beste, out of thy stal!
Know thy contree, look up, thank God of al;
Hold the heye wey, and lat thy gost [spirit] thee lede;
And trouthe thee shal delivere, it is no drede.

Envoy

Therefor, thou Vache, leve thyn owld wrecchednesse;
Unto the world leve now to be thral;
Crye him mercy, that of his hy goodnesse
Made thee of noght, and in especial
Draw unto him, and pray in general
For thee, an eek for other, hevenlich mede;
And trouthe thee shal delivere, it is no drede.

One of Chaucer's most admired short poems, the '*Balade de Bon Conseyl*' was traditionally believed to be Chaucer's parting counsel, composed on his deathbed, but this is doubtful. It seems more likely to have been written to give advice and encouragement to his young friend Sir Philip de la Vache when the latter was out of favour in court (between 1386 and 1389). The refrain recalls John, 8, 32: 'And ye shall know the truth, and the truth shall make you free'. (F. N. Robinson, ed., *The Complete Works of Geoffrey Chaucer*, Oxford, 1974.)

Heremon: QUEENS, II, 1: Heremon and Heber, the first **Milesian** princes of 1000 BC, are accredited in Bardic tradition as having brought the **lute** to Ireland. (C.A. Harris & Mary Hargreave, *The Story of British Music*.)

Heresy: CASTLE, I, 8: **Mary Tudor** did her best to reinstitute the structure and creed of the Roman Catholic church in England, which had been so greatly undermined by her father and half-brother. One of the main ways of restoring faith by threats was the Heresy Act of 1554. It restored the medieval authority of the Bishops' Courts to punish heresy, by death if necessary. The burning of many prominent and devout Protestants led to charges of brutality against the bishops and earned the monarch the title of 'Bloody Mary' from the repressed Protestants.

The Statute of Repeal, also in 1554, reversed all religious policy statements of Henry VIII and **Edward VI**, and led to England being invited back into the papal fold. The one thing it did not repeal was the dissolution of the monasteries, thus it allowed the nobility to remain in control of church lands seized under Henry VIII. If Philip and Mary had forced the return of these territories to either the crown or church, it would have severely threatened the support given to the monarchy from most of the wealthy (and landed) nobility. (Beatrice White, *Mary Tudor*, 1935; A.G. Dickens & D. Carr, eds, *The Reformation in England*, London, 1982.)

Hermaphrodite: QUEENS, II, 2: Hermaphroditús, the son of Hermes and Aphrodite, was endowed with the physical attributes of both deities. The nymph of the fountain of Salmacis had been rejected by Hermaphroditus, and so she prayed to the gods that she might be totally united with him. It is from this prayer that the creature encompassing the attributes of both sexes was formed.

HERRIES, Agnes: See **Maxwell, John.**

Heterocrania: CHECKMATE, IV, 2: See **Migraine.**

Heu prodiga ventris hi, nives, illi glaciem potant: PAWN, 21: Comment by Pierre Bellon (or Belon) on the subject of storing snow underground in Constantinople. A traveller in Greece, Asia, Egypt, Judaea and Arabia, he wrote an account in Latin of his travels from 1546 to 1549 in which he quoted Pliny on the ancient Romans having learned the same trick. In the time of Nero, water was boiled and then placed in a glass in the snow store. The water would cool to ice, and thus new cool liquids could be produced all summer long without depleting the original stock of winter snow brought down from the mountains. (Pierre Belon, *Petri Bellonii, Cenomani, 1546–1549,* 1589.)

Heureux qui, comme Ulysse, a fait un beau voyage: PAWN, 27: A sonnet of
Joachim du Bellay (1522–1560):

> Heureux qui, comme Ulysse, a fait un beau voyage,
> Ou comme ceslui-là qui conquit la toison,
> Et puis est retourné, plein d'usage et raison,
> Vivre entre ses parents le reste de son âge!
>
> Quand reverrai-je, hélas! de mon petit village
> Fumer la cheminée, et en quelle saison
> Reverrai-je le clos de ma pauvre maison,
> Quoi m'est une province, et beaucoup davantage?
>
> Plus me plait le séjour qu'ont bâti mes aïeux
> Que des palais romains le front audacieux:
> Plus que le marbre dur me plait l'ardoise fine,
>
> Plus mon Loire gaulois que le Tibre latin,
> Plus mon petit Liré que le mont Palatin,
> Et plus que l'air marin la douceur angevine.

Happy the man who has made a fine voyage like Ulysses,
Or he who seized the Golden Fleece
And then, wise and mature,
Returned home to live out his life with his family.

When, alas, will I see again the chimney-smoke of
My little village. When see again
The yard of my humble house:
To me a kingdom, and more.

The home built by my forebears moves me more
Than the most extravagant spectacle of a palace in Rome
As I prefer fine slate to hard marble.

As I prefer my Gallic Loire to the Tiber of the Latins,
My little Liré to the Palatine Hill
And the soft air of my sweet Angevin countryside
To the taste of the sea.

(Tr. D.D.)

Hic jacet arte Plato, Cato, Tullius: PAWN, 20: 'Here lie together a Plato, a
Cato, a Tully: worms eat their bodies; their souls seek the stars'. (Fynes
Moryson, Gent., *An Itinerary*, 1617.)

Hic turtur gemit: KINGS, IV, 3: 'Here the dove moans'. Referring to the brutal Roman subjugation of the Britons.

Hilarion, St: SCORPIONS: The principal fortress of Cyprus, named after the ascetic saint who sought sanctuary in the Egyptian desert. Unfortunately, he was so plagued with pilgrims and visitors that he was forced to travel to Cyprus for some respite from popular acclaim. Hilarion found the solitude he desired on a mountain peak in the north of the island, and lived in peace there until his death. The palace which grew up on the site of his retreat became the summer palace of the **Lusignans**. As it developed, it had strategic importance also as a fortress, but was finally dismantled by the Venetians in 1489.

Hippocras: A heavy red wine, formerly considered medicinal cordial. It is spiced with sugar, a tablespoon of ground cinnamon, ¾ tablespoon of ground ginger, and a teaspoon each of cloves, nutmeg, marjoram, cardamon, galingale, spikenard, long pepper and grains of paradise. To make your own, first take 2 litres of red wine and 175 grammes of white sugar. Heat the wine until it steams, then add the sugar. When the sugar has fully dissolved in the wine, mix together all of the above listed spices, and add them to the liquid to taste. Simmer the potion gently for ten minutes or so, then strain the mixture through muslin or a jelly bag. When it has cooled, bottle and cork the piment. It will keep for approximately one week. (Maggie Black, *The Medieval Cookbook*, British Museum Press, 1992.)

Hippocrenes: KINGS, IV, 2: The fountain of the Muses; struck out of Mount Helicon by the hoof of Pegasus.

His children let be fatherles, Hys wife a wydow make: CHECKMATE, I, 5: Psalm 109, vv 9–13. The version used is that of the Geneva Psalms, published by John Crespin in 1569 (extract):

> Fewe be hys dayes, his charge also
> Let thou an other take:
> his children let be fatherles,
> his wyfe a wydoe make.
> Let hys ofspring be vagabondes,
> To beg and seke their bread:
> Wandring out of the wasted place,
> Where erst they have bene fed.
>
> Let courteous extortion:
> Catch all his goods and store,
> And let the strangers spoyle the fruites

Of all his toyle before.
Let there be none to pitie him,
Let there be none at all:
That on his children fatherles,
Will let theyr mercy fall.

Hiver sans feu, vieillesse sans maison: KNIGHTS, II, 6; PAWN, 11: Sixteenth-century poem of Mellin de Saint-Gelais (1487–1558), '*Malediction contre un Envieux*', 'A curse upon a Jealous Man', (extract):

> *Je prie à Dieu, qu'il vous doint pauvreté,*
> *Hiver sans feu, vieillesse sans maison,*
> *Grenier sans bled en l'arrière-saison,*
> *Cave sans vin tout le long de l'été.*
>
> *Je prie à Dieu, qu'a bon droit et raison*
> *N'ayez chez vous rien que ne vous déplaise,*
> *Tant que pour estre un peu mieux à votre aise*
> *Vous pourchassiez d'estre mis en prison ...*
>
> *Je prie à Dieu, le roi de paradis,*
> *Que mendiant, vostre pain alliez querre,*
> *Seul, inconnu, et en étrange terre,*
> *Non entendu par signes, ni par dits ...*
>
> *Je prie à Dieu, que pour honneur acquerre,*
> *Et mériter couronne de laurier,*
> *Vous ne pensiez qu'à vous tenir gourrier,*
> *Brave en la paix, et couard en la guerre.*
>
> *Je prie à Dieu, qu'il vous prenne un accès*
> *De froid peur, et longue jalousie.*
> *Qu'un autre n'ait votre femme choisie*
> *Pour l'épouser après votre décès.*

I pray that the Lord gives you poverty,
Cold hearth in the winter,
Old age without roof,
Barns bare of wheat, when autumn is ending,
Cellars empty of wine
All the long summer through.

I pray that the Lord makes you dwell
In a place of ill ease

So that no comfort beckons
But prison.

I pray that the Lord makes you beg
For your bread in strange lands
Unrecognised and alone: understood, signs or words
By no person.

I pray that the Lord will attend
Lest in war you find haven,
Let you conquer in peace
And in battle turn craven.

I pray that the Lord will bestow
A cold fear upon you: a hot jealousy too.
I pray that when you are dead, another will take your beloved
And marry her.

Ho Ho: say you so; Money shall make my mare to go: KINGS, I, 2: From the Scots poem:

> 'Wilt thou lend me thy mare to ride but a mile?'
> No, she's lame going over a stile.
> 'But if thou wilt her to me spare
> Thou shalt have money for thy mare.'
> Ho ho: say you so;
> Money shall make my mare to go.

DE HOMEDÈS, Juan: KNIGHTS: (1473–1553) Grand Master of the **Knights of St John** on Malta. Elected to the head of the order in 1536 by the Emperor and Pope, de Homedes had previously been bailiff of Capua, and had shown great courage at the siege of Rhodes, where he lost an eye. His election proved the power of Emperor **Charles V** and bribery over the choice of Grand Master. A Spanish Knight had to be elected, as the Order was currently beholden to the Emperor. After seven years of wandering, Charles had given them the island of Malta in 1530 on condition that they would guard Tripoli and Gozo and drive the Turk from North Africa.

De Homedes was ambitious, arrogant and cruel. When he was elected Grand Master, he waited fifteen months in Spain before finally bothering to go to Malta. In his fifteen years there, he built no defences against the Turk, wasting the Order's money on lavish grants to his nephews. His own excuse for the Order's shortage of funds was the high price of imported grain and corn from Sicily. Blame for the Order's defeats was placed on others, not de Homedes himself. **D'Aramon**, for example, who had done much to rescue both the French and Spanish Knights after the fall of Tripoli, was personally blamed as a traitor by de Homedes, who refused the French Ambassador entry into Malta's harbour, saying that the Frenchman had helped the Turks attack. D'Aramon appealed to the French King, and, under pressure, de Homedes was forced to write an apology to the Ambassador, retracting his slanders against the King's representative.

One of his few good points seems to have been his interest in natural history; collecting birds, plants and animals from everywhere in Europe. De Homedes also spent much of his time in religious contemplation, or studying the customs of the Maltese, whom he ruled with a rod of iron.

It is said his death was not lamented amongst the brothers of the Order, who received the sad news 'with the most edifying resignation'. He had bled the Order so dry that many Knights recommended that his nephews should pay for his funeral rather than the Order, as they had profited more from his rule than the fighting brothers. Eventually the Order did foot the bill for burial of their late and little-lamented Grand Master, if only to exhibit that they still possessed a fragment of Christian charity and the grandeur of former days. (Henry Seddall, *Malta, Past and Present*, 1870.)

Hondeslagers: RISING, 4: The recognised Bruges **Guild** of Dog-killers. Dogs and pigs roamed the streets of Bruges at will, but the number of loosed dogs began to present such a nuisance that canine control groups with leaden clubs were appointed to dispose of the unwanted menace. They were to confine themselves to strays of no value or breed. The bread these dogs consumed was to be distributed to the worthy poor of the city instead of feeding unwanted mongrels. Under no circumstances were the dog-killers to touch hunting dogs, or those owned by nobles. These dogs were recognisable by their brands or collars and if one was killed by mistake, the offending hondeslager risked public flogging.

In return for their humane work, the guild was allowed to keep and sell the skin and fat from the slaughtered animals. It was lucrative work; in 1455 the guild is recorded as having killed 1,121 dogs for the city, and from 1470 to 1473, 11,000 were disposed of. (Malcolm Letts, *Bruges and its Past*.)

Hoopooe: PAWN, 22; RAM, 27: A small crested bird, revered by the ancients, especially the Egyptians, and known to the Arabs as the *upapa* (UNICORN, 36). It appears on the sceptre of Horus, and symbolised joy and filial affection. According to Arabic legend Solomon's hoopooe called Ya'fur could speak and told its master secrets. It was also able to detect the presence of water under the ground, and was thus invaluable to the King on long journeys. It was a most faithful and trustworthy bird, up until the point where it went missing in transit, having made close friends with the hoopooe belonging to the Queen of Sheba. The friendship of the birds gave Solomon an opportunity to introduce himself to the beautiful queen of the Yemen. (H. Howarth & I. Shakrullah, eds, *Images From the Arab World*, London, 1944.)

Hosea's wife: KINGS, IV, 1: A reference to the biblical book of Hosea and the prophet's adulterous wife; the analogy used to describe the covenant between God and his chosen people where only one partner in the relationship remained faithful.

Hourglass: SCALES, 19: The main timepiece on fifteenth-century sea journeys, essential for the plotting of courses and to estimate the distances travelled in a certain period. Clocks were fairly advanced by the time **Prince Henry**'s navigators discovered West Africa, but as individual items they were too fragile and precious to risk on board ships.

Hourglasses were also delicate, manufactured in **Venice** which led the world in the production of fine glassware. They were difficult to export in one piece. Mariners would take as many as eighteen on a single journey to counteract the high probability of breakages. Hourglasses were prone to grave discrepancies, which could be attributed to a number of causes. Firstly, the ship might have sailed a substantial distance either to the east or west, or rough weather might have restricted the passing of the sand crystals. If the sand had passed through the glass quicker than expected, then warm weather could be to blame. More likely was the possibility of the cabin boy on watch having deliberately warmed the glass with the intention of shortening his tedious long shift. This would cause the glass to expand and the sand to run through faster than it ought to; dire penalties would be inflicted on those suspected of such an act of wanton misleading. (John Ure, *Prince Henry the Navigator*, London, 1977.)

Houri: PAWN, 15: Persian Arabic for a nymph, sexual angel or temple prostitute. Houris were dancing 'ladies of the night' who kept time in heaven and tended to the souls of the stars. Egyptian temple women performed the same function, protecting the solar boat of Ra in the Underworld. Each woman would guard over the god for her allotted hour. The Holy Koran talks of the paradise of 'houris made of musk'. (Aytoun Ellis, *Essence of Beauty*.)

Hunting causeth a man to eschew the Seven Deadly Sins: CASTLE, II, 12: The premise of the argument is that in pursuit of venery, man remains on the move, and his quality of life and achievements are subsequently enhanced. Those who do not hunt, are not seen as morally ascendant:

> For such men have no wish but always to
> abide in one place and think in pride, or in

avarice, or in wrath, or in sloth, or in
gluttony, or in lechery, or in envy.
(Edward, Second Duke of York, *The Master of Game,* 1413, tr. from Gaston
III, 1904.)

I

I abide and abide and better abide: CHECKMATE, I, I: Sonnet by Sir **Thomas Wyatt:**

> I abide and abide and better abide,
> And after the olde proverbe the happie daye;
> And ever my ladye to me dothe saye
> 'Let me alone and I will provyde.'
> I abide and abide and tarrye the tyde
> And with abiding spede well ye maye;
> Thus do I abide I wott [believe] allwaye,
> Neither obtayning nor yet denied.
> Ay me! this long abiding
> Semithe to me as who sayethe
> A prolonging of a dieng dethe
> Or a refusing of a desyrid thing:
> Moch ware it bettre for to be playne,
> Then to saye abide and yet shall not obtayne.

(Gerald Bullett, ed., *Silver Poets of the Sixteenth Century*, London, 1970.)

I am but one mad man that thou hast here met: KINGS, I, 2: From the fourteenth-century Scots poem relating an encounter between the Emperor Charlemagne and a collier, 'The Tale of Rauf [Ralph] Coilzear' (extract):

> I am bot ane mad man that thow hes heir met
> I haue na myster to matche with maisterfull men
> Fairand ouir the feildis fewell to fet
> And oft fylit my feit in mony foull fen
> Gangand with laidis my gouerning to get . . .

(David Laing, ed., *Early Popular Poetry of Scotland*, Vol. I, London, 1895.)

I am naught but the lewd compilator of the labour of old astrologians: PAWN, 18: Geoffrey Chaucer (c. 1345–1400), *Treatise on the Astrolabe*, written for his son Lewis. (Chaucer, *Complete Works*, ed. F.N. Robinson, Oxford University Press, 1985.)

I am thi master: wilt thou fight?: KINGS, III, 2: From the medieval mystery play *The Killing of Abel*. (J.Q. Adams, *Chief Pre-Shakespearean Dramas*, Boston, 1924.)

I bring, lover, I bring the news glad: KINGS, I, 1: From the Scots poem, 'The Kingis Quair', attributed to King James I of Scotland (1394–1437). See also **Hast thou no mind of love? Where is thy make?** (extract):

> Awake! Awake! I bring lufar, I bring
> The newis glad, that blissful been, and sure,
> Of thy comfort; now laugh, and play, and sing,
> That art beside [near] so glad an adventure.

(J. Ross, ed., *The Book of Scottish Poems*, Edinburgh, 1878.)

I can say naught but Hoy gee ho!: KINGS, I, 3: The anonymous ballad 'Quoth John to Joan', also known as the **'Wooing o' Jock and Jenny'**:

> Quoth John to Joan, wilt thou have me?
> I prithee now, wilt? And I'se marry with thee
> My cow, my calf, my house, my rents,
> And all my lands and tenements:
> O say, my Joan, say my Joan, wilt not that do?
> I cannot come ev'ry day to woo.
>
> I've corn and hay in the barn hard by
> And three fat hogs pent up in the sty:
> I have a mare, and she is coal-black,
> I ride on her tail to save her back:
> O say, my Joan, say my Joan, wilt not that do?
> I cannot come ev'ry day to woo.
>
> I have a cheese upon the shelf
> And I cannot eat it all myself:
> I've three good marks that lie in a rag
> In the nook of the chimney instead of a bag:
> O say, my Joan, say my Joan, wilt not that do?
> I cannot come ev'ry day to woo.
>
> To marry I would have thy consent
> But, faith, I never could compliment.
> I can say naught but 'hoy, gee ho',
> Words that belong to the cart and the plough:
> Then say, my Joan, say my Joan, wilt that not do?
> I cannot come every day to woo.

I cannot eat but little meat: QUEENS, II, 6: The song attributed to John Still, Bishop of Bath and Wells. It appears in his play *Gammer Gurton's* Needle (c. 1566), but is older still:

> I cannot eat but little meat
> My stomach is not good;
> But sure I think that I can drink
> With him that wears a hood.
>
> Though I go bare, take ye no care
> I nothing am a-cold;
> I stuff my skin so full within
> Of jolly good ale and old.
>
> Back and side go bare, go bare;
> Both feet and hand go cold;
> But belly, God send thee good ale enough,
> Whether it be new or old.

(Reginald Nettel, *Seven Centuries of Popular Song.*)

I geid the gait wes nevir gaine: CHECKMATE, V, 9: A traditional ironic Scots narrative on the perfidy of women (extract):

> I geid [took] the gait [path] wes nevir gane [taken]:
> I fand [found] the thing wes nevir fund:
> I saw under ane tre [tree] bowane [bowing],
> A lowes [free] man lyand bund [lying bound]:
> Ane dum man hard [heard] I full lowd speik:
> Ane deid man hard I sing:
> Ye may knaw be my talking eik [still],
> That this is no lesing [lie].
> And als ane blindman hard I reid [read],
> Vpoun [upon] a buke allane [alone]:
> Ane handles [handless] man I saw but dreid [without fear],
> In caichepule [catch-ball] saft [easily] playane [playing] . . .
>
> The air [court of justice] come hirpland [limping] to that toun,
> The preistis [priests] to leir [teach] to spell:
> The hurcheon [hedgehog] to the kirk [church] maid boun [went],
> To ring the commoun bell:
> The mowes [mouse] grat [cried] that the cat was deid [dead],
> That all hir [her] kin mycht [might] rew [rue]:
> Quhen [when] all thir [these] tailis [tales] are trew in deid,
> A' [all] wemen [women] will be trew.

I have a young sister: PAWN, 28: Anonymous sonnet quoted in full in the text. The original spelling is given below:

> I have a zong suster fer bezondyn the se,
> Many be the drowryis that che sente me.

> Che sente me the cherye, withoutyn ony ston,
> And so che dede [the] dowe, withoutyn ony bon.
> Sche sente me the brere, withoutyn ony rynde,
> Sche bad me love my lemman withoute longyng.

> How xuld ony cherye be withoute ston?
> And how xuld ony dowe ben withoute bon?
> How xuld ony brere ben withoute rynde?
> How xuld y love myn lemman without longyng?

> Quan the cherye was a flour, than hadde it non ston;
> Quan the dowe was an ey, than hadde it non bon:
> Quan the brere was onbred, than hadde it non rynd:
> Quan the mayden hazt that che lovit, che is without longyng.

I have peper and piones, and a pound of garlik: KINGS, I, 1: From *The Vision of Piers Plowman* (c. 1372–1389). These are the words of Betty the Brewer to the character of Gluttony as she persuades him to sup her spiced ale rather than go to church.

I, King of Flesh, flourishing in my flowers: QUEENS, III, 1: A quote taken from the medieval mystery play, *Mary Magdalene* (J.Q. Adams, *Chief Pre-Shakespearean Dramas*, Boston, 1924.)

I love the love that loves not me: CHECKMATE, II, 9: From the anonymous Scottish sixteenth-century poem, 'The Murning Maiden' (extract):

> Still under the leavis green,
> This hinder day, I went alone;
> I heard ane mai [maiden] sair murne and meyne [moan];
> To the king of love she made her moan,
> She sighèd sely [wretched] sore:
> Said 'Lord, I love thy lore
> Mair woe dreeit [endured] never woman one!
> O langsome life and [if] thou were gone,
> Than should I murne no more!'

As red gold-wire shinèd her hair;
And all in green the mai she glaid;
Ane bent bow in her hand she bare;
Under her belt were arrows braid.
I followèd on that fre [lady],
That seemly was to see.
With still murning her moan she made.
That bird [burd, lady], under a bank she bade,
And leanèd to ane tree.

'Wanweird [unhappy lot],' she said, 'What have I wrought,
That on me kytht has [to me has caused] all this care?
True love so dear I have thee bought!
Certes so shall I do no mare.
Sen that I go beguiled
With ane that faith has filed.
That gars me of sighs such full sair,
And walk among the holtis hair [forests hoar]
Within the woodis wild.

This great disease for love I dree [suffer],
There is no tongue can tell the woe!
I love the love that loves not me;
I may not mend, but murning mo [must grieve].
Quhill [will] God send some remead [remedy],
Through destiny, or dead [death].
I am his friend, and he my foe;
My sweet, alas! why does he so?
I wrought him never nae feid [no ill]!
(J. Ross, ed., *The Book of Scottish Poems*, Edinburgh, 1878.)

I shall send gems of lapis lazuli, I shall make her fields into vineyards:
CHECKMATE, V, 11; SCORPIONS 28: From the writings of Yarih of Nikkal.

I'd give unto her Indian mole Bokhara town and Samarkand: CHECKMATE,
IV, 8: From the Divan (a collection of poems) of the Persian lyrical poet, Hafiz,
pseudonym of Shams ad-Din Mohammed (d. 1388), translated by Gertrude
Lowthian Bell (extract):

Oh Turkish maid of Shiraz! In thy hand
If thou'lt take my heart, for the mole on thy cheek
I would barter Bokhara and Samarkand.
Bring, Cup-bearer, all that is left of thy wine!
In the Garden of Paradise vainly thou'lt seek

The lip of the fountain of Ruknabad
And the bower of Mosalla where roses twine.

They have filled the city with blood and broil,
Those soft-voiced Lulis for whom we sigh;
As Turkish robbers fall on the spoil,
They have robbed and plundered the peace of my heart.
Dowered is my mistress, a beggar am I;
What shall I bring her? A beautiful face
Needs nor jewel nor mole nor the tiring-maid's art . . .

The song is sung, and the pearl is strung:
Come hither, oh Hafiz, and sing again!
And the listening Heavens above thee hung
Shall loose o'er thy verses the Pleiades' chain.

The sobriquet 'Hafiz' means 'Remember', and is therefore applied to one who has learned the Koran by heart.

I'll trip upon trenchers; I'll dance upon dishes: KINGS, I, 1: A comic verse to accompany the popular late sixteenth-century 'cushion dance'. There is a *double entendre*, of course, in the meaning of 'barm' as the froth of a yeast-fermented liquid (such as beer) and its use to leaven:

I'll trip upon trenchers [clogs],
I'll dance upon dishes [iron-heeled shoes],
My mither sent me for barm, for barm!
And thro' the kirkyard I met wi the laird,
The silly poor body could do me no harm.
But down i' the park, I met with the clerk,
And he gied me my barm, my barm!

Ida, la bergère phrygienne: QUEENS, IV, 5: Ida, the shepherdess or nymph of Crete, who went into Phrygia, where she gave her name to a mountain of that country. She was also the mother of Minos, King of Crete. (J. Lempriere, *A Classical Dictionary*, London, 1815.)

If any be afflicted, let hym praye: CHECKMATE, II, 2: The words of King James V of Scotland; taken from the title page of the Geneva Psalms, published by John Crespin in London in 1569.

If they place the sun in my right hand and the moon in my left: CHECK-MATE, I, 4: The words of the Prophet Mohammed:

If they place the sun in my right hand and the moon in my left and ask
me to give up my mission, I will not give it up until the truth prevails or
I myself perish in the attempt.
(*The Holy Koran*, tr. Maulvi Muhammad Ali, 1920.)

Igor, my own brother, my own bright light, thou?: CHECKMATE, III, 3: From
the Russian ballad, 'The Song of Igor's Campaign'.

Il n'est soing que quant on a fain [faim]: QUEENS, I, 6: 'The only worry is
when you are hungry'.

Il se gratte les fesses et conte des apologues: PAWN, 18: 'He scratches his bottom and starts to recount fables'.

*Il sera vraisemblable que Calais on assiège Quand le fer ou le plomb nagera
comme liège:* CHECKMATE, II, 5: 'It is as likely that someone will besiege Calais
As that iron or lead should float like cork'. Having held the port for so long,
the English dogmatically believed that Hell would freeze over before they
were finally forced out of France.

Il y a des accommodements avec le ciel: KNIGHTS, II, 4: 'One may come to an
understanding with Heaven'.

Ils mentirent donc: QUEENS, III, 1: 'So they lied'.

In aurum coruscante et crispante capillo: KINGS, II, 3: 'Golden hair, waving
and glittering'. Such was the hair of Jason, Castor, Pollux, Achilles and Cupid.

In bocca serrata mai non entrò mosca: CHECKMATE, III, 2: Italian proverb: 'no
flies enter a closed mouth'.

In Moab I will washe my feete, Over Edom throw my shoo: CHECKMATE, I,
6: Psalm 60, 8. The translation used is that of the Geneva Psalms, printed by
John Crespin in 1569.

In the battlefield he was a lion wielding a dagger: CHECKMATE, IV, 2: A contemporary poetic quote from 1524 referring to Shah Tahmasp of Persia
(1514–1576). (E.G. Brown, *Persian Literature in Modern Times.*)

In the name of God and of Profit: RAM, 19: The two deities of the Renaissance
merchant. The regular opening of Renaissance ledger accounts and used
among others by the Datini family of Prato. Francesco Datini (c. 1335–1410)
inscribed the phrase at the beginning of each of his trade ledgers. (I. Origo,
The Merchant of Prato: The Journal of Francesco Datini, 1957.)

Incidi in Scyllam, cupiens vitare Charibdim: PAWN, 7: The Latin version of 'Out of the frying pan and into the fire'; 'seeking to avoid Charybdis, I fell into Scylla'.

Incubators: KNIGHTS, II, 7; UNICORN, 39: The Arabs are accredited with having developed the incubator well before their Western rivals had even considered the idea. The practice in fact dates back to Ancient Egypt. The incubators themselves were fairly large rooms, with a narrow entrance and consisting of two rows of ovens on each side. They were in constant use from January to mid-June. The eggs would lie in the lower ovens on a cushion of flax, dung, then matting. On either side of the ovens, there were trenches of loam in which the fuel necessary to heat the ovens would be placed. The main fuel used was camel dung, which was in plentiful supply and provided a stifling heat without smoke or any vile odour. (See also **Camels.**)

The eggs were turned daily, and remained in the lower ovens for eight days after being laid. Then they would be examined by holding each between the eye and a lamp. Those not developing would be discarded; the remainder would be left in the lower ovens for another two days before the fires were extinguished. Then the eggs would be moved to the top ovens, and left in the sealed compartments for a further ten days. After this period, the chicks would all hatch at once.

Nicolas de Nicolay in his account of his travels in the Far East noted the plentiful supply of fowl in Algiers, hatched in hothouses without the need for a mother hen. Poulterers were well established in Cairo and in the Sublime Porte of Sultan **Suleiman the Magnificent**, there were over 400 fowl merchants with 105 shops between them. Their patron saint was the Arabic alchemist Karun, a great breeder of birds and first to discover the secret of hatching chicks in ovens. Larger ovens could hold up to six thousand eggs. (John Harris, ed., *Navigantium atque Itinerantium Bibliotheca: Collection of Voyages and Travels*, 1705; Alex Pallis, *In the Days of the Janissaries*; Stanley Mayers, *An Organ for the Sultan,* London, 1956.)

Infidel bells: PAWN, 18: Muslims forbade the sounding of bells in Constantinople, as presumably they were considered to be amongst the instruments disapproved of by the Prophet, in addition to their role of calling the unholy Christians to prayer. Christian churches in the Muslim capital were only allowed to call their congregations to prayer with the use of an iron bar, or wooden block (used at Easter) hit by a hammer.

Inishmurray sweating house: QUEENS, I, 2: Most famous of the ancient Irish vapour houses, or *tigh'n alluis*. A turf fire would be kindled inside the house, then swept out and cold water thrown on the stones below to cause a rapid effusion of steam. The person wishing to enjoy the medicinal benefits of the sweating experience would then enter the room, wrapped in a blanket, and remain there for an hour, followed by a plunge in cold water.

Initium sapientiae est timor Domini: KINGS, IV, 1: Proverbs, 9, 10: 'The fear of the Lord is the beginning of wisdom'. *Dominus* can also be translated as 'Master', hence a pun on the loyalty and obedience demanded by the fictional character.

Io: KNIGHTS, III, 16: First priestess of Hera at Argos. Zeus fell in love with her, and out of jealousy, Hera turned her into a white heifer, sending Argus of the hundred eyes to guard her. Zeus sent Hermes to kill Argus, but Hera would not relent, and sent a gadfly to bother Io continually. She wandered across the continents of the world (Io meaning 'the wanderer'), and every strait of water she crossed still bears her name (Oxford, Bosphorus, etc.). In Egypt, she found rest at last, returning to her original shape and becoming the mother of Ephasus, founder of Memphis. She is closely identified with the Egyptian deity Isis; represented with cow's horns.

Io baccio la sua cortese e valorosa mano: KNIGHTS, III, 10: 'I kiss your courteous and valorous hand'.

Ipse ego dum vivam et post dura fata sepultus: UNICORN, 43: 'So long as I live, I shall devote myself to thy will, and even when I lie, worn by toil, in my tomb, Still my spirit will serve thee'. Jan Adorne's tribute to his father **Anselm Adorne** in the account he wrote in Latin of their pilgrimage to the Holy Land.

It is the crown of dead men to see the sun before they are buried: CASTLE, II, 11: The tale of Muscovites storing their winter corpses in church belfries until the spring softens the earth for burial was a widely spread story in sixteenth- and early–seventeenth-century Europe and is quoted from the account of Fynes Moryson, an early–seventeenth-century traveller who noted many such customs; as did **Sigismund von Herberstein.** (Fynes Moryson, Gent., *An Itinerary*, 1617.)

It was the Frogge on the wall: KINGS, IV, 2: Old Scots rhyme quoted under **The Frogge would a wooing ride.**

IVAN IV, Tsar of Russia: CASTLE: (1530–1584) Also known as Ivan the Terrible, owing to the fearful acts he perpetrated on his downhill slide to total insanity (see **Elephant hacked to death . . .**). Ivan took power at the age of fourteen, after enduring total humiliation at the hands of the Boyar nobles who had ruled since the death of Ivan's mother Helen, regent until 1538. He was crowned Tsar in 1547. His first priority as ruler was to begin a wave of brutal retribution against the Boyars, his real and imagined persecutors, and institute a rule of absolute despotic autocracy. Tall, strong and powerful, the charismatic but dangerously imbalanced Tsar would personally torture and murder those who stood in his way.

His treatment of the seventy Pskov men who came to him in his first year as ruler with a reasonable complaint is symptomatic of early signs of this brutality; he covered them in flammable liquid, and teasingly set fire to their hair and beards with a candle. He then ordered that they be stripped naked. Fire was to turn against the Tsar's family that same year; in the spring, Moscow experienced its worst-ever outbreak, killing an estimated 17,000 of his subjects. His enemies blamed the Tsar's own family, saying that his grandmother and his uncles had steeped human hearts in water, and the resultant combustible liquid had been deliberately spread around the city. Ivan's uncle, attempting to seek sanctuary in the Upensky cathedral, was stoned to death by an angry mob, and the Tsar, apparently as a result of the fires, publicly repented of his former cruelties. He appointed a new council of advisers, amongst whom was Alexei Adashev. Adashev was from the minor gentry, but became the *de facto* head of the government from 1549.

Ivan reformed the army and administrative organisation of his kingdom, founding the Streltsy musketeers as the nucleus of his new standing army. Victorious in Kazan and Astrakhan, by 1556 Ivan was in control of the whole of the Volga. The prolonged and ultimately unsuccessful war over the territory of Livonia (1558–1582) destroyed Ivan's hopes of establishing an expansive Orthodox Empire and advancing their position in the Baltic; and by the first decade of the sixteenth century, Russia had lost its access to the Baltic coast.

The Tsar had a towering ego and belief in his own justice and intellect. He loved public debate (so long as he won) and scorned elective monarchies, claiming his own rule, chosen by God alone, was far superior to any other chosen by a mob of ignoble citizens. In later adulthood, his youthful passion for tormenting animals was transferred to an equal contempt for human life. As well as his first wife Anastasia (d. 1560), he had a string of fifty concubines. If any of them proved troublesome to the Tsar, he would strangle, stab or bury them alive; failing this there was the more public torture of being ripped to pieces by wild bears. The insane Tsar was nothing if not imaginative when it came to the punishment of his unruly subjects. He having been chosen by God, there was little his mortal subjects were capable of doing against him.

Ivan's son Dmitri was murdered in 1591, heralding the last of the insane Rurik dynasty. He was succeeded by the Boyar Boris Gudunov, elected Tsar in 1598, and ultimately by the House of Romanov, which established control in 1613. (Ronald Hingley, *The Tsars*, London, 1968.)

Jabatek ummek wahad f'il-dunya: KNIGHTS, III, 17: Stock Arabic poetic phrase, 'Thy mother made thee unique in the world'.

Jaffa, Count of: SCORPIONS, 20: See **Carlotta, Queen of Cyprus.**

JAMES II, King of Cyprus: SCORPIONS: See **Zacco, King of Cyprus.**

JAMES II, King of Scotland: RISING: (1430–1460) Called 'Fiery Face', on account of a red birthmark on one side of his face, the popular monarch succeeded to the throne on the murder of his father James I (b. 1394) in 1437, and became one of many of Scotland's boy kings. Authority over the realm lay mostly with his mother until such time as the King should reach adulthood. In 1447, **Philip the Good** recommended Mary of Gueldres as a suitable spouse for the young King and they were duly married in 1449. The conclusion of negotiations between Flanders and Scotland was celebrated with a magnificent tournament attended by the famous **Jacques de Lalaing.** The marriage increased the links between Scotland and Burgundy, already developed by James's father.

James was a popular king, encouraging learning although not himself exhibiting literary traits like his poet-king predecessor. Relations with England were as bad as ever during his reign; James supported the Lancastrian side, but the Douglas family took the Yorkist side of **Edward IV** and the nation was once more drawn into conflict with the English. James's entire lowland army besieged the town of Roxburgh in 1460; it was here that a wedge from one of the siege bombards killed the King.

JAMES III, King of Scotland: RISING: (1452–1488) Son of **James II** and Mary of Gueldres, the young king inherited the throne at the age of only eight, and grew up during the critical period of the Wars of the Roses in England, when his Flemish mother, helped by the late King's cousin, Bishop **Kennedy,** and an able circle of other advisers had to steer a difficult course between the two claimants to the English throne and competing claims for alliances with Burgundy and with France. Among the nobles who took advantage of the young King to advance their own power were the **Boyd** family, monopolising the offices of the kingdom and laying hands on the boy himself. Much against the King's will, a marriage took place between Thomas Boyd and James's older sister Mary. In due course, Boyd was sent abroad with a mission to negotiate the King's marriage to the twelve-year-old Margaret of Denmark, which was to bring Scotland not only a bride but the islands of Orkney and Shetland. In Boyd's absence the King discredited the powerful family, forcing Boyd, now Earl of Arran, to flee with his wife to avoid execution. When, after much travelling, Boyd sought asylum with his princess in the home of **Anselm Adorne** in **Bruges**, diplomats had to sort out the resulting tangle between Scotland and Burgundy.

James's marriage, though fruitful, was a difficult one, as was the second half of his reign. Pressed hard by two competitive younger brothers, James was less interested than they in war and chivalry, although he tried to persuade his Parliament, once he came to power, to allow him to lead an army to France, and to pursue his claims to the duchy of Gueldres. He was especially aware of his European heritage, linked as he was to France, to Burgundy and to the Tyrol by the diplomatic marriages of his aunts. Although the court was far from rich, James attempted to follow some of the civilised practices of the great courts of the Italian states and of Burgundy, neglecting other aspects of statecraft and sowing the seeds of discontent, which were later to mar his reign.

JAMES IV, King of Scotland: (1473–1513) Son of James III of Scotland, and husband of Henry VIII's sister, Margaret Tudor. Despite temporary peace between the nations of Scotland and England, culminating in the Union of the Thistle and the Rose (as the marriage was known), James once more turned Scotland against his own brother-in-law. He personally led an army of over eighty thousand Scots troops to their doom; despite many prophecies that the conflict would not end in Scotland's favour.

James was a chivalric and courageous fighter, a wise legislator and energetic diplomat, but an incompetent general. By siding wholeheartedly with the French, James dragged Scotland once more into war against England; culminating in the disastrous battle of Flodden in 1513, where the King and the flower of the Scottish nobility were massacred. Despite a string of mistresses and bastards, he left only one legitimate heir; **James V** of Scotland.

JAMES V, King of Scotland: (1512–1542) Another of Scotland's child-kings, James was crowned immediately after his father's death in 1513, and was, like earlier Stuarts, to lose his life and his crown to the armies of England. His mother's rapid marriage to **Archibald Douglas** lost her the respect of the nobility, and also the powerful role of Regent. The Duke of Albany was named as the Protector and Governor of Scotland instead. Margaret Tudor took her son and heir to Stirling and refused to hand him over to the new Regent until she was obliged to do so by force; besieged by Albany and an army of seven thousand men. Douglas and Albany then fought between them

EDINBURGH

Oriens · Meridies · Occidēs

Letha

Brachiú maris — Septétrio

as to who should have control over the King; consequently, James became the second Scottish monarch to employ a guard of Royal **Archers** to protect him from the nobility (**James III** having briefly employed similar guards).

Like his father before him, James relied on France as a powerful outside ally; in 1536 he arrived in France to view Marie de Bourbon, daughter of the Duke de Vendôme, as a potential bride. However, the King, with his definite eye for the ladies, did not feel attracted to Marie physically, nor was it as politically appealing as the alternative. He chose instead Madeleine, the consumptive daughter of **Francis I**. The marriage lasted less than a year as the frail new queen could not cope with the Scottish climate. Shortly after she had died in his arms in July 1537, James was on the lookout for a new spouse. His next bride was to be the tall (and more physically robust) **Mary de Guise**, the mother of **Mary Queen of Scots**; the queen who was only days old when her father died, following the Scots defeat at the battle of Solway Moss in 1542.

Janissaries: From the Turkish *yeni-ceri*, meaning 'new troops', the Janissaries were the infantry corps of the Ottoman army. They were supposedly founded in 1326 when the new recruits to the army were blessed by Hacci Bektas, founder of the **Bektashi** order of dervishes. The troops then adopted the flap that fell behind their white felt caps as a symbol of the holy leader's broad sleeve raised in benediction. It is more likely that the corps was founded from captured and converted prisoners of war.

The Bektashi dervishes maintained their links with the troops, acting as their chaplains, living in the barracks with the soldiers and accompanying them on parade. The troops consisted almost wholly of ex-Christian converts. The main source of new troops was the **Devshirmé,** instigated in 1438, from which Muslims were normally exempt. By the sixteenth century, over one thousand boys were conscripted every year. The most promising trained as pages in the Seraglio, and rose to positions of government. The rest were set to farm labour and manual work, until physically strong and well indoctrinated into the Muslim faith. Then they became trainee Janissaries; *acemî oglan.* Janissaries remained bachelors, dedicated only to war, although **Sulieman the Magnificent** relaxed the legislation somewhat, often giving wives to individual troopers as a sign of favour. Once fully trained, the men would become cavalry officers or military and administrative leaders. Each regiment or *orta* would have its own emblem, tattooed on its tents, flags and the skin of its soldiers. Rank was similarly displayed on the body: a quill in the turban indicated that the soldier had been castrated, but a quill through a fold of skin above the temples was an indication of upper rank. The Janissaries formed the backbone of the Ottoman Empire's military prowess and conquests. In the time of **Mehmet II**, there were 12,000 Janissaries; by the time of Sultan Suleiman, their number had risen to 20,000. The troops were normally stationed in Constantinople, but economic crisis and provincial revolt forced Suleiman to disperse the Janissaries throughout his Empire as garrison troops. Because of their method of recruitment, the troops were a heterogenous mix of Greeks, Poles, Bohemians, Russians, Italians and Germans; captives of war in addition to the children of tribute.

The Janissaries had the greatest reputation (even amongst their hated enemies) as a clean, orderly and highly disciplined fighting force. They could only be disciplined by their own officers, and were not even answerable to the Grand Vizier. When condemned to die, they had the dubious honour of being strangled, rather than the more horrific forms of prolonged torture often saved for commoners or Christians. Their barrack dormitories were kept lit all night, and constantly patrolled, so the troops could learn to sleep even in the midst of an alarm. On campaign, their camps were meticulously run, and free from the disorderly rabble which often followed Christian forces into battle.

Suleiman the Magnificent was himself an honorary Janissary, and would formally present himself before the Aga, the head of the Janissaries, to receive his pay as a private. He would accept a cup of sherbet from the Aga, while he gave the toast, 'We shall see each other again at the Red Apple'; meaning after death, the Red Apple being the Eternal City.

It is said that when Mohammed saw the Throne of God, the Almighty turned and looked down at him. Mohammed became so nervous that he began to perspire. As he wiped the sweat from his brow, six drops fell to earth. The first drop produced the rose, the second produced rice. This explains the Janissaries' strict injunction against trampling on roses, the first blessing of God. Similarly, they were strictly forbidden from pasturing their horses on cultivated grass or flowers, even in enemy territory. The punishment was thirty or forty blows with the **bastinado**, enough to cripple a man for two months. (David Nicolle, *Armies of the Ottoman Turks: 1300–1774*, London, 1990; Alexander Pallis, *In the Days of the Janissaries*.)

Jannequin, Clément: QUEENS, I, 6: (c. 1485–1558) Prolific composer of the court of **Francis I** of France. His talents included the creation of courtly and narrative chansons, one of the most famous being '*La Guerre*', quoted elsewhere in the Lymond Chronicles. See *Soyez hardis, en joye mis.* (LP: The Kings Singers, *A French Collection*, 1973, EMI, CSD 3740.)

Janus: KNIGHTS, III, 4: The Roman god invoked before Jupiter as the divinity who presided over the beginning of all things. He opens the year and the seasons, and is also the doorkeeper of heaven. Cronus gave Janus knowledge of both past and future; hence the two-faced appearance of the god. As a door has two sides, so Janus looks to past and future at once. See *Qui bifrons fueram, gallis sum gallicus una fronte Deus.*

Japhet: CASTLE, III, 8: The ancestors of the Slavonic peoples were said to have descended from Japhet, the son of Noah, when they dispersed across the world after the Flood. The early history of the tribes and nation has been lost due to its reliance upon oral tradition; they did not even develop an alphabet until much later. In the ninth century, Michael III, King of Constantinople, sent two Thessalonian brothers, Cyrillus and Methodius, to Bulgaria, with the task of translating the scriptures into the Slavonic language. They are credited with having invented the Cyrillic alphabet.

J'ay bien nourry sept ans ung joly gay: PAWN, 29:

> For seven years I fed and watered a handsome young magpie,
> In a cage.
> And when came the first day of May,
> My handsome young bird flew away.

Je fille quant Dieu me donne de quoy: CHECKMATE, I, 1: Song by Philip de Vuildre (d. 1530). The *double entendre* is obvious:

> *Je fille quant Dieu me donne de quoy*
> *Je fille ma quenouille au voy*
> *Je fille quant Dieu me donne de quoy*
> *Je fille ma quenouille au voy.*
>
> *En un jardin m'en entray*
> *Je fille quant Dieu me donne de quoy*
> *Trois fleurs d'amour j'y trouvay*

Je vois, je viens, je vois, je viens
Je tourne, je fille, je tons, je raiz
Je danse, je saute, je ris, je chante,
Je chauffe mon four
Je garde mes quailles du long
Je fille ma quenouille au voy.

Je fille quant Dieu me donne de quoy
Je fille ma quenouille au voy
Je fille quant Dieu me donne de quoy
Je fille ma quenouille au voy.

When God gives me the means to spin
I wield my distaff openly

And to a garden make my way
When God gives me the means, I spin.
Three sprigs of love I find this day—
I see, I come, I see, I come
I spin, I clip, I cut, I turn
I leap, I laugh, I sing, I glide—
My oven I keep ready warm .
And all my quails I keep beside
I wield my distaff openly.
When God gives me the means to spin
I wield my distaff openly.

(Tr. D.D. LP, The Kings Singers, *A French Collection*, 1973, EMI, CSD 3740.)

Je prie à Dieu qu'il vous doint pauvreté: PAWN, 11: See **Hiver sans feu, vieillesse sans maison.**

Je suis oiseau; voyez mes ailes . . . Je suis souris; vivent les rats: KINGS, I, 6: 'I am a bird; see my wings . . . I am a mouse, long live rats!' The lines come from the fable of the bat and the weasels, popularised by La Fontaine (1621–1695), concerning those who adapt best to circumstance. One of the weasels detests rats, the other hates birds, but as the bat is half mouse and half bird, it can live quite amicably with both of them.

Jelal-ud-Din: PAWN, 13: See **Ottoman poetry.**

Jemmy bands: KNIGHTS, III, 7: Or Jammy-bandis; window hinges. Glassing bands are metal strips used to secure the glass for windows. (H.M. Paton, *Accounts of the Masters of Works*, Vol. I, 1529–1615.)

Jephthah: UNICORN: The Old Testament judge (Judges, 11, 30ff) who vowed that if God would help him defeat the Ammonites, on his return home from battle, he would offer as a burnt offering the first living thing which appeared out of his house. It turned out to be his only daughter, who had come out to welcome her victorious father. Jephthah kept to his promise, and presumably God taught him a valuable lesson. The daughter was kindly given two months' leave to roam the hills and lament the fact that she would not now have the chance to get married.

Jerome, St: CASTLE: III, 7: (c. 342–420) Eusebius Heronymus; biblical scholar, hermit and priest, also papal secretary. His letter to **Eustochion** and her mother **Paula** urging them to adopt an ascetic lifestyle away from the corruption of Rome caused such scandal that he was forced to leave Rome with them. In 386 he settled in Bethlehem where he ruled a newly founded men's monastery and devoted his life to study. His scholarship was unsurpassed in the early church, comprising biblical commentaries, and his translation of the Bible into Latin from its original tongues. (F.L. Cross, *The Oxford Dictionary of the Christian Church*, London, 1974.)

Jerusalemkirk: RISING, 21: The **Adorne** Chapel of the Holy Sepulchre, founded in 1427 by Anselm Adorne's father and uncle, Peter and James Adorne, and probably completed by 1465. See **Adorne, Anselm.** (Wilfrid C. Robinson, *Bruges, An Historical Sketch*, Bruges, 1899.)

Jeu de paume: CHECKMATE, V, 3: see **Handball.**

Jeune, galant, frisque, dehait, bien adèxtre, hardi, adventureaux, delibéré: KNIGHTS, III, 13: 'Young, gallant, lively, alert, agile, bold, adventurous, determined, tall, slender, with a decisive mouth, well-endowed with a nose'.

J'irai donc maugré toy: CHECKMATE, IV, 4, 7: From the sonnet by Oliver de Magny, 'Magny et Caron':

Magny: *Hola Caron,Caron, nautonier infernal.*
Caron: *Qui est cet importun qui si pressé m'appelle?*
Magny: *C'est le coeur éploré d'un amoureux fidèle,*
       Lequel pour bien aimer n'eut jamais que du mal.
Caron: *Que cherches-tu de moi?*
Magny: *Le passage fatal.*
Caron: *Quelle est ton homicide?*
Magny: *O demande cruelle!*
       Amour m'a fait mourir.
Caron: *Jamais dans ma nacelle*
       Nul sujet à l'Amour je ne conduis à val.

Magny: Eh! de grâce, Caron, conduis-moi dans ta barque.
Caron: Cherche un autre nocher: car ni moi ni la Parque
        N'entreprenons jamais sur ce maître des dieux.
Magny: J'irai donc malgré toi: car je porte dans l'âme
        Tant de traits amoureux, tant de larmes aux yeux,
        Que je serais le fleuve, et la barque, et la rame.

Magny: Charon, dreadful boatman.
Charon: Who dares to call there?
Magny: A lover whose faith has
         But brought him despair.
Charon: What seek you from me?
Magny: But my passage from life.
Charon: What occasions your death?
Magny: Bitter question! My love.
Charon: Never subject of Love
         To the Vale would I carry.
Magny: Take me, Charon, I beg you.
Charon: Find another to ferry:
         I will not challenge the might
         Of the master of Gods.
Magny: I shall go despite you, for I bear in my soul
         Such harsh traces of love: of sunk tears such a store
         That I shall be the stream, and the barque, and the oar.
(Tr. D.D.)

Jiwaka, who gave an aperient to the great Buddha himself: CHECKMATE, I, 5: From the Buddhist scriptures. (Samuel Beal, *Texts from the Buddhist Canon, The Dhammapada*, London, 1902.)

Job: PAWN, 2: See The prayer of Job upon the dunghill . . .

Jodelle, Etienne: CHECKMATE, III, 2: (1532–1573) Court poet and dramatist to **Henri II** of France, Jodelle was the first to attempt to create a French tragedy along the lines of the Greek classics. He was also responsible for the evening masque at the Hôtel de Ville, the antique triumph for the heroes of Calais, 'Les Argonautes'. This masquerade for twelve people in Alexandrine verse was, unfortunately, played very badly indeed; not one of his dramatic triumphs. Jodelle was amply provided with cloths of gold and silver for his players, and a room for his company to rehearse in. Unfortunately, on the evening of the performance itself the singers were hoarse and there was so much confusion with the overcrowding in the Grand Salle that the masque was abandoned; a total waste of time and money for Jodelle, his performers and the burghers footing the bill. Henri II was to have taken a part in the performance, and never forgave Jodelle that his scene was missed out because of an inept scene shifter.

Whether it was supposed to be or not, the antique triumph that his cast attempted to perform was called a 'comedy' by those present. Jodelle made sure, at least, that he and his players received recompense for the Calais travesty; they were ordered (on pain of arrest) to return all the silk and gilded clothes worn for their performance to the Hôtel de Ville, but all that was eventually returned were a few of the masks, not even worth the paltry sum of five sols. Inventive, impetuous and independently minded, Jodelle was also a reckless spendthrift, who died in utter poverty. (Cimber & Danjou, *Archives Curieuses de l'Histoire de France*, 1835.)

Joliba: SCALES: Meaning 'Great River', it is one of the African names for the River Niger. Many of the devout Muslims (with their leather neck pouches containing verses from the Holy Koran) still appease the water spirits of the river with the sacrifice of the occasional hen, and carry a baby chick in their river canoes for luck. (Georg Gerster, 'River of Sorrow, River of Hope', *National Geographic Magazine*, August 1975.)

Jouissance vous donneray: KINGS, IV, 2: Poem of Clément Marot (1496–1544):

> *Jouissance vous donneray*
> *et vous méneray*
> *Là où prétend*
> *Votre espérance*
> *Vivante ne vous laisseray*
> *Encores quand morte seray*
> *L'esprit en aura souvenance.*
> *L'esprit en aura souvenance.*
>
> I would give you happiness
> Take you
> To the bourne of all your longing.
> Living, I shall never leave you
> And dead
> My soul will carry still
> Remembrance
> Of this.

(Tr. D.D.)

Judge, like the widow did to the: QUEENS, I, 5: See **Bring the skin up over my ears.**

Judith and Holofernes: RAM, 3: The popular Jewish heroine of the Apocrypha who nearly sacrificed her honour to save the people of Bethulia. She crept into the tent of the Assyrian general Holofernes, and decapitated him. Her victory has been suspiciously considered to be a somewhat subversive message of female rebellion; **Donatello**'s statue of the couple was described as too unsettling for public display, and was originally exhibited at the Medici Palazzo, although it is now in the Piazza della Signoria in Florence.

Julius III: CASTLE: (1487–1555) Pope Gianmaria Ciocchi del Monte studied jurisprudence and held administrative posts in the church under Popes **Clement VII** and **Paul III** before rising to the ultimate office in 1550. He advanced the Jesuit order worldwide and was also responsible for Cardinal **Pole**'s return to England as papal legate. Pole helped restore England to the fold of the Catholic church, until it was alienated once more by **Philip II**'s war against the papacy.

Juste ciel: PAWN, 23: 'Heavens above'; literally it means 'the just heavens'.

K

Kamen Woronucha: CASTLE, II, 1: See **Oatmeal butter smeared on the . . .**

KEITH, Sir William: CASTLE: See **Dunnottar Castle.**

KENNEDY, Bishop James: RISING: (1408–1465) The astute and active Bishop of St Andrews in the time of **James II** and **James III** of Scotland. Kennedy was one of the sons of Mary, daughter of King Robert III of Scotland, by her marriage to James Kennedy of Dalrymple. From his mother, Kennedy therefore received royal blood. He also received a useful if motley band of kinsmen through his mother's four other marriages—to George Douglas, Earl of Angus, to Sir William Cunningham of Kilmaurs, to Sir William Graham (the grandfather of Kennedy's successor at St Andrews, Patrick Graham) and to Sir William Edmonston of Culloden. Statesman, trader, ecclesiastical leader and ambassador for his country, Kennedy was trained for the church in the university of St Andrews in 1426, and from 1430 to 1431 studied at the university of **Louvain** in Flanders, the home of Mary of Gueldres, future Queen of James II.

By 1437, Kennedy's first cousin James II had taken the throne, and Kennedy rose quickly to take a leading role in the affairs of the kingdom, both at home and abroad. In 1437 he was created Bishop of Dunkeld. Two years later, he was sent as Scottish envoy to the papal curia, and became from then onwards a loyal supporter of the papal throne. He was probably among the princes and churchmen who attended the famous Council of Florence to discuss the future of the Eastern and Western forms of Christian faith.

In 1440 Kennedy became Bishop of St Andrews, and in the 1440s arranged at least one of the highly advantageous foreign marriages of his royal cousin's six sisters—that of the lady Mary to Wolfaert van Borselen of Veere in 1444. Of the King's other sisters, Margaret was married to the future **Louis XI** of France; Eleanor became the wife of **Sigismond of the Tyrol**; and Isabella married Francis I, Duke of Brittany. (Joan and Annabella were returned home unmarried; Annabella after a brief betrothal to Louis, Count of Geneva, the future husband of **Carlotta** of Cyprus, and Joan, unwanted because of her deafness).

Affected by faction struggles at home, Kennedy continued to receive the favour of Rome which he visited in 1451, taking part in the Holy Blood Procession at **Bruges** on his way home. When James II was killed in 1460, Kennedy was again absent on his way to an embassy, at the outset of which he conducted to Bruges the King's young second son, Alexander (future Duke of **Albany**).

During the difficult times of the battles in England between the Lancastrian and Yorkist claimants to the throne, both Kennedy and the Queen Mother were at first pro-Lancastrian, the fugitive Henry VI and his Queen Margaret of Anjou finding shelter in Linlithgow Palace in Scotland, and surrendering the town of **Berwick** as the price of Scottish support. By 1463, the Bishop was preparing with the Queen Mother and the young James III to launch an army into England in support of Henry VI, but the failure of the Lancastrian cause led to diplomatic reversals, and a douceur from the English treasury accompanied the forthcoming truce.

In 1450, a few months before the foundation of Glasgow University, Bishop Kennedy founded the College of St Salvator at St Andrews, intended to combine the teaching of clerics with the functions of a collegiate church. The Bishop gave the scheme his personal attention from the start, bringing building materials in the 'Bishop's Barge' from Sluys, and putting his factors to the purchase and collection of treasure to adorn it, which were later to prove a bone of contention between the College and the nephew who succeeded him. When Kennedy died, however, the College remained as his monument, and the crown in the person of a thirteen-year-old King James III was seemingly strong, even though the shadow of the rising **Boyd** family was already in place.

Kentigern, St: CHECKMATE, II, 8: (d. 603) Also known as St Mungo, the patron saint of Glasgow. Legend credits him with being the grandson of a British prince in southern Scotland, and subsequently trained by St Scrf at Culross. He became a missionary to the Britons of Strathclyde, and was later consecrated as their bishop. He was driven out of Scotland by persecution, but managed to return to Glasgow, where he restored the city to Christianity and baptised the inhabitants. St Mungo's crypt stands at the base of the city's cathedral. The legend about Kentigern's robin comes from an account of his miracles, in which he restored the dead bird to life by joining its head to its body again.

KERR, Sir John of Ferniehurst: KNIGHTS: (d. c. 1562) Head of the Ferniehurst Kerrs, and kin to the Cessford Kerrs (see below). Eleven of the Kerr family came to Edinburgh in 1552 to murder **Buccleuch.**

KERR, Sir Walter of Cessford: KNIGHTS: (d. c. 1584) Sir Walter's father Sir Andrew Kerr was killed by **Buccleuch**'s men in 1526, thus beginning the family feud which culminated in the murder of Buccleuch in Edinburgh in 1552.

Accompanied by John Home (or Hume) of Coldenknowes, the Kerrs set upon Wat Buccleuch; Home stabbed him, shouting to Walter Kerr, 'Strike, traitor! Ane strike for thy father's sake!' Home then flung the body of their victim into one of the booths by the side of **St Giles**, saying 'Lie there with my malison [curse], for I had rather gang by thy grave nor [than] thy door'. Two of Home's servants, passing by later, realised that Buccleuch was not yet dead, and finished him off, striking him three or four times each, and stripping him of his cloak and hat. When questioned by passersby, they put the state of the corpse down to an advanced state of intoxication, saying simply that they had just come across 'ane lad fallen'. Home's men escaped to England, but were later declared rebels and outlawed.

Originally banished to France, Walter and the rest of the Kerr family were given a full pardon in 1553. Walter became one of the chief opponents of **Mary Queen of Scots** when she returned to Scotland. (*County Histories of Roxburgh, Selkirk and Peebles*, 1899.)

Kevin, St: CHECKMATE, III, 1: Irish saint of the sixth century. It is said that he retired to an island where he vowed that no woman would ever land. Contrary to his strict instructions, Kathleen followed him there, and to keep his vow, the saint was obliged to fling her from his rock, killing her in the process. It is said that her ghost still haunts the spot, at Glendalough, County Wicklow. The saint's devout life extended beyond chastity to the rigours of his prayer life: Kevin worshipped so steadfastly that the birds would come and nest in the palms of his outstretched hands. (P.W. Joyce, *Social History of Ancient Ireland*.)

KHATUN, Sara: RAM: See **Uzum Hasan**.

KHUSHCADAM: SCORPIONS: (ruled 1461–1467) The first Greek-born Sultan of Egypt and Syria, a position he attained by a series of merciless coups. Bought by Sultan Sheikh as a page, he rose over a period of fifty years to become Governor of Damascus and an army commander. He proved an unpopular ruler, unable to moderate the barbarities of his Mameluke bodyguard, which continued uncontrolled throughout his reign, despite his policy of exporting the worst offenders to the small standing army he maintained in Cyprus (see **Tzani-Bey** and **Zacco, King of Cyprus**). He was politically adept, setting opposing factions against each other at home, and countering the growing dangers abroad from the Ottoman Turks and the Turcoman armies threatening Syria. Egypt's relations with the Ottoman Empire nevertheless became increasingly strained under Khushcadam, leading to open conflict under his successor Sultan **Qayt Bey**. (Franz Babinger, *Mehmed the Conqueror*, tr. F. Bruckmann, Princeton, 1978.)

Kiaya Khátún: PAWN, 2: Arabic for 'Mother of Maids'; the female examiner of the Seraglio girls. If any of the three hundred or so inmates of the Seraglio had not been chosen for the Sultan's favour by the time they were twenty-five, they would be given in marriage to the **Spahis**.

KINLOCH, John Gosyn of: RISING: (b. c. 1408) Chaplain to the Scots merchants in **Bruges** from 1450. Little is known about the Scottish Chaplain, other than his possible date of birth. He first appears in the Scottish records in 1438, as Sir John de Kinloch, chaplain to the friar Andrew Meldrum, brother of the Hospital of St John of Jerusalem in Scotland.

Kirk cow and the upmost cloth: CHECKMATE, V, 5: Regular early funeral fee due to the officiating priest in sixteenth-century Scotland, regardless of obvious poverty:

> First to complain on our Vicar.
> The puir cottat being like to die,
> Hanand small infants twa or three,
> And has twa kye [cows] withouten mair,
> The vicar must have ane of thac,
> With the gret coat that haps the bed,
> Howbeit the wife be puirly cled!

> And gif the wife die on the morn,
> Though all the bairns should be forlorn,
> The other cow he cleeks away,
> With the puir coat of raploch grey.

(Sir David Lindsay, *Ane Satyre of the Thrie Estates*, ed. Robert Kemp, Edinburgh, 1985.)

KIRKALDY OF GRANGE, William: QUEENS: (c. 1530–1573) Eldest son of Sir James Kirkaldy, Lord High Treasurer to **James V** of Scotland. From a Reformed family, Kirkaldy was described by fellow Protestants as humble, gentle, brave and eloquent. He was one of the envoys sent to Henry VIII to seek aid for Scottish Protestants, in return for which they would do their best to promote the marriage of **Edward VI** to the young **Mary Queen of Scots**. Kirkaldy was present at the siege of St Andrews in 1547, after the murder of Cardinal Beaton by the Protestants, and along with **John Knox** was made a galley slave, normally a punishment for vagrants and common criminals. He escaped after two years, and returned to England, where he was given a pension by Edward VI. Deprived of patronage under **Mary Tudor**, Kirkaldy sought military service in France, and by 1553 was captain of a troop of light horse with the **Scottish Archers**. He was regarded as a valiant soldier by the French King, although he remained personally hostile to French interference in Scotland. His offer to spy on both France and Scotland was apparently turned down by Mary Tudor.

Kirkaldy was finally pardoned by **Mary de Guise** in 1558 and recalled from exile. His daughter married Thomas Kerr of Ferniehurst, the son of **Buccleuch**'s murderer. Kirkaldy was one of the Scots counsellors who opposed Mary Queen of Scots on her marriage to Henry Darnley. (*Memoirs and Adventures of Sir William Kennedy*.)

Kiti: SCORPIONS, 22: Kittim, the great-grandson of Noah who settled on the island of Cyprus after the flood, gave his name to Kiti, now called Larnaca. The first Bishop of Kiti was none other than St Lazarus, who was put into a boat at Jaffa and left to the mercy of the waves. A propitious wind blew him to Cyprus where he spread the Christian doctrine; his own resurrection being a shining example of its efficacy. (Rupert Gunnis, *Historic Cyprus*, Cyprus, 1936.)

Knight of the Ass: KNIGHTS, III, 15: A reference to the tenth-century religious revolt against the Christians in Tunisia, where a leading prelate was caught and executed. His body was then stuffed with cotton and exhibited in a cage alongside two monkeys. (Alan Houghton Broderick, *Parts of Barbary*.)

Knights of St John: KNIGHTS, SCORPIONS: The Order began not as the Knights of Jerusalem but as an order of Hospitallers; a brotherhood of religious and aristocratic men vowed to relieve the suffering of pilgrims, to found and maintain hospitals and serve those suffering from earthquake, epidemic and war. They were not always (as in their crusading days) vowed to the oaths of chastity and poverty. They saw themselves as religious monks and warriors,

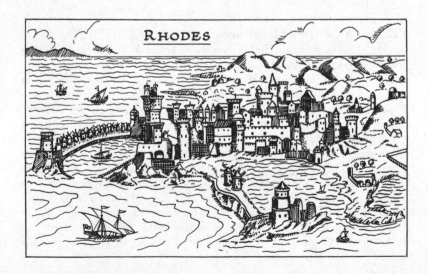

RHODES

first and foremost servants of any poor and distressed Christians harried by Saracens.

The Order began in Jerusalem as a charitable institution for pilgrims, funded and entrusted in 1023 to the Benedictine monks by merchants of Amalfi. It had grown considerably by the time of **Blessed Gerard**, Master of the Hospital at Jerusalem in 1113. Thanks to donations from devout merchants, he was able to found another hospice at St Giles, near Arles in France, for pilgrims awaiting the departure of the galleys to the Holy Land. Under his successor, Master Raymond du Puy, the military aspect was added to the brotherhood, with the intention of safeguarding recent Christian conquests in Palestine. This required a permanent, well-trained army and the Knights became the top rank of the Order, followed by Chaplains, then the common serving brothers, or sergeants. The initial patron of the Order was St John the Almoner, reflecting their charitable heritage, but was later exchanged for St John the Baptist as the crusading spirit ruled supreme.

The earliest houses of the Order were called Preceptories, and the Knight chosen to administer the hospice was a Preceptor, Master or Prior. From the thirteenth century, the most common name for the hospital or lodging house was a Commanderie, and its leader was the Commander. The eight-pointed cross appeared on all the goods and clothing of the Order by 1259, symbolising the Beatitudes from Christ's Sermon on the Mount.

Hospitality was later prioritised not necessarily for the sick, or for the poor, but for pilgrims of all social status. For example, the Priory of Clerkenwell in London housed all brothers coming to and from London, and the monarch and his household also had the right to expect free entertainment from the brothers. The small Order soon grew in size and wealth from pious donations in money and land, spreading its property and influence from one end of Europe to the other. They also gained considerably from the dissolution of the Knights Templar in the fourteenth century as many of their properties came straight to the Knights of St John.

The Knights were forced out of Jerusalem in 1187; reestablishing their headquarters at Acre, until it too fell to the infidel in 1291. From there, the Knights moved their base to Cyprus, onto land held since 1210. Then they moved to Rhodes, conquered in 1522 by Ottoman Turks, and finally to Malta, where the Order remained until finally excised by Napoleon. Originally a land-based fighting force, the Knights became the greatest Christian naval power left to defend Christendom against the ever-encroaching Turk. (Edward J. King, *The Knights of St John in England*, London, 1926; Roderick Cavaliero, *The Last of the Crusaders*; Elizabeth Schermerhorn, *On the Trail of the Eight-Pointed Cross*, London, 1940; I. Cowan, P. Mackay & A. Macquarrie, *The Knights of St John of Jerusalem in Scotland*, Edinburgh, 1983.)

Knollys, William: UNICORN: (d. 1510) Brother of the Order of **Knights of St John** in Scotland. In 1466, he was Preceptor of their house at Torphichen, and treasurer in 1488. He also had a career as Ambassador and public servant to the crown. His worldly and secular links did not stop there; Knollys was also a successful merchant with his own ships trading on the English coast. (I. Cowan, P. Mackay & A. Macquarrie, *The Knights of St John of Jerusalem in Scotland*, Edinburgh, 1983.)

Knots on a string: CASTLE, III, 13: See **Quipus.**

Know that this world's life is only sport: PAWN, 21: From the Holy Koran (extract):

> Know that this world's life is only sport and play and gaiety and boasting among yourselves, and a vying in the multiplication of wealth and children, like the rain, whose causing the vegetation to grow, pleases the husbandman . . . Hasten to forgiveness from your Lord and to a garden . . .
> (*The Holy Koran*, tr. Maulvi Muhammad Ali, 1920.)

KNOX, John: CHECKMATE: (1505–1572) Protestant preacher who first joined the Reformers of the Church in his late thirties, having come under the influence of **George Wishart.** Knox was not amongst the murderers of Cardinal Beaton of St Andrews (see **Wishart, George**) but joined the Reformers at St Andrews and preached there for the first time in 1547. Along with several of the other Reformers, Knox was sentenced to become a galley slave for the French fleet. On his release from the galleys he came to England, but left when **Mary Tudor** came to power. Knox went to Geneva and studied with **John Calvin** for three years.

He returned to Scotland briefly in 1555 and gleaned from his visit that the Reformation must have the support of the nobility, not just the lesser gentry and burgesses if it were to succeed. Some Reformers were more interested in obtaining church lands for themselves than a reform of doctrine. They did have their nationalism in common; the Scottish love of independence that Knox encountered not merely relied on a dislike of English intervention, but encapsulated a growing dislike of the French who controlled many fortresses and positions of responsibility in Scotland in return for their military and financial support in the war against England. A religious separateness from the French was another sign of their distinctive political and national identity. As long as **Mary de Guise**, the Queen Dowager, remained tolerant to their religious views, the Reformers would have no real excuse for the type of revolution Knox advocated. Up until 1557 Knox was advised by other Reformers in Scotland that he should not yet return, as they were making do with private worship rather than pushing for full public status. The new religion was tolerated by the Dowager, and by the French. Until the **de Guises** had safely married the young **Mary Queen of Scots** to the French Dauphin, the Dowager needed all the supporters she could find in Scotland, regardless of their religious persuasion.

Knox considered the Queen Dowager ruling as Regent from 1554 a contemptible state of affairs: 'And a crown put upon her head, as seemly a sight as to put a saddle on the back of an unruly cow'. His nose had been further put out of joint the previous year when he exhorted that she must leave the follies of Rome for the sake of her own soul and the nation. Needless to say she did not consider the request seriously.

Knox had a particular talent for alienating the female rulers of his day. The publication of his tract 'The First Blast of the Trumpet against the Monstrous Regiment of Women' (1559) angered Queen **Elizabeth** and lost him much potential support. Its publication coincided with Mary de Guise's repression of her recalcitrant Protestant subjects. Despite the inclusion of Protestant Commissioners in the wedding negotiations, the marriage of Mary Queen of Scots to the Dauphin meant that religious orthodoxy would be upheld in Scotland—by more French troops if necessary—at the expense of the Reformers' political and religious ambition. The moderates who had advocated peaceful reform were bitterly disappointed that the Queen Dowager no longer needed their support. Civil war seemed inevitable as zealots like Knox were now in the ascendant. Their moment came in 1560 with the death of the Dowager, closely followed by the decline of the de Guise family's power in France. In August 1560 the Protestant Lords of the Congregation abolished the Pope's jurisdiction over Scotland, authorised a new Protestant confession and outlawed the saying and hearing of Mass in Scotland. Knox became the first Protestant minister of the High Kirk of **St Giles** in Edinburgh. He remained its minister until his death, proving to be a thorn in the flesh of Mary Queen of Scots as he had been to her mother.

Kola nuts: SCALES, 20: *Gorro:* the African nut with certain stimulating properties. Kola nuts have a bitter taste, and were widely regarded as a cure for impotency. The name of the nut is now better known as a caffeine-rich sugared soft drink. The nut itself has two interlocking kernels, so closely linked that they became a symbol of friendship, and the giving and receiving of kola nuts accompanied almost every exchange. Oaths were commonly sworn on the nut as a sign of undying faithfulness and friendship. (E.W. Bovill, *The Golden Trade of the Moors*, London, 1958.)

Kolossi: SCORPIONS, 9: The Cypriot outpost and home of the **Knights of St John.** Its fortress was constructed in 1454, with walls three feet thick and seventy-five feet high. After the fall of Acre, Cyprus became the home of the Knights. The base was placed in a difficult position when it came to the internecine warring between **Carlotta** and **Zacco.** The Knights did not want to alienate both of the warring parties and risk losing their foothold on the island in retaliation.

The wine made by the Commanderie on Cyprus was said to be the best on the island, and was widely exported as its reputation spread. The island also takes credit for having introduced fine wines to France. In the thirteenth century, Thibault IV, Count of Champagne, came to Cyprus to visit his cousin, Queen Alice of Cyprus. During his stay, one of the King's nobles was condemned to death for sneaking into the apartment of his beloved, a lady in the Queen's retinue. Thibault interceded for the young man's life; it was agreed that he would be spared if he would leave Cyprus immediately with the generous Count. This he did, but missed his lady so much that he begged (successfully) to be allowed to return home for her. For a year, the Count of Champagne heard no more about the lovers' fate, until the elated young noble and his sweetheart eventually returned to Champagne, now husband and wife. In thanks for the Count's generosity and patronage, the couple presented him with a sweet-scented rose bush and a bunch of cuttings from the vines of Mount Olympus. The vines flourished, and yielded the fine grapes which when pressed matured into the distinctive wine of the region.

It was the Commanderie wine which eventually tempted the conqueror of the island, Sultan Selim II (d. 1574) to break his vow of temperance, earning him the nickname 'Selim the Sot'. It could be said that the Knights indirectly killed him; while drunk on their wine, he slipped on the marble-tiled floor of his bath in the Seraglio and split his skull open.

The Knights' fortress fell into the hands of the **Corner** family with the death of King Zacco, and remained in their control until Cyprus fell to the Ottoman Empire in 1571. The fortress is still in good condition, and the great millstone from its medieval stone **sugar** mill can still be seen. (Rupert Gunnis, *Historic Cyprus*, Cyprus, 1936; Sir Harry Luke, *Cyprus*, London, 1965.)

Kouklia: SCORPIONS, 12: Site of the famous temple of **Aphrodite** on Cyprus. The settlement of Kouklia itself dates from the late Mycenaean period, and the cult held sway until the goddess of love was finally supplanted by Christianity and Islam between them.

The goddess was worshipped in the form of a conical (phallic) stone, often smeared with olive oil and accompanied by prayer, fire and incense. The altar of the open-air temple was to be kept clear of both blood and rain. It is interesting that in the vogue for human sacrifice, only males were sacrificed to the goddess at this particular location. (Rupert Gunnis, *Historic Cyprus*, Cyprus, 1936; Sir Harry Luke, *Cyprus*, London, 1965.)

Krishna: KINGS, III, 2: Hindu god of love. His adventures with the *Gopis* (milkmaids) present a classic scenario of religious erotica, or pornography, depending on one's moral standpoint.

Kvass: CASTLE, I, 5: Russian beer, brewed from black rye bread, yeast and water. It is the less alcoholic (four per cent) alternative to vodka or *Gorelka* (CHECK-

MATE, IV, 1), and Russia's other national drink. It is fairly easy to produce in large quantities, if you have a large enough bucket. The required ingredients are: 500 grammes sliced black rye bread; 8 litres of water; 25 grammes of fresh yeast, 225 grammes of sugar, 4 tbsp lukewarm water, an untreated lemon, 2 tbsp raisins and two bunches of fresh mint. Firstly, dry the rye bread in the oven for about forty-five minutes at 200° C. Bring the water to the boil, and crumble the dry bread into the water and leave to stand for four hours. Just before the four hours are up, crumble the starch in a bowl, adding the lukewarm water and 1 tsp of sugar and leave to rise for fifteen minutes. Strain the bread out of the water mixture (using a sieve) and add the yeast, the rest of the sugar, and the clean lemon peel. Leave this overnight to ferment, then strain the liquid once more (using a tea-towel or jelly bag). Now pour the liquid into clean (and hopefully sterile) bottles. Add a piece of lemon peel, some fresh mint and a few raisins to each bottle. Cork the bottles and store in a cool place for another day or so. When the raisins have floated to the top, the kvass is ready. Strain it again and pour it back into the freshly cleaned bottles. Refrigerate for four hours before serving.

At its best, the beer forms a good head, and tastes sweet and sour. At its worst, when it has stopped fermenting, the kvass will be flat and lifeless. The flavour can be enhanced with the addition of malt, lemon juice, mint, honey or fresh orange juice. Adding more sugar takes longer, but results in a stronger brew. (Marianne Saul, *Perestroika: The Dinner Party*, Berlin, 1989.)

L'absence de discipline est la source de tout mal: PAWN, 4: 'The absence of discipline is the source of all evil: the admiral should eviscerate anyone who disobeys', the motto of Pietro Mocenigo, general of the Venetian galleys in 1420, who maintained order on his galleys using a strict code of fines and punishments. (Juvien de la Gravière, *Les Derniers Jours de la Marine à Rames.*)

L'amor' è cieco y rede niente, Ma non son' cieche l'altre gente: PAWN, 15: 'Love is blind, but other people are not'.

La guerre a ses douceurs, l'hymen a ses alarmes: QUEENS, III, 6: 'War has its comforts, marriage has its anxieties'.

La mer des cronicques et mirouer hystorial de France: CHECKMATE, III, 2: 'The mother of chronicles and historical mirror of France'.

La musique recrée l'homme et lui donne volupté: CHECKMATE, IV, 1: 'Music refreshes man and gives him delight'; one of the more positive comments of **John Calvin.**

La piquure du scorpion par le scorpion mesme: CHECKMATE, IV, 7: 'The scorpion stung by the scorpion itself'.

La plus belle de la ville, c'est moi: CHECKMATE, I, 1: Song by **Clément Jannequin** (pub. 1553):

> *La plus belle de la ville, c'est moy*
> *Non est, sy est, je vous jure ma foy*
>
> *Mon amy m'a dit que je suis celle*
> *'M'ayme je tiens pour la plus belle'*
>
> *Mon amy m'a dit que je suis celle*
> *La plus frique et plus habille*
> *Au boys*

La vostre est une faulse femelle
Vous estes laide, orde et rebelle
La vostre est une faulse femelle
Je suis la plus belle fille
Au boys

T'amye ne vault une groselle
Tais toy, je te repute pour telle
T'amye ne vault une groselle
Tire ailleurs, plus ne babille
Au boys

The fairest maiden in the town, 'tis I
It's not, it is, I swear in faith ('tis I).

My lover told me I was the one.
'My love you are the fairest (one).'
My lover told me I was the one,
The liveliest and the brightest one.
To the woods.

As for yours, she's a false female.
'You are ugly, rough and unyielding.'
As for yours, she's a false female,
I am the fairest maiden.
To the woods.

Your love is not worth a fig.
Be quiet! That's my opinion anyway.
Your love is not worth a fig.
Try someone else: babble no more!
To the woods.

(LP: Purcell Consort of Voices, *Doulce Memoire: French Chansons of the Sixteenth Century*, 1972, Decca, ZRG 667.)

La plus belle des savantes et la plus savante des belles: CHECKMATE, III, 4: Mademoiselle d'Heilly: 'the most beautiful of scholars and the most scholarly beauty', greatly admired by the poet Clément Marot. He said of her:

> *Dix-huit ans je vous donne*
> *Belle et bonne*
> *Mais à votre sens rassis*

> *Trente-cinq et trente-six*
> *J'en ordonne*

'I'd call you eighteen years pretty but wise thirty-six'.

La plus belle me devoit avoir: UNICORN, 16: See **Paris.**

La plus gaie demoiselle qui soit d'ici en Italie: KNIGHTS, III, 4: 'The merriest damsel between here and Italy'.

La rhume écclesiastique: PAWN, 20: 'An ecclesiastical cold in the head'.

La sphere en rond, de circuit lassée: PAWN, 29: Poem of Pontus de Tyard:

> The round sphere, weary of turning
> In my favour, despite its symmetry
> Has changed its course and thrown itself against me . . .

(Tr. D. D.)

LA VALETTE, Jean Parisot de: KNIGHTS: (1494–1568) Grand Master of the **Knights of St John** after **Juan de Homedes.** From an ancient Provençal family, Parisot joined the Order at the age of twenty and dedicated the rest of his life to the fulfilment of the Order's chivalric and crusading vows. Described as tall, handsome and unemotional, La Valette spoke French, Italian, Spanish, Greek, Turkish and Arabic fluently. His knowledge of the last two came in the year he spent as a galley slave after his capture by the Turks. Whilst a captive, he met the great corsair **Dragut Rais**, who personally saw that La Valette was kept in better conditions until he was eventually released in an exchange of prisoners between the Order and the Barbary corsairs. The tables were turned several years later when Dragut was captured by Giannettino Doria of the **Knights of St John.** La Valette sympathised with the corsair's anger at his treatment, saying, 'Monsieur Dragut, it is the custom of war', to which Dragut replied, 'And change of Fortune'.

In his life with the Order, La Valette successively held nearly all of the important posts, including becoming the first non-Italian commander of the Order's galleys. A born soldier and dedicated leader of the Order, it was said of him that he was equally capable of converting a Protestant or governing a kingdom. His mastership of the Order certainly compared favourably with the wanton profligacy of his predecessor.

La Valette died at the age of seventy-four, having had a stroke following a day's hawking, and was the first to be buried in the crypt of St John's cathedral in Valetta, the new fortress of the Knights of Malta which he had founded. (Ernle Bradford, *The Great Siege*, London, 1961.)

Lacoön: QUEENS, I, 5: Son of Priam and Hecuba; priest of Apollo during the Trojan wars. Lacoön was the only one to suspect that the wooden horse left outside Troy was not a sacred idol to the gods. He almost succeeded in dissuading the Trojans from letting the horse inside, when **Pallas-Athene** (Minerva) took an active part in the proceedings. Lacoön and his two sons were preparing a sacrifice to Poseidon, when two huge serpents came from the sea crushing all three of them to death. The Trojans saw this as a punishment from Zeus, and to avoid further retribution they accepted the wooden horse.

Laisser courrer: QUEENS, II, 2: Hunting term, meaning to let the hounds run.

Lalaing, Jacques, Seigneur de Bugnicourt: UNICORN, 5: (1421–1453) 'Beautiful as Paris, pious as Aeneas, wise as Ulysses—debonnaire and humble as a rule, but in battle, glorious in rage as Hector the Trojan'. The anonymous *Livre des Faits* extols the courage and deeds of the legendary ideal knight of Hainault, home of this fifteenth-century Flower of Chivalry. Jacques de Lalaing was the eldest son of a Burgundian nobleman and descended from a long line of seigneurs, one of whom had served St Louis on Crusade. The greatest swordsman of his day, he reputedly visited in turn the courts of France, Spain and Portugal, fighting in the lists against all challengers.

In 1445 he arranged the jousts at Nancy for the wedding between Margaret of Anjou and King Henry VI of England, which took place in the presence of Margaret of Scotland, by now Dauphine of France. Jacques and his uncle Simon de Lalaing were both Chevaliers of the **Order of the Golden Fleece**, and consequent on this encounter Jacques, Simon and a French lord, de Longueville, elected in 1449 to travel to Scotland to challenge a Scottish chevalier of great reputation: James, brother of William, Earl of Douglas. The French-Burgundians fought three against three in the lists at Stirling with lance, sword, axe and dagger and appeared to have gained the advantage when the Scottish King (**James II**), as was his prerogative, prematurely halted the combat before either life or honour was lost. When, four months later, Mary of Gueldres arrived for her wedding to James, she brought Isabelle de Lalaing, sister of Jacques, in her train.

Jacques the chevalier was not always welcome—the English refused him a licence to fight, and in Naples King **Alfonso**, for love of **Philip the Good of Burgundy**, forbade his subjects to challenge him. In 1450, the Duke himself was so offended when—as he thought—Jacques spared his seventeen-year-old son **Charles** in a practice bout in the ducal park at Brussels that the duel had to be repeated. The most spectacular of all Jacques' performances took place in 1450 at Chalon-sur-Saône, at the legendary *pas d'armes* of the Fontaine des Fleurs, of which the centrepiece was a damsel tending a **unicorn**. He had just, in 1453, won the prize of the encounter at Loheren when he was unexpectedly and ironically killed in real battle by a stray cannonball in the military campaign at Ghent. When it came to real warfare, siege artillery was already starting to win over chivalric conduct (see **Cannon**); Lalaing was the last of a breed. At the feet of his tomb effigy there lies a replica of the gun which killed him, rather than the symbols of chivalry which accompanied his colourful life. (Margaret Wade Labarge, *Medieval Travellers: The Rich and the Restless*, London, 1982; Maurice Keen, *Chivalry*.)

Lámdhia: QUEENS, II, 5: Gaelic, literally 'handgod'; a portable idol, pertaining to the pagan gods of Ireland supplanted by St Patrick and the introduction of Christianity. (P.W. Joyce, *Social History of Ancient Ireland*.)

Lapps: CASTLE, II, 10: **Sigismund von Herberstein** is responsible for much of the material available concerning sixteenth-century Lapps; including the fact that they liked to leave their wives in the company of foreign merchants. If when they came back from a long journey, they saw that their wife was happy, they would give great presents to the foreign merchant rather than punish him for turning the husband into a cuckold.

Lateen rigging: A new method of rigging sails, instituted by **Henry the Navigator**, especially on **caravels**. It allowed the boats to sail a course closer to the wind; 55° rather than 67°. This enabled the caravels to sail more efficiently against the prevailing winds, especially on their return journeys from Africa. It saved many weeks of unnecessary sailing, improving the efficiency and speed of journeys to the new continent and the confidence of their navigators. (John Ure, *Prince Henry the Navigator*, London, 1977.)

Latin: The primary medieval language of study and learning; the use of Latin is not anachronistic to the transfer of ideas in the Renaissance; indeed in some senses it was the easiest language of common communication across national boundaries. Before the advent of printing the literate world consisted mainly of scholars, merchants, and of course the clergy. Latin as the language of discourse created a close intellectual solidarity; a book could travel easily from Prague to Oxford and its impact could be assimilated immediately without the need for an intimate working knowledge of any language other than Latin.

Lazaretto: PAWN, 10: Not just a precaution against the spread of specific skin diseases such as leprosy. Isolation in quarantine was one way to limit the impact of severely infectious diseases in a mercantile community. Anyone with business in Zakynthos would have to stay in the Lazaretto until they had clearance from the Signiors of Health, which would take between twenty and forty days. As in the text, if any infectious disease broke out during this time, the stay would be extended for another forty days. Although the merchants or travellers would be allowed no visitors, the Lazaretto was made as hospitable as possible, especially for long-stay visitors. If any friends or fellow travellers made the mistake of going too close to their companions in the quarantine area, they would be forced to join them for the duration. Before release, all clothing and bedding was disinfected by scenting with brimstone.

Fynes Moryson, a seventeenth-century visitor to the isle of 'Candia', then under Venetian control, was also obliged to spend forty days in the Lazaretto, and had to write to the Provisioner General and Inquisitor of the city affirming that he and his company had travelled from a plague-free region. A long stay in the Lazaretto not only ensured that travellers brought no disease, it was also the perfect way to confine foreign travellers and learn their business before letting them loose on the area's trade. (Fynes Moryson, Gent., *An Itinerary*, 1617.)

Le bouclier de la foy, le fort de la Chréstienté et le fléau des infidèles: CHECK-MATE, II, 1: 'The shield of faith, the bastion of Christendom and the scourge of the infidel', referring to the Order of the **Knights of St John.**

L'échange de deux fantasies et le contact de deux épidermes: CHECKMATE, I, 3: 'The exchange of two fantasies and the touch of two bodies'.

Le corps sauvé, les branches se reconquesteront tousjours: CHECKMATE, V, 7: 'The trunk saved, the branches will grow again'.

Le douzièm' mois de l'an Que donner à ma mie: KINGS, I, 5: The whole of this song, reminiscent of 'The Twelve Days of Christmas', appears within a few pages of the text; a free translation follows:

> At the end of the twelvemonth,
> What shall I give my sweet?
> Twelve jolly hoglets
> Eleven juicy hambones
> Ten pouting turkeys
> Nine horned bullocks
> Eight sheared sheep
> Seven running hounds
> Six country hares
> Five coneys skipping
> Four mallards flying
> Three pigeons cooing
> Two turtle doves
> One partridge wise
> Which flies and flies and flies
> From the brake to the field of his love.

(Tr. D.D.)

Le mal preveu ne donne pas un grand coup: CHECKMATE, III, 9: French proverb, 'Misfortune foreseen has less impact'.

Le malheureux lion, languissant, triste et morne . . . Peut à peine rugir: KNIGHTS, III, 15: 'The unhappy lion, listless, sad and doleful . . . can hardly roar'.

Le monde est ennuyé de moy, Et moy pareillement de lui: QUEENS, IV, 3: 'The world is bored with me, and I equally with it'.

Le temps a laissé son manteau: PAWN, 11: Poem by Charles d'Orléans (1394–1465). Born in Paris at the Hôtel Saint-Pol, Charles was the son of Louis, Duke of Orléans and grandson of Charles V of France. He was captured at the battle of Agincourt in 1415 and spent the next twenty-five years as a prisoner in England.

> Winter has cast his cloak away,
> His cloak of wind and cold and wet
> And donn'd his broider'd doublet
> Of pattern 'd sunshine brave and gay,
> Each beast and bird without delay
> 'Gins cry or sing its roundelet,
> Winter has cast his cloak away,
> His cloak of wind and cold and wet.
> See, in the livery of May,
> Spring and river and rivulet,
> With silver and gold and jewels set,
> The world is all new clad to-day,
> Winter has cast his cloak away.

(André Mary, *La Fleur de la Poésie Française*, Paris, 1951; tr. in Anne Macdonell, *Touraine and its History*.)

Leda, swan-seduced: UNICORN, 2: The daughter of Thestius and wife of Tyndareus, King of Sparta. Leda was loved by Zeus who had taken the form of a swan, and gave birth to an egg from which hatched Helen and Polydeuces. This seduction by the swan has been a powerful image in art since ancient times, reproduced by Renaissance painters; it is also a recurrent image in English poetry.

Lee penny: KINGS, I, 7: Said to be a small dark red stone, which came from the Holy Sepulchre. It was brought back from the Holy Land by Simon of Lockhart in the fourteenth century, and preserved by his family, the Lockharts of Lee in Lanarkshire. The stone was set in the reverse of a silver groat of **Edward**

IV, and like many other holy relics was said to possess miraculous powers. It provided the basis for Sir Walter Scott's romantic novel, *The Talisman*.

Leet oath: PAWN, 24: The oath given in the text is from the Domesday Book of Ipswich, and is the frank-pledge taken annually, ensuring that the subjects will answer to the authorities in a considerate and submissive fashion, and that they will pay their tithes to the church and their master as requested. (Sir Travers Twiss, *The Black Book of the Admiralty*, 1871.)

Lemand lamp of lechery: KNIGHTS, III, 14: Lemand meaning glimmering, a satirical description of the Roman papacy from **Sir David Lindsay's** satire:

> Believe ye, sir, that lechery be sin?
> Na, trow nocht that! This is my reason why.
> First at the Roman Court will ye begin,
> Whilk is the lemand lamp of lechery,
> Where cardinals and bishops generally
> To love ladies they think a pleasant sport.

(Sir David Lindsay, *Ane Satyre of the Thrie Estatis*, ed. Robert Kemp, Edinburgh, 1985.)

LENNOX, Margaret: KINGS: (1515–1578) Lady Margaret Douglas, the daughter of Margaret Tudor (sister of Henry VIII) and her second husband **Archibald Douglas**, Earl of Angus. Margaret spent the first eighteen months of her life in Henry VIII's court then returned north. She was taken by her father at the age of three and was brought up in Tantallon Castle. From the age of seven she was totally separated from her mother and was taught by the Douglases to look upon Margaret Tudor as her worst enemy. Her father's flatterers treated her as a Princess of Scotland, encouraging her in her presumption and arrogance. Her permanent friendship with **Mary Tudor** began around 1530, when Margaret was described as even more devout than Mary in her strict adherence to Catholicism. She and her father were generally favoured by Henry VIII. When Anne Boleyn gave birth to **Elizabeth** in 1533 Margaret was appointed her first Lady of Honour, thus giving Anne the prestige she sought as a royal lady of standing. When Mary was disinherited Margaret Douglas was—after Elizabeth—the nearest blood royal to the English throne.

With the fall of Anne Boleyn in 1536, Margaret Douglas's fortunes took a turn for the worse. Anne had encouraged the secret betrothal of Margaret and her own youngest uncle Lord Thomas Howard. With Anne's execution, Howard and Margaret were sent to the Tower of London and accused of treason; both faced execution. Margaret became ill with fever and blind terror. Henry VIII would not listen to the pleas of his sister to let his young niece return to Scotland in safety. She was, however, moved to the former Abbey of Sion on the Thames near Isleworth. Margaret was promised the King's favour if she gave up Thomas Howard and renounced their secret marriage as invalid. She rapidly did so, avowing she had never married him in the first place. She was thus released after the birth of **Edward VI**, but her lover proved to be more steadfast and would not give her up; Howard died in the Tower of London in October 1537. Four days after his death Margaret took part in the funeral procession of Queen Jane Seymour as 'Lady Margaret Howard'. She redeemed herself enough to become first lady to Anne of Cleves and then to Katherine Howard, but was banished again in 1540 because of her love for another Howard: Lord Charles, third brother of the Queen. She and Mary Tudor were both considered a threat to the succession, but Margaret was released in 1541.

Because of Henry VIII's wars against Scotland, Margaret was totally parted from her father and all his family. She remained a widow for seven years but was then used as bait by Henry VIII to lure **Matthew Lennox** to relinquish his Franco-Scottish loyalties. (Lennox's father had been killed by Margaret's father in a long-standing feud between the families, and Matthew and his three brothers had been taken to France to escape.) Lennox and Margaret were married in 1544. They had eight children, two of whom survived into adulthood, Henry Darnley (1545–1567) and his younger brother Charles, later to be the Earl of Lennox. Margaret chose to live at Temple Newsome so her children could be brought up as strict Catholics, and later she and Matthew moved to Yorkshire. Having not achieved the ultimate position of Queen or Consort, Margaret was determined that her son Henry should realise her ambitions for her. Under Mary Tudor, Margaret was favoured once again, becoming First Lady-in-Waiting, Mistress of the Robes and Queen's Purse-Bearer. Elizabeth was jealous of the Queen's interest in Henry Darnley although there was little she could do at the time.

On the death of her father in 1556, Margaret became sole heir to his estates and Countess of Angus. In the opinion of **Mary de Guise** the Queen Dowager, and the Scots parliament, the estates were too important to be lawfully ceded to the wife of a traitor, and although Margaret received her day in Chancery her claim was not successful. If she were to improve the family's standing, it would have to be achieved by other means. Margaret's scheming appeared to pay off in the land of her birth in 1565 when **Mary Queen of Scots** chose Henry Darnley, Margaret's eldest surviving son, as her second husband. The tall foppish King Henry, father of King James VI of Scotland, reigned for only a year and a half before his murder in 1567. Margaret lived to witness her blue-eyed boy's triumphant rise to power and ignominious murder, for which she openly blamed the Queen of Scots. In 1577 she also witnessed the death from consumption of her younger son Charles.

Margaret Lennox died in poverty and was interred at royal cost in Westminster Abbey. The altar tomb was erected by her grandson, King James VI of

Scotland, who placed Henry Darnley next to her. (Agnes Strickland, *The Lady Margaret Douglas, Countess of Lennox.*)

LENNOX, Matthew: KINGS: (1516–1571) Of Scots and French ancestry, Lennox was educated in France, and early on earned himself a reputation for valour, campaigning in the Italian wars of **Francis I** of France, and as the head of the company of one hundred **Scottish Archers**. He remained in France until Cardinal Beaton enticed him back to Scotland with the promise of marriage to **Mary de Guise**, the Queen Dowager. He quarrelled again with the Douglases, but tried to woo Mary for a year before losing heart. In 1543 Lennox reappraised his political allegiance. He stole ten thousand crowns destined for the Dowager and relieved Dumbarton of its artillery, fleeing to Carlisle. He promised to betray the castles of Dumbarton and Rothesay to England and prevent the young **Mary Queen of Scots** from being taken to France. Lennox was further lured by Henry VIII's promise of the Lord Governorship of Scotland if he could conquer and subdue the country, the hand of **Margaret Douglas (Lennox)** and a pension of five hundred English merks per annum. Lennox accepted the deal and turned traitor. Henry VIII talked of their heirs succeeding to the throne of England if his own bloodline failed; after all, Lennox had married the King's niece.

Having forfeited his Scottish estates, Lennox waged war on the Scottish Borders while Margaret stayed at the court of Katherine Parr. The French retaliated to his treason by imprisoning his brother **John d'Aubigny**, depriving him of his office and honours. (He was later released by **Henri II**.) Lennox's northern military campaigns against Scotland were typified by cold brutality. In 1547 Lennox ordered the wholesale hanging of the child hostages held at Annan, as their Scottish fathers had deserted them. This was not to be the best of years for Lennox. His large and lucrative French estates had been confiscated and he subsequently fell ill, afflicted with a phobia for silence and solitude, and could not bear to be left alone. He retired to Settrington House in south-east Yorkshire. The English government still suspected that politically he was playing a double game; trading with **Mary de Guise** through his servant Lawrence Nisbet and the French Ambassador. In 1559 the Scottish government suspected the same, and both sides turned against him; Nisbet was imprisoned in London in 1560 as a known enemy to the Reformed religion and for 'trafikking with papists'. Lennox's life of religious expediency, however, made for an easier passage than that of his wife from the rule of **Mary Tudor** to that of **Elizabeth**: having not affected deep Roman Catholic beliefs he was more than tolerated by the new Queen Elizabeth.

LEO X: QUEENS, I, 4: (1475–1521) Giovanni de' Medici, the second son of **Lorenzo** the Magnificent. His father ensured that the family's contacts were used to best advantage to secure a future in the church for young Giovanni. Elected to the papacy as Leo X in 1513, he is reputed to have said, 'Let us enjoy the papacy since God has given it to us'. It is certainly true that he used the divine office for his personal aggrandisement, and for the opportunity to indulge in many of the material benefits offered by his position. One way in which he improved the finances of the papacy was by formally licensing the sale of indulgences; a lucrative policy so greatly abused that it drew direct fire from Luther.

Les Dames de Dieppe: QUEENS, IV, 1: Pierre Grognet on the ladies of Dieppe (1520):

> Les Dames de Dieppe font
> Confrairies qui belles sont
> Et donnent prix aux balladeurs
> Et orateurs et rondeleurs
> Et si présentent la couronne
> Au mieux disnat que l'on luy donne.

'The beautiful ladies of Dieppe create, and give prizes to balladeers, orators and composers of rondos. And they present the crown to the finest speaker.' (René Herval, *Dieppe*.)

Les executeurs de la justice de Dieu: KNIGHTS, III, 6: 'Those who carry out divine justice'.

LESLIE, George, Earl of Rothes: CHECKMATE: See **Rothes, George Leslie, Earl of.**

Let all stand still, for the master of the house has come: RAM, 18, 42: From the writings of the seventh-century philosopher Isaac of Nineveh, whose works in Syriac were translated into Greek in the ninth century by the monks of St Sabas in Palestine. The Orthodox church believed that the spirit, having travailed to attain the purity of *apatheia*, should then withdraw to the holy quiet of *hesychia*, there to receive in peace and silence the illumination of God: 'All must stand still, for the master of the house has come'.

Let every godly man close the mouth of his stomach, lest he be disturbed: CHECKMATE, IV, 9: A quote from **Richard Eden.** The stomach embodied all physical appetites; especially—in this reference—those for lust and anger (as in 'I haven't the stomach for it'), not just the desire for food. (Richard Eden, *The First Three English Books on America: 1511–1555*.)

Lewy: QUEENS, I, 5: The king of ancient Ireland who was struck dead by a 'mallet' of lightning, hence the proverbial use of his name in this context. (P.W. Joyce, *Social History of Ancient Ireland*.)

L'*homme armé*: KINGS, IV, 2: The name of an old French *chanson*, the melody of which was adopted by some of the great masters of the fifteenth and sixteenth centuries, including **Palestrina.** The tune is mentioned in the text; a version of the anonymous lyric is given below:

> *L'homme, l'homme, l'homme armé, l'homme armé.*
> *L'homme armé doibt on doubter, doibt on doubter.*
> *On a fait partout crier*
> *Que chascun se viegne armer*
> *D'un haubregin de fer.*

> Man in armour, man in harness
> Watch him, heed him without fail
> Every man has heard the order
> Come attired in coat of mail.

(Tr. D.D.)

Li *jalous Envious de cor rous*: KINGS, I, 7:

> Jealous, grudging and tart
> Death can haunt him
> Sweet and vivid and fond—
> Then I want him.

(Tr. D.D.)

Li *rosignox est mon père, qui chante sur le ramée*: KINGS, I, 2: From the anonymous French song, '*Volez vous que je vos chant un son d'amors avenant?*':

> *Volez vous que je vos chant*
> *Un son d'amors avenant?*
> *Vilain nel fist mie,*
> *Ainz le fist un chevalier*
> *Soz l'onbre d'un olivier*
> *Entre les braz s'amie.*

> *Chemisete avoir de lin*
> *Et blanc pelicon hermin*
> *Et bliaut de soie:*
> *Chauces out de jaglolai*
> *Et solers de flors de mai,*
> *Estroitement chaucade.*

Cainturcte avoit de fueille
Qui verdist quant li tens mueille,
D'or ert boutonade.
L'aumosniere estoit d'amor,
Li pendant furent de flor:
Par amors fu donade.

Et chevauchoit une mule:
D'argent ert la ferreure,
La sele ert dorade:
Sus la crope par derriers
Avoit plante trois rosiers
Por fere li onbrage.

Si s'en vey aval la pree:
Chevaliers l'ont encontree,
Biau l'ont saluade.
'Bele, dont estes vos nee?'
'De France sui la loee,
Du plus haut parage.

Li rosignox est mon pere,
Qui chante sor la ramee
Et plus haut boscage.
La seraine ele est ma mere,
Qui chante en la mer salee
El plus haut rivage.'

'Bele, bon fussiez vos nee:
Bien estes en parentee
Et de haut parage.
Pleust a dieu nostre pere
Que vos me fussiez donee
A fame esposade!'

I have for you a tale of love
As once a sweet knight made
When lying in his lady's arms
Beneath an olive's shade.

She had a shift of linen fine
And silks all heaped with fur
Her hose of tiger lilies cut
Her shoes of petals were.

Green leaves in rain her girdle made
Her buttons all were golden
Her flower-hung wallet shaped for love
Was from her love a token.

She rode a palfrey silver-shod
Upon her golden saddle
Three rose trees hung behind her head
To give their lady shadow.

Those knights she met when riding free
Would come on her to wait
Would, 'Lady!' say, 'Where were you born?'
'In France, of high estate.

My father is the nightingale
Who trills on tallest tree
From soaring wave my mother sings
By birth a mermaid she.'

'High-born indeed were you, my love
And sprung of high degree.
Pray God that now you may be given
A wedded wife to me!'

(Tr. D.D.)

Li tens, qui s'en vait nuit et jour: CHECKMATE, II, 1: From the thirteenth-century French allegorical romance, the *'Roman de la Rose'*, later translated by Chaucer (extract):

> The tyme, that passeth nyght and day,
> And restled travayleth ay,
> And steleth from us so priveley
> That to us semeth sykerly
> That it in oon poynt dwelleth ever,
> But goeth so fast and passeth ay . . .
> The tyme eke, that chaungith all,
> And all doth waxe and fostred be,
> And alle thing distroieth he . . .

(Geoffrey Chaucer, *The Complete Works*, ed. F.N. Robinson, Oxford, 1985.)

Liam aboo!: QUEENS, I, 1: Ancient Gaelic war cry, 'Liam to victory!'

Liepard laisse au ciel extend son oeil: CHECKMATE, Chapter Headings: 'Leopard looks up to heaven and sees an eagle playing round the sun'. This and all the subsequent chapter headings are taken from the *Centuries* of **Nostradamus**, of which there is a plethora of variously interpreted translations. (Erica Cheetham, *The Prophecies of Nostradamus*, London, 1973.)

Limousin, Leonard: QUEENS, III, 1: (c. 1505–1577) Painter in ordinary and enameller to **Henri II**. Originally from Limoges, he was the most famous and skilled enameller of his time. His work was particularly appreciated by **Catherine de Médicis** who collected enamels, having 259 in total of the finest pieces available.

Lindsay, Sir David: KINGS, IV, 4: (c. 1486–1555) Scottish court poet and Lyon King of Arms; usher to Prince James (1513–1542, later **James V** of Scotland); author of *Ane Satyre of the Thrie Estatis* (See **Three Estates**), the morality play satirising the abuses of court and authority. Amongst his other works is *The Testament and Complaynt of our Soverane Lordis Papyngo* (1530), using the mouth of the parrot to give both advice to the King and a stem moral warning to courtiers.

Lindsé rutter: KNIGHTS, II, 5: For the chart drawn by Alec Lindsé, or Lindesay (CASTLE, III, 7) see **Nicolay, Nicolas de.**

Lion suet: SCALES, 36: Reputedly good for the ears, but also the fat was known to scare away dogs. Resourceful Tunisian robbers used to smear themselves in the fat to clear the area of canines prior to their nocturnal burglaries. (Alan Houghton Broderick, *Parts of Barbary*.)

Lisáni: PAWN, 28: Poet, who died in 1533. For details on Ottoman verse, see **Ottoman poetry.**

Liticontestation: KNIGHTS, III, 10: Legal term, meaning the end of the preliminary arguments and the beginning of the actual case.

Lo siento, señor . . . ¿No duermes? . . . Duermo y guardo: PAWN, 1: 'I'm sorry, sir' . . . 'Can't you sleep?' . . . 'I sleep and I guard'. The two characters are speaking alternately.

Loi, foi, nation que ce soit: PAWN, 22: 'Whatever law, faith, or nation it might be'. See also **Night is the stranger's** and *Sive Idolatra.*

LOMELLINI: SCALES: Genoese merchant family, a branch of which lived in **Bruges.** In 1425, Julien Lomellini lent money to finance François Spinola's expedition against the Catalans, and was eventually reimbursed by the city for his expenses. In 1470, Gregory Lomellini was put in charge of the annual payment of £30 from the city of Bruges to the wife and children of **Anselm Adorne**, to be paid to them in his absences in Scotland and the Holy Land. The Adornes invested the payments in housing for themselves and Adorne's brothers. They also used the funds on a house they owned on Spangnaerts Street which was left to them by their father. Tobias Lomellini was at this time treasurer of the Order of the **Knights of St John** on Rhodes (SCORPIONS). Another branch of the same family was resident in Lisbon, and in the 1470s received permits to trade with the Moors, although strictly limited to goods which might not be used for waging war; no iron, weapons, lumber, ropes or any naval equipment.

Long Peter, Brigand of the Forest of Jurthen: PAWN, 2: Mentioned in the journal of a German medical student in Montpellier, travelling near the forest in 1552. Long Peter was later captured, and taken to Berne where he was broken on the wheel and confessed to his crimes. (*The Journal of Felix Platter* (*1539–1614*), tr. Sean Jennet.)

LONGUEVILLE, Francis, Duke de: QUEENS: (1534–1550) Eldest son of **Mary de Guise** from her first marriage to Louis, Duke of Longueville. Francis was brought up by his grandmother when Mary married **James V** of Scotland. He died shortly after Mary's first visit back to France to see her daughter **Mary Queen of Scots** in 1550.

Lord is there nothing in the cup for me?: CHECKMATE, V, 9: From the Arabic poet Al Mutanabbi (915–965). The two-line fragment quoted in the text is all that appears in the source. (Herbert Howarth & Ibrahim Shukrallah, *Images from the Arab World*, London, 1944.)

LORRAINE, Cardinal of: QUEENS: See De Guise, Charles.

Lotophagi, land of the: PAWN, 11: The Lotus-Eaters in Homer's *Odyssey*, Book IX:

> I sent some of my comrades to find what manner of human beings were those who lived here. They went at once, and soon were among the Lotus-Eaters, who had no thoughts of making away with my companions, but gave them lotus to taste instead. Those of my men who ate the honey-sweet lotus fruit had no desire to retrace their steps and come back with news; their only wish was to linger there with the Lotus-Eaters, to feed on the fruit and put aside all thought of a voyage home.

(Homer, *The Odyssey*, tr. Walter Shewring, Oxford, 1980.)

LOUIS XI, King of France: RAM: (1423–1483) Nicknamed 'The Universal Spider', Louis was one of the cleverest men of his age, intellectually and physically agile, a tireless horseman and huntsman and a ferocious letter-writer. Although ugly, thick-tongued and plainly dressed, he was a man of wit and quenchless vitality who could attract not only by gold but by the force of his personality. His father was **Charles VII** of France, his mother Marie of Anjou, the sister of **René of Anjou** and Provence. René was thus his uncle and vassal. Louis's sister Catherine, who died young, was the first wife of **Charles the Bold**, future Duke of Burgundy. Louis's first marriage, when he was thirteen, was to Margaret, eleven-year-old sister of King **James II** of Scotland. Margaret died childless at the age of twenty and Louis then married, in 1451, Charlotte of Savoy, but without obtaining permission from his father, thus straining further their hostile relationship. Louis's sister Yolande also married into the House of Savoy: her husband the Duke was brother to Louis of Savoy who became King of Cyprus (briefly) by marrying **Carlotta** de Lusignan.

The resulting network of kinsmen was formidable, and open to every kind of exploitation by the best manipulator of his day. Louis began by falling out with his father and after various missions, campaigns and periods of virtual exile, was sufficiently wary of the King to resist his demands to stop causing trouble and return to his side. When in 1456 King Charles began to move troops towards his son's domain of Dauphiné (Charles had banished his son to Brabant for four months in 1446 as a punishment for court intrigues, and the Dauphin had remained there permanently), Louis fled to the Flemish court of his '*bel oncle de Bourgogne*'. Duke **Philip the Good** was his late sister's father-in-law, his own uncle-by-marriage—and his father's vassal, kinsman and enemy. This was, therefore, a considerable snub, which worsened the already difficult relations between France and Burgundy. Duke Philip, who was having problems with his own son Charles (he once offered to swap sons with King Charles), generously accommodated the Dauphin, giving him an allowance and making over Genappe near Brussels as his home. Despite veiled threats, Louis stayed away (attending **Louvain** University, hunting and plotting) until after his father's death, an event which he certainly greeted with undisguised pleasure.

Returning to France as King in 1461, Louis lost no time in making it clear that he owed nothing to Duke Philip or his son. Indeed he was to spend the rest of his life in a gleeful and vituperative tug of war in which sections of the frontier land between France and Flanders changed hands like playing cards, while he played off England and Scotland against one another and against Burgundy and Brittany. At the same time he intrigued everywhere his spies could reach, suborning his enemies' friends and household officials and buying influence in Rome and Genoa and the Swiss Confederate States—yet, unscrupulous though he could be, men deserted the brilliant court of Charles of Burgundy to serve him.

Living as he did, the King's life was often at risk. He moved about a great deal, often to heavily fortified châteaux. He also secured his own safety through a bodyguard of **Scottish Archers** and men at arms who were well rewarded, often with land and advancement, as well as being usefully connected in Scotland. One of his minor achievements, envied in the rest of Europe, was his establishment of a fast courier service operated through a chain of royal stables, which brought him the latest news, wherever he was.

His purpose throughout was consistent: to ensure that France had control over the largest territorial area it possibly could. Endemic warfare with England and now Burgundy had left the French crown with considerable possessions in its own right, but this was offset by the great lands of semi-autonomous magnates considered by Louis still to be royal vassals. These included those of the Dukes of Burgundy in the north and east, those of the Dukes of Brittany in the west, and the provinces of the House of Anjou. Many magnates, also drawing on alliances and resources outwith French borders, wielded great power and wished to extend their semi-autonomous status. Louis did his best to curtail such ambitions. (Paul Murray Kendall, *Louis XI*; Philippe de Commynes, *The Universal Spider: The Life of Louis XI of France*, tr. and ed. by Paul Kendall, London, 1973.)

Louvain University: RISING: Founded in 1426 with a constitution very similar to the university at Paris. Because Paris was dominated by the English at this time, Scots were no longer welcome there, hence the founding not only of Louvain, but of the university of St Andrews in 1411. Amongst the students at Louvain were Bishop **James Kennedy** of St Andrews, and **Duns Scotus**, who matriculated in 1431 and returned as a member of the arts faculty at Louvain in 1442.

Louvain offered passes on three levels for candidates to mastership. Firstly, the 'honour men', or *rigorosi*; secondly the *transibiles*, or 'pass men', and finally the 'charity passes', or *gratiosi*. A fourth class was identified as those who would not pass at all. Louvain's competitive nature boosted its reputation as a place of education, and it remained strictly anti-Reformation in the seventeenth century. (Hastings Rashdall, *The Universities of Europe in the Middle Ages*, Vol. II, Oxford, 1936.)

Love potion: See *Poculum amatorium ad venerem*.

Luadhaus: QUEENS, II, 2: Gaelic for 'speed'; compare *luath* meaning swift or fast, and *luathas*, swiftness of foot. *Luadh* is also Gaelic for a beloved object (*mo luaidh*: my dearest dear). Luath was the hound of Cú Chulainn (or Cuthullian), the legendary hero of Ulster mentioned by 'Ossian'. (Edmund Hogan, *The Irish Wolfdog*; James Macpherson, tr., *Poems of Ossian*, London, 1888.)

Lucullus: CHECKMATE, IV, 3: (d. c. 57 BC) Roman senator and general celebrated in Plutarch's *Lives* as the conqueror of Mithridates. On his return to
Rome in 67 BC, he devoted himself to a life of indolence and luxury. He was
the first to introduce cherries to Italy brought from Cerasus (Kerasous). His
name has become a byword for extravagance, but Lucullus was not merely a
sensualist. He owned one of the finest libraries in Rome, which he opened to
the public. He also enjoyed the company of philosophers and scholars, and
counted Cicero as one of his friends.

LUDOVICO de Severi da Bologna: RISING: (b. c. 1410) Latin Patriarch of
Antioch. One of the great (and most chaotic) characters of the fifteenth century, lumbering still only half-recognised through Greek, Persian, Syrian, Burgundian and papal records in the decades following the fall of Constantinople
to the Turks. Ludovico da Bologna was the second son of a wealthy timber
merchant from Bologna. By 1438 the family home and warehouse had moved
to Ferrara, where the business was run after the father's death by Ludovico's
married brother Filippo, and flourished to the extent that a private fleet was
contemplated to transport the timber (Ferrara was close to Venice and on its
waterway network). The family did equally well in the duchy of Ferrara, the
cousins and nephews of Ludovico obtaining important notarial posts at the
artistic and glamorous court of Borso and then Ercole d'Este (husband of
Eleanor of Aragon); one serving as Chancellor of the ducal secretariat.

In contrast to his worldly relatives, Ludovico became a member of the strict
Observatine branch of the Franciscan Order, a mendicant order of 'pilgrims
and strangers', committed to poverty. His early education is unknown, but it
seems likely that he shared in the family's leaning towards jurisprudence—but
whatever he lacked, he certainly made up for in terms of his confidence in
himself and his decisions. The initial driving force behind his future wandering appeared to stem first from the sustained and passionate attempts of the
religious leaders of the period to reunite the Christian churches of the East
and the West and persuade them to defend Christendom against the Turks.
Ludovico also came to think of himself as a pastor to the scattered colonies of
Western or Latin Christians embedded among the Greeks and the Muslims
in the lands bordering the Eastern Mediterranean and stretching up past the
Black Sea towards Muscovy.

Ludovico first appears in 1431 as one of the chapter of six brethren learned
in law summoned before Pope Eugenius IV (1431–1447) to discuss Eastern
doctrine and the threat of the Turk. With him was his Vicar-General, John of
Capistrano, and Alberto da Sarteano, the Reader of Jerusalem, where the
Observatines had a convent, and where Ludovico went to live for several
years. He appeared, however, to be at home in Ferrara for the great event of
1437–1438, the Council of Florence (held in Ferrara) where Pope Eugenius
welcomed princes and religious leaders of East and West to discuss possible
union. Among those attending was Emperor John VI Paleologus of Constan-

tinople, accompanied by Cardinal **Bessarion** and **George Amiroutzes**, the Great Chancellor of **Trebizond**, with Michael Alighieri, Florentine merchant in Trebizond. Delegates from the West and the North included representatives of both England and Scotland, the latter sending several churchmen of whom Bishop **James Kennedy** was probably one. At some point in 1437, Ludovico was again received by the Pope and dispatched with two companions on his travels again, possibly back to Jerusalem.

After the fall of Constantinople in 1453, the need to stem the advance of the Turk became a Christian priority, in which the union of the Eastern and Western churches remained an important if diminishing factor. Ludovico, resident in Jerusalem, was encouraged to attempt to reach Ethiopia (believed to be a potential Christian ally) and India, which traded with both the Turk and the Christian West. This he was never able to do. After a year, he returned to report to the newly elected Catalan Pope **Calixtus III** (1455–1458), with whom he achieved a immediate rapport. Now seventy-six years old, Calixtus had been a practising lawyer as Alfonso de Borgia before entering holy orders, and had been employed as royal secretary and chief councillor to King **Alfonso V of Aragon**, assuming in 1436 the training of **Ferrante**, the King's natural son who eventually became King of Naples. The future Pope had led the Aragonese envoys at the Council of Florence, at which he met Cardinal Bessarion, the future protector of the Order of Minorite Friars and Papal Legate to Bologna from 1450 to 1455.

The seven centuries of war Spain had waged with the Moors had sharpened Borgia's resolution to oppose the Turks, and immediately on becoming Pope, he dispatched legates through Europe. He consulted frequently with the Brother responsible for Caffa and other houses in the East, and received Ludovico enthusiastically, talking to him sometimes for two hours at a time, eventually dispatching him with appeals to Persia and Georgia. Returning in 1456, Ludovico reported that he had found many Christians within the Muslim communities, and brought back letters of courtesy from the rulers he had visited. He also brought a delegation of eight Coptic monks from Ethiopia who appeared to have promised to take him to their King (see **Prester John**). Impressed, Calixtus immediately sent Ludovico back to the Christian Latins in Asia (the Christian Greeks had their own pastors), with letters appointing him formally as the papal nuncio, to be their chief and direct them if he chose. Although not a priest, he was permitted to preach, to hear confessions, to confer sacraments and to baptise.

The exhortations were repeated after the death of Calixtus by the new Pope, **Pius II**, hoping equally to spread Christian belief and to arrange a crusade with the help of the rulers of Armenia, Georgia, Persia and the Emperor of Trebizond, to whom he presented Ludovico da Bologna as Apostolic Nuncio for the Christian faith. At first, it seemed that the friar had achieved great success, travelling though Hungary, Germany, Venice and Florence to distribute letters from the princes of the Orient to the rulers of the West, and appearing finally before Pope Pius in Rome in 1461 with a group of envoys from the Emperor of Trebizond, the King of Georgia and the rulers of Persia and Armenia and Ethiopia. These envoys ranged from the familiar Michael Alighieri to the ambassador of the King of Georgia who wore two crowns on top of his head, rings in his ears, and possessed 'a face and a beard like a monkey'. The sensibilities of the Pope were offended, and further inflamed when the letters from these exotic rulers all appeared suspiciously uniform, even that from the Muslim chief Uzum Hasan, beginning 'Vale in Christo' (Hail to thee in Christ), although helpfully addressed as from 'castris nostris prope tentorium' (our own palace of tents). It is to be presumed that the letters, in many different languages, had necessarily all been translated into Latin by Ludovico himself who, commonly employing Greek, Persian and Italian (at the very least) in his travels, confessed unashamedly that his Latin was rusty.

Sent on their way nevertheless with money to finance their journeys to Burgundy and France, Ludovico's party was in time to reach the deathbed and attend the funeral for King Charles VII of France in 1461. Ludovico remained for the coronation of King Louis XI, but did not extract the promise of help for a crusade from the new monarch. The delegates were similarly unfortunate with the Duke of Burgundy, Philip the Good, despite lingering at St Omer, where a lavish meeting of the Order of the Golden Fleece was being held. By the time of their return, Pope Pius had apparently lost confidence in Ludovico and the authenticity of his emissaries' credentials, particularly since Ludovico had begun to grant lavish dispensations and to use the title of Latin Patriarch of Antioch (or Patriarch of the Latin Christians in the East) without waiting for papal confirmation. When the Patriarch removed himself to the friendlier climate of Venice (where he took the chance to enter the priesthood and obtained episcopal consecration without the Pope's leave), he left a fulminating Pope Pius who later claimed to have sent orders to have him put in prison.

Pius's successor Pope Paul II is credited with sending Ludovico in 1465 as Legate to the Khan of the Crimea, after which the Patriarch visited King Casimir of Poland. In 1468 he travelled to see King Christian of Denmark, passing from there to Uppsala in Sweden, by which time he was described as Patriarch of all Europe, or Patriarch of Antioch, or Patriarch of the Latins, and assumed to have Imperial credentials. His reception indicated that he was considered at least to have received his authority from the Pope. By 1471 he had made his way again to the court of Uzum Hasan, the ruler of Persia, and to the Genoese-controlled town of Caffa in the Crimea, from whence he brought letters back to the Pope. Sixtus IV, who succeeded Pope Paul in 1471, was impressed enough by the Patriarch to restore to him the full confidence of the papacy, and in April 1472 sent him overseas again to consult with the princes of the East, and especially Persia. Single-minded, tactless, unprepossessing but indomitable, Ludovico da Bologna devoted his life to his faith, travelling as far as and further than the most energetic merchant of his day, without money or comfort, sustained by his indefatigable belief in himself, his Order, and his God.

Lug of the Long Arms: CHECKMATE, III, 9: One of the principal exponents of the Irish sling. According to tradition, Luga of the Long Arms used his weapon with specially prepared balls composed of 'mystic mixtures' (including the brains of former adversaries). With these, and incredible accuracy in shooting, he was able to slaughter Balor of the Mighty Blows. (P.W. Joyce, *Social History of Ancient Ireland.*)

Lupercalia: QUEENS, IV, 3: Roman festival in honour of Faunus, similar to the Greek god Pan, worshipped under the name of Lupercus. The festival was held on February 15, a celebration of purification and expiation; to give new life and fruitfulness to the fields, flocks and people, hence February from *februare*, to purify.

Lusignan: SCORPIONS: See **Carlotta, Queen of Cyprus,** and **Zacco, King of Cyprus.**

Lute: PAWN, 13: Late medieval and early modern stringed instrument; shaped like a pear cut in half, with five or six pairs of strings. Keeping the instrument in tune was difficult and expensive, as strings regularly needed replacing. (C. Harris & M. Hargreaves, *The Story of British Music;* CD set, Musica Reservata of London, *The Instruments of the Middle Ages and Renaissance,* 1993, Vanguard Classics, 08 9060 72.)

Lydgate: KINGS, I, 1: (c. 1370–c. 1451) John Lydgate, a very prolific English poet, born at Lydgate near Newmarket. He was a Benedictine monk at Bury

St Edmunds and wrote in the Chaucerian style. See **Come my friend, my brother most enteere.**

Lying about being amended in corners: KNIGHTS, III, 13: From one of the letters of Sir Richard Morison, 'Merry Morisine', English Ambassador to the imperial court of **Charles V** at Augsburg in 1552. It refers to his previously unsent dispatches, no doubt altered by his diplomatic secretary, **Roger Ascham.** Morison was censured on the frivolity he included in his diplomatic dispatches. This time he is perhaps misquoting the character of Goods from the medieval morality play *Everyman:*

> Who calleth me? Everyman? What? hast thou haste!
> I lie here in corners, trussed and piled so high,
> And in chests I am locked so fast,
> Also sacked in bags—thou mayest see with thine eye
> I cannot stir—in packs low I lie.

(G. A. Lester, ed., *Three Late Medieval Morality Plays*, London, 1981.)

Lyre: PAWN, 13: Ancient musical instrument like the harp, formerly used as an accompaniment to the recitation of poems, hence lyric poetry.

Ma mie: QUEENS, IV, 6: 'My beloved'.

Macarius: KINGS, IV, 1: Macarius, son of Aedus; committed incest with his sister Canace, the mistress of Poseidon. After her suicide, Macarius fled to Delphi where he became the priest of Apollo.

Madame, il n'y a là aucun mal: QUEENS, II, 5: 'Madame, there is no harm in this, I am only chatting'. **Henri II** of France's words to **Diane de Poitiers** on being caught leaving **Jenny Fleming's** apartments. As subsequent issue proved, i.e. Jenny Fleming's pregnancy, there was more to the matter than mere conversation. (Adrien Thierry, *Diane de Poitiers*.)

Madge Mumblecrust: KNIGHTS, III, 13: Character from the play *Ralph Roister Doister,* written by Udall (see **Royster-Doister** . . .). Madge or Margery is the gullible nurse of Dame Christian. (Karl J. Holzknecht, *Tudor and Stuart Plays in Outline,* London, 1963.)

Madre Dios! Caballeros, su ayuda, su venganza! Ladrones!: KINGS, I, 5: 'Mother of God! Gentlemen, help me, avenge me! Robbers!'

Maecenas, sleeping for: QUEENS, III, 2: Meaning that **Catherine de Médicis** will turn a blind eye to the presence of one mistress, but nothing and no one else will escape her attention. Maecenas (d. c. 37 BC), a rich, dissolute patron of letters, was the lifelong friend and adviser to the Roman Emperor Augustus. Plutarch relates how a Roman called Galba invited Maecenas to supper. Seeing how greatly Maecenas was enamoured of his wife, Galba courteously pretended to fall asleep at table, so the two of them could take what licence they wished, but when a slave thought it was safe to steal a vase from the table, Galba jumped up and caught him, saying, 'Stop! I sleep only for Maecenas!'

Magna pars libertatis est bene moratus venter: PAWN, 3: 'A great part of freedom is a well-behaved stomach', a quote from Seneca, Epistle 123. See also **Sea-sickness.**

Majnú and Leylí: CASTLE, II, 5: Names given to the stars of Sirius and Betelgeuse by the Arabs. The couple in question are famous lovers of a Persian poem: the Romeo and Juliet of the East. (E. J. W. Gibb, *History of Ottoman Poetry*.)

Make thou fast, Gabriel, the gates of hell: PAWN, 11: See **Gabriel**. (E. J. W. Gibb, *History of Ottoman Poetry*.)

Mal' Maritate: CHECKMATE, III, 4: A convent for women unhappily married, wishing to escape their spouses in a climate disapproving of divorce. By the time of the Reformation it became commonplace to satirise convents as a hotbed of sexual intrigue rather than a pious retreat for the devout.

Mal sur mal ne font pas santé: CHECKMATE, V, 10: Roughly speaking, 'Two wrongs don't make a right'.

MALATESTA, Sigismondo Pandolfo: SCORPIONS: (1417–1468) Lord of Rimini. Illegitimate son of Pandfolfo Malatesta, ruler of Fano, Sigismondo followed his uncle Carlo as lord of Rimini in 1432. His career and fortune were made as a mercenary. Malatesta had the reputation of a scandalously immoral and irreligious (but incredibly successful) soldier. He served King Alfonso of Naples, but was not the most trustworthy of *condottieri*: he defected in the middle of the battle for Naples without refunding the contract money paid in advance. He was also a committed and lifelong enemy both of **Urbino** and **Sforza**. Towards Urbino the grudge was more than personal, as the Duke consistently tried to expand his own empire at the expense of the Prince of Rimini.

For his desertions, Malatesta was excommunicated by Pope **Pius II** in 1459. The pope could hardly make it any clearer that he hated Malatesta, but he did, literally telling Malatesta to go to hell; in 1462, he specifically canonized the mercenary to eternal damnation, the only time the papacy has ever been so direct.

After the siege of Fano in 1463 Sigismondo lost all but Rimini, but went on to serve Venice against the Turks in southern Greece from 1464 to 1466 before dying in Rimini. In private life, he remained 'constant in passion' for his mistress Isotta degli Atti, who survived two marriages. The death of Malatesta's second wife Polissena Sforza in 1449 was rumoured to be due to poison: at any rate he married Isotta in 1456. Although he left many illegitimate sons, he had no lawful heirs.

Despite his irreligious reputation, Malatesta did commission the rebuilding of the San Francesco church in Rimini along classical lines. It was known as the Malatesta temple, and its inscriptions in Greek, Italian and Latin attempt to bolster his reputation as a great ruler, military tactician and pious Christian, although they contained some profane features as well. His patronage of poets and artists epitomised the image of the Renaissance Prince. His reputation as an aesthete reached Constantinople: twenty years before Bellini travelled to the Sublime Porte to paint the Sultan, **Mehmet** asked Malatesta, through the Venetian Ambassador, to send him Matteo de' Pasti of Verona, a famous painter and medallist who had worked on the Temple. Matteo did go to Constantinople in about 1463, accompanied by a manuscript of *De Re Militari*, a gift from Malatesta on a subject which the Sultan might be thought to have mastered rather too well already. (P. Jones, *The Malatesta of Rimini.*)

Mamelukes: KNIGHTS; SCORPIONS: From the past participle of the verb *mallak*, 'to possess', and originally signifying the Egyptian slave or bondsman. As the slave population of medieval Egypt expanded, they were freed, trained in the art of warfare, and formed the bodyguard of the Egyptian Eyyubite sultans. By the late thirteenth century, the Mamelukes had gained control of the sultanate for themselves.

These former slaves kept themselves apart as a race from the Egyptian peoples they governed. There was no concept of hereditary succession for their rulers; the next Emir was likely to be the most ruthless and the one cunning enough to murder his opponents before they attempted to do the same to him. Their oligarchic rule was typified by the cruelty with which they dealt with their rivals and enemies, and they were renowned for their invention in the arts of torture, such as crucifixion on a wooden board, which was then paraded on the back of a camel.

In 1517, the Mamelukes were finally subjugated by the Ottoman Sultan Selim II, but they retained their control over Cairo. Hereditary succession was still denied; the head slave could inherit from his master, alternatively all property and belongings would revert to the state. Accumulated wealth thus only profited one generation. In the Mameluke kingdom, the Sultan was always a Mameluke or a descendant of one, no different from any other who had completed his training; all theoretically had the same right to rule, provided they were strong enough. Even then the rule was tenuous; a Sultan could only rely on the absolute support of the trained soldiers he had formerly owned, not the military leaders of his predecessor. Waves of executions often followed a change of Sultan, as the new incumbent culled and replaced all former favourites.

The Mamelukes became the light horse infantry of the Ottoman Empire, renowned for their skill on horseback. Their pride and obsessive reliance upon the horse is one of the main causes of their sixteenth-century subjugation by the Turk. The Mamelukes were among the last to embrace firearms; because the early arquebus required both hands to load and fire, it could not be used on horseback. The Mamelukes rejected artillery because it reduced them to the status of common foot soldiers, a degrading position which was seen as contrary to their chivalric and moral code. The Mameluke cavalry was only finally disbanded in 1811. (Sir William Muir, *The Mameluke or Slave Dynasty of Egypt: 1260–1517*, London, 1896; David Ayalon, *Gunpowder and Firearms in the Mameluke Kingdom*, London, 1956.)

Manco passioni humane: PAWN, 15: 'I lack human passions'.

Mandeville: KINGS, I, 2; CASTLE, II, 9: Sir John Mandeville (1300–1372) English explorer who published extravagant written accounts of his supposed travels; a compilation of history, geography, romance and fables, fantastical in the extreme. The account was first written in French, probably around 1375, and purports to be the journal of the English knight who set out on his travels in 1322. Mandeville was amongst the favourite reading of **James III** of Scotland. (W. Peacock, *English Prose from Mandeville to Ruskin*, Oxford University Press, 1903; *The Travels of Sir John Mandeville*, introduction by Jules Bramont, Everyman's Library, London, n.d.)

Mandragora: CHECKMATE, V, 9: A powerful medicinal herb. When mixed with wine the root was a cross between a drug and a poison, popular before the full value and side effects of opiates had been discovered, and with the additional properties of an aphrodisiac. According to Pliny, when bears were fed on mandrake, they could lick up and eat ants without any ill effects. A small dose induces the taker to be vain about his looks, but a large dose will turn him into a fool. The root itself was dangerous to collect as it was fatal to hear the scream of the perishing herb. One of the best ways to dig up the living plant was to tie a dog to the herb, and then retreat, calling the dog to you. As the running animal pulled up the roots of the plant, it would be killed by the shriek of the dying plant, not you. (Douglas Guthrie, *King James VI of Scotland: His Influence on Medicine and Science*.)

Manerly Margery, Mylk, and Ale: KINGS, III, 4: A song in three parts from c. 1510, by John Skelton, (c. 1460–1529). The clerk's lines are in quotation marks; Margery sings the rest, apart from the chorus lines which are sung by a bass.

> Aye, beshrew you, by my fay,
> These wanton clerks be nice [foolish] alway,
> Avaunt, avaunt my popinjay!
> 'What will you do nothing but play?'
> Tilly, vally straw, let be I say!
> Gup [Go up], Christian Clout, gup, Jack of the Vale!
> With Mannerly Margery milk and ale.
>
> 'By God ye be a pretty pode [toad],
> And I love you an whole cartload.'

Straw, James Foder, ye play the fode [deceiver, seducer]
I am no hackney for your rod [riding]:
Go watch a bull, your back is broad!
Gup, Christian Clout, gup, Jack of the Vale!
With Mannerly Margery milk and ale.

Ywis ye deal uncourteously;
What would ye frumple [tumble] me? now fie!
'What, and ye shall not be my pignsy [darling]?'
By Christ, ye shall not, no hardily:
I will not be japped [tricked] bodily!
Gup, Christian Clout, gup, Jack of the Vale!
With Mannerly Margery milk and ale.

'Walk forth your way, ye cost me nought;
Now have I found that I have sought:
The best cheap flesh that ever I bought.'
Yet for his love that hath all wrought,
Wed me, or else I die for thought.
Gup Christian Clout your breath is stale!
Go Mannerly Margery milk and ale!
Gup, Christian Clout, gup, Jack of the Vale!
With Mannerly Margery milk and ale.

(*Norton Anthology of English Literature*, Vol. I, fourth edn, 1979.)

MANSION, Colard: RISING: (fl. 1450–1482) A Flemish resident of **Bruges**, and Dean of the Manuscript Writers and Booksellers' Guild of St John the Evangelist. Mansion was a renowned illustrator of manuscripts; in 1450 he illuminated a romance for **Philip the Good**, Duke of Burgundy, and was regularly given work by his patron, **Louis de Gruuthuse**, owner of the very fine library admired by **Edward IV** amongst others.

He was also amongst the first residents of the city to try his hand at using a printing press. **William Caxton** printed six books in Bruges, including the first book to be written in English, all of which were printed in Mansion's workshop and using his typeface. Despite being Dean of the Guild twice in the years 1454 to 1473, his name does not appear in the rolls of the guild from 1476 to 1482. This absence can be explained in several ways: Mansion may have been excluded from the guild for some misdemeanour; or may have fallen on hard times and been too poor to pay the subscription charge for full membership. However, as these years coincide with the busiest period for his printing press, it may have more to do with the diversification of his career than penury. (Wilfrid C. Robinson, *Bruges, An Historical Sketch*, Bruges, 1899.)

Marco Polo: CASTLE, II, 10: (1254–1324) Venetian explorer who became an envoy of the Mongol prince Kublai Khan, he was one of the first to travel the Orient and leave a full written account of his journeys and experiences abroad. His stories about the great wealth of the East, like those of **Mandeville** and Pliny, were not believed, earning him his reputation as a teller of tall tales, Il Milione, 'the man who talks in thousands'. He is credited with introducing the West to paper money and, of course, pasta.

Margot labourez les Vignes: CHECKMATE, V, 9: Court chanson by Jacques Arcadelt (c. 1514–1557). The version used as the source is a four-part vocal harmony. The entire song appears within a page or so of the text, so only the translation is given below:

> Margot till the vineyard
> Vineyard, vineyard, vineyard-o
> Margot till the vineyard soon now.
> On my way back from Lorraine
> Margot, I met with three captains
> Vineyard, vineyard, vineyard-o
> Margot till the vineyard soon now.
> They did hail me, wicked wench,
> Margot, I am their quartain ague,
> Vineyard, vineyard, vineyard-o
> Margot till the vineyard soon now.

(Tr. Frank Dobbins; LP, The Purcell Concert of Voices, *Doulce Memoire*, 1972, DECCA, ZRG 667.)

Marie sonne Marie ne donne: QUEENS, II, 5: Contemporary lampoon against **Diane de Poitiers**, to whom **Henri II** gave the revenues of the tax on church bells. The verse names one bell in Blois and plays on the jewels (or horse collar) which Diane, wife of the seneschal of Normandy, will purchase with the income from the tax.

> Marie rings out
> Marie gives out
> Nothing but gear
> For the Seneschale-mare.

Marsh fever: RISING, 35: Malaria.

Marry never a priest's get: CHECKMATE, V, 11: 'Get' meaning illegitimate offspring. It was the advice offered by **James V** of Scotland to the prospective husband of one of Cardinal Beaton's daughters (not **Janet Beaton**, wife of **Buccleuch**). (D. Hay Fleming, *The Reformation in Scotland.*)

Marthambles: CASTLE, II, 9: Popular collective term for any number of divergent symptoms or diseases noted and 'treated' by a mountebank. If particularly fortunate, the patient might also be relieved of the symptoms of the Rockogrogle. Fictitious diseases still cost good money to cure. (W. S. C. Copeman, *Doctors and Disease in Tudor Times.*)

Martinmas hog: KNIGHTS, III, 2: The feast of St Martin (November 11) was the traditional time for the slaughter of livestock, after which it was salted to see the farmer and his family through the long winter ahead. It is used as an extended metaphor to remind man of his mortality and the inevitability of his own death, as in 'his Martinmas will come'. (E. Cobham Brewer, *The Dictionary of Phrase and Fable*, London, 1894 edn.) See also **At Martinmas I kill my swine.**

MARY Queen of Scots: KINGS: (1542–1587) Daughter of **James V** of Scotland and his French bride **Mary de Guise.** Born at Linlithgow shortly after the defeat of her father's army at Solway Moss, Mary was the only surviving heir to a kingdom at war. Within a week of her birth, she was its queen. Henry VIII's campaigns ceased for a brief respite of mourning for her father, but he soon concentrated his attacks on the sovereignty and independence of Scotland once more. Peace would only be made between the two countries on Henry VIII's terms. According to the Treaty of Greenwich, Henry proposed that Mary should become the bride of young **Edward VI.** If the betrothal went ahead, the young Scottish queen would be taken to England, educated with her husband-to-be, and grow up in the English court. The Scots were unlikely to approve of these proposals except under duress, for by such an agreement, the monarchy and reins of power would leave Scottish soil; the union of the crowns would cost Scotland her independence in return for peace. It would also leave a power vacuum that would inevitably cause a religious and baronial power struggle north of the border. As soon as the majority of the fifteen thousand Scots captured at Solway Moss had been returned north, the Treaty of Greenwich was revoked, and Henry VIII was forced to gain a bride for his son by more brutal means. For the following six years, Henry unsuccessfully pursued the 'Rough Wooing' of Mary and the Scots; a campaign of terror involving regular despoilatory incursions onto Scottish soil.

In 1548, as the English pushed further north, Mary was sent to France to the relative safety of her uncles in the French court. It kept her away from the armies of Henry, and was the first physical step for the ambitious **de Guise** family in uniting the French and Scottish crowns. Her route to the continent, round the north coast of Scotland, accompanied by the French galleys of **Leone Strozzi**, was reliant upon information gleaned from the **Lindsé** (Lindesay) **rutter**, the coastal map of Scotland by a Scots pilot of James V which was gifted back to Scotland by **Nicolas de Nicolay**, who himself had received it as a gift from the Admiral of England, Lord Dudley (later the Earl of **Warwick**). It was a fitting irony that it was next used to safeguard Mary from the English army.

When Mary arrived in France, her mother's family stopped at nothing to ensure the promised marriage between the royal houses of Scotland and France. If Mary were married to the Dauphin, the future **Francis II**, it would cement the 'Auld Alliance' between the two countries, and would place the powerful de Guise family on an even more significant position *vis-à-vis* the actual power behind the French throne. The secret papers that Mary signed (probably on the diplomatic insistence of her French uncles) before the wedding in 1558 prove that the alliance was not purely to the advantage of an independent Scotland. If Mary did not produce an heir from the marriage, and if she were to die before the Dauphin, she agreed that the French would then be paid the sum of one million pounds which would go towards recouping their recent military investments in the defence of Scotland. Even up to the year 1548, the French had spent 1,600,000 crowns on Scotland. Failing this, the French would be given the right to rule Scotland. No doubt Mary considered that this promise was illusory, and there would never be cause to pay, but it immediately undermined the Earl of **Arran**'s position; he had already been promised the governorship of Scotland if Mary were to die childless. Also, if it were already suspected that the Dauphin might be impotent, Mary had as good as given Scotland away.

Mary and her betrothed were eventually married in Paris at Notre Dame in 1558, but this phase of her life was to be short. With the death of **Mary Tudor**, Mary was encouraged to pursue her claim to the English throne; the first step being to quarter her arms with those of England. It was a dynastic threat that **Elizabeth** was not to forget, particularly when Mary no longer had the French to support her. Things started to move very rapidly for the young Queen of Scots: her father-in-law **Henri II** was killed in a freak jousting accident in 1559; Mary and her young husband were crowned in September of the same year. Her peace and prosperity were to be short-lived, for in 1560, disaster seemed to follow Mary's every move. Her husband Francis died of an ear infection; her mother, still acting as Regent in Scotland, also died; and the Protestant Lords of the Congregation took advantage of the situation to declare Scotland a Protestant country, outlawing the Catholic religion she had espoused all her life.

The Scotland to which Mary returned in 1561 was not the nation of loyal subjects she had left in her childhood. Within six brief years she was to marry disastrously twice, be widowed once, and then deposed by her own subjects. Her apparent complicity in the murder of Henry Darnley and the hurried marriage to the Earl of Bothwell (a co-conspirator in the plot) finally lost the headstrong monarch the support of France and Rome. In 1567 she was forced to flee to England and seek sanctuary in Elizabeth's territory. As Elizabeth had been a rallying point for England's Protestants, so Mary Queen of Scots proved to be the same for her cousin Elizabeth's Catholic subjects. Eventually, after nineteen years of captivity in England, Mary was implicated in Sir Anthony Babington's plot against Elizabeth, duly tried and executed the following year. (Antonia Fraser, *Mary Queen of Scots*; Rosalind K. Marshall, *Queen of Scots*, Edinburgh, 1986.)

MARY TUDOR: CASTLE: (1515–1558) Daughter of Henry VIII and Catherine of Aragon. Her childhood ambitions and potential marriage proposals were destroyed with her parents' divorce. When Mary was disinherited, she had no bargaining power to make her attractive to other monarchs and princes, and her beauty was apparently not great enough to sustain a love match on its own merit. After **Elizabeth** was born, seventeen-year-old Mary was downgraded in rank, not even permitted to call herself a princess. She refused to recognise Elizabeth as a sister, and would not acknowledge that she was even the daughter of Henry VIII, but the offspring of one of Anne Boleyn's acts of promiscuity.

With the death of **Edward VI** and the end of Lady Jane Grey's abortive nine-day reign, Mary was proclaimed Queen in 1553. On her accession to the throne at the age of thirty-seven, one of Mary's first acts was to repeal the acts of her father; legitimising herself and having Elizabeth bastardised. She had her half-sister constantly watched and confined when popular support for Anne Boleyn's daughter seemed a threat to her own rule. To secure the Catholic succession, Mary would have to find a husband and produce an heir.

In 1554, she received a pencil portrait of **Philip II** by Titian, sent by his aunt, the Regent of the Netherlands. Even though it erred on the flattering side, and was over three years out of date, Mary immediately fell for the King of Spain who was eleven years her junior. The inscription on the back of the portrait said that it was to be returned to its owner when Mary was in possession of the living original. Despite the protests of Cardinal **Pole**, who thought that the devoutly religious queen should remain a bride to Christ alone, the couple were married. The marriage treaty specifically stated that Philip should not drag England into his own European wars, but England was embroiled as Mary helped fund her husband's 'defensive' war against the Pope; somewhat ironically since their royal entry to London had been lyrically overlaid with **Elder**'s verses, proclaiming Philip as the heroic embodiment of England's religious salvation. Despite the fact that Philip had a well-established mistress at home, Mary naïvely believed he had eyes for her alone. The Spanish could not believe that Mary was so pure that she had no crude words whatsoever in her vocabulary; nor could she even understand what they meant. They did admit that they had seldom seen one so assiduous in prayer.

Mary was described as small, flabby rather than fat, with fair skin, reddish hair and no eyebrows. The Spanish state papers are somewhat scathing on their first impressions of the new bride for Philip II; commenting on how unflattering the English clothes were to her figure, and that neither was she the able statesman they had been led to believe. They did let up on the point of her religious devotions and her affection for Philip, describing her some- what patronisingly as a 'good soul'. The Venetian Ambassador to the English court was similarly realistic in his appraisal of Mary's charms, commenting, 'Were not her years on the decline, she might be called handsome'. Her health had never been particularly good; being blooded regularly, and suffer- ing from amenorrhoea, it was unlikely that she could have conceived a Catholic heir for England. She remained obsessively hopeful, despite the dispiriting false alarms.

Mary died in 1558, surrounded by her loyal Catholic retinue, including **Jane Dormer**, but notable by his absence was her husband. Her last hours are touchingly described: she comforted her grieving courtiers and told them of her calming dreams of little children, like angels, who played and sang before her. Before passing away, after grudgingly naming Elizabeth as her successor, she reminded them that all things are for the best and that God would be mer- ciful. (Helen Simpson, *The Spanish Marriage*; Beatrice White, *Mary Tudor*, 1935.)

Marzocco: RAM, 6: See **Donatello.**

Mas veen quatro ojos que no dos: KINGS, I, 5: 'Four eyes see better than two'.

Match-lock carbines: PAWN, 4: One of the earliest of the trigger-fired weapons. A piece of cord impregnated with combustible material was lit, and fitted into a moveable arm, called the serpentine. When the trigger was squeezed, the serpentine swung forward and ignited the priming powder, which then made contact with the main charge of gunpowder, causing the explosion which would eventually propel the projectile from the barrel. See also **Guns.**

Mauldicte soit trestoute la lignye: KNIGHTS, III, 8: 'Accursed be all their line'.

Mauro, Fra: SCALES, 4: Fifteenth-century cartographer of the Camaldolite Monastery of San Michele at Murano, Venice. King Alfonso of Portugal per- suaded **Henry the Navigator** to create a map of the world, charting the great Portuguese discoveries in West **Africa** which he had encouraged. The work was entrusted to Fra Mauro, a Venetian monk, and Andrea Bianco, another Venetian cartographer. The map was completed in 1459, and included all the information from **Ca'da Mosto**'s journeys and every other journey made up to that point.

The Portuguese were obsessively secretive about the map, fearing that it might encourage others to infringe on their hard-won monopolies in West Africa. The Doge of Venice, Francesco Foscari, was allowed to see the map whilst it was being made and wrote back to Portugal that the map should hopefully encourage Prince Henry to continue his great explorations. (John Ure, *Prince Henry the Navigator*, London, 1977; Ernle Bradford, *Southward the Caravels: The Story of Henry the Navigator*, London, 1961.)

Maximilian's pelican: QUEENS, II, 1: The favourite bird of Maximilian II, nephew of **Charles V**, and founder of the menagerie at Ebersdorf in 1552. It is said the bird flew everywhere with him, even into battle. **Roger Ascham** mentions having seen the bird in 1550, when he was travelling as secretary to the English Ambassador at Augsburg, Sir Richard Morison. It was the first pelican Ascham had ever seen and he was astounded at the bird's ability to swallow (without difficulty) an entire white English Penny loaf. (Lawrence V. Ryan, *Roger Ascham*.)

MAXWELL, John: KINGS: (1512–1583) Sir John of Terregles, Master of Maxwell and fourth Baron Herries. John was the second son of Robert, fifth Baron Maxwell and his wife Janet Douglas (daughter of William Douglas of Drumlanrig). He was described by **John Knox** as 'a man stout and wittie', of 'great judgement and experience', proving to be a valuable adviser to the crown in times of peace and war. In 1547 he married Agnes Herries, the eldest daughter and heir apparent of William, the third baron of the name. The couple were related within prohibited degree, but neglected to apply for a papal dispensation. In 1555, they received an absolution from the Pope and grace of dispensation was awarded, despite Maxwell's Reformed views. Agnes was originally promised to the Earl of **Arran**'s son, but seemingly love took its course over the ambitious plans of the scheming Governor of Scotland. The marriage was very fruitful, producing four sons and seven daughters who all lived to adulthood.

In 1551, John was appointed as Warden of the East and Middle Marches, the border territories between Scotland and England, although he resigned in 1553 and the office was transferred to his uncle. He took the office again when **Mary Queen of Scots** returned. Although amongst the religious Reformers, Maxwell gave his political support to the Queen, particularly after her secretary David Riccio was murdered before her eyes. Maxwell fought on the Queen's side at the battle of Langside in 1568, and accompanied the Queen the same year when she fled Scotland. He advised that she should go to France, but Mary was determined that she would receive help from her cousin **Elizabeth** in England. (See also **Wharton, Thomas**.) (Sir John Maxwell of Terregles, *Historical Memoirs of the Reign of Mary Queen of Scots*.)

M. d'Orleans, a large round face, who does nothing but give blows: QUEENS, I, 3: A description of the future **Henri II** of France when he was only eleven years of age. Because of the war between his father **Francis I** and the Empire of **Charles V**, Henri and his brother spent much of their childhood as prisoners of Charles V, cooped up in the citadel of Pedraza, in sparse, isolated conditions; with no wall hangings and only straw mattresses. Even the view out of the window was constrained by iron bars. Henri was allowed no entertainment or pastimes, and all the two brothers had for company were two pet dogs.

On their return to France, their father had no time for his 'dreamy, sullen, sleepy children'. Henri was morose, and psychologically damaged by the series of petty humiliations his captors had inflicted upon him. Francis ignored his two elder boys, who had been scapegoats for his policies, and instead lavished his attention on their younger brother Charles, aged nine. (H. Noel Williams, *Henri II.*)

Meddáh: PAWN, 21: Arabic storyteller who gives an eloquent and animated rendition of traditional and contemporary popular folk tales. They were a strong part of the oral culture of the city, and most Constantinople coffeehouses would employ a *Meddáh* as entertainment. They served a dual role, whereby they could be primed by the government (or its opposition) to warn the populace of or reconcile it to unpopular measures. (James Dallaway, *Constantinople*, 1797.)

Medea: CHECKMATE, I, 5; RAM, 5: Daughter of Aëtes, King of Colchis (the Crimea), and chief votary of Hecate. Celebrated for her skills in magic and as the bitterly scorned wife of Jason. Medea's father had refused to honour his promise to give the Golden Fleece to Jason so Medea, by this time absolutely smitten with the heroic Argonaut, led him into the sacred grove where the fleece hung from the top bough of a great oak tree. The fleece itself was guarded by a dragon which never slept. Medea used a magic potion to drug the beast, thus enabling her lover to secure the object of his quest. The couple then boarded the *Argo* with the stolen fleece, and fled.

Medea's love for Jason knew no bounds. She assented to the premeditated murder of her own brother to help Jason's escape, but her fidelity was not ultimately rewarded. After settling in Corinth and having three children together, Jason soon found himself attracted instead to the daughter of the resident King. He did his best to persuade Medea to release him from his vows of faithfulness, claiming that he wanted to marry the Princess Glauce for political reasons and that his affection was still only for Medea. She outwardly agreed to the divorce, dissembling the perfect embodiment of amicable separation, and magnanimously sending her replacement a golden robe as a wedding present. Glauce readily accepted the gift, but as soon as it touched her skin, it burned the flesh so deeply that Glauce perished in agony. Medea's revenge was only beginning; not content with destroying the most recent object of her husband's affection, she then slaughtered their three sons. Jason soon arrived at the scene of carnage, vowing revenge, but Medea escaped his clutches by taking to the skies in a chariot drawn by winged dragons. In his desolation,

Jason fittingly committed suicide. (E.M. Berens, *Myths and Legends of Greece and Rome*, London.)

MEDICI, Cosimo de': RISING: (1389–1464) Sole controller of the powerful Medici banking empire from the time of his brother Lorenzo's death in 1440, until **Pierfrancesco** was old enough to take over his father's share. Lorenzo was also the *de facto* ruler of the republic of Florence. When the two brothers inherited the banking empire in 1429, its assets already totalled 180,000 florins, with branches in Florence, **Bruges**, London, **Venice**, Pisa, Avignon, Milan, Geneva (moving to Lyons by 1466) and Naples. Each branch was run as a separate partnership by its profit-sharing manager, rather than by a purely salaried 'factor'. Each manager was ultimately answerable to the Medici and was not free to engage in mercantile ventures without the approval of the bank's general manager.

Diversification was the key to the bank's success, hence the Medici's involvement in textile manufacture in addition to banking and bills of exchange. The Medici possessed a considerable number of wool and silk factories in Florence—over 300 firms, with a workforce estimated at 10,000. The fifteenth century was characterised by a shortage in actual hard currency, so barter and bills of exchange provided a viable alternative for the success of trade and enterprise. Bills of exchange enabled merchants to transfer assets and purchasing power without having to transfer hard currency across dangerous routes. The Medici bank managed to increase their own profits by successfully speculating on currency exchanges, allowing them to lend money at a profit. Technically, this was forbidden by the Christian church, but commission taken on exchanges from one currency to another allowed the bank to circumvent the strict ecclesiastical ruling on usury. Reliable couriers were employed to carry the reports of each junior profit-sharing partner back to the headquarters in Florence. The secrecy of these dealings guaranteed their rate of profit. The dispatches were always coded, so the details of their commerce were never revealed to rivals. Anyone able to break the Medici cipher could sell his secrets to the highest bidder and potentially undermine the bank's profit margin or destroy an investor.

Cosimo virtually retired from the day-to-day running of the decentralised branches in 1451, when gout severely impaired his ability to participate on a practical level. The assets of the company, then estimated at 54,000 florins, were split between the general manager of the Medici empire, Giovanni d'Amerigo Benci, Cosimo's two sons **Piero** and **Giovanni**, and his nephew, Pierfrancesco. After Benci's death in 1455, the bank never found another general manager who was able to keep a tight rein on the activities of its branch managers. **Tommaso Portinari**, of the Bruges branch, was thus able to break Cosimo's ultimate banking injunction, that the branches and managers should not lend money to princes, courts or the upper aristocracy. Such debts could easily become impossible to redeem. The bank's decentralised struc-

ture caused problems later, especially in Bruges when the Medici bank as a whole became responsible for bad debts incurred by the reckless decisions of its semiautonomous managers.

Cosimo and his sons virtually ran Florence between them; not by overtly seizing power, but by controlling the voting system of the republic. They placed their allies in strategic positions and alienated or exiled their enemies (like the **Strozzi**). In addition to his financial support for the city, Cosimo was also a great patron of the arts and of learning. He commissioned many works from **Donatello** and Michelozzo, who designed the Palazzo Medici. His simple tomb at the family's church of San Lorenzo belies the reality of the inscription, *pater patriae* (father of his country) as the Medici family continued to control Florence both politically and financially. (Raymond de Roover, *The Rise and Decline of the Medici Bank*, Harvard, 1963.)

MEDICI, Giovanni de': RAM: (1421–1463) Son of **Cosimo**, but eclipsed in control of the bank by his brother **Piero**, who survived him by six years.

MEDICI, Giovanni de': See **Leo X**.

MEDICI, Giulio de': See **Clement VII**.

MEDICI, Lorenzo de', the Magnificent: (1449–1492) Son of **Piero**, but more concerned with politics and statesmanship than the fortunes of the family's banking empire. The bank was to decline under Lorenzo as he increasingly concentrated on the domination of Florence, ruling his 'Republic' as a powerful oligarchy. Like his grandfather **Cosimo**, Lorenzo was a great patron of the arts and the Renaissance humanists flourished under his regime.

Lorenzo greatly encouraged the Platonic Academy of Florence. Unlike Cosimo, Lorenzo and Piero collected great artistic works for their own private collections rather than for public buildings.

Lorenzo's control over Florence was not without its opponents. His Florentine rivals and enemies the Pazzi plotted against the Medici, particularly because of the family's political and dynastic aspirations. The rebellion against Lorenzo was helped by Pope **Sixtus IV**, and culminated in the Pazzi assassination plot of 1478. The Pazzi were unsuccessful in their attempt to dethrone Lorenzo, although relations between the Medici and the papacy did not improve.

MEDICI, Pierfrancesco de': RISING: (1430–1476) Nephew to **Cosimo de' Medici**, and husband of Laudomia **Acciajuoli**. This link with the most powerful banking house of the fifteenth century allowed the fortunes of the Acciajuoli to improve not only financially, but in terms of court and curia appointments in the latter half of the century.

MEDICI, Piero de': SCALES: (1416–1469) Son of, and successor to **Cosimo**, he outlived his father and brother **Giovanni de' Medici** to become the next leader of the bank. As the younger brother, his inclination had been more towards the study of humanism than finance, but he did his best to control the lending levels of individual branches during the five years he was to act as its titular head. Like his father, Piero was crippled by gout, and spent much of his leadership bedridden.

War in the Levant was endemic from 1463 to 1479, and any Venetian bank with investments risked forfeiture with the enlargement of the Ottoman Empire. Economic depression was bound to follow, and Piero did his best to consolidate the bank's holdings and assess the level of debt for each branch. Following his death, the branch passed on to his sons **Lorenzo** and Giuliano, but management of the branches devolved to Francesco de Tommaso Sassetti.

MEDICI, Prosper Schiaffino de Camulio de': RISING, 33: See **Camulio, Prosper Schiaffino de' Medici**.

MÉDICIS, Catherine de: QUEENS: (1519–1589) Wife of Henri II of France, she was the daughter of **Lorenzo de' Medici**, Duke of Urbino, and Madeleine de la Tour d'Auvergne. Described from contemporary accounts as tall, with large dark brown eyes, and dark hair, the least flattering summation of her facial attributes (based on the portraits) concentrates on the plain, sallow face with its baggy cheeks and 'goggle-eyes'.

An orphan at three weeks of age, she was reared by her grandmother, who sent her to Rome to be closer to her relative, Pope **Leo X**. With the death of her grandmother in 1520, and Leo in 1521, her aunt Clarice became her new guardian. Clarice married **Filippo Strozzi**, friend of Pope **Clement VII**

(Clarice's second cousin twice removed. Catherine was also related to the king's mistress, **Diane de Poitiers**, again through Clarice).

Catherine was educated in Florence at the convent of Santa Lucia, and then at Murate, which kept her out of the way of the Medici family's many enemies, and was betrothed when thirteen. Her marriage contract with **Henri II** was signed at **Anet**, with the celebrations lasting thirty-four days. The marriage followed in 1534, giving her enough time to learn the language of her new husband and subjects. The first years of marriage were without issue (other than rumours of her infertility, or that of the king); the elderly Cardinal de Guise offered to help her apparent sexual problems by reading her the most lascivious verses of Horace, but she declined, having no taste for '*les beaux poètes du diable*'. The court physician, Jean Fernel, is eventually said to have cured her with a course of myrrh pills, having already performed a minor operation on Henri II, which suggests the medical problem was her husband's. (See **A *Madame la Dauphine***.) Their first child was born in 1544: **Francis**, Dauphin of France; followed by a steady succession of other potential heirs.

Catherine de Médicis adapted well to the artistic and cultural possibilities offered by French court life, employing **Della Robbia** and **Limousin** amongst others. She also had a passion for enamels, astrology and alchemy. Her library was extensive, comprising 4,500 books, and 776 ancient manuscripts, many of which came from the libraries of **Piero Strozzi** and **Lorenzo de' Medici**. Her range of conversation was extensive, and she was regarded as a generous and accomplished hostess, holding regular concerts, often several times a week. Dance music was her favourite, especially those which required delicacy and precision, such as the pavane.

In public, she was often severely dressed, saving her rich clothes imported from Italy for court receptions. It was Catherine who introduced the ruff and the corset to the court; essential to the maintenance of a thirteen-inch waist which was her ideal of feminine perfection. Her court etiquette was similarly remarked upon as a model of perfection: she behaved with wit and verve in public, yet was said to have blind rages in privacy. Given the discrepancy between public masque and private behaviour, courtiers were said to be somewhat alarmed when she referred to them as '*mon ami*'. In rivalry to the King's mistress, Diana the huntress, Catherine de Médicis showed her skill and courage when hunting. She always carried an *arbaletre* (crossbow) and is credited with having been the first woman to ride side-saddle.

After the death of her husband in 1559 and the eldest of their sons the following year, as Regent Catherine attempted to pursue a policy of conciliation between the **de Guise** and Bourbon families, and also favoured toleration of the Protestants. In 1561 during the minority of Charles IX, she issued an Edict of Toleration for those of the Reformed religion. The attempt to pacify the Protestants ended in 1568 after the second civil war; when it became clear that the militant Protestants sought equality rather than just toleration. Despite her attempts to alleviate religious conflict, by the end of her life, France had been split in two by its religious wars. (Francis Watson, *Life and Times of Catherine de Medici*; Baron Alphonse de Ruble, *La Première Jeunesse de Marie Stuart*; Louis Battifol, *The Century of the Renaissance*, tr. E.F. Buckley, London, 1916.)

Medusa: KINGS, I, 7: Medusa the Gorgon, one of three beautiful sisters, was transformed into a monster with hair of snakes as a punishment for sleeping with Poseidon. She could turn anyone who looked on her to stone, but was eventually destroyed by Perseus.

Megrim: CHECKMATE, V, 9: See **Migraine.**

MEHMET II: RAM: (1432–1481) Also known as Mehmet the Conqueror, the head of the Ottoman Empire came to power in 1451, and ruled for the next thirty years. He made fratricide a monarchical policy, slaughtering his brothers to ensure he would be the sole successor, without any sibling rivalry to interfere in his great military campaigns. The son of a Christian mother, Mehmet was without doubt a devout Muslim, despite Pope **Pius's** optimistic attempts to convert him,

Within two years of coming to power, he attacked and conquered Constantinople. Military and naval superiority ensured victory for the Ottomans, and led to the creation of Constantinople (or Stamboul) as their new imperial capital. It was at this point that the young Sultan earned the epithet of 'Conqueror' and created the Empire's symbol of sovereignty: the crescent and star on the blood-red flag. A creative poet and inspired leader, his aim was to build an empire which would surpass that of Alexander the Great and, more to the point, be Muslim-controlled, spreading from East to West. Having obtained the capital of the Byzantine Empire, he then set about collecting its colonies, including **Trebizond.** Serbia and Bosnia soon followed, and only Albania held out against him until 1468, under **Skanderbeg.** In total, Mehmet conquered twelve kingdoms and two hundred cities. Religious tolerance was guaranteed to his new subjects if they paid the appropriate infidel tax. In a catalogue of ruthless campaigns and great loss of life, perhaps one of his more humane campaigns was the attempt to depose Prince Vlad III of Walachia (better known as Vlad the Impaler, or Dracul 'the devil', the character behind Bram Stoker's fictional vampire), replacing him with his non-bloodthirsty brother Radu in 1462. (Franz Babinger, *Mehmet the Conqueror and His Time*, tr. Ralph Manheim, Princeton, 1978.)

Mehterkhané: PAWN, 20: The first military band formed by the Turks to accompany them into battle. It consisted of trumpets, fifes, drums and cymbals; each regiment would have its own band. The Prophet Mohammed initially banned all musical instruments, but lifted the injunction on the above exceptions.

The Ottoman Sultans would have a consort of the best musicians playing in the Seraglio twice a day and would also send them to play outside the windows of foreign ambassadors on the days they were to be received in audiences by the Sultan. (Alexander Pallis, *In the Days of the Janissaries*.)

Melita: KNIGHTS, II, 2: The island of honey. Originally called Maleth (a haven) by the Phoenicians, corrupted to Melita by the Greeks.

Melpomene: KINGS, IV, 2: One of the nine muses; the singing goddess who presided over tragedy.

Melusine: SCORPIONS, 9, 15: See **Fairy Melusine**.

Men live, not while they breathe, but while they live well: CHECKMATE, II, 9: Contemporary quote from the *Panegyricus*, printed in Paris in 1540, urging the moral reform of French life.

Mene, Mene, Tekel, Upharsin: KINGS, I, 3: The fateful warning which appeared on the wall at Belshazzar's feast, as interpreted in Daniel, 5, 25ff.

Mercenaries: RAM: Or *condottiere*, from the Italian *condotta*, meaning the contractual period of labour for hire. In the endemic Italian wars of the fifteenth century, many groups of mercenaries were headed by foreign, entrepreneurial captains, commanding their battle-hardened companies to lucrative profits. The Italian city-states needed imported mercenaries to guard their frontiers against ambitious neighbours. The companies themselves comprised mixed bands of heavy cavalry, accompanied by infantry and mounted crossbowmen, in addition to the standard men at arms. The contract itself was seen as a business venture. A *condotta* or contract would be signed between the mercenary and his employer, arranging for the provision of a certain number of troops for a certain period of time. In return, the captain would receive a guaranteed rate of pay for his men (and often the profits from looting).

Mercenaries were not only attracted by the statutory rate of pay, or the glory of honour on the battlefield, but also by the possibilities of booty following a victorious battle or siege. Many renegades and campaigners rose to fame and fortune during the Italian wars. **Sir John Hawkwood** took advantage of the end of the Hundred Years War to move his veterans to Italy. Known as the **White Company**, Hawkwood's men were renowned for the unity and loyalty they exhibited in the field.

Mercenary captains could be motivated by intense personal hatred in addition to the financial reward for their service: the bitter feud which raged between **Urbino** and **Sigismondo Malatesta** lay behind the war for Naples as much as if not more than the territorial ambition of its rulers.

Handgunners, in addition to cavalry and foot soldiers, were an increasing feature of hired labour when it came to the Italian wars (see **Guns**). Hand firearms were increasingly used to harass the enemy, protect the flanks of an advancing troop, and to mow down the opposition's men at arms, easily piercing their armour.

Campaigns took place in the spring and autumn, when the weather was most clement for fighting, and when most damage could be done to crops. A scorched-earth policy could shatter a state's economy better than a prolonged siege. Starvation and disease were two of the most effective weapons of warfare. Often more troops would die from camp fever than on the battlefield itself. (Michael Mallett, *Mercenaries and their Masters*, London, 1974.)

Mercury: KINGS, II, 2: Messenger of the gods; equivalent to the Greek Hermes. Inventive and versatile, with a special talent for trickery and cunning. Born in the morning, by midday he had invented the lyre and by the evening he had stolen fifty head of cattle from his brother Apollo which could not be found. Mercury or Hermes is herald to all the gods and guide of the dead in Hades, and also the god of sleep and dreams. Amongst his other roles, he is the god of mining and digging for lost or buried treasure. As messenger, he doubles as the god of roads, and patron of tradespeople and thieves.

Merry Report the Vice, court-crier and squire: PAWN, 18: A character appearing in the play by John Heywood (c. 1497–c. 1578): *The Play of the Weather* (1533). Mortals complain to the Greek gods that the present climate is unsuitable to their particular needs. Each character from the Miller to the Laundress demands a contradictory change. To please all of them Merry Report gives each character the weather they request, hence the changeable nature of the British climate. (Karl J. Holzknecht, *Tudor and Stuart Plays in Outline*, London, 1963.)

Meskale: PAWN, 13: Turkish pan pipes, said to have been invented by Moses. (Alexander Pallis, *In the Days of the Janissaries*.)

Mesnevi verse: PAWN, 13: See **Ottoman poetry.**

Messalina: KINGS, II, 2: The third wife of Emperor Claudius; notorious for profligate and licentious behaviour; especially with reference to her conduct in public brothels. She was eventually executed for her supposed involvement in a plot against the Emperor's, her husband's, life.

Meum est propositum: CASTLE, II, 10: Quoted in full in the text; one of the greatest early drinking songs popularised by the goliards (travelling scholars) of the twelfth and thirteenth centuries:

> I would die where I would dine
> In a tavern to recline

> Then would angels pray the glibber
> God have mercy on this bibber.

Midas: KINGS, I, 1: King of Phrygia, and friend of **Dionysus** who granted him the power to turn everything he touched to gold. When Pan and Apollo were having a musical contest on flute and lyre, they chose Midas to be the judge. When Midas decided in favour of Pan, Apollo took his revenge by giving Midas the ears of an ass. Midas tried to hide them under his cap, but the servant who cut his hair discovered his secret. This knowledge obsessed the barber, but not daring to tell another living soul, he dug a hole in the ground, whispered into it, 'King Midas has asses ears', then filled it up. Unfortunately, a reed grew up on the exact site, which in its whispers betrayed the secret.

Migraine: CASTLE, III, 7: An acute and debilitating headache, often preceded by symptoms including the total or partial loss of vision, loss of coordination and nausea. The headache itself can last for several days. There are several sixteenth-century cures for the 'heterocrania' or 'blue devils'; one of the more drastic suggestions is to place a hangman's noose round the patient's forehead. The 'brain pan of the blessed St Michael' (CASTLE, III, 11) is a cure suggested in the play by John Heywood (c. 1497–c. 1578), *The Pardoner and the Friar*. A traditional fifteenth-century cure for the migraine was the recipe below, used as a tried and tested poultice:

> Take half a dishful of barley, one handful each of betony, vervain, and other herbs that are good for the head; and when they be well boiled together, take them up and wrap them in a cloth and lay them to the sick head, and it shall be whole.

Vervain, or 'holy herb', was a very powerful antidote and supposed to cure scrofula, counteract rabies, cancel out poison, and consolidate friendship. As a pledge of good faith, it was worn and carried by **heralds**. It is still common in nerve tonics and the treatment of both migraine and depression. The temporary relief of migraine's early symptoms can also be effected by eating raisins, which contain natural aspirin, and the consumption of alcohol. (CHECKMATE, III, 3). (Karl J. Holzknecht, *Tudor and Stuart Plays in Outline*, London, 1963; Stephen Paget, *Ambroise Paré and His Times*; Maggie Black, *The Medieval Cookbook*, London, 1993.)

MILAN, Duke of: RISING: See **Sforza, Francesco.**

Milanese armour: KINGS, I, 3: Milanese craftsmen were the finest of the sixteenth century in the engraving and gilding of steel morions, corselets, point de fers, pikes, halberds and even cannon and arquebuses. Easier to keep than traditional iron armour (which required polishing to avoid rust), Milanese armour was popular amongst professional soldiers for its visual and practical appeal. The armour of **Henri II** of France was made in Paris and Milan by two Milanese brothers, César and Baptiste Gamber. (J. Quicherat, *Histoire du Costume en France.*)

Milesian: RAM, 18: The Milesians were amongst the early colonists of Ireland, tall and fair, compared with the **firbolg** natives. The Milesians are descendants of the mythical Spanish king Milesius whose sons conquered the island and its natives, calling themselves *Gaels.*

Mille douceurs, mille bons mots, mille plaisirs: KNIGHTS, III, 13: See **A la fontaine je voudrais.**

Milo: KINGS, Gambit: (c. 6th century BC) Celebrated athlete of Crotona. He carried a four-year-old heifer on his shoulders through the stadium at Olympia, eating the whole of it in a single day. In his old age Milo was passing through a forest where he saw the trunk of a tree split open by woodcutters. Testing his strength on the trunk, he attempted to split the tree further, but his hands became trapped in the crack. Thus pinioned, Milo was attacked and devoured by wolves. (Harry Thurston Peck, ed., *Harper's Dictionary of Classical Literature and Antiquities,* NY, 1962.)

Mind, voice, study, power and will, Is only set to love thee, Philip, still: CASTLE III, 8: Translation of the welcoming placards erected in London for the Royal Entry of Queen **Mary Tudor** and her new husband, King **Philip II.** The verses in question were written in Latin by **John Elder** and held aloft by two 'giants', standing on London Bridge. See also **O noble Prince, sole hope of Caesar's side.** (Helen Simpson, *The Spanish Marriage.*)

Minerva: QUEENS, IV, 3: Roman goddess; also known to the Greeks as **Pallas-Athene.** Goddess of wisdom, war and the liberal arts. Credited with playing the flute before Juno and Venus; a skill she abandoned when she saw how much her concentration on playing the instrument distorted her face. She was particularly worshipped on Rhodes; it is said that Jupiter rained a shower of gold upon the island which had held his daughter in such high esteem, hence the golden sands of the rivers.

Mis arreos son las armas: PAWN, 29: The anonymous Spanish lyric 'Romance della Constancia':

> *Mis arreos son las armas, mi descanso es pelear,*
> *Mi cama las duras peñas, mi dormir siempre velar,*
> *Las manidas son escuras, los caminos por usar,*
> *El cielo con sus mudanzas ha por bien de me dañar,*

> *Andando de sierra en sierra, por orillas de la mar,*
> *Por probar si mi ventura hay lugar donde avadar.*
> *Pero por vos, mi señora, todo se ha de comportar.*

> My ornaments are tools of war,
> My sweet repose is battle,
> My mattress is of bitter pain,
> My time of sleep is wakeful.

> My shelter is a public way,
> My road unbending ranges,
> The sky instead of gentle climes
> Afflicts me with its changes.

> From land to land, by running wave
> I seek some other fortune,
> While finding, lady, as your slave,
> No respite from this burden.

(Tr. D.D.)

Mnemosyne: CHECKMATE, III, 2: Daughter of Uranus and **Gaea**, symbolic of the marriage of Heaven and Earth. She was one of the Titanides and the goddess of memory, considered also to be the mother of the Muses, in the company of whom she was generally worshipped.

Mo chridh: PAWN, 26: 'My love'.

Momus: KINGS, III, 4: The god of mockery and ridicule, whose main aim was to find fault in anything and everything. When Hephaestus showed him the first man he had created, Momus criticised the mortal, saying Hephaestus should have included an aperture in the breast so the gods could see his innermost thoughts. He even found fault with **Aphrodite**; she was too talkative and her sandals made too much noise when she walked.

Mon Dieu qui m'as créé, je te supplie, gardemoy: CHECKMATE, V, 7: The prayer of Blaise de Montluc:

O Lord Who made me: help me this day keep untarnished my wit and my judgment, which Thou hast given me, and which I hold only from Thou. And if it is Thy will that I shall die, let me keep in death the good name I strive to deserve, through every danger. I do not ask for my life, for Thy wish is mine also. Thy will be done: I submit the whole to Thy divine mercy.

(Tr. D.D.)

MONTEFELTRO, Federigo da, Duke of Urbino: RISING: See **Urbino, Federigo da Montefeltro, Duke of.**

MONTMORENCY, Anne de: QUEENS: (1491–1576) Marshal, Grand Master and Constable of France. In exile from 1541 until **Henri II's** accession, when he was brought back to court by **Diane de Poitiers.** The Constable of France and the King were so close that it was said of them 'one is the breath of the other'. Described as having a fringe beard and moustache, short crewcut hair, a fleshy nose and a pug-like face with pouched eyes, and known unaffectionately as Le Grand Rabroueur, 'the great snubber'. He was considered to be a harsh, arrogant and sometimes brutal disciplinarian, as proved by his suppression of the Salt Tax revolt. In 1548 the institution of the *Gabelle*, or Salt Tax, caused a revolt in Bordeaux, resulting in the murder of Governor Monniens at the hands of the rebellious citizens. Montmorency and **François de Guise** were sent to control the situation: Montmorency wasted no time on concessions or negotiations but immediately sent in troops and cannon to raze the town hall and abolish the privileges of the city. In action and parades, when it came to a show of military force, Montmorency preferred cold unadorned steel to flashy displays of arms; he was furious at Bonnivet's troops returning from Piedmont to suppress Guyene when they arrived resplendent with gilded weaponry.

Montmorency became distanced from the King, owing to the influence held by the King's principal mistress Diane de Poitiers and the increasing power of his hereditary enemies, the **de Guises,** and he became an ally of **Catherine de Médicis.** Placing **Jenny Fleming** in Henri's path caused a rift between Diane and the Constable that was not resolved until 1556 when the rivals for the King's affection united their offspring in several alliances. The eldest of Montmorency's eleven sons married Diane's daughter, while his second-eldest son married Diane de Poitiers' granddaughter. Montmorency lived to the age of seventy-six, having served under five French kings. He died as he had lived, on the field of battle. (Paul van Dyke, *Catherine de Medici.*)

Mopsus: CHECKMATE, III, 2: Son of Ampyx and Chlonis from Thessaly. He was the prophet and soothsayer of Jason and his Argonauts but died on his return from Colchis when bitten by a serpent.

More, Sir Thomas: KNIGHTS, III, 16: (1478–1535) Humanist scholar and Lord Chancellor of England from 1529 until 1532, and the author of *Utopia* (published in 1516). A lifelong correspondent with Erasmus, More would not agree to Henry VIII's church reforms. As a devout Catholic, More refused to take any oath that undermined the authority of the Pope, for which Henry VIII had him confined to the Tower of London. He was found guilty of high treason and executed in 1535.

Mors sine morte, finis sine fine: QUEENS, IV, 6: From the Latin, meaning 'Death without Death, end without ending'.

Mouldiewarp: KINGS, Gambit: Scots and old English word for the common mole.

Mount Sinai: UNICORN: See **Sinai, Mount.**

Muchos Grisones, y pocos Bayardos: CHECKMATE, II, 7: 'Too many Grisones (plodding Swiss) and not enough Bayards (dashing heroes)'; a Spanish comment on the composition of the French army.

Multum in parvo: CASTLE, III, 9: 'Much in small bulk'.

Mummification: CASTLE, I, 1: Powdered mummies were often used in medieval physicians' remedies, to be taken internally. Ambroise Paré, the sixteenth-century French surgeon, was much against Christians eating Jews, Egyptians and Chaldees who had been embalmed; particularly when low-class embalming was only so much asphalt. Counterfeit mummies were relatively easy to produce: eviscerated gallows bodies were dried in ovens, then dipped in pitch to give them the appearance and consistency of their Egyptian lookalikes. It is not recorded if the taste of the end product was similar. (Stephen Paget, *Ambroise Paré and His Times.*)

Mumsconduren: PAWN, 17: Base Latin term used to describe the **Bektashi,** meaning 'putters out of the candle' from the proverb 'when the candle goes out the girl/daughter cannot be distinguished from the woman/wife'. It was believed that the Bektashi practised incest as a feature of their ecstatic religious devotion. (E. J. W. Gibb, *History of Ottoman Poetry.*)

Murraghach: QUEENS, II, 2: Or merrow; Gaelic for 'mermaid'.

Muscovy Company: CASTLE; See **Chancellor, Diccon.**

Mustapha: PAWN, 18: The handsome and popular eldest son of **Suleiman's** favourite Sultana, Gulbehar (Rose of Spring). She was supplanted in his affections by **Roxelana,** who wished to make her own son-in-law Rustem Pasha the Grand Vizier instead of Mustapha. Suleiman had given his eldest son positions of power, but under the influence of Roxelana began to fear Mustapha's ambition. The narrative account of Mustapha's execution as engineered by Roxelana is accurate. When the Sultan summoned Mustapha to his headquarters at Eregli in 1553, his son feared the worst but would not be dissuaded from answering the command, saying, 'If he were to lose his life he could wish to do no better than to give it back to him from whom he had received it'.

Suleiman is said to have silently watched as his son struggled against the three mutes ordered to strangle him with a bow string. Mustapha had been very popular with his **Janissaries**, but they were soon pacified with a bribe of 600,000 ducats. Rustem Pasha diplomatically withdrew for the time being, to be replaced by Ahmet Pasha, who himself fell victim to a similar plot and was beheaded in 1555. Roxelana's son-in-law then nobly stepped in as Grand Vizier. (Roger B. Merriman, *Suleiman the Magnificent, 1520–1566*, London, 1944.)

My beloved is unto me as a cluster of camphire in the vineyards of Engedi: PAWN, 11: SCORPIONS, 9: From the biblical Song of Solomon, I, 14. The Engedi referred to in the 'Song of Songs' is in the Holy Land, not the Engedi referred to in SCORPIONS, 9, which is in Cyprus. See also **A garden enclosed is my sister, my spouse.**

My bird Willie, my boy Willie: KINGS, II, 2: The anonymous Scots 'Ballad of Child Maurice'. The ballad itself is older than the form in which it is presented. See also **Ye leid, ye leid, ye filthy nurse.** Extract:

> Child Maurice was an erle's son
> His name it waxed wide;
> It was nac for his great riches
> Nor yit his meikle [great] pride,
> But it was for his mother gay
> Wha liv'd on Carron side.
>
> 'Whar sall I get a bonny boy
> 'That will win hose and shoen,
> 'That will gae to lord Barnard's ha [hall],
> 'And bid his lady come?
>
> 'And ye maun rin [must run] errand, Willie,
> 'And ye maun rin wi speid [speed];
> 'When ither boys gang on their feet
> 'Ye sall ha [have] prancing steid.'
>
> 'Oh no! oh no! my master deir,
> 'I dar na [dare not] for my life:
> 'I'll no gae to the bauld barons,
> For to triest furth [tryst forth] his wife.'
>
> 'My bird Willie, my boy Willie,
> 'My deir Willie,' he said.
> 'How can ye strive against the streim?
> 'For I sall be obeyed.'

My heid did yak yester nicht: CHECKMATE, III, 3: William Dunbar's (c. 1460–1520) sixteenth-century poem, 'On His Heid-Ake', mainly quoted within the text.

> My heid did yak yester nicht,
> This day to mak that I na micht,
> So sair [sore] the magryme dois me menyie [accompany],
> Perseing my brow as ony ganyie [dart],
> That scant I luik may on the licht.
>
> And now, schir, laitlie, eftir mes [Mass],
> To dyt [poem] thocht I begowthe to dres [write],
> The sentence lay full evill till [hard to] find,
> Unsleipit in my heid behind,
> Dulkt in dulness and distres.
>
> Full oft at morrow I upryse,
> Quehn that my curage sleipeing lyis,
> For mirth, for menstrallie [minstrelsy] and play,
> For din nor danceing nore deray [revelry],
> It will nocht walkin [waken] me no wise.

(Tom Scott, *Late Medieval Scots Poetry*, London, 1967.)

My joy, cry peip! where ever thou be!: KINGS, III, 4: See **Cry peip! where ever thou be!**

My lute, awake! perform the last: QUEENS, IV, 4: The poem by Sir **Thomas Wyatt**, 'My Lute Awake!' Partly quoted within the text, the full poem is given below:

> My lute awake! perform the last
> Labour that thou and I shall waste,
> And end that I have now begun:
> And when this song is sung and past,
> My lute be still, for I have done.
>
> As to be heard where ear is none,
> As lead to grave in marble stone,
> My song may pierce her heart as soon.
> Should we then sigh, or sing, or moan?
> No, no, my lute, for I have done.
>
> The rocks do not so cruelly
> Repulse the waves continually

As she my suit and affection,
So that I am past remedy;
Whereby my lute and I have done.

Proud of the spoil that thou hast got
Of simple hearts through Love's shot,
By whom, unkind, thou hast them won:
Think not he hath his bow forgot,
Although my lute and I have done.

Vengeance shall fall on thy disdain
That makest but game on earnest pain;
Think not alone under the sun
Unquit to cause thy lovers plain;
Although my lute and I have done.

May chance thee lie withered and old
In winter nights that are so cold,
Plaining in vain unto the moon;
Thy wishes then dare not be told:
Care then who list, for I have done.

And then may chance thee to repent
The time that thou hast lost and spent
To cause thy lovers sigh and swoon:
Then shalt thou know beauty but lent,
And wish and want as I have done.

Now cease my lute: this is the last
Labour that thou and I shall waste,
And ended is that we begun.
Now is this song both sung and past:
My lute be still, for I have done.

(Gerald Bullett, ed., *Silver Poets of the Sixteenth Century*, London, 1970.)

Ná buail do choin gan chinaid: QUEENS, II, 2: 'Without a fault of his, beat not thy hound'. Advice from the Irish hero, Finn, master of three hundred hounds and two hundred pups. His favourite hound, Conbec, slept in the same bed as his master. (Edmund Hogan, *The Irish Wolfdog*.)

Naft: SCORPIONS, 24: The Arabic word for firearms, not necessarily **naphtha**. The term is first used in the Arabic records from around 1460, and clearly refers to weapons which fire solid projectiles rather than combustible materials. Their efficacy relied on the development of gunpowder (the mixture of charcoal, sulphur and saltpetre) and of field artillery. The **cannon** came first, followed by the increasing sophistication of handguns (see **Guns**). Firearms were used by the Ottomans long before the **Mamelukes** lowered themselves to their use, one of the main reasons that the Ottomans were able to conquer the rival Egyptian kingdom. (David Ayalon, *Gunpowder and Firearms in the Mameluke Kingdom*, London, 1956.)

Nailed for . . . horabull lyes and sedyssyous wordes: CASTLE, III, 12: A humiliating form of corporal punishm.... meted out to agitators and scandalmongers in London at the time of **Wyatt**'s execution in April 1554. Common as a punishment throughout Scotland and England; the miscreant's ear would be nailed to a fixed post at a prominent public place; often at the marketplace. As specifically noted in this case, the victim was nailed by his ear to the pillory at Cheap in London. (*Machlyn's Diary*, 1554, as printed by the Camden Society.)

Naphtha: SCORPIONS, 24: The proper name for the combustible weapon also called 'Greek fire' (KINGS, IV, 1) or wildfire, which was greatly used by the Christians during the Crusades. Although the exact recipe of the weapon was kept a secret, the formula basically consisted of a mixture of saltpetre, pounded sulphur, unrefined ammoniacal salt, resin and turps; a highly combustible assortment of chemicals. The mixture was packed into thin pots, small enough to fit into the hand. The mouth of the pot would be sealed with paper or linen, then secured by cords soaked in sulphur. The free ends of the cord were lit just prior to throwing the weapon, to ensure that it would ignite and explode as soon as it reached the enemy. The devastation it caused was a cross between that resulting from the use of a hand grenade and a flame thrower.

Naphtha was particularly popular as a siege weapon during the Crusades, especially when used against siege towers or other large flammable fixed targets. The **Janissaries** with their long flowing white robes made excellent targets; two or three men could be set on fire with one shot. Also popular with the **Knights of St John** was their refinement on the above, the **fire hoop**. (Ernle Bradford, *The Great Siege*, 1961.)

National characteristics: There are many allusions—not always flattering—to national characteristics in the Lymond Chronicles. These references include 'Germans woo like lions, Italians like foxes, Spaniards like friars and French like stinging bees' (CASTLE, III, 7); 'Greeks in bed, Italians at table, are most neat' (CASTLE, III, 13); 'To pass over grief . . . the Italian sleeps; the Frenchman sings; the German drinks; the Spaniard laments, and the Englishman goes to plays' (PAWN, 5). These are all taken from Fynes Moryson's notes on his travels in Europe from 1615 to 1617. See also *Eine Deutscher bulet wie ein bawar*. (Fynes Moryson, Gent., *An Itinerary*, 1617.)

Natura sunt Turcae avari et pecuniarium avide: PAWN, 22: 'The Turks are by nature greedy and desirous of money'.

NAVES, Sor de: SCORPIONS. See **Carlotta, Queen of Cyprus.**

Nay brother, I wyll not daunce: KINGS, IV, 3: From the medieval morality play *Mankind*; the reference is to the character of Mercy who will not join in with the irreverent foolery of Naught, Nowadays and Newguise. (G. A. Lester, *Three Late Medieval Morality Plays*, London, 1981.)

Naxos: Much of the fifteenth-century political manoeuvring which took place in the Levant after the fall of Constantinople came about through the opportune marriages, not to mention guile, of the princesses of the island of Naxos in the eastern Mediterranean, the largest and most beautiful of the Cyclades, and famous—apart from its marble and lemons—as the place where Ariadne was abandoned by the legendary Theseus. In real life, Naxos was seized in 1207 by a Venetian, Marco Sanudi, who later put himself under the protection of the Latin Emperor Henry of Flanders, and was eventually made Duke of the Archipelago. The Sanudi, and the following dynasty of the Crespi, ruled over much of the Cyclades for 360 years.

About 1441, Niccolò Crespo, Duke of Naxos, took in marriage Valencia, daughter of John IV, the Grand Comnenos, Emperor of **Trebizond**. It was a marriage of extraordinary importance, since Valencia's sister Theodora married the Prince **Uzum Hasan**, leader of the White Sheep Tribe of Persia, while her first cousin was the wife of King George VIII of Georgia—both being potential allies against the Ottoman Turk. When Valencia's father John died in 1455, his brother **David Conmenos**, Valencia's uncle, became the next and last Emperor of Trebizond. Having adequately supplied themselves with powerful uncles, in-laws and cousins, the Duke and Duchess of Naxos then set about marrying off their own daughters, of whom there were at least seven, to Venetians. Of these seven, Violante married and had a son Paul by **Caterino Zeno**, of a powerful family already linked with the Crespi in the Levant. Caterino, a Venetian merchant and diplomat, spent some time at the court of Uzum Hasan (and was invited to visit him in bed with his wife). Valenza married Giovanni Loredano of a famous seagoing family, who became Venetian Vice-Baillie in Cyprus, and Fiorenza married **Marco Corner**, who ran the vast **sugar** plantations at Episkopi, Cyprus, and whose daughter **Caterina** was to marry King **Zacco** and become Queen of Cyprus. Had the states of the West been less deeply embroiled in their own conflicts, the network of marriage and trade might have provided the means of stopping the western advance of Sultan **Mehmet II**: as it was, it certainly delayed it.

Ne suis pas abandoné A chascun qui dit 'Vien ça': CHECKMATE, I, 5: 'I am not at the mercy Of anyone who says "Come here"'.

Nemesis: KINGS, III, 4: Daughter of night and the goddess of equilibrium and restraint in all things. She rewards the modest and humble, but punishes the arrogant, boastful and evil. Because she found the world so full of sin and pride, the goddess is more often employed in chastising the worthless than rewarding the meek.

NEPEJA, Osep Grigorievich: CASTLE: The first Russian Ambassador to England, as brought to the English court by **Diccon Chancellor** in 1556. Little is known about Nepeja's sea journey, although the fated landing at Pitsligo is fully noted by Pitscottie, the chronicler of Scotland:

> In the zeir of God 1556 thair landit ane schip of Muscowe at Aberdein quhilk [which] schip was richlie leidnit [laden] with all kynd of coistlie wairis [wares]. So our northland lordis and lairdis seand [seeing] this schip cum in into Aberdeine they zeid [seized] and tuik [took] all thair geir frome thame and let thame nothing nor wald [would) pay thame for the samyn to the maister of the schip. So the maister of the schip seand this passit [remitted the matter] to the quein [queen, i.e. **Mary de Guise**] thinkand [thinking] to have gottin ae remedie at [from] hir [her] and so thay pleinzeit [petitioned] to hir and I beleive that they gat bot ane littil answer to effectt. And than thay past to Ingland quhilk causit thame to speik meikill [much] evill of Scotland thair.

Nepeja and the other survivors did not therefore arrive in England with a glowing tribute to the Pitsligo residents who had saved their lives but stolen their

Arms of the Muscovy Company

goods. The Queen Dowager did her best to remedy the matter, presenting Nepeja with gifts, but the Pitsligo locals remained intransigent over the matter of the liberated cargo. The total value of the *Edward Bonaventure*'s cargo was estimated at £20,000, but of this only £1,000 worth was salvaged, and only half of this amount was ever returned to the Muscovy Company and its associates.

When Nepeja arrived in London, he was presented with a gold chain to the value of £100, and several items of silver gilt. Unlike European ambassadors, who were allowed to accept presents for themselves, Nepeja had to hand over all personal gifts to the Tsar when he returned home. This was also the case for visiting ambassadors to Muscovy who were clothed by the Tsar; it was not so much a gift as a loan, a fact which shocked Western ambassadors when they were ordered to return their rich robes to the crown prince (CASTLE, II, I). (Charles Oman, *English Silver in the Kremlin*; A.E. Mackay, ed., *Pitscottie's Chronicles of Scotland*, Vol. II, Edinburgh, 1899.)

Nero: KINGS, I, 1: (AD 37–68) Roman Emperor Claudius Caesar, who took the epithet of 'brave' as his imperial title. The first five years of his reign were distinguished by outward modesty and clemency, underpinned though they were with personal excess. In the tenth year of his reign, rumour blamed him for the fire which burned Rome to the ground (which he is said to have watched whilst merrily singing 'The Burning of Troy'). Nero supervised the wholesale persecution of the Christians as scapegoats for the fire; a controversial campaign which some said was for his own pleasure rather than justifiable retribution. He was finally deposed by a rebellion of the Senate and Praetorian guard, and committed suicide with the help of a servant.

New moon in the arms of the old: CHECKMATE, V, 9: It was considered both unlucky to travel and a dangerous sign for sailors to set sail when an outline of the full moon could be seen between the horns of the new moon, as it presages vile weather. Compare the Scots ballad 'Sir Patrick Spens':

> Make haste, make haste, my mirry men all
> Our guid ship sails the morn.
> Or say na sae, my master dear,
> For I fear a deadly storm.

> Late late yestre'en I saw the new moon
> Wi' the auld moon in her arm,
> And I fear, I fear, my dear master,
> That we will come to harm.

Next after dark night, the mirthful morrow: CHECKMATE, I, 3: William Dunbar's (c. 1460–1520) poem: 'The Changes of Life':

> I seek about this world unstable,
> To find one sentence convenable;
> But I can not, in all my wit,
> So true a sentence find of it,
> As say it is deceivable.

> For yesterday I did declare
> How that the time was soft and fair,
> Come in as fresh as peacock feather;
> This day it stingis like an adder,
> Concluding all in my contrair.

> Yesterday fair upsprang the flowers,
> This day they are all slain with showers;
> And fowls in forest that sang clear,
> Now weepis with a dreary cheer,
> Full cold are both their beds and bowers.

> So next to Summer, Winter been;
> Next after comfort, cares keen;
> Next after night, the mirthful morrow;
> Next after joy, aye comes sorrow:
> So is this world and aye has been.

(H. Macaulay Fitzgibbon, ed., *Early English Poetry*, London, n.d.)

Nicholas, St: RISING; RAM, 15: The third-century Bishop of Myra in Lycia, and one of the most popular saints of both the Greek and Latin churches. He is the patron saint of scholars, boys, virgins, brides, parish clerks, thieves and sailors.

One of his most popular miracles concerns the fate of three young virgins. A certain father was preparing to sell his daughters as prostitutes, because he could neither afford to keep them nor give them each a dowry. An angel warned Nicholas of the potential fate of the three girls, whereupon the saint visited their house by night and left a purse of gold on the window ledge of each, more than enough for their dowries.

Another legend tells of three young scholars sent by their father to school in Athens. He implored them to receive a benediction from the bishop *en route*, but when they stopped overnight at Smyrna, they were murdered by the innkeeper who pickled their corpses in a pork tub, planning to sell the tender young flesh as pork. The saint saw the fate of the three boys in a dream and travelled to Smyrna to confront the innkeeper, who in terror confessed to his crime. Nicholas then miraculously brought the three boys back to life.

Honest and devout, Nicholas became the patron of thieves from his intercession that they be forgiven: having confronted a group of villains he made them repent and return their stolen plunder. He is also chosen as the intercessor for mariners and sailors because he calmed a storm whilst on his way to the Holy Land.

The saint is represented iconographically with three gold purses or balls; a symbol which was appropriated both by the **Medici** and pawnbrokers (although there is apparently no connection). Gold bezants are the traditional symbol for money in art and heraldry, whilst the round pills of the Medici were also used as an iconographic representation of the medical profession.

NICOLAY, Nicolas de: KNIGHTS: (1517–c. 1583) Cosmographer to **Henri II** of France. Nicolay began his travels at the age of twenty-five, and accompanied **d'Aramon** on his last mission to Constantinople in 1551. The fifteen years he spent abroad included visits to Germany, Denmark, Sweden, Livonia, Zeeland, England, Scotland, Spain and the Barbary coast. During this time he became fluent in nearly all European languages. Nicolay was also known as 'Nicholas the Painter', from his early training as an artist. This he used to his advantage in the construction of harbour plans and coastal charts. In 1546, after Nicolay had completed a tour of northern Europe, Lord Dudley, Admiral of England (later the Earl of **Warwick**) saw his maps and invited him to return to England with him. Nicolay stayed for a year in the English court, where he was apparently well received.

In 1548 it was brought to the attention of the court that Nicolay had taken copies of English maps back to France. Admiral Dudley had also been rash enough to confide in the loyal Frenchman, and give him a map of the Scottish coastline (the **Lindsé rutter**), which was taken from the Scots pilot Lindsey's observations on his tour of Scotland with **James V** in 1540. Nicolay took this map to France with him, where he had the Scots names translated by a Piedmontese scholar who was familiar with the language. The resulting rutter and chart were given to the King, who passed them on to the Master of the French Galleys, **Leone Strozzi**. The rutter was then used to bring **Mary Queen of Scots** safely to France in 1548.

Nicolay left several of his maps for posterity, including a marine map of the New World which was published in 1554 and a further map of the Orkneys, Hebrides and Scottish coast which was published in Paris in 1583. The rutter used for Mary's escape to France is in the possession of the National Library of Scotland. (E.G.R. Taylor, *Tudor Geography, 1485–1583*.)

Nicosia: SCORPIONS: Capital of Cyprus since the bronze age. The Lusignan monarchy made it their home and the city prospered until it was pillaged by the **Mamelukes** in 1426. The city soon recovered, and by the later fifteenth century it is estimated that the city was home to over 50,000 inhabitants, and covered an area of seven miles. The sprawling nature of the city made it very difficult to defend against possible attack, hence the reason that **Carlotta** concentrated her defences on Kyrenia and **Famagusta** and allowed **Zacco** to take control of the capital so easily in 1460. It was to take him a further four years to subdue the rest of the island.

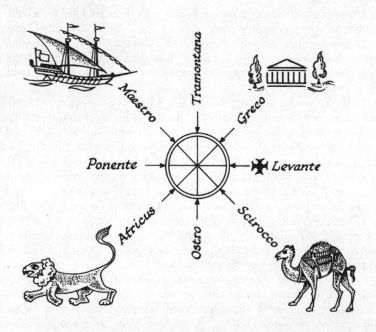

The indefensible nature of the city was permissible in times of peace, but in the later sixteenth century when the Ottoman Empire threatened Venetian control over the city, the decision was made to reduce its circumference by three miles: all churches, buildings and monuments outwith the new walls were razed to the ground. Nevertheless, the city still fell to the Turk in 1570, after a six-week siege, and 20,000 inhabitants died in the fighting which followed. (Rupert Gunnis, *Historic Cyprus*, Cyprus, 1936.)

Night is the stranger's: PAWN, 22: Traditional Turkish proverb on the visitor's rights to hospitality. See also *Loi, foi, nation que ce soit.* (E. J. W. Gibb, *History of Ottoman Poetry.*)

Nil est tam populare quam bonitas: KNIGHTS, III, 13: Latin proverb, possibly from Cicero: 'Nothing is as endearing as goodness'.

Nilometer: UNICORN, 38: Situated on the island of Rawdah (Roda). There has been a working Nilometer at this site since the days of the ancient pharaohs. The current Nilometer dates from the ninth century, although the roof of the building is a modern replica. The purpose of the meter is both financial and hydrographic: the annual flooding of the Nile has always been seen as a heavenly blessing to the inhabitants of the Nile delta, and the greater the water level, then the more abundant will be the crops from the well-irrigated land. The level of water measured on the Nilometer showed the height of the flood to come. Above a certain level was a warning of disastrous flooding, below the level would indicate the certainty of drought. Importantly, this also regulated the level of land tax which could be exacted from the farming population. If the Nilometer showed the height to be under sixteen cubits (thirty-two feet), then no tax would be charged, but the higher the water, then the better the crop, and in direct proportion to that, the greater would be the tax. (John Rodenbeck, ed., *Cairo: Insight City Guides*, Cairo, 1992.)

Ninguno cierre las puertas: QUEENS, IV, 5: 'Let no one shut the doors', line from a *villancico*, a verse form that derives from the Arabic *zéjel*, used by Spanish court poets during the early Renaissance.

No te quiero. No te quiero, Juliano: CHECKMATE, III, 2: This phrase became popular in the French court from 1554, on the occasion of a duel between two Spaniards in the presence of the King. It seems to have been more of a lovers' disagreement rather than slighted chivalric honour. Only the name of the less petulant combatant has been recorded for posterity; one Julian Romero. Julian did not wish to fight and backed off, pursued by his would-be opponent calling, 'No te quiero, Juliano!', 'I don't love you!'. (Brantôme, *Les Vies des Grands Capitaines François*, Vol. IV.)

Non minime ex parte: KINGS, IV, 4: 'Not in the very least'.

Non si puo: il signor e accompagnato: QUEENS, II, 3: 'The gentleman cannot oblige, he is engaged'. A courtesan's warning (*'La signora e accompagnata'*). The gender is changed to that of a man in the text.

NOSTRADAMUS, Michael: CASTLE: (1503–1566) The reputation and prophecies of the doctor and visionary from Provence are almost so well known as to make repetition unnecessary. Michael Nostradamus was the eldest of four children, his family having converted to Christianity from Judaism when he was a child. Nostradamus studied at Avignon, and in 1522 began to study medicine at Montpellier. He graduated with his licence to practise and immediately began to treat victims of the virulent plague sweeping the countryside. Despite his successful experiments with various cures, both his children and his first wife died in a further epidemic of the disease in 1534.

By 1554, he had settled in Marseilles, and had already begun to illuminate others with his prophecies. He was successful in treating an outbreak of plague in Aix, and dealing with the whooping cough in Lyons the same year. His reputation as an astrologer and prophet was spreading: in 1555, the first three hundred of his quatrain prophecies and a part of the fourth *Century* were published. Nostradamus was summoned to the court of **Henri II** the following year. Perhaps diplomatically, he seemed to have told the King and Queen the opposite of the fates of their respective children.

Nostradamus was described as agile, despite later arthritic gout and dropsy, and although taciturn in nature the explanation given for his saying little was that he was devoting all his energies to thinking rather than wasting his time on idle chatter. Even though he came close to heresy for his dabbling in the occult, Nostradamus was a devout Roman Catholic and had no time for Lutherans. His justification for revealing his prophecies was not that he sought self-proclamation or even the hero worship associated with foretelling the future. Nostradamus reasoned that his revelations came directly from God, and revealed his plans for mankind. Thus his inspired prophecies fitted in perfectly with his conception of his faith.

The respect and patronage elicited by the publication of his prophecies drew him away from the practice of medicine, although after his court appearance he was made physician, astrologer and councillor in ordinary to the King. For the next decade, Nostradamus concentrated mostly upon his annual almanacs and completing the rest of the prophecies. He was found dead in his house at Salon in 1566, having accurately predicted the manner of his own demise. The rest of his prophecies were published posthumously in 1568. See **Liepard laisse an ciel extend son œil,** and **Pisse-pot prophet.** (Erica Cheetham, *The Prophecies of Nostradamus*, London, 1975; Charles A. Ward, *The Oracles of Nostradamus.*)

Not alike are the inmates of the fire and the dwellers of the garden: CASTLE, II, 6: Quoted from the Holy Koran. The quote closes with the line 'the dwellers of the garden are they that are the achievers'.

Not as the fragrance of him who walks according to the precepts: QUEENS, IV, 3: From the Buddhist scriptures of the Dhammapada (extract):

> The scent of sandal-wood and the Tagara, of the Lotus and Vassikî flower, although real and sensible, is not as the fragrance of [him who walks according to] the precepts. Mean and false in comparison is the scent of the rarest flowers with the same of him who holds by virtue, the excellency of whose conduct rises to heaven.

(Samuel Beal, tr., *Texts from the Buddhist Canon: The Dhammapada*, London, 1902.)

Nous devons à la Mort et nous et nos ouvrages: QUEENS: IV, 6: French proverb: 'Both ourselves and our creations are a debt owed to Death'.

Nouvelle amour, nouvelle affection, nouvelles fleurs parmi l'herbe nouvelle: KINGS, Gambit: 'New-sprung love, new-sprung affection, new-sprung flowers among the new-sprung grass'; quoted from Maurice Scève.

Now in dry, now in wete: KINGS, III, 4. Quoted within the text, the verse comes from a medieval mystery play, *The Second Shepherd's Play*. (Clement Adams, *Chief Pre-Shakespearean Drama*, 1924.)

Now the spider spins his web in Caesar's palace hall: PAWN, 23: Ottoman verse on the entry of Sultan **Mehmet II** to Constantinople:

> The spider spins his web in the Palace of the Caesars
> And the owl keeps watch on the Tower of Afrasiâb.

The Byzantine capital was finally crushed and reestablished as the capital of Mehmet's Muslim empire (Alexander Pallis, *In the Days of the Janissaries.*)

O Bhikshu! Empty this boat!: PAWN, 6: From the Buddhist scriptural canon, the Dhammapada: the entire verse is given within the text. A Bhikshu is a mendicant follower of Buddha and his wisdom. (Samuel Beal, tr., *Texts from the Buddhist Canon: The Dhammapada*, London, 1902.)

O cruell mars, thou dedly god of war: CHECKMATE, V, 2: From the poem by John Skelton (c. 1460–1529) 'Upon the death of the Earl of Northumberland'.

O Dermyne, O Donnall, O Dochardy droch: KINGS, I, 2: From the **Buke of the Howlat**. These are the words of the rook, the Celtic bard of the piece, giving a farcical picture of the bard's Gaelic and genealogy:

> Sa came the Ruke with a rerd [fart], and a rane roch [coarse babble],
> A bard out of Irland, with Banachadee;
> Said, Gluntowguk dynyd dach hala mischy doch;
> Raike hir a rug of the rost, or scho sal ryive the.
> Mich macmory ach mach mometir moch loch;
> Set hir dovne, gif her drink: quhat Dele alis the [what the devil ails thee]?
> O Deremyne, O Donnall, O Dochardy droch;
> Thir ar his Irland kingis of the Irisherye:
> O Krewlyn, O Conochor, O Gregre Makgrane,
> The Schenachy, the Clarsach,
> The Ben schene, the Ballach,
> The Crekery, the Corach,
> Scho kennis [knows] thaim ilkane [every one].

O England, the Hell of Horses, the Purgatory of Servants and the Paradise of Women: PAWN, 2: The view of John Florio (c. 1553–1625); as quoted in his *Second Fruites*, 1591.

O England thou garden of delights: KNIGHTS, II, 3: Pope Innocent III (1198–1213) exhorting Europe to a new crusade. (Pearl Binder, *Muffs and Morals*.)

O God breake thou theyr teeth at once: CHECKMATE, I, 6: Psalm 58, 6. The version used is the Geneva Psalms printed by John Crespin in London, 1569.

O Kama, Kama: with thy bow made of sugar cane: PAWN, 12: Kama being the Hindu God of Love, who rides on the back of a sparrow and carries a bow made of sugar cane, strung with bees. He carries five arrows tipped with flowers, signifying the physical senses.

O Lord, I am not puft in mynde: CHECKMATE, II, 5: Psalm 131; a profession of humility. The version used is the Geneva Psalms printed by John Crespin in London, 1569.

O *mea cella, vale*: KINGS, Gambit: From the Latin poem by Fredugis:

> *O mea cella, mihi habitatio, dulcis,*
> *Amata semper in aeternum,*
> *O mea cella, vale.*

> *O my cell, my sweet dwelling long loved,*
> O farewell, my cell.

O mill, what hast thou ground?: PAWN, 14, CHECKMATE, V, 7: Fragment of Irish verse:

> O mill, what hast thou ground? Precious thy wheat!
> It is not oats thou hast ground, but the offspring of Kervall
> The grain which the mill has ground
> Is not oats but blood-red wheat
> With the scions of the great tree Mailoran's mill was fed.

The lament relates the death of Donogh and Conall, sons of Blathmac who was one of the joint Kings of ancient Ireland. Escaping from their enemies, Blathmac's two sons hid in the wheel shaft of a water mill owned by Mailoran, son of Dima Crón. Their pursuers forced the woman in charge of the mill to open the sluice gates and let the water run. As the mill turned, the two brothers were crushed to death in its workings. (Kuno Meyer, *Hibernia Minoria*; P.W. Joyce, *Social History of Ancient Ireland*.)

O'n aird tuaid tic in chabair: QUEENS, I, 2: Gaelic proverb; 'Out of the north airt [direction or region] is it that succour comes'. (Gerard A. Hayes-McCoy, *Scots Mercenary Forces in Ireland*.)

O noble Prince, sole hope of Caesar's side: CASTLE, III, 8: **John Elder's** verse in homage to **Philip II** on the occasion of his royal entry to London following his marriage to **Mary Tudor**. The verse, written on a placard, was held aloft by the two traditional London pageant giants Corineus Brittanicus and Gogmagog Albionus. See also **Mind, voice, study, power and will, Is only set to love thee, Philip, still.** (Beatrice White, *Mary Tudor*, 1935.)

O row my lady in satin and silk: KINGS, III, 3: From the anonymous Scottish 'Ballad of Cospatrick' (extract):

> But I wad gie a' my ha's and tours [halls and towers],
> I had that bright burd in my bours [bowers]:
>
> 'But I wad gie my very life,
> I had that ladye to my wife!'
>
> 'Now keep, my son, your ha's and tours,
> Ye have that bright burd in your bours.
>
> 'And keep, my son, your very life,
> Ye have that ladye to your wife.'
>
> Now, or [before] a month was come and gane,
> The ladye bore him a bonny son.
>
> And it was well written on his breast-bane,
> 'Cospatrick is my father's name'.
>
> 'O rowe [wrap] my ladye in satin and silk
> And wash my son in the morning milk.'

O wow' quo' he, were I as free: KINGS, I, 1: Poem attributed to **James V** of Scotland, 'The Gaberlunzie Man', a Gaberlunzie man being the Scots term for a mendicant or beggar. It describes the rather willing seduction of a young girl by a beggar (extract):

> The pawky [sly] auld carle [churl] came o'er the lee,
> Wi' many good e'ens and days to me,
> Saying, Goodwife [mistress of the house, lady farmer], for your courtesie,
> Will you lodge a silly poor man?
> The night was cauld, the carle was wat [wet],
> And down ayont the ingle [beyond the fire] he sat:
> My daughter's shoulders he 'gan to clap,
> And cadgily [merrily] ranted and sang.

O wow! quo' he, were I as free
As first when I saw this countrie,
How blyth and merry wad I be!
And I wad never think lang.
He grew canty [affectionate], and she grew fain,
But little did her auld minny [mother] ken
What thir slee twa thegither [those sly two together] were say'ng,
When wooing they were sae thrang [intimate].

And O, quo' he, an' [if] ye were as black
As e'er the croun of my daddy's hat,
'Tis I wad lay thee by my back,
And awa' wi' me thou shou'd gang.
And O, quo' she, an' I were as white
As e'er the snaw lay on the dike,
I'd cleed [clad] me braw [fine] and lady-like,
And awa' wi' thee I would gang.

Between the twa was made a plot:
They rose a wee before the cock,
And wilily they shot the lock,
And fast to the bent [afield] are they gane.
Up in the morn the auld wife raise,
And at her leisure pat on her claise [clothes]:
Syne [then] to the servant's bed she gaes,
To speer [inquire] for the silly poor man.

She gaed to the bed where the beggar lay:
The strae [straw] was cauld, he was away,
She clapt her hands, cry'd Waladay,
For some of our gear will be gane [gone]!
Some ran to coffer, and some to kist [chest],
But nought was stown [stolen] that could be mist [missed]:
She danced her lane [by herself], cry'd Praise be blest.
I have lodged a leal [honest] poor man!

Since naething's awa', as we can learn,
The kirn's [churn] to kirn, and milk to earn:
Gae but the house, lass, and waken my bairn,
And bid her come quickly ben.
The servant gaed where the daughter lay,
The sheet were cauld, she was away,
And fast to her goodwife did say,
She's aff with the gaberlunzie man.

Meantime far 'hind out o'er the lee,
Fu' snug in a glen, where nane cou'd see,
The twa, with kindly sport and glee,
Cut drae a new cheese a whang [slice]:
The priving [tasting] was good, it pleas'd them baith,
To lo'e [love] her for ay, he gae her his aith [oath],
Quo' she, To leave thee I will be laith [loth],
My winsome gaberlunzie man.

(H. Macaulay Fitzgibbon, *Early English Poetry*, London, n.d.)

Oatmeal butter smeared on the Kamen Woronucha: CASTLE, II, 1: Described by **Richard Eden** as the pilot's votive offering on reaching Cape Holy Nose. Rather like **Charybdis**, there was a cave with a whirlpool which swallowed the sea every six hours. It was the habit of the pilots to climb out of the boat and smear butter mixed with oatmeal on the stone outcrop to pacify the winds, no doubt in the hope of a safe passage through the treacherous waters. (Richard Eden, *The First Three English Books on America 1511–1555*.)

Ochone: QUEENS, IV, 5: Gaelic; 'Alas; an exclamation of sorrow'.

Of Cat, nor Fall, nor trap I haif nae Dreid: KINGS, II, 1: From Scottish poet Robert Henryson's (c. 1430–1506) poem, 'The Upland Mouse and the Burgess Mouse'; the urban mouse boasts of the opulent luxury of her life in the big house as opposed to her sister in the humble hedgerow. See also **Cry peip! where ever thou be!** (extract):

'Let be this hole, and come into my place,
I shall you show, by good experience,
My Good Friday is better nor [than] your Pace [Easter feast],
My dish washings is worth your hale expense;
I have houses enow of great defence,
Of cat, nor of fall trap, I have nae dread.'
'I grant,' quoth she, and on together they yied [went].

(J. Ross, ed., *The Book of Scottish Poems*, Edinburgh, 1878.)

Oimè el cor, oimè la testa: KINGS, Gambit: The first line of a Spanish poem, which, with the second line, translates thus: 'What says the heart? Listen: what says the head? He who does not love does not understand.'

Old Man of the Mountains: KINGS, I, 7: A reference to Hassan, Subah of Nish'apour, the eleventh-century captain of the marauding band of Carmathians who had their headquarters at Mount Lebanon. Before attacking their enemies, they are said to have drunk a potent brew containing hashish to elevate them to a violent frenzy. From this the Carmathians earned their popular name of 'assassins'.

Olla Podrida: KINGS, Gambit: Spanish miscellaneous mixed stew of meat and vegetables; a hotch-potch. Not to be confused with *Olla Bethbar:* Arabic for 'God is Alone'.

Ollave: QUEENS, I, 1: Title given to a graduate of the ancient bardic schools of Ireland; versed in history, poetry and literature. After twelve years of study the diligent pupil would have mastered at least 350 tales; at which point he could properly call himself an ollave. The schools had seven different degrees of wisdom; the first level, the *Caogdach* or fifty-man, consisted in the ability to recite from memory fifty psalms in Latin. The ultimate degree, the *Druimcli*, would have a perfect awareness of all gleanable knowledge, from the smallest book to the largest. (P.W. Joyce, *Social History of Ancient Ireland.*)

On touche toujours sur le cheval qui tire: CHECKMATE, I, 4: 'The horse that draws best is most whipped'.

Ophites: KINGS, III, 3: Opheltes was the son of Lycurgus, King of Nemea. The infant child was left in the care of Hypsipylé (a Lemnian princess sold into slavery). She left the child lying on the grass while she gave the new commander of the army directions to a nearby spring. When she returned, the child had been killed by a poisonous serpent. Amphiaraüs, soothsayer and warrior, saw this as a bad omen, and posthumously called the child Archemorus; 'Fate beginner', indicative of the evils which would then befall their race.

Opus plumarum: PAWN, 24: 'Feathered work', a type of embroidery, used as a pun in the text.

Or se chante: QUEENS, III, 3: 'Now it is sung'. The formula that introduces each section of the early *Chantfables* (prose and verse chorus). The reference here is to **Aucassin and Nicolette**.

Orcades flowed with Saxon gore, the: QUEENS, I, 4: Claudian, on the Romans in Ireland driving out the Picts and the Saxons: the Orcades being the Roman name for the Orkneys; 'Thule [Shetland] became warm with the blood of the Picts and icy Erin [Ireland] wept for her heaps of slaughtered Scots'. (P. W. Joyce, *Social History of Ancient Ireland.*)

Order of St Michael: QUEENS: France's principal order of chivalry. The legend behind the choice of St Michael as defender of France was the belief that every time an enemy fleet approached Mont St Michel, the Archangel would excite a tempest to disperse them; hence the motto of the Order *Immensi tremor Oceani*. The King was Grand Master of the Order, and during the reign of **Henri II**, Cardinal Charles **de Guise** was its Chancellor.

The Order's decoration was a gold four-armed cross with eight points, enamelled in white and bordered with gold, and seeded with *fleurs-de-lys*. In the centre of the decoration was an oval medallion with St Michael trampling the dragon. Knights dressed in white, with a one-armed silver cloak, black cross sash (on which was pinned the decoration), and a heavy golden collar of silver fluted shells. The thirty-six Knights of noble birth admitted to the order vowed to uphold virtue, concord, fidelity, friendship, nobility, grandeur and equality. The full regalia would only be worn by members either on St Michael's Day, or when a new member was elected. (Theodore Godefroy, *Le Ceremonial François*, 1649; Helen W. Henderson, *Diane de Poytiers*.)

Order of the Garter: QUEENS: Founded in 1348 by Edward III of England, in honour of the Virgin Mary, St George and St Edward the Confessor. Originally limited to twenty-five Knights and the monarch, but enlarged in 1810 and 1834. The garter in question was of dark blue velvet, edged in gold with the motto of the Order, *Honi soit qui mal y pense* (Shame on him who thinks evil of it), also in gold; the garter to be worn below the left knee. Dress for the Order included garter, mantle, surcoat, hood, star and collar. The insignia hung from the collar on a string of pearls (similar to that of the **Order of St Michael**) is George killing the dragon, signifying the triumph of good over evil. (Major L. Gordon, *British Orders and Awards*.)

Order of the Golden Fleece: RISING: The Toison d'Or, founded by **Philip the Good**, Duke of Burgundy, in 1429 to coincide with his marriage to Isabella of Portugal. Membership was limited to twenty-four knights of noble, legitimate birth and chosen by the King from the nobility and gentry of French Flanders, Artois and Burgundy. Participation and enrolment in the new chivalric Order was not merely a picturesque honour for the Knights, it exemplified a shrewd attempt on behalf of the Duke to unite the nobility of the different Burgundian territories and to tie them in personal dependence to their benefactor. It was also used by the Duke as a prestigious gift to cement good relations with neighbouring rulers and potential allies.

The Order would meet once every year, in solemn chapter, to solve disputes amongst themselves, and humbly criticise the chivalric conduct of each other and the Duke. Philip was bound by oath to listen to the judgements of his peers. There was no direct connection between the Order and the crusading aspirations of the Duke, nor did it play any significant part in the day-to-day running of the Burgundian state; it has been described more as the 'Order of Making and Keeping Friends for Burgundy'.

· BURGUNDY ·

The original inspiration for the Order was Jason, leader of the Argonauts, but in the fleece's Christian incarnation, the Old Testament leader Gideon was also drawn into the heraldic *mélange*. In 1448 Duke Philip commissioned a series of tapestries specifically for the Order, entitled 'Gideon and the Golden Fleece'. This intertwining of Christian and classical references is characteristic of the cultural influences in fifteenth-century Renaissance Burgundy.

The Order originally celebrated its foundation and held its chapter meetings and feasts on St Andrew's Day. Until the French Revolution, a salvo of artillery was fired from the ramparts of Bruges on November 30 in honour of the Golden Fleece. (Richard Vaughan, *Philip the Good, The Apogee of Burgundy*, London, 1970.)

Order of the Knights of St John of Jerusalem: See **Knights of St John.**

Order of the Sword: SCORPIONS: Founded by Peter I, King of Cyprus, Jerusalem and Armenia (1359–1369), the motto being *C'est pour Loïauté Maintenir*, 'For the maintenance of loyalty'. Peter I carried the sword as a symbol of his new order, as his predecessors had carried the sceptre. The last to bear the heraldic imagery on her grave was **Catherine Corner**, Queen of Cyprus. (Sir Harry Luke, *Cyprus: A Portrait and Appreciation*, London, 1965.)

Order of the Unicorn: UNICORN: Granted by **James III** of Scotland to the Flemish knight **Anselm Adorne** in 1469, the Collar of this Order can be seen on Adorne's funeral effigy in the **Jerusalemkirk** in **Bruges**, together with carved and painted versions of the Adorne arms surrounded by a collar from which hangs a unicorn couchant. It was the first Collar of Honour granted as an order of chivalry by a Scottish monarch, and was perhaps prompted by the founding by the King's father-in-law of the Order of the Elephant in 1462. No one else is known to have received the Collar.

The unicorn appeared as a royal symbol in Scotland at the beginning of the fifteenth century, and a heraldic Office of Arms named after the Unicorn has existed since at least 1426. By 1439 a signet was in use showing the lozenge shield of Joan Beaufort, Queen of James I, and displaying a unicorn on the dexter side. By 1454 a manuscript thought to have been owned by Eleanor, Duchess of the Tyrol (a daughter of James I) shows a painting of the Scottish Royal Arms supported by two unicorns. (Unicorns were already popular on the continent—one of the great tourneying Brotherhoods of the fifteenth century was the Brotherhood of the Unicorn in Thuringia). Back in Scotland, a Signet of the Unicorn was employed by **James II** as early as 1460. When James III came to the throne, he made even more use of the unicorn as a royal beast. His second privy seal in 1482 bore a unicorn; a fine gold coin showing one was struck in his reign, and the hangings of his bed were embroidered with unicorns. The unicorn was removed from the chivalric order on the death of James III and replaced with St Andrew, patron saint of Scotland. There is cause to believe that the Order is the origin of the Most Ancient and Most Noble Order of the Thistle, revived and named as Scotland's order of chivalry by James VII of Scotland and II of England in the seventeenth century.

A copy of the original order is in Edinburgh castle, created for the tercentenary of the Order's revival in 1987; and a second was presented to Queen Elizabeth II. (Charles Burnett, 'Reflections on the Order of the Thistle', *Journal of the Heraldry Society of Scotland, No 5*; Charles & Helen Burnett, *The Green Mantle*.)

ORKNEY, Bishop of: CHECKMATE: See **Reid, Robert, Bishop of Orkney.**

Orpheus: KINGS, III, 4: Most celebrated of the mythical poets. According to Virgil and Ovid, the death of his beloved Euridyce led him to follow her to Hades, where the charms of his lyre temporarily suspended the torment of the damned. On failing to rescue Euridyce from the underworld, his grief was overwhelming, to the point that he treated all members of the opposite sex with contempt. It was this coldness to their advances which caused the Thracian women to tear him to death in the sexual frenzy of their Bacchanalia. Orpheus was buried by the Muses at Leibethra, at the foot of Mount Olympus, where nightingales sing sweetly over his grave.

Osiris: KINGS, IV, 3: Egyptian male god of life and fertility, and the cause of the Nile's annual overflow. Originally he ruled as King of Egypt, where he introduced agriculture, worship of the gods, and a code of morals. His brother Set tried to murder Osiris by trapping him in a chest and filling it with molten lead before throwing it into the Nile. Osiris's wife and sister Isis, the moon goddess, rescued the chest and concealed it from her brother. Set discovered the corpse, and cut his brother into fourteen pieces, leaving Isis to bury the remains. Revenge came in the shape of Isis and Osiris's son, Horus, who eventually defeated Set in battle. Osiris became the sun god, where he rules over the earth for six months of the year; the rest of the time he spends in the underworld. His physical incarnation is that of the black bull, Apis, the symbol of his favour and the continuation of life in this world and the next.

Osman: PAWN, 18: (1281–1326) Son of the leader of the Ogus tribe of Asia Minor and independent Sultan of the area, Osman was the founder of a dynasty and the Ottoman Empire. Osman dreamed of his expanding power and influence as a great tree which would overshadow the world. His son Orchan founded the **Janissaries.** Their sultanate was originally based upon free and hereditary rule, somewhat limited by later reigns, such as that of **Mehmet II,** who legislated that, for the sake of order and peace, it was the Sultan's duty to slaughter his brothers, thus avoiding dynastic conflict.

At its greatest extent in the sixteenth century, under **Suleiman the Magnificent,** the Empire stretched from Syria in the east to Hungary and Transylvania in the north. It only finally crumbled at the turn of this century; precipitating crisis in the Balkans and the First World War. (William Holden Hutton, *Constantinople.*)

Ottoman poetry: PAWN, 13: The eighteen varieties of verse are described in Gibb's analysis of the poetic form, including the Turkish, Turki and Sharquí forms. Every letter of the alphabet has a corresponding numerical value; thus as well as describing events, the verse can also indicate the date on which the incident took place.

The first book written in Turkish was the ethical and moral *Qudatqu Bilik, The Book of Auspicious Knowledge* (1070); written in *mesnevi* verse, or rhyming couplets. Another favourite verse form was the *gházel;* four to fifteen couplets, similar to a sonnet and generally about love. (See **I'd give unto her Indian mole . . .**) Amongst popular poets of the period are Anvari (d. 1191) and Jclal-ud-Din; the finest writers in Persian. Jelal wrote the great *mesnevi* of three thousand couplets, considered the best of its type. The fifteenth century saw the development of the first secular poetry, reaching its peak under Sultan **Suleiman,** as compared with the mystic and religious verse of earlier periods. There is no gender distinction in the poetry, so one cannot check if the verse is addressed to male or female. (E. J. W. Gibb, *History of Ottoman Poetry;* E. G. Brown, *Persian Literature in Modern Times.*)

Où est la très sage Helloïs . . . Pour qui chastré fut, et puis moyne?: KNIGHTS, III, 13: A reference to the woeful tale of the twelfth-century romance between Abelard and Eloise, retold through the centuries: 'Where is the virtuous Héloïse . . . On account of whom he [Abelard] was castrated and became a monk?'

Oüez, oüez, oüez. Et vous taisez si vous pouvez: KNIGHTS, III, 13: Carnival rhyme, commonly spoken by a crier, herald or carnival barker; 'Listen and be quiet if you can'.

Out, alas! Now goeth away my prisoners and all my prey: KINGS, III, 2: The words of Satan in the medieval mystery play *The Harrowing of Hell,* as performed by the Cooks and Innkeepers of Chester. The legend of the Harrowing, where Jesus descends into the Underworld and rescues the righteous souls, comes from the apocryphal gospel of Nicodemus. (A. C. Cawley, ed., *Everyman and Medieval Mystery Plays*, London, 1986.)

Paestum: KINGS, II, 1: The city in Lucania, near the Gulf of Salerno, colonised by the **Sybarites** in the sixth century BC. It was a flourishing and powerful colony, but sank into obscurity under domination by the Roman Empire. By the time of the Emperor Augustus, it was mentioned only on account of its beautiful roses which bloomed twice a year.

PAGET, Sir William: CASTLE: (1505–1563) Lord Chancellor of England. He was not from the upper echelons of English society, but was the base-born son of a London shearman and barber; less aristocratic but more conscientious than many of his counterparts. Paget studied in Paris, and became clerk to the Privy Council in the English Embassy to France of 1540. He was made Lord Paget of Beaudesert in 1549.

The tremendous cost of war under Henry VIII had placed the English economy in a precarious state, forcing the sale of massive tracts of monastic land and the devaluation of coinage. Paget, as Secretary of State (since 1543), was sworn to secrecy about the conduct of the mint and the debasement of coins, lest the population panic and throw the economy further into disorder.

He fell from grace in 1552 because of his loyalty to Protector **Somerset**, but his strict adherence to Catholicism allowed him to climb back into power under **Mary Tudor**. He was disliked and mistrusted by **Philip II** because of his indiscretions in the peace talks between the Empire of **Charles V**, England and France; also because of his frank letters to colleagues abroad declaring that Mary Tudor's pregnancy was a false alarm, unlikely ever to come to fruition. (Penry Williams, *The Tudor Regime*, Oxford, 1979.)

Pairidaeza: CHECKMATE, III, 3: Paradise. The Persian origin of the term denotes an enclosed park or pleasure ground.

Pale, The: QUEENS: The area of Ireland controlled by the English from the 1172 conquests of King John I onwards. The dominions of the English crown were referred to as the 'pale', or the part paled off. The verb 'to pale' refers to an area staked off and enclosed, from the French, *pal*, and Latin, *palus*, a stake.

Paleologus, Thomas: RAM, 23: (d. 1465) Brother of Constantine, last Emperor of Constantinople. Thomas and his other brother Demetrius (d. 1470) were joint Despots (rulers) of the Morea. They were deposed by **Mehmet II** after a series of disagreements over the level of tribute due to the Ottoman Empire. Demetrius' revenues were withdrawn by the Sultan, and he was moved from Edime to Dimotika in 1467, living in a state of near poverty. He became a monk, living under the name of David, and died three years later.

Thomas fled to Corfu, and in 1460 sought financial help and personal safety from Pope **Pius II**, promising in return to send the head of St Andrew (RAM, 9, 23) to the Pope. In 1461 he arrived in Rome and was honoured by the Pope with the gift of a golden rose, and an annual income of 6,000 ducats. Thomas maintained his personal claim to the conquered throne of Byzantium, still calling himself Emperor up until the time of his death.

In 1472 Thomas's daughter Zoë Paleologus, pensioner of the Tolfa **alum** fund and living under the protection of **Bessarion**, was given 4,400 ducats from the papal alum fund to pay for her travelling expenses to Russia as the bride of the grand Duke Ivan III Vasilievich, better known as Ivan the Great, then reigning as Grand Duke of Muscovy. Zoë's marriage united the line of the Byzantium Emperors with the rising Russian Empire, and the hereditary claim to the Byzantine throne thus passed to Russia. (Franz Babinger, *Mehmet the Conqueror,* tr. Ralph Manheim, Princeton, 1978.)

Palestrina: QUEENS, I, 6: Giovanni Pierluigi da Palestrina (c. 1524–1594), Italian composer and innovator of sixteenth-century sacred music. He received his musical education at Rome, returning to become the organist of his home town of Palestrina. In 1551, Pope **Julius III** appointed him musical instructor of the Cappella Giulia of St Peter's in Rome, with the title of *Magister Capellae.* In 1555, despite being married, he was made a member of the papal choir, but was forced to resign by Pope **Paul IV**. In 1570, he became Composer of the Papal Chapel; a post specifically created for him, and in the following year he became Choirmaster of St Peter's. Palestrina produced a massive number of masses and motets, amongst his most famous works are the *Improperia* and the *Missa Papae Marcelli.* His music was deeply religious; epitomising the intensity of the Counter-Reformation and a period of vigorous ecclesiastical reform.

Palissy, Bernard: QUEENS, IV, 4: (c. 1509–1589) Geometric surveyor from southern France, most famous for discovering the Italian secret of glazing earthenware. Palissy's famous iridescent glazes gave the effect of lapis lazuli, agate and precious jewels to the lizards, crayfish and animals which decorated his vases and bowls, highly sought after in sixteenth-century France. He is less well remembered for his translation of the works of Pliny and his teaching in the natural sciences.

Pall-mall: QUEENS, II, 6: Also known as *palemaille* and *parmaille*; the game involves striking a ball with a mallet (or cudgel of medlar wood) through a high iron arch; similar to golf and considered to be the ancestor of croquet. (George H. Powell, *Duelling Stories of the Sixteenth Century*, tr. from Brantôme.)

Pallas: CHECKMATE, III, 6: Pallas-Athene; **Minerva**, daughter of Jupiter; and the Greek goddess of armed resistance. Her name has two origins: firstly from her clothing made from the flayed skin of the slayed Titan Pallas; and secondly from the shield with the head of the Medusa which she swung to ward off anatagonists (from the Greek *pallo*, 'I swing'). In the fifth century BC it was a sign of war to gild the statues of Pallas on the Greek ships. (Juvien de la Gravière, *Les Derniers Jours de la Marine à Rames*; E.M. Berens, *Myths and Legends of Ancient Greece and Rome*.)

Palm wine: SCALES, 20: As noted by **Ca'da Mosto** on his voyages of discovery to Africa, this liquid called *mignol* by the natives was gathered from the wild (not cultivated) trees of the area which he described as similar in type to date trees, although not plentiful. The sap of the trees was collected almost all year round. Ca'da Mosto described the liquid as 'sweet as the sweetest wine in the world' when first collected. After a few days he noted that the wine began to lose its sweetness and turned sour, although it tasted better to him after this period of maturing than the cloying sweetness of the freshly collected liquid. In strength he claimed it was as potent as wine if water was not added.

Another name for the distilled juice of the raphia palm is *kakai*, which in the African Ijaw language also means 'headache'. (G. Crone, ed., *The Voyages of Cadamosto*, Hakluyt Society, 1937; Georg Gerster, 'River of Sorrow, River of Hope', *National Geographic*, Vol. 148, No. 2, August 1975.)

PALMER, Sir Thomas: KINGS: (d. 1558) Soldier and engineer by trade; the third and youngest son of Sir Edward Palmer. From a noble and established Sussex family, Thomas was attached to court from his early years. In 1515 he was mentioned as serving at Tournay, and in 1519 was made a gentleman usher to King Henry VIII. In 1532 he received his knighthood at Calais. His later military career was not peppered with success; he was taken prisoner in France in an expedition from Guines in the 1540s, and was forced to ransom himself. Back in England, he joined the campaigns against Scotland where the English defeat and loss of **Grey of Wilton**'s troops at Haddington were blamed on his rashness.

In 1551, he was arrested for acting as a spy for Protector **Somerset**. Palmer had initially supported the Protector, but had resented his command. **Warwick** promised he would help to advance Palmer if he would denounce Somerset. Thomas fabricated a plot against the Protector, and stood as the main witness against him at his trial. In return, Palmer was fully pardoned in 1552 and given several grants of monastic land as well as the post of councillor for the division of the Debatable Lands. He busied himself building a house in Stroud with his profits, but had risen too far under Warwick to escape unscathed when the Earl was embroiled in the attempt to put Lady Jane Grey on the throne. He was sent to the Tower of London, and was condemned in 1553, dying as a Protestant.

Thomas Palmer had two brothers: the eldest, Buskin Palmer, also in the service of Henry VIII, was reputedly hanged for earning the King's disfavour at the gaming table. Henry Palmer (d. 1558) was a soldier and helped to hold Guines for **Mary Tudor** and **Philip II**. He was mortally wounded when the town fell to the French in January 1557, and was ransomed to Monsieur Sipierre, the French military commander in charge of the French assault on the English fortress, in whose arms he died.

Pan: KINGS, II, 2: The god of nature, and of flocks and herds; as a satyr, his lower half was that of a goat. He was also the god of all pastoral life and the inventor of the shepherd's flute. According to Elizabeth Barrett Browning (1806–1861), when Christ died on the cross, a cry went across the oceans of the world, 'Great Pan is dead!'.

Panter, David: KINGS, IV, 1: Bishop of Ross, and Scots Ambassador in France. He also negotiated the transfer of the Scottish Regency to **Mary de Guise**.

Par temperance ay acquis grand renom; Cyncinnatus Quintus est mon vray nom: CHECKMATE, III, 5: 'By temperance I have acquired great renown; Cyncinnatus Quintus is my real name'.

Paracelsus: KINGS, I, 1: (1493–1541) Noted alchemist, born in Schwitz, he travelled from university to university practising the arts of magic, alchemy and astrology. He was consulted by Erasmus, but was generally despised and reviled as a charlatan. Paracelsus' reputation as one of the fathers of modern chemistry is tainted somewhat by his announcement in all seriousness that he had discovered the **Philosopher's Stone**.

PARENTI, Marco: RISING: (1422–1497) Florentine merchant and husband of Caterina Strozzi (d. 1481), the daughter of **Alessandra Strozzi**. Described by his mother-in-law as 'worthy and virtuous', Marco was the only son and heir of his father's silk workshop in Florence. Well-educated and wealthy, Parenti was first elected to the governing body of the city, the Signoria, in 1454, at a relatively young age.

Although well below the Strozzi family in terms of their former political standing, Parenti was an excellent contact for Alessandra's exiled sons. He was one of the governing class of Florence, and his links with the exiled Strozzi did not halt his slow rise to the patriciate of the city. An excellent source of information on Parenti and his links with the Strozzi comes from the recently discovered and translated manuscript of his memoirs (1464–1467) and his correspondence. (Mark Phillips, *The Memoir of Marco Parenti*, London, 1989.)

Parfitières: QUEENS, II, 2: The last relay of hounds in a hunt. Hounds were divided into three relays: the *vaunt chasse*, the *midel* and the *parfitières* which were the most reliable dogs of the three. (C.E. Hare, *The Language of Field Sports*, Glasgow, 1939.)

Paris: KINGS, IV, 2: Also called Alexander; the second son of Priam, King of Troy, brought up as a shepherd and in ignorance of his parentage. At the marriage of Peleus and Thetis, the goddess Discord (who was not among the invited) threw a golden apple into the assembly. On it were written the words, 'Let the most beautiful among you take me' ('*La plus belle me devoit avoir*' UNICORN, 16). Hera, Aphrodite and **Pallas-Athene** all laid claim to the apple. Paris was named by Zeus as the mortal who should choose which goddess was most deserving of the prize. To secure the apple, Hera offered him dominion over the world; Athene offered martial fame and glory, but Aphrodite promised him the most beautiful woman in the world to be his wife; consequently Paris decided Aphrodite should get the apple. She was thus universally acclaimed as the goddess of beauty, but the hatred of the losing goddesses was later to cause Paris immense problems.

Paris, fontaine de toutes sciences: CHECKMATE, III, 2: 'Paris, fountain-head of all knowledge'.

Patrick, St: QUEENS, III, 4: (c. 390–460): Apostle and patron saint of the Irish, born in Scotland from mixed British and Roman parentage. At the age of sixteen, he was captured by Irish pirates, and spent six years amongst 'the children of the wood of Fochut' in County Mayo. Turning to God in his captivity, he received a divine message that he would escape. He went back to Britain and trained for the church before returning to Ireland in AD 432 as a bishop, spending the rest of his life evangelising and ordaining others in religious orders.

Paul, St: KNIGHTS, II, 3: The Christian saint sought sanctuary on Malta in AD 60, and was housed by the chief of the island, Publius. St Paul converted the Phoenician population there. The Maltese are considered to be the oldest converted Christian population in the world.

PAUL II: RISING: (1417–1471) Pietro Barbo, the Venetian who was elected Pope in 1464, a devoted collector of antiquities. Like his predecessor **Pius II**, Paul attempted to draw support for a crusade against the Turkish empire. Unlike his predecessors, however, be succeeded in alienating the Italian humanist movement, drawing a clear distinction between the pagan philosophies of the ancient world and that espoused by the Catholic church.

PAUL III: KINGS: (1468–1549) Alessandro Farnese; patron of arts and letters, he was amongst the greatest of the sixteenth-century humanist popes. Farnese was the protégé of both Pope Alexander VI and his successor **Clement VII.** Farnese owed part of his rapid rise to apostolic power to Alexander's attraction for his sister; a relationship which earned Alessandro the title of the 'petticoat cardinal'. He did not share his sister with Clement, who, having the same humanist and political views, was soon to be his successor, elected pope in 1534. His papacy went a long way towards restoring both the fortunes and fabric of the city of Rome.

PAUL IV: CASTLE: (1475–1559) Giovanni Pietro Caraffa, the Cardinal and Archbishop of Naples, elected Pope in 1555 at the age of seventy-nine. Considered to be one of the finest classical scholars of the sixteenth century, as Cardinal and later as Archbishop of Naples he corresponded with Erasmus and other great humanists, but in his pontificate he was later forced to prohibit works he had earlier encouraged.

When elected to the ultimate office, Caraffa's austerity gave way to luxurious excess and nepotism. He is reported as having held lunches lasting for more than three hours at which he conducted his public audiences, but his guests were not invited to dine or drink with the Pope his favourite thick black wine of Naples, *mangiaguerra*.

His hatred of the Spanish was longstanding; as early as 1513, when a papal nuncio, he recommended that Naples should be annexed by the Holy See, and not left in the hands of the Spanish, claiming it was humiliating for Italy to be ruled by masters who had once been their cooks. He made one of his nephews a cardinal, and the other a duke, and used them both to further his schemes against the Holy Roman Empire of **Charles V.** His nephew the cardinal was sent to France in 1555 to arrange a secret treaty to recover Naples. Within two months, however, **Henri II** had signed the peace of Vaucelles with Emperor **Charles V** which was supposed to last for five years. Pope Paul was furious, and sent Cardinal Caraffa to encourage the French to break the treaty; promising to create a new batch of French cardinals in Rome, and to give the French, and any of Charles's subjects (including the heretical German Lutherans) absolution for breaking their oath to the Emperor.

The second secret treaty between the Pope and the French was signed in July 1556; Venice declined to join the new 'Little League' against the Empire, but did send them gunpowder. Caraffa and his French allies each promised to raise twelve thousand foot soldiers, five hundred horse, and five hundred men at arms to recover Naples. Financially, the French would also provide 350,000 ducats to fund the war, and Paul would raise an additional 150,000. In return for their investment of men and money, the crown of Naples would go to the younger son of Henri II, restoring their old Angevin inheritance. Some of the land would go to create estates for Caraffa's nephews; the rest would go to the papacy. The French were also encouraged by the Pope to get Sultan **Suleiman** to join them against the Calabrians. The French were victorious in Piedmont in the autumn of 1556, and Paul, feeling confident, renewed conflict against Philip's close adviser, the Duke of Alva. In April 1557, Alva marched from Naples against the papacy, with 25,000 men.

Back in France, when St Quentin fell to the forces of the Empire, the French troops in Piedmont (under **François, Duke de Guise, Piero Strozzi** and **Claude de Guise**, Duke d'Aumale) were recalled. Paul was left to face the wrath of the Empire alone, saying bitterly to Piero Strozzi, 'Go then, and take with you the consciousness of having done little for your king, still less for the church and nothing for your own honour'. Following the flood of the River Tiber in late September 1557, the Duke of Alva entered Rome and Pope Paul was forced to make peace with the enemy. With the end of the war and the demise of the Pope's attempts to recover Naples, the Caraffa nephews were deprived of office and publicly executed. For the last years of his reign, Paul was obliged to redirect his energies towards reforming the church rather than pursuing personal grudges.

Paula: CASTLE, III, 7: (347–404) Mother of **Eustochion** and follower of **St Jerome**.

Pavia: RISING: 14: Pavia was famous as a law school before it was usurped by the reputation earned by Bologna. The university began as a capitulary school founded by Lothair in 825 and was revived as a school of law in the fourteenth century. By the early fifteenth century the university already had a well-established reputation for the study of medicine and law, becoming the university town of the Milanese and attracting students both from the surrounding area and abroad. See also **Giammattco Ferrari da Grado**, one of Pavia's most famous physicians. (Hastings Rashdall, *The Universities of Europe in the Middle Ages*, Vol. II, Oxford, 1936.)

Pawnbroking: RISING: Pawnbrokers managed to evade the church's prohibition on usury by lending money on secured pledges. A certain degree of trade has always been part of the business, if only to dispose of unredeemed pledges. This earned them the dubious reputation (still retained) as 'fences' for the resale of stolen goods. Pawnbrokers were restricted by law as to the goods they were allowed to accept in pledges, and were strictly forbidden to capitalise by lending on church ornaments or liturgical vestments.

Each town laid down specific laws on lending, dependent upon the social structure of the economy. For example, Louvain pawnbrokers were not allowed to lend to students if they pledged their school texts; and in Troyes, they were forbidden to accept loans on agricultural implements. In Valenciennes, any wool or unfinished pieces of cloth could not be pawned unless it could be conclusively proved that they were the property of the applicant rather than his employer. These regulations at least meant that the brokers remained within the limit of the law when it came to the provenance of their pledges, if not the interest rates charged.

In addition to their banking and speculative investments, pawnbrokers occasionally invested directly in trade. In **Bruges** in 1447, the Lombard pawnbrokers accepted money on deposit and also speculated on commodities such as wool, although the strong **guild** structure barred them from cloth production. The bankruptcy of the Lombards in fifteenth-century Bruges was due to their over-optimistic speculation in fluctuating markets, which lost them more than they gained. (Malcolm Letts, *Bruges and its Past*, London, 1924.)

Peacock: KNIGHTS, II, 9; PAWN, 20: The bird, 'whose plumage shone like pearl and emerald, and whose voice was so sweet that he was appointed to sing the daily praise of God'. The legend is that Allah made the peacock the angel above all others in the garden of Paradise. According to the Muslim version of the Fall, it was the peacock, or the Paon of Paradise as he is also known, that induced the serpent to bring Satan into the Garden, carrying him in his tooth. For this act of malicious evil, God deprived the bird of his beautiful voice. (E.J.W. Gibb, *A History of Ottoman Poetry*, Vol. II.)

Pearl divers: PAWN, 10: There are many accounts of pearl divers in the Ottoman empire. According to one account, in the reign of **Suleiman** the island of Symi off Rhodes was famed for its divers; all four thousand Greek inhabitants of the island could dive. They would fill their mouths with oil and plunge as deep as seventy fathoms. On reaching the bottom, they would spit out the oil, and the particles would act like a series of magnifying glasses to make visible any valuable items on the sea bottom. In addition to diving for pearls, they could use their talents for sponge diving or even recovery of booty from sunken ships. Henry Blount, an English traveller to the Levant in 1634, also noted the divers off Rhodes, saying that they lived on a diet of dry biscuits to keep them lean, and none were allowed to marry until they were capable of holding their breath under water for at least half an hour. Later visitors relate the same tale. (Alexander Pallis, *In the Days of the Janissaries; Harleian Collection of Voyages*, Vol. I; James Dallaway, *Constantinople*, 1797.)

Peg-a-Ramsay, little: KINGS, I, 1: The Scots riddle (name the flower):

> Little Peg-a-Ramsay
> With the yellow hair,
> Double ruff around her neck
> And ne'er a shirt to wear.

Peine Forte et Dure: KINGS, IV, 1: A form of punishment permitted against those who remained mute in the face of a legal accusation and refused to plead guilty or not guilty. Iron weights were successively loaded upon the silent victim until he was literally pressed to death.

Pelops: KINGS, IV, 4: Meaning 'black face', he was the grandson of Zeus and son of Tantalus and Dioné. Tantalus, wishing to test the gods, invited them to a great banquet. He murdered his own son Pelops to serve up as the main course. None of the gods would touch the cannibal repast apart from **Demeter**, who was so distracted at the loss of her daughter that she was not aware that she had consumed Pelops' shoulder. The gods ordered Hermes (**Mercury**) to place Pelops' corpse in a cauldron, and restore him to life. **Clotho** lifted him out of the cauldron and replaced his missing shoulder with one made of ivory. It is said that his descendants from the Peloponnesus peninsula of Greece still have one white shoulder.

Pentecost: CASTLE, I, 7: See **Worship the buttock-bone of . . .**

Per qual dignitade, l'uom si creasse: QUEENS, II, 6: 'For which dignity man is conceived' (Giovanni Boccacio, c. 1313–1375); used in an ironic sense in the text. (D.B. Wyndham Lewis, *The Soul of Marshal Gilles de Raiz.*)

Perun: CASTLE, II, 7: One of the gods of pagan Russia. A statue of the god, with a silver head and gold mouth, was in Kiev up until the conversion of Vladimir in AD 988.

According to **Herberstein**, an idol of Perun used to stand in Novgorod, later replaced by the Perunski cathedral. When the city was converted and the people baptised, the idol was thrown into the river. Witnesses swore that the idol swam against the stream, and when it reached the bridge over the river, called out, 'This is for you, O inhabitants of Novgorod, in memory of me'. A rope miraculously appeared on the bridge. Herberstein was told that the voice still sounded from time to time, and when this happened the citizens would run together and lash each other with ropes. No further explanation is given to explain whether the voice and rope represent a curse on the people of Novgorod for deserting their time-honoured idol, or a warning. (Sigismund von Herberstein, *Notes Upon Russia*, Vol. II.)

Petite coquette (co co co co dae) qu'esse cy?: CHECKMATE, II, 7: From the song '*Il est bel et bon*' by Passereau (c. 1485–1548), on the traditional theme of dominant wives and cuckoldry:

> *Il est bel et bon, commère, mon mary,*
> *Il estoit deux femmes toutes d'ung pays*

Disans l'une à l'aultre—'Avez bon mary?'
Il est bel et bon . . .
Il ne me courrousse, ne me bat aussy.
Il faict le mesnaige, il donne aux poulailles,
Et je prens mes plaisirs.
Commère, c'est pour rire.
Quant les poullailles crient:
Petite coquette (co co co co dae), qu'esse cy?
Il est bel et bon . . .

My husband's fine and good, neighbour.
There were two women in the same neighbourhood
Asking one another—'Have you a good husband?'
My husband's fine and good . . .
He doesn't annoy me nor does he beat me.
He does the housework and feeds the chickens,
And I enjoy myself.
(I tell you) neighbour, it's a laugh
When the chickens cry
Little coquette (cock a doodle doo) that's what it is!
My husband's fine and good . . .
(Tr. Frank Dobbin, from the LP: The Kings Singers, A *French Collection*, 1973, EMI CSD 3740.)

Petite Pucelle of Ireland: QUEENS, IV, 3: Compare Joan of Arc to the Dauphin of France, *'Gentil Dauphin, j'ai nom Jehannes la Pucelle'*; *pucelle* meaning virgin. (Alan Houghton Brodrick, *Touraine*.)

PETRE, Sir William: CASTLE: (1505–1572) Another of the base-born but shrewd advisers who rose to prominence under Henry VIII. Sir William was the son of a rich tanner, educated at Oxford University in canon and civil law. Under both Henry and **Edward VI** he served as a Privy Councillor, and was sent to Oxford University to examine potential Catholic heretics in his former place of study. Petre was zealous in helping to eradicate the Catholic church in England and was knighted for his service to the crown in 1543. He held over two dozen properties in six counties; many of his accquisitions were former monastic and chantry lands gained by Petre after Henry VIII's dissolution of the monasteries.

Under **Mary Tudor**, his tenure and possessions seemed uncertain, as a persecutor of Catholics in the former regimes. However, with a diplomatic about-face in his religious opinions and his zeal for Mary's marriage, he soon consolidated his position once again, retiring only in 1557 due to ill health. Apart from his chameleon-like religious sympathies, his political career was otherwise blameless. He gained much by saying little; rather than bargaining, he waited for the opposition to make suggestions most favourable to England. When Petre was Ambassador to negotiate the English handover of Boulogne in 1556, Châtillon, the French councillor, claimed that the French would have saved a fortune in payments and would not have had to guarantee their payments with hostages 'had it not been for the man who said nothing'. Petre was also a great patron of learning and collector of rare manuscripts, forever asking English envoys abroad to search out books on his behalf.

Petroneus: KINGS, III, 2: (d. AD 66) Roman novelist; close companion to the Emperor **Nero** and director in chief of his Imperial entertainment. Nero accused him of treason, and Petroneus resolved to die as he had lived; exciting admiration and attention for the frivolous eccentricity of his suicide. He opened his veins, but from time to time stopped the bleeding by applying bandages. During the apparently extensive time it took him to die, he met with his friends and chose to be seen in public. He eventually collapsed and died in the street; one of his last acts having been to send a vituperative document to Nero, condemning him for his brutality and excesses.

Peut-il naître de cette Agar autres enfants que des Ismaëlites et bâtards?: CHECKMATE, V, 9: 'Can this Hagar give birth to children other than Ishmaelites and bastards?' See Genesis, 16, 11–12: 'And the angel of the Lord said unto her, Behold, thou [Hagar] art with child, and shalt bear a son, and shalt call his name Ishmael; because the Lord hath heard thy affliction. And he will be a wild man; his hand will be against every man, and every man's hand against him; and he shall dwell in the presence of all his brethren'. Ishmael is regarded as the father of the nomadic Arab peoples.

Philemon and Baucis: KINGS, IV, 1: An elderly married couple of Phrygian legend. When Zeus and Hermes wandered through the countryside in human form, the couple were the only ones to offer food and shelter to the gods. Zeus and Hermes sent floods to punish the surrounding area for its inhospitable behaviour, but rewarded Philemon and Baucis by turning their humble cottage into a magnificent temple. In their religious devotions as the chosen representatives of the gods, they prayed that they would not be separated by death. When they died within the same hour, the gods answered their petition by turning them into a pair of intertwined trees.

PHILIP II: CASTLE: (1527–1598) King of Spain and husband of **Mary Tudor**. Described as having large, heavy-lidded blue eyes, arched thick brows, small ears, and a small trim beard. An excellent likeness is visible in the enamelled silver head sculpted by Leone Leoni in 1556 (Kunsthistorisches Museum, Vienna). He was described as the image of his father, the Emperor **Charles V**, in looks, actions and lifestyle, although more grave and reserved than his father. Philip spoke nothing but Spanish, and surrounded himself with Spanish courtiers and confidants. He is said to have laughed in public only once: at Brussels when he saw a procession float of a bear playing an organ (the organ consisting of twenty cages of cats with their tails tied to the keys to make them scream). It was at this point that the Queen Dowager of Hungary (Charles V's sister) began to dislike him. Philip also hated getting up early in the morning, and would avoid field sports and chivalric display whenever possible; preferring to regulate his weight by rigorous dieting rather than exercise.

Despite these apparent character flaws, as heir to the massive empire of his father he was described in his youth as the most eligible bachelor in the world. In 1543 he was married to Infanta Mary, the daughter of John III of Portugal and Catherine (his father's sister). He had only one legitimate son by his first wife: Don Carlos (executed at the age of twenty-three for having conspired to murder his father). In 1554 he married Mary Tudor, hoping to keep England as an ally and provide fresh blood for the Catholic succession. Under the terms of the marriage alliance, Philip promised not to involve England in the Empire's wars against France, but French involvement in **Paul IV**'s attempt to recover Naples, and the French-backed abortive invasion of **Sir Thomas Stafford**, gave him the excuse to muster troops and drag England into his 'defensive' war against the Pope and his allies.

In addition to the Kingdom of Spain (including Castile, Aragon and Granada), Philip was also ruler of Naples, Sicily, the Netherlands, Milan; Lord of the Franche Comté, Low Countries, the Cape Verde Islands, the Canaries, Tunis, Oran, the Philippines, the Spice Islands, West Indies, Mexico and Peru. Even without becoming Emperor on his father's death, Philip's dominions covered the world; as would be said later of the British Empire, the sun never set on Philip's land. Despite the scale of his territories, he was overwhelmed by debt and spent most of his reign attempting to extract as much money out of his possessions as was possible without totally bleeding them dry. Religious and political wars, combined with rampant inflation, crippled his economy. He was constantly strapped for cash; a situation not eased on his arrival in England in 1555 when the French flooded London with counterfeit Spanish money, increasing the existing English distrust of foreigners.

His bride desperately needed an heir, but despite early encouraging symptoms (later diagnosed as dropsy), their marriage was not to prove fruitful. He returned to the Low Countries in 1557 to wage war against the French, and never saw Mary alive again. England had never welcomed the Spaniard and his court with open arms and after Mary's death it was most unlikely that they would be tolerated for longer now that their monarch and protector was gone. The Venetian Ambassador to England was well aware of the xenophobia of the citizens, commenting on their attitude towards not just the Spanish, but 'the perverse hatred of these people and their most inveterate detestation of foreigners'. Philip's subsequent failure to court Mary's Protestant half-sister **Elizabeth** culminated in the attempted invasion of the Spanish Armada in

1588, when England finally shook off the last of its lip-service to Spain and the Empire.

On returning to Spain, Philip ran his Empire from the Escorial near Madrid, an ambitious complex of buildings including a library, church and mausoleum. It was commissioned by Philip and built from 1563 to 1584, after the biblical description of Solomon's temple. Despite his war against the Spanish-hating papacy, Philip was as fanatical as his English wife when it came to the maintenance of Orthodox Catholicism; the Inquisition in Spain was at its height during his rule. (W.H. Prescott, *History of the Reign of Philip the Second*; Geoffrey Parker, *Philip II.*)

PHILIP THE GOOD, Duke of Burgundy: RISING: (1396–1467) Renowned as one of the foremost patrons of music, painting, jewellery and many other arts and crafts, Philip's court represented the zenith of chivalry and artistic endeavour. He employed the Flemish painter **Jan Van Eyck** as court painter from 1425 until Van Eyck's death in 1441. The Duke was famous amongst his contemporaries for his sense of humour, his love of dancing, feasting and romantic fiction. He often turned day into night, revelling into the small hours, and subsequently received a special dispensation from the Pope to allow him to hear Mass in the early afternoon rather than the morning. Tall, handsome and lean, the Duke was not short of admirers. The greatest reckoning of his paramours and sexual conquests estimates that there were thirty-three mistresses in all, with a total of twenty-six children. These 'Bastards of Burgundy' were treated well at court and often honoured with political or army appointments. Their mothers were given financial support, but discreetly left unnamed in most of the records.

Philip was the founder of a new order of chivalry, the **Order of the Golden Fleece.** His crusading aspirations are further embodied in the famous Feast of the Pheasant in 1454 which was perhaps the last great gathering of chivalric heroes. The feast proclaimed Philip's dream of a new crusade against the Turk, and was to encourage the knights and nobles present to make their crusading vows. Later historians have explained the devout and extravagant oaths pledged at these festivities as a perfect example of infectious bombast and the power of the wine rather than exemplifying a realistic plan for a new crusade. Indeed, bad relations between Burgundy and France delayed the prospective crusade for ten years. By 1464 it did seem possible that it might at last take place, with Anthony, Bastard of Burgundy leading, but the death of Pope **Pius II** ultimately halted the elderly Duke's advanced preparations.

The Duke's sense of humour and the eccentricities of his old age are well documented. When Philip fell ill in 1462, one of his doctors recommended that to effect a full cure, the duke would have to shave his head. Philip retorted that he was not going to be the only bald fool at court, and henceforth ordered over five hundred of his courtiers to comply with this new trend. The ducal castle of Hesdin represented the pinnacle of his taste for practical jokes and mechanical toys, with a room specially constructed to delight his guests. In it were devices which would squirt water at every conceivable angle and statues which appeared to talk. Even though he seldom spent time there, Philip would invest several thousand ducats on its upkeep each year.

One particular hobby of his dotage was to retire to a specially constructed room and amuse himself threading needles, fixing broken glasses, mending knives and making clogs. The skills of the Duke turned artisan were scorned by his only son and heir **Charles the Bold**, who took great pleasure in ordering the destruction of his father's playthings as soon as he succeeded him to the duchy.

The glory and luxuries of Burgundian court life were offset against almost permanent conflict with France and the threat of war. In 1456, the Dauphin of France, the future **Louis XI**, had fled the wrath of his father and had been openly welcomed by Philip against the wishes of the French King. This put a severe strain on relations between the duchy and its former feudal sovereign which spilled over to the next generation. (Richard Vaughan, *Philip the Good: The Apogee of Burgundy*, London, 1970.)

Philosopher's stone: KINGS: The substance by which all base metals could be transmuted into gold. Alchemists, the first empirical chemists, strove in vain to perfect the process by which their elixir would effect the change; mountebanks often doing better financially than those striving for the genuine article. (Ripley, *The Compound of Alchemy*, 1471.)

PICCOLOMINI, Aeneas: RAM: See **Pius II**.

Pigged with a full set of teeth: PAWN, 1: See *Animal gregale*.

Pilgrims: UNICORN: On the Venice-to-Jaffa route to the Holy Land, most pilgrims would first visit Rome in time for the Easter celebrations, then go to Venice in time for the festivities of St Mark. Failing that, they would arrive at their point of departure in time for the Doge's espousal to the sea on Ascension Day, or Corpus Christi, which showed the great wealth of Venice and its **guilds** in procession. The **Venetian galleys** would leave in May or June for the East. Three methods of transport were available for the medieval pilgrim. First was the special galley belonging to the Venetian state, which would be hired out by the Signoria to noble and wealthy pilgrims. These VIP galleys were more luxurious and less crowded than the second method for the six-week journey, which were the pilgrim galleys owned and operated by private citizens of Venice. The third option was a smaller sailing ship, also privately owned and chartered, often by groups who had made the journey together, or had met in Venice.

The second option, of the pilgrim galley, was the most popular—and over-crowded. It was also an excellent souce of income to the state and its citizens. Potential pilgrims would require food and bedding for the journey; everything from bedding to camp stoves could be purchased at the point of departure, new and second hand. Those fortunate enough to return from their tour of the Holy Land could sell back their slightly soiled goods and recoup a fraction of their initial investment in the trip. Amongst the necessary items for a sojourn on the common pilgrim galleys were a mattress, two pillows, two pairs of sheets, a quilt, cooking provisions (e.g. a crate of hens) and utensils, medicines, laxatives and a chest with a strong lock. On board the galley the travellers would be allotted their sleeping area, chalked out on the floor of the lower deck. The appropriate medicines were a must; epidemics were rife on the galleys, due to both overcrowding and poor sanitation. Such conditions made the journey to the Holy Land almost as perilous as the dangers encountered on arrival. (Margaret Wade Labarge, *Medieval Travellers, The Rich and the Restless*, London, 1982; William Wey, *Itineraries to Jerusalem*, 1458, pub. Roxburghe Club, 1857; *The Book of Margery Kempe*, London, 1987.)

Pisse-pot prophet: CHECKMATE, II, 7: *The Pisse-Pot Prophet* is a book by Thomas Brian. In the text, the unflattering name is given to **Nostradamus**, who was both a prophet and a physician diagnosing through urine tests, one of the mainstays of medieval medicine. See **Urine glasses.**

Pistacia lentiscus: PAWN, 19: The evergreen tree, common to **Chios.** The resin from the tree was gathered from June to September. The gum was regarded as medicinal by the ancients, but later used as a flavouring. The sixteenth-century Greeks used it in their drink called *masicha*, and the Arabs used it in their sweetmeats. In more modern times it has also been used as a varnish. The mastic plant only grows on the south side of the island of Chios, and its gum is referred to as 'tears' because it symbolises the anguish of St Theodora as she was led across the south side of the island to her martyrdom.

PIUS II: RAM: (1405–1464) Perhaps most famous of Renaissance popes, Aeneas Silvio Piccolomini was one of the foremost humanists, womanisers and lyric writers of his day. This is in contrast to his devout crusading stance as pontiff but does not indicate a degree of hypocrisy. Piccolomini only entered Holy Orders at the age of forty-six. Prior to this point, he had been secretary to prominent ecclesiastics and laymen, such as Emperor Frederick III of Austria. Like many of his contemporaries, he thought little of the artistic culture of Austria and Germany, comparing the love of letters in Italy to the attitude prevalent in the north where 'princes pay more attention to horses and dogs than to poets'.

Piccolomini also visited Scotland during his pre-papal libidinous phase, in

1435, to visit **James I**, himself a poet and writer of distinction. The winter crossing over the North Sea was so rough that the papal legate was in fear of his safety. He vowed that if he survived the crossing, he would walk barefoot from his point of arrival to the nearest shrine of Our Lady. He managed the pilgrimage, but Pius was subsequently to blame Scotland as the cause of the gout which plagued him for the rest of his life. It was in Scotland that the Italian scholar was first introduced to **coal**. The Scots were not averse to beguiling such early tourists: having seen for his own eyes the wonders of these sulphurous black stones burned by the locals, he was then regaled with the Scottish tale of the swan-fruit tree. It is said that a certain tree grew close to the river, and when the fruit dropped to the ground, that which landed in the water would sink and rise to the surface as a fully grown swan, whereas the fruit which landed on the earth would simply shrivel and die. Piccolomini asked at several junctures where this tree could be found, and like later travellers was always given the vague instruction 'further north'. He was ultimately given directions to Orkney where he was assured he would find the tree in question.

Following his induction to the church, Piccolomini was papal secretary to three popes, during which time he received his bishopric and cardinal's hat, finally rising to the supreme office in 1458. First and foremost, Pius attempted to reform the church and give the Christian world a sense of purpose and motivation in a new crusade to recover Constantinople, lost to the Ottoman Empire only five years before. Despite his hopes and promises from other rulers such as **Philip the Good**, the planned crusade did not come to fruition. Pius II died in Ancona, waiting to see the beginning of what he hoped would be a great Christian fleet sent to reconquer the East. (F.A. Gragg, tr., *Memoirs of a Renaissance Pope: The Commentaries of Pius II*, London, 1959.)

Plague cures: There are many alternative and optimistic fifteenth- and sixteenth-century cures for the plague, but few of them were ever capable of alleviating the symptoms, let alone curing the bubonic and pneumonic plagues which ravaged late medieval Europe, dispatching an estimated third of the population. In 1546, **Nostradamus** did attempt to deal with the plague caused by stagnant water in the town of Aix. He had already noted that plague tended to follow the course of rivers and spent years experimenting with fumigation techniques and herbal treatments, but believed that vinegar and rosewater would take the venom from the water-borne disease. One of his life-saving pomades was a combination of powdered lapis lazuli, coral and gold leaf.

He recommended that a powder should be made, requiring an ounce of green cyprus, six ounces of Provence iris, three ounces of cloves, three drachms of *calami odorati* and six ounces of aloes wood. The ingredients were to be powdered, then mixed with red rose petals, picked before the dew. The mixture was then made into pills, and left to dry in the shade. They were to be carried in the mouth in order to dispel evil smells, believed to cause the plague. All who took Nostradamus' various potions survived the Provence epidemics, and he was handsomely rewarded with money, gifts and a pension for life. (Jean Moura & Paul Louvet, *La Vie de Nostradamus*, Paris, 1936.)

Platfut he bobbit up with bendis: CHECKMATE, III, 9: From the poem, 'Christ's Kirk on the Green', reputedly written by James I of Scotland (1394–1437) (extract):

Was never in Scotland heard nor seen
Sic dancing nor deray [revelry],
Neither at Falkland on the green,
Nor Peblis at the Play;
As was of wowaris [wooers] as I wen
At Christ's-Kirk on a day;
There came our Kitties [country girls] washen clean,
In their new kirtillis [gowns] of gray,
Full gay,
At Christ's-Kirk on the green, that day.

To dance thir damysellis them dicht [made themselves ready],
Thir lasses licht of laitis [nimble];
Their gloves were of the raffel right [roe skin],
Their shune were of the straitis [Cordovan leather],
Their kirtles were of lyncome light,
Well prest with many plaitis;
They were so nyss [shy] when men them nigh'd [approached them]
They squeilit like any gaitis [goats],
Full loud,
At Christ's-Kirk on the green, that day.

Of all these maidens mild as meid,
Was none so gymp [slender] as Gillie;
As any rose her rude [complexion] was red,
Her lyre [neck, bosom] was like the lily:
Fow yellow, yellow was her head,
But she of love was silly,
Though all her kin had sworn her dead,
She would have but sweet Willy,
Alone,
At Christ's-Kirk on the green, that day.

She scornèd Jock and skraipit at him,
And murgeon'd him with mocks,

He would have luvit, she would not let him,
For all his yellow locks;
He cherisht her, she bad go chat him [hang himself],
She comptit him not two clocks [beetles];
So shamefully his short gown set him,
His limbs were like two rocks,
She said,
At Christ's-Kirk on the green, that day . . .

Then Stephen came stepping in with stends [bounds]
No rink [strong man] might him arrest [make him stop],
Splayfoot he bobbit up with bends [leaps]
For Maud [the name of a dance] he made request:
He lap [did leap] till he lay on his lends [all his length]
But rising he was prest,
Till that he hostit [broke wind], at both ends,
For honour of the feast,
That day,
At Christ's-kirk on the green, that day.
(J. Ross, ed., *The Book of Scottish Poems*, Edinburgh, 1878.)

Plures crapula quam ensis: CHECKMATE, III, 1: Latin proverb; 'Inebriation (or
over-indulgence in wine) kills more than the sword'.

Plus étroit que la vigne à l'ormeau se marie: CHECKMATE, IV, 6: Poem of Pierre
de Ronsard (1524–1585) (extract):

> *Plus estroit que la vigne à l'Ormeau se marie*
> *De bras souplement-forts.*
> *Du lien de tes mains, Maistresse, je te prie,*
> *Enlace-moy le corps.*
> *Et feignant de dormir, d'une mignarde face*
> *Sur mon front panche toy:*
> *Inspire, en me baisant, ton haleine et ta grace*
> *Et ton coeur dedans moy.*
> *Puis appuyant ton sein sur le mien qui se paine,*
> *Pour mon mal appaiser,*
> *Serre plus fort mon col, et me redonna l'âme*
> *Par l'esprit d'un baiser.*
> *Si tu me fais ce bien, par tes yeux je te jure,*
> *Serment qui m'est si cher,*
> *Que de tes bras aimez jamais autre aventure*
> *Ne pourra m'arracher:*

> *Mais souffrant doucement le joug de ton Empire,*
> *Tant soit-il rigoureux,*
> *Dans les champs Elisez une mesme navire*
> *Nous passera tous deux.*

Hold me close; closer than vine about elm
With these soft, supple arms.
My body embrace with thy hands
And while seeming to sleep,
With these gentling lips
Linger over my brow.
Breathe, in kissing, your soul and your grace
And your heart into mine;
Then bending on mine your smooth breast
Ease the place of my hurt.
Hold me tight and restore me my soul
With the flame of a kiss.
If you do this for me, by your eyes let me swear,
Oath I hold passing dear,
That from these loving arms
No wayward adventure will tear me.
But bearing lightly the yoke of your reign
Rigorous though it prove,
We shall reach the Elysian Fields
Together, we two.

(Tr. D.D.)

Pluto: KINGS, III, 2: The Roman King of the Underworld, or Hades, as the Greeks called it.

Plûtot souffrir que mourir; c'est la devise des hommes: KNIGHTS, II, 5: 'On the whole men would rather suffer than die'.

Poculum amatorium ad venerem: CHECKMATE, III, 4: A particularly potent love potion recorded by **Nostradamus** as guaranteed to make the object of your desire frantic with unbridled passion. The ingredients and method are as follows. First, take three apples from the mandragora, plucked at sunrise, and wrap in the leaves of verbena and molly grass and leave overnight. Then take ¼ oz of magnetised stone, pulverised in a marble mortar and moistened with the juice of mandragora. Add to the above the blood of seven male sparrows bathed in their left wings, 2 oz of ambergris, ¼ oz of musk, 13 oz of cinnamon bark, cloves and lignum aloes. Then add fairly large quantities of purple fish's eyes in honey, calamint, the root of *lyris illyrica, racina apirisus* and lime water.

The resultant concoction must then be carefully mixed in a marble mortar with a wooden pestle and silver spoon. Boil the sludge in a glass vessel until the mixture has reached a écu's syrupy consistency. Place only in a glass, gold or silver vessel. If half an écu's weight of this potion is placed in the lover's mouth, it will render him or her insensible with sexual desire, and will kill them unless they either immediately make mad, passionate love to you, or spit out the potion. The good doctor Nostradamus does not say which is the advisable option. (Jean Moura & Paul Lovet, *La Vie de Nostradamus*, Paris, 1930.)

Podicicinist: QUEENS, II, 4: One who breaks wind as a form of public entertainment. Skilled exponents of the art could imitate sounds, extinguish candles, and even play musical instruments. (Bulletin of the University of London, No 26, June 1975; Jean Nohain & F. Caradec, *Le Pétomane*, London, 1967.)

Poison Plot: QUEENS: There was indeed a genuine attempt 'by one Stewart' against the life of **Mary Queen of Scots** during her minority in France. The perpetrator is named as Gilbert, Robert or Robin Stewart, depending upon the sources consulted. Stewart, a Royal **Archer** of the Guard, was caught and tortured, but would not be drawn to admit his motives, methods, or accomplices in the plot. Stewart had fled to England in April 1551, and boasted of his plans to **Brice Harison**, a translator in the employ of Protector **Somerset**, who turned him over to the English authorities. Harison told de Chémault, French Ambassador in London, that Stewart had the means to poison the Scottish Queen through knowing officers in her kitchen and her tastes, and had asked Harison to tell the English Privy Council, hoping to please them. Stewart was sent back to France as a prisoner in June 1551, where he was questioned by **Henri II** at Calais and again at Plessis-Macé, before being tortured and then executed.

His plot, if carried through, would have cleared the way for **Matthew Lennox** to succeed to the Scottish throne and advance the claim of **Margaret Lennox** to the crowns of Scotland and England. Lennox and his brother **d'Aubigny**'s involvement in the plot was refuted by **Warwick** when he discussed the matter with the French herald, Vervassal. Little is recorded about Stewart as a person, other than the suggestion that prior to his service in the King of France's Scottish Guard, Stewart had been recently released from servitude as a French galley slave. He is described as a 'Castilian' who preferred servitude on the galleys to punishment in Scotland for his part in the murder of Cardinal Beaton at St Andrews, for which **John Knox** also ended up on *travaux forcés*. The existence of the plot reveals the undercurrent of radical Reformed politics holding sway in Scotland in the Queen Dowager **Mary de Guise**'s absence. (E. Mavianne & H. McKerlie, *Mary of Guise-Lorraine*; Francique-Michel, *Les Ecossais en France*; A. Teulet, *Papiers d'État Rélatifs à L'Histoire de L'Écosse, 16ème siècle*, Vol. I, Bannatyne Club.)

POITIERS, Diane de: QUEENS: See **Diane de Poitiers.**

POLE, Cardinal Reginald: CASTLE: (1501–1558) Archbishop of Canterbury. He spent most of his life in Italy, firstly through choice and later due to involuntary exile. Pole began his academic studies at Oxford, but travelled to Padua in 1521 where he stayed for a number of years. Described as ascetic, kind and gentle; with large sad eyes, and a Plantagenet face. Pole was the last surviving Plantagenet in line to the throne: his mother was the daughter of the Duke of Clarence (King **Edward IV**'s brother), and his father was a cousin of Henry VIII. When Pole disagreed with Henry VIII over the matter of serial divorce, he was forced to flee England and sought involuntary exile in Rome, where Pope **Paul III** made him a cardinal. Despite Henry VIII's numerous attempts to assassinate the popular prelate, 'Pole the Angel' seems to have led a charmed life. Henry contented himself with executing Pole's family instead; including his mother the Countess of Salisbury, his brother Lord Montacute and his cousin Henry Courtenay, Marquis of Exeter.

He was considered to be the favoured choice as pope after the death of Paul III in 1549 (the odds in the Rome betting shops were in his favour at eighty to one), but the votes were split evenly between Pole and Cardinal Caraffa, later to be **Paul IV.** As the conclave could not agree on either of them, they elected Gianmaria Ciocchi Del Monte, described as 'that sybaritic sodomite', as Pope **Julius III.** Whilst in Italy, Pole converted **Vittoria Colonna** to strict Catholicism; she later had great influence over Michelangelo, with whom Pole also cultivated a friendship. Michelangelo honoured the cardinal by representing him as the prophet Ezekiel in the Sistine Chapel.

After spending most of his life abroad, he was recalled to England in 1553, when **Mary Tudor** came to the throne. Pole had been a childhood friend of Mary, and although not ambitious he had a good claim to the throne on his own merits. Before his ordination he was considered as a possible suitor for Mary, but is said to have thought **Courtenay** more suitable for that role if Mary were to marry at all.

Although he would have preferred Mary to remain dedicated as a bride of Christ rather than to marry, he did not provide an obstacle to her marriage, but remained out of England until after 1554, when as papal legate to England he received Imperial permission to return. He also did his best to avoid **Philip II** when the latter was waging war against Pope Paul IV. Cardinal Pole's life and death were inextricably linked to the royal line; having eventually returned home after a life in exile, he died exactly twelve hours after Mary Tudor. (H. Ross Williamson, 'Cardinal Pole in Italy', *History Today*, January, 1970.)

Polycarp: KINGS, III, 4: (AD c. 69–c. 155) One of the early Christian fathers; said to have been a disciple of John, who consecrated Polycarp as Bishop of Smyrna. On returning from Rome in AD 155, he was arrested during a pagan festival. Proclaiming that he had served Christ for eighty-six years of his life, he refused to recant, and was condemned to die at the stake. Tradition has it that burning was, however, unsuccessful (the flames refused to come near him) and he had to be despatched with a dagger.

Poorterslogie: RISING: The meeting place of the burghers of **Bruges**, and the headquarters of the **White Bear Society**, who set their emblem on the corner of the building in 1417. The house itself takes its name from the status of Bruges as a trading town or *poort*; its burghers thus being the *poorters*. The *poorters* were the wealthy oligarchy of the town, living on their personal incomes, or from the ample opportunities to trade. They represented the governing class of Bruges, with full rights of citizenship, as compared to the artisans and journeymen of the town who had little or no say in the day-to-day running of their town. (Malcolm Letts, *Bruges and its Past*, London, 1924.)

Porphyrius, wonder of the Blues: RAM, 34: From the fourth century onwards, teams taking part in sporting events in the Hippodrome of Constantinople were distinguished by colours, originally those of Green, Blue, Red and White. The custom was supposed to date back to Rome and the legendary Romulus (Caligula and **Nero** supported the Greens). When established on Roman lines in Constantinople, the factions became so powerful that it was necessary to reorganise them in the form of militia-type clubs. They aroused frenetic partisan support, and the leading charioteers were the bullfighter/TV stars of their time, statues to their honour being erected in public places with inscriptions of suitable fervour. That to the most famous of all ran as follows: 'Porphyrius, wonder of the Blues, having defeated every charioteer on earth, does well to rise and race towards heaven. For he, victorious over every driver here below, mounts to join the sun on its course'.

Pordative organ: SCALES, 6: A small, fully portable organ, as its name suggests, which could be played with one hand while the other hand worked the bellows necessary to provide the instrument with air for the pipes. (CD Set: Musica Reservata, *The Instruments of the Middle Ages and Renaissance*, 1993, Vanguard Classics, 08 9060 72.)

PORTINARI, Tommaso: RISING: (c. 1425–1501) Manager of the **Medici** bank in **Bruges**, a handsome young Florentine who spent most of his life in Burgundian Flanders and nearly wrecked himself and his company with his inveterate social climbing and overspending. The Portinari were an old Florentine family (Folco di Ricovero Portinari was the father of Beatrice Portinari, associated with the poet Dante in the thirteenth century) who found exercise for their quick wits and gifts of numeracy as part of the managerial network of **Cosimo de' Medici**. Two of Tommaso's brothers managed the Medici bank in Milan; his cousin Bernardo was head of the **Bruges** branch when Tommaso began his apprenticeship there in 1437 as a *giovane*, or office boy, a post he was to give in turn twenty-eight years later to his young nephew Folco.

The years in Bruges under Bernardo were gloomy. Bernardo's father had managed the Venetian branch of the Medici and Bernardo was solidly capable, and stayed thirteen years. Advancement was slow in coming; but in 1465 Tommaso finally became a junior partner and governor of the Bruges office after twenty-five years as a factor and a great deal of grumbling. The occasionally rash financial dealings of the branch had not gone unnoticed by the head of the bank in Florence. Cosimo de' Medici kept a tight rein on young men with expensive ideas, and had he not died in 1464, Tommaso might not have been allowed to embark on his happy programme of lending money to princes at rates that made him highly acceptable, while ignoring the £6,000 annual limit imposed by his contract.

Bruges was now at the height of its expansion, and the business of the bank allowed plenty of scope for the ambitious and inventive. It dealt with the exchange of money in all its sly fifteenth-century modes, calculated to evade the usury statutes. It sold letters of credit to travellers and collected dues for the Apostolic Chamber in Rome. It also handled the ordering and selling of luxury goods from tapestry cushions and paintings to horses (chandeliers crossed the Alps in numbered pieces packed in barrels of wool. Chapel singers had less comfortable journeys).

The bank in Bruges imported spices and exported cloth and wool and crossbow wires: it replaced the Arnolfini as chief supplier of Italian silks to the Burgundian court. It also imported **alum** on a vast scale for the dyeing and leather industries, running Tommaso into a series of skirmishes involving his own branch in Rome, the Duke of Burgundy and the Vatican, which wished to fix prices and supplies to protect its own papal alum mines. Private transport was useful for alum, and Tommaso was triumphant in obtaining for the Medici the use of two unused crusading galleys built in 1464 in Pisa for **Philip the Good. Piero de' Medici,** spotting trouble ahead, died just too soon to ensure that Tommaso got rid of them.

In due course Tommaso became a counsellor to the much-indebted Duke **Charles the Bold,** wielding erratic but genuine power at his court. He also plunged into the world of subterranean diplomacy, sending long busy reports to the Duke of Milan, a close associate of the Medici family and their managers: Tommaso's brother Pigello had been financial adviser to Duke Francesco. Tommaso was employed in the secret negotiations which led to the marriage of Duke Charles with Margaret of York. The Medici bank, with its chain of influence, heard everything and knew everything, and was courted by almost everyone.

After years of repression, Tommaso flourished. With the approval of Piero de' Medici, who lacked the astute cynicism of his father Cosimo, Tommaso bought in 1466 the Hôtel Bladelin. This magnificent house in the Rue des Aiguilles, Bruges, had belonged to Pierre Bladelin, the dyer's son who had risen to become Controller of the Duke's household and a treasurer of the **Order of the Golden Fleece** and who (like Tommaso in time to come) had his portrait painted by the leading artist of his day. Tommaso's new acquisition now became the base for the enlarged accountancy staff of the bank as well as a residence for visiting Florentine colleages; and a fully staffed home for the manager (himself).

By 1469 he was ready to consider founding a family. Naturally, his wife must be Florentine, and well born, and favoured by the Medici family. The choice of Piero de' Medici (Tommaso's personal preference was never recorded) fell upon Maria Bandini Baroncelli, a member of a family involved with the rival banking company of the Pazzi. Piero's reasons were no doubt political but Tommaso, desperate to return to Florence, was not likely to object, even though the girl was thirty-one years his junior—indeed so young that after the marriage (in 1470) she was left at home for a year. (**Alessandra Strozzi**, with her finger equally on the erratic pulse of Florentine political advancement, married her son to Maria's sister.)

Resigned, on the death of Piero, to accepting a renewal of his contract in Bruges, Tommaso settled down once more to his eventful life. Seven more good years remained. Among all the ills that befell him then, the success of his marriage must have been his greatest comfort. In 1471 his bride presented him with his first child, a daughter named Margherita after the Duchess Margaret of Burgundy. He was to have nine more children, some of them visible in the paintings by Hans Memling and Hugo van der Goes still extant, which show Tommaso at his best: dark, long-nosed, eager but eternally ostentatious. (Raymond de Roover, *The Rise and Decline of the Medici Bank*, Harvard, 1963; Raymond de Roover, *Money, Banking and Credit in Medieval Bruges*; L. Gilliodts van Severen, *Cartulaires de Bruges*; A. Grunzweig, *Correspondance de la Filiale de Bruges des Medicis*.)

Prelude to the Salt: QUEENS, II, 6: Theme for the harp, with twenty-four variations, played in the court of King Arthur to accompany the salter being placed on the board. (C.A. Harris & Mary Hargreave, *The Story of British Music*.)

Prester John: SCALES, 4: The legendary Christian (Coptic) King of Africa; Prester meaning priest. The myth of the magical ruler can be traced back as far as the twelfth century, when a letter purporting to be from Prester John arrived at the court of the Eastern Emperor Manuel and the German Emperor Frederick I. It came from a ruler whose territories were somewhat vaguely situated in Asia. The Tower of Babel was included in its dominions, as was the Fountain of Youth. The great Christian King ruled over seventy-two other kings, who were tributaries of his empire. Also in his kingdom were a variety of miraculous beasts: huge ants which dug up gold, fish that exuded imperial dye, and salamanders which lived in the heart of fires. The magical gems of the kingdom were without parallel, including mystic pebbles which would restore sight to the blind. Prester John was so powerful that he could alter the course of the Nile if he so wished. His sole reason for maintaining its traditional course was to protect the Egyptian Christians whom he did not want to die of thirst.

The great legends of Prester John (some of which are explicable) were amplified and believed well into the fifteenth century. In 1440, the papal records of Rome make reference to John, Patriarch of Copts, living in Cairo. **Ludovico de Severi da Bologna**'s colourful group of ambassadors included representatives of Zara Ya'qob, Emperor of Ethiopia. Christians from the West desperately tried to reach him; not for the wealth and power of his magical kingdom, but to harness his influence as a Christian ally in a new crusade against the Turk. In 1442, Fra Tommaso da Firenze consistently tried to find Prester John, not overland from Egypt, but overland from Constantinople. Each time he was stopped, imprisoned and ransomed. He only abandoned his search in 1446 after the third attempt, having spent a year or so languishing in prison. (John Ure, *Prince Henry the Navigator*, London, 1977.)

Prick song: QUEENS, II, 3; CASTLE, III, 7: A song set to music, or laid out in parts, where the notes are literally pricked onto paper. When used as a verb, it refers to the ability to sight-read music.

Priés pour l'âme de Jean Maugué, qui nouvellement est allé de vie à trespas entre le Ciel et la terre, au service du Roi notre Sire: CHECKMATE, II, 1: 'Pray for the soul of Jean Maugué, recently passed from life to death between Heaven and earth in the service of our lord the King'.

Primaticcio, Francesco: QUEENS, II, 3: (1504–1570) Italian sculptor, commissioned by **Francis I** and **Henri II**. Francis invited the architect and sculptor to decorate the chateau of **Fontainebleau** with his elegant style of sensuous and erotic female nudes. Along with Il Rosso, he was the founder of the Italianate style of art and architecture developing in France, later known as the Fontainebleau school. Primaticcio continued to live and work in France until his death.

Princenhof: RISING: 1: The grand palace of the **Duke of Burgundy** in **Bruges**, which has existed in one form or another since 1350. In 1446, the bathing arrangements of the ducal residence were overhauled and renewed. Heating and drying rooms were provided for the Duke and his guests, as were barbers' shops. The star attraction of the refurbishment was a great bathing basin, made at Valenciennes and brought to Bruges by canal. It took thirty-three men to drag the bath from the bridge at Notre Dame to the palace. When it eventually arrived, a large hole had to be made in the wall of the palace as it was too immense to fit through the doors. In 1468, alterations to the palace culminated in its enlargement in time for the wedding of **Charles**

the **Bold** to Margaret of York. (Malcolm Letts, *Bruges and its Past*, London, 1924.)

Principibus placuisse viris non ultima laus est: CHECKMATE, III, 5: 'Flattery of distinguished men is not the most glorious of achievements'.

Prior exiit, prior intravit: KINGS, III, 3: Latin proverb: 'First in, first out'.

Priscian's grammar: CASTLE, I, 8: Priscian was a Latin grammarian of Mauretania in the sixth century BC, and teacher in Constantinople. He is remembered as the compiler of *Institutiones Grammaticae*; eighteen volumes of the most complete and systematic Latin grammar to have survived intact. It was considered to be the standard reference book for all Latin school exercises throughout the Middle Ages.

Proponi in publicum: CASTLE, II, 9: Legal term: 'publicly pronounced'.

Prophète de malheur, babillarde: KINGS, IV, 1: 'Prophet of misfortune, chatterer'.

Propissimus, honestissimus et eruditissimus: QUEENS, III, 4: 'The most gracious, most virtuous and most learned'. Said by Pliny the Younger of the grammarian Suetonius, commending him to the Emperor Trajan.

PROTECTOR SOMERSET: KNIGHTS, III, 3: See **Somerset, Duke of.**

Proxime et immediate sequens: CASTLE, II, 4: Legal term: 'next and immediately following'.

Psaltery: SCALES, 6: Triangular box-shaped flat instrument, made of wood. The wire strings could be plucked either with the fingers or with a quill. The sound is lighter and softer than the dulcimer which, although similar, is hit with small hammers, resulting in a more metallic sound. (CD Set: Musica Reservata, *The Music of the Middle Ages and Renaissance*, 1993, Vanguard Classics, 08 9060 72.)

Psyche: PAWN, 8: The personification of the human soul. The youngest of three royal daughters and eternal lover of Eros.

Ptolemies: QUEENS, I, 5: The incestuous monarchs of ancient Egypt from the fourth to the second century BC; descendants of Ptolemy Sotar (323–285 BC); the son of Lagos, and friend and comrade in arms of **Alexander the Great.**

Pyrrha: KINGS, I, 1: A girl's name (and therefore insulting in this context) used by the poet Horace to denote auburn hair (extract):

> What slim and scented youth is courting you now, Pyrrha, amid the roses of that pleasant grotto? For whom are you making those artful, though simple-looking toilettes?

Pythia: KINGS, III, 3: The high priestess who delivered the oracles of Apollo at Delphi. Named after the serpent killed by Apollo, the priestess would bathe in the waters of the Castilian spring before installing herself in the temple set above a cave producing sulphurous vapours. In the midst of the obscuring fog, the priestess would prophesy and make her ambiguously interpreted predictions.

Qahveh: PAWN, 2: The Arabic drink of coffee has been in popular use since the fourteenth century. It is said that a Syrian monastery goatherd found that his goats did not need their afternoon siesta when they had spent the morning browsing on the leaves and fruit of a certain strange bush. He then suggested that the plant should be tested on the monks who were prone to sleep through their evening prayers.

By the mid-fifteenth century, the brew had become particularly popular in Arabian towns; each with a plethora of coffeehouses. With the caravan trains, trade and pilgrims to Mecca, the fashion for coffee spread throughout the Muslim world, across the Persian Gulf to northern India and northward to Cairo and Stamboul. At its best, coffee would quicken the wit, restore the weary and enable the faithful to spend all night at their prayers and devotions. The coffeehouses became popular meeting places for merchants, traders, officials and officers to discuss politics. Their very popularity caused outrage from the Muftis, who saw their mosques empty as the coffeehouses filled. Although not mentioned in the Koran, coffee was condemned for a while as being contrary to its teachings: not being strictly like wine, it was likened to charcoal. Coffeehouses were closed in Mecca in 1511, and repeatedly forbidden.

Sultan Selim I not only greatly expanded the Ottoman Empire from 1515 to 1520, taking control of Syria, Arabia and Egypt, he also revoked the interdict on coffee, spreading its appeal even further. Not only was it more popular than ever, it was a capital offence to criticise its medicinal value; Selim hanged two Persian doctors who claimed that it was injurious to health. However, the Sultan's favourite brew was outlawed by his successors and by 1633 all coffee and tobacco were forbidden on pain of death.

Mocha undoubtably supplied the best coffee, and for two centuries Arabia provided all the beans for the expanding market. European travellers to the Ottoman Empire had described the plant and its potent beans in the 1570s, but it took half a century before the drink began to spread into Europe. Dutch traders brought coffee beans back from Aden in 1614, and a special shipment came from Mocha in 1640. From Constantinople it spread directly to Venice in 1624 and to Rome by the following year. Marseilles was the first French town to embrace 'the Turkish berry drink' which arrived in bales from Egypt.

In 1650 it eventually reached England, courtesy of a Jewish traveller from the Lebanon. (B.E. Dahlgren, *Coffee*, 1938.)

QAYT BEY: UNICORN: (ruled 1468–1496) Qayt Bey came to power as Sultan of **Mameluke** Egypt and Syria at the age of fifty-six. Of Circassian birth, he was bought as a boy for fifty dinars and later put to the service of Sultan Djaqmaq (1438–1453), rising to become Marshal of Armies, a post which often led to the throne of the Sultan. The last Mameluke ruler of strength, he was also one of the greatest of their builders, his cartouche appearing on edifices throughout the Middle East, as well as in Cairo and Alexandria, where in 1480 he commanded a splendid fort to be built as a coastal defence against the Ottoman Turks. It was erected on Pharos island on the site of the Lighthouse which in the third century BC was one of the seven wonders of the world, standing some five hundred feet high with a lantern which threw a beam thirty-five miles out to sea. (Tumbled stones from the Pharos were still visible in the fifteenth century.) In Cairo, Qayt Bey's Mausoleum, completed in 1474, has been described as one of the jewels of Mameluke architecture.

With a frequently empty Treasury, Qayt Bey helped to finance the costs of war and of his luxurious building by controlling and participating in the profitable spice trade between Europe and the Indies, soon to be vitiated by the

Portuguese discovery of alternative sea routes round **Africa**. He also had to deal with the threat to Syria of the Ottoman forces which had plagued his predecessors, while conducting trade negotiations and forming shifting alliances with Christian Venice and Rhodes, or whoever would best preserve him from conquest. The perpetual menace from undisciplined Mamelukes within his own country was successfully countered by the immense personal bulwark of his loyal slaves. Qayt Bey, an accomplished spearman in his youth, never lost his charisma as a leader, being described by Jan Adorne in 1470 as tall, thin, white-haired and brave as a lion in combat. At eighty he was still handsome, and 'upright as a reed'. He died at the age of eighty-six, having ruled longer than any Sultan but al-Nasr.

Qedeshet, Mistress of all the Gods: CHECKMATE, IV, 13: From the Arabic *qadisha* or the Hebrew *kadesha*; meaning sacred harlot or holy virgin. Qedeshet was also the title of the Syrian goddess Astarte. In the Koran, it is the name used for the Prophet Mohammed's first wife Khadija whose money financed his endeavours. (Barbara G. Walker, *The Woman's Encyclopedia of Myths and Secrets*, San Francisco, 1983.)

Quand le bâtiment va, tout va: CHECKMATE, III, 2: 'When the trade is doing well, everything does well'.

Quartain ague: CHECKMATE, V, 9: A fever or series of pains which recurs at regular intervals, with paroxysms occurring every fourth day (tertian ague occurring every third day and so on). Quartain and tertian fevers were included amongst twenty types of English fever in the sixteenth century, including marsh fever or malaria. The pain could be alleviated with homegrown opium: coagulated poppy juice pressed into pellets, cultivated in the Fen district. With the addition of spiders' webs, it was the standard Tudor treatment. Another suggested French cure for a quartain fever (a palliative not currently recommended) was to drink wine which had been stirred with a sword just used for human decapitation. (W.S.C. Copeman, *Doctors and Disease in Tudor Times*; Stephen Paget, *Ambroise Paré and His Times*.)

Qué lástima: PAWN, 8: 'What a pity'.

Quel changement . . . quantum mutatus ab illo Hectore!: CHECKMATE, V, 1: 'What a change . . . How brave Hector was altered'. From *The Aeneid*, Book 2.

Quenouille: CHECKMATE, I, 1: Distaff: See *Je fille quant Dieu me donne de quoy* for the numerous *double entendres* presented by its use.

Qu'es casado el Rey Ricardo: KINGS, Gambit: 'King Richard is married'.

Quetzalcoatl, Lord of the Toltecs: QUEENS, II, 3: Saviour god of the ancient Aztecs; a two-faced deity of creation and destruction united back to back with his brother Death. He represents the corn, death and resurrection; linked with the seasons of planting, growth and harvest. After the flood, he gave blood from his penis to recreate the human race, and thus became one of the 'Castrated Fathers' amongst the gods. He was sacrificed, descended into hell and rose from the dead; his Second Coming is still expected. (Barbara G. Walker, *The Woman's Encyclopaedia* of *Myths and Secrets*, San Francisco, 1983.)

Qui bifrons fueram, gallis sum gallicus una fronte deus: CHECKMATE, III, 2: 'I, the two-faced, am for the Gauls a gallic God with one visage'. Spoken by the god **Janus** in **Etienne Jodelle's** play.

Qui Fortunam vincit, vincit et invidiat: CHECKMATE, V, 5: 'It's nice to triumph over Fortune, but watch out, all the same'.

Qui [que] maudit soit les pieds d'escot, Et les pieds d'escots qui les suivent: CHECKMATE, III, 5: 'Accursed be those fools of Scots, and the fools of Scots who follow them'.

Qui nescit orare, discat navigare: PAWN, 9: Latin proverb, 'If you don't know how to pray, learn to sail', an ironic proverb. Fear induced by the power of the unbiddable elements would soon teach the mariner to remember and trust in his saviour (see **Candles**). For those who took a more pragmatic view of their faith, this seaman's prayer offers an alternative relationship between God and man:

> O Lord, I am no common beggar, I do not trouble thee every day, for I have never prayed to thee before; and if it pleases thee to deliver me this once, I will never pray to thee again as long as I live.

(*Harleian Collection of Voyages*, 1745, Vol. I.)

Qui peut de tous bois faire flèches: CHECKMATE, III, 9: Literally, 'Who can make arrows of any wood', meaning one who can turn any situation to his or her advantage.

Qui vero in Indiam, Persiam, aliasque Orientis regiones profisci cupient semper istic negociatores reperiunt: PAWN, 16: 'Those who really wish to set out for India, Persia and other regions of the East, always find there merchants to pass to and fro on that side and this'. A quote from Pierre Bellon (or Belon) (1517–1564), the French naturalist who travelled extensively in the Levant, referring to the great market of Aleppo.

Quick and Merry Dialogues: QUEENS, IV, 3: Title of one of the prose works of Sir Thomas Elyot (1499–1546). Elyot's *Dictionary* (Latin and English), published in 1538, was the first book of its kind to bear this title. (Henry Craik, ed., *English Prose Selections*, Vol. I.)

Quicquid libet, licet: KINGS, I, 1: A quotation associated with the dissolute Roman Emperor Antoninus (Caracalla, ruled AD 211–217): 'Ah, si, licevit, Quicquid libet, licet' ('Ah, if it were allowed, Whatever you wished, you could do').

Quid melius Roma? Scythio quid frigore peius?: CHECKMATE, II, 5: 'What is better than Rome? What worse than the Scythian cold?' (De Breul, *Antiquité de Paris*, 1612.)

Quiere Vd comer? ¡Está servido un poquito, poquito: KNIGHTS, III, 8: 'Does my lord wish to eat? I have prepared a morsel . . . a morsel'.

Quince paste: QUEENS, II, 5: The young **Mary Queen of Scots** was particularly fond of making *cotignac*, or quince paste; a simple recipe for a child (with help) to follow. Peel, quarter and core the ripe quinces, putting them in cold water to avoid discoloration. Bring the water to the boil, and simmer until the fruit is soft. Strain the fruit and pound the flesh with an equal quantity of powdered white sugar. Pour the mixture into trays or dishes ⅛ inch deep, and leave to stand for four to five days. Cut the paste into strips and store in a closed jar. Because of the high sugar content, the paste should keep for a year. (Le Baron Alphonse de Ruble, *La Première Jeunesse de Marie Stuart*, Paris, 1891.)

Quintain: QUEENS, II, 1: By the sixteenth century this referred to a wooden saracen on a revolving post with a shield on its left arm and a club in its right; used for jousting and target practice. If the quintain was not hit correctly, it would swing round and the club would neatly catch the human assailant in the back. Another popular pastime was to tilt at a water butt; again if the stroke was not accurate, the misguided flower of chivalry would receive a sound drenching. (Joseph Strutt, *Sports and Pastimes of the People of England*, 1801.)

Quipus: QUEENS, III, 2: The Inca language of knots on string (CASTLE, III, 13), by which messages are passed using a specific arrangement of the order, type and colour of threads used.

Quod purpura non potest, saccus potest: KINGS, IV, 4: 'What high dignity [imperial purple robes] can't, sackcloth can'.

Qu'on lui ferme la porte au nez, il reviendra par les fenêtres: KINGS, IV, 2: 'It's no good closing the door in his face, he'll come back through the window'.

Quum [cum] infirmi sumus, optimi sumus: KINGS, IV, 4: 'We are at our most virtuous when sick'.

RAIS, DRAGUT: See **Dragut Rais.**

Rebec: KINGS, IV, 2: Small violin-type instrument of two or three strings, played with a bow; introduced to Spain by the Moors. (C.A. Harris & M. Hargreave, *The Story of British Music; The Earlier French Musicians.*)

Red wise, Brown trusty: KINGS, Gambit: Quoted from the old Scots advice on colour and temperament:

> To a Red man read thy Reade [counsel, advice],
> With a Brown man break thy bread,
> At a Pale man draw thy knife,
> From a Black man keep thy wife.
> The Red is wise, the Brown trusty,
> The Pale envious and the Black lusty.

The advice on colour coding for women is somewhat different:

> Fair and foolish, little and loud,
> Long and lusty, black and proud,
> Fat and merry, lean and sad,
> Pale and pettish, Red and bad,
> High colour choler shows,
> And she's unwholesome that like sorrel grows.
> Naught are the peevish, proud malicious,
> But worst of all the red shrill, jealous.

REID, Robert, Bishop of Orkney: CHECKMATE: (d. 1558) Educated first at the University of St Andrews. After graduating in 1515, Reid went to France. In 1528 he was anointed Abbot of Kinloss and nominated for the College of Justice in 1532. Reid was one of **James V**'s closest advisers and his secretary. In 1541 he was made Bishop of Orkney; the title of Kinloss officially passed to his nephew, but Reid maintained his other abbacy in his title. In 1548, he was appointed President of the Court of Session.

Reid was James V's chosen ambassador to three popes and the Kings of France and England, and in 1558 he was one of the Scots Commissioners chosen to negotiate the marriage between the Scots Queen and the French Dauphin. He was aboard the boat which sank *en route*, but he and the **Earl of Rothes** were saved by a fishing boat which came to their rescue. Along with several others, Reid never made it home alive.

Although **John Knox** called him a miser, and specifically made note of the fact Reid slept on his coffers of gold, even when close to death, few others comment on the miserly nature of the prelate; even **Buchanan** called him 'a man of consummate wisdom'. His interests outside the church and diplomacy included the maintenance of his library and garden: he constructed a fireproof room for his books at Kinloss and brought a gardener skilled in grafting fruit trees over from France. He left 8,000 merks in his will to found a university in Edinburgh, used in 1581 to buy the precincts from the last provost of Kirk o' Field. It was on this site that the university buildings were first constructed.

RENÉ (Renatus), Duke of Anjou, Bar and Lorraine, Count of Provence, King of Naples: RISING: (1409–1480) A delightful Renaissance prince and much-loved ruler who lacked, however, the military brilliance of an **Urbino**. Despite his titles, René did not at the end of his life control a single foot of soil—not even the island of Majorca which he gave his daughter Margaret as a wedding present for her marriage to Henry VI of England.

Born in the castle of Angers to Louis II, King of Sicily, Duke of Anjou, Count of Provence, and Yolande, daughter of John I, King of Aragon, his favourite homeland always remained the Loire valley of France. René grew up in Anjou and in Provence. An early marriage to Isabella, the daughter of the Duke of Lorraine, brought René, when old enough, to fight for France (and Joan of Arc) against England and her ally Burgundy in the Hundred Years' War. When his father-in-law died in 1431 René inherited the Duchy of Lorraine, but lost it to a rival claimant backed by the Duke of Burgundy. Defeated and captured at the battle of Bulgnéville that same year, René was imprisoned by Duke **Philip the Good** in his Dijon fortress, where he remained intermittently for five years under threat of a punishing ransom of 400,000 gold crowns. While in prison he occupied himself by painting: it is said that he took lessons from the Flemish painter Jan Van Eyck, then attached to the Burgundian court.

René emerged from Dijon in 1436 after the death of his brother to find that he was now Duke of Anjou, with a claim to the crown of Naples and Sicily. In this claim Genoa and Milan were his allies. In 1438 René travelled via Genoa to take up his kingdom in Naples, but after four years of fighting against his rival claimant **Alfonso V of Aragon** was forced to abandon Naples in 1442 and return to Provence, King of Sicily only in name. A further series of battles against Alfonso in 1453–1454 was inconclusive. The war for Naples was not, however, completely lost until 1462 when his son John, Duke of Calabria, was routed at Troia. Losing Naples, John turned his attention to Aragon, but died in 1470 in Barcelona, to his father's great sorrow, before he could enforce his claim to the crown.

Meanwhile there had taken place some important alliances. In 1445 René's daughter Margaret married the Lancastrian King Henry VI of England, and would in time seek the support of both Scotland and her cousin **Louis XI** of France against the Yorkish claimants to the English throne. René's young daughter Yolande and her husband were given the duchy of Lorraine, which was to fall in turn to Yolande's nephew Nicholas and then her son René, named after his grandfather.

At the court of René himself, the high artistic skills of the Duke flourished between and after the periods of battle. The opulent port of Marseilles brought him the treasures of the Orient he so admired; in Provence and Angers he established his menageries of exotic birds and beasts, at both courts he welcomed musicians and artists and made possible the commissioning of lavish spectacles, whether of plays or magnificent tournaments. A poet and painter himself, René was an admirable patron of art and literature. In his private life he was equally fortunate. Isabella of Lorraine was a loyal and loving wife, active in his interests all through his imprisonment. On her death, he married in 1454 Jeanne de Laval, twenty-four years his junior, a Breton lady whom he held in deep affection and who, although childless herself, was unfailingly kind to her stepchildren. His poem 'Regnault and Jeanneton' celebrated their union, lightly disguised, on the lines of 'The Kingis Quair' of James I of Scotland (see **Hast thou no mind of love? Where is thy make?**). In addition, René did have at least one mistress, and a natural daughter, Blanche.

René's sister had married **Charles VII** of France, under whom René held his French lands in vassaldom. Relations between René and King Charles's son Louis XI were less harmonious, and in time were to lose René his delightful houses on the Loire and send him to end his days in Provence where even the wine could not compare with that of the vignobles of his stately Loire. (A. Lecoy de la Marche, *Le Roi René*; F. Unterkircher, *King René's Book of Love*.)

Rest to the soul, food to the spirit: KNIGHTS, II, 6: The hawking cry of the five hundred or so sherbet vendors in sixteenth-century Constantinople. The nonalcoholic spiced water of the Arabs was also described as 'the sherbet of the soul'. The sherbet was basically water, sweetened with rhubarb, rose leaves, lemon, lotus, tamarind and grapes. The best sherbet sellers would gather at the Scutari landing stage, but there were plenty of rivals with inferior products, sweet nonetheless. The itinerant sellers of the sweet syrup *ighdá* would lurk in the alleys, selling the liquid from the cask. Since they were always selling or consuming their own sweet product, it was claimed that even the most timid animal could be tamed by their sugar-sweet nature. Their sweetness was also said to help them when it came to romantic entanglements, as the syrup was supposed to make their saccharine-tinged terms of endearment irresistible to the opposite sex. See also **The love of sweetmeats comes from the Faith**. (Alexander Pallis, *In the Days of the Janissaries*.)

Rex Nemorensis: KINGS, I, 5: King of the Grove. The high priest who presided over the sacrifices to Diana of Aricia; the temple being on the north shore of Lake Nemi, sixteen miles south of Rome, on the Appian Way. The priest in question was always a runaway slave who obtained his post by slaughtering his predecessor in single combat.

Riding of O'Neill: QUEENS, II, 6: '*Marcuighecht U'Néill*': ancient Irish song-verse which imitates the monotonous hoof-beats of a cavalcade. (Richard Henebry, *Handbook of Irish Music*.)

Ríg-domna: QUEENS, II, 4: Irish Gaelic for 'king material'.

Right so came an adder out of a little heath bush: QUEENS, IV, 1: From Sir Thomas Malory's (c. 1405–1471) *Le Morte D'Arthur*. The appearance of the adder causes the peace between Sir Mordred and King Arthur to be untimely broken:

> And so they met as their pointment [arrangement] was and were agreed and accorded throughout. And wine was fetched and they drank together. Right so came an adder out of a little heath-bush, and it stung a knight in the foot. And so when the knight felt him so stung, he looked down and saw the adder. And anon he drew his sword to slay the adder, and thought [meant] none other harm. And when the host on both parties saw that sword drawn, then they blew beams, trumpets, and horns, and shouted grimly.

(*Norton Anthology of English Literature*, Vol. I, N.Y., 1979.)

RIMINI, Lord of: SCORPIONS: See **Malatesta, Sigismondo Pandolfo**.

Ring the bells backwards: KINGS, II, 1: A muffled noise which warns of disaster, or expresses dismay rather than joy.

Riza: CASTLE, II, 2: The silver covering frame of an icon, usually embellished with precious metals and jewels.

Robbia, Luca della: KINGS, IV, 1; PAWN, 29: See **Della Robbia, Luca**.

ROGER, Will: UNICORN: An English musician who flourished in Scotland in the reign of **James III**, but about whom reports conflict. Some sources refer to him as 'Dr' William Roger, who may have come to Scotland in the train of an English embassy, and remained to enjoy the patronage of the King. Other reports, with perhaps less credibility, claim that **Edward IV** sent Roger to the

Scottish court, and that he was eventually given a knighthood. The historian Ferrerius calls Roger '*rarissimus musicus ex Anglia*'. One might speculate that one of the attractions to Roger himself was the strong link between the Scottish court and that of Burgundy, which was at the time highly sophisticated in musical matters. By 1467, he was Clerk of the Chapel Royal in Scotland, and was promised twenty pounds annually for life from the Customs returns for Haddington (which also paid the expenses of the lady Margaret, the King's sister, who was being reared at Haddington Priory). By 1468, Roger was master of the hospital of St Leonard, near Peebles, a hospital for the poor founded under another name before 1305, from which he received payment through Peebles customs. In 1469 Roger was awarded the lands of Traquair, beside Peebles, which had reverted to the Crown with the forfeiture of Robert, Lord **Boyd**, but in 1476 was required to resign them (as happened to many others) when the King came of age. It is hard to tell how many of these appointments were simply means of supplying Roger with a livelihood to enable him to continue to advise the King on music. It seems likely that he helped James III with his plans to establish the Chapel Royal as a music conservatory. It is not known how far this work progressed, but Ferrerius recorded that in 1529 he met several people who claimed to have studied at a school of musicians founded by Roger. No music by Roger is known. He seems to have had a home in North Leith, but probably stayed at or near court with the King's other musicians. The splendid organ for Trinity College which appears in the painting of **Edward Bonkle** by Hugo van der Goes was presumably one of the instruments in Roger's care. He was also no doubt responsible for the dispatch of a succession of Scottish court musicians—mostly 'lutars'—to **Bruges** for instrumental instruction.

Rooftop race: QUEENS, II, 5: During the reign of **Francis I**, there was a brief fashion for wagers to be laid that one would enter the precincts of a town by jumping only from roof to roof, not touching the ground at all but using the narrow overcrowded late medieval towns of France to their best advantage, jumping across the narrow streets. Another 'dare' was to set a wood on fire and then gallop through it without causing injury to either the horse or the rider. Such feats of bravado were excellent training for the budding gentleman skilled in games and warfare. (Clarisse Coignet, *Francis the First and His Times*.)

Rosa das rosas, et fror das frores: KINGS, II, 2:

> *Rosa das rosas, et fror das frores*
> *Dona das donas, senor das sennores*
> *Rosa de beldad et de parecer*
> *et fror d'allegria et de prazer* . . .

> Rose among roses and flower among flowers
> Maiden of maidens and lord of her bower

> Blossom of beauty, of bearing, of mien
> and flower of happiness, courtly, serene . . .

(Tr. D.D.)

Rosault, vomit three ways . . . like the: CHECKMATE, III, 2: According to ancient Celtic myth, the Rosault was a deadly sea monster which could vomit into the sea, killing fish and wrecking ships; into the air, where its vile fumes slew the birds; or onto the land, whereby it caused a pestilent rain. No doubt the Rosault more than made up for the absence of snakes in Ireland.

ROTHES, George Leslie, Earl of: CHECKMATE: (d. 1558) Scottish Protestant, Lord of the Court of Session from 1541. Rothes had been present at the marriage of **James V** to his first French wife in 1536. Both his brother and son were prime movers in the murder of Cardinal Beaton in St Andrews in 1546 (see **Wishart, George**), but Rothes kept himself apart from the plotting and, although tried, was acquitted of any involvement in the murder. In 1550 he was appointed Scottish Ambassador to Denmark, and in 1558 he was amongst the Scots Councillors sent to France to oversee the wedding plans of **Mary Queen of Scots**. Along with several others of the Councillors, he succumbed to illness on his return to Scotland and died in Dieppe on or around November 8.

Rotz's Differential Quadrant: CASTLE, II, 9: Jean Rotz was a Dieppe-born geographer appointed as a salaried Hydrographer by Henry VIII of England in 1542. He was ranked amongst the top cosmographers and explorers of his day, and received preferment after presenting Henry with an elaborate meridional compass and a treatise in French on the intricacies of nautical science. Rotz tried to solve the problem mariners had in assessing longitude by examining the differences between compasses. All compasses were produced allowing for local deviation, thus when they were taken abroad, they were unreliable. For example, Columbus found that his Genoese and Flemish needles gave contradictory readings. (E.G.R. Taylor, *Tudor Geography: 1485–1583*.)

Round ship: SCALES: Built primarily for stability and heavy cargoes, the round ship was a merchant's craft, capable of carrying 100 deadweight tons or more. The ship depended completely on sailpower. Large round ships (of 240 tons or more) carried heavy cargoes on the same routes as the **galleys**; such as alum, cotton, stone, oil, salt and slaves. The Venetian round ships were not built or owned by the Signoria, but by private enterprise in private shipyards.

In the mid-fifteenth century, the rigging of these ships changed dramatically. Instead of being one-masted cogs, the round ship developed into a fully rigged three-masted ship complete with spritsail, topsail and mizzen lateen sails. In simple terms, this dramatically improved their manoeuvrability. The concurrent development of superior artillery enabled them adequately to defend

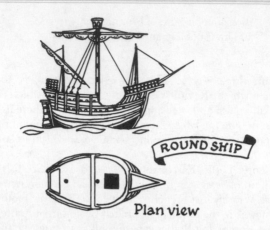

ROUND SHIP

Plan view

themselves without the need for large armed crews of soldiers. The high sides of the round ship also made them harder to board than the low narrow galleys. (Frederick C. Lane, *Venice and History: Collected Papers*, Baltimore, 1966.)

ROXELANA, Sultana: PAWN: Also known as Khurrem, 'The Laughing One', she was brought to Constantinople from Galicia in 1523 by Turkish raiders. Slight, graceful, witty and very astute, she bore at least one son to Sultan **Suleiman**, and became the first legal wife of a sultan in a century and a half. Roxelana obtained and maintained her position by manipulating Suleiman's great affection for her. She told her master that she desired to build a temple for the good of her soul, but that the Mufti said that the pious works of a slave turn only to the advantage of his or her lord. Suleiman declared her to be free forthwith. However, she then explained that being free, the Mufti also said that to sleep with the Sultan (now she was not forced to do so as a bondswoman) would also be a sin. In desperation to keep his beautiful former slave, Suleiman was obliged to marry her.

She was jealous of all possible rivals, and encouraged her husband to marry off the most attractive girls of the Seraglio. She also did her best to advance the case of her son-in-law, **Rustem Pasha**, at the expense of Suleiman's favourite son **Mustapha**. (Roger B. Merriman, *Suleiman the Magnificent*, 1944; William Holden Hutton, *Constantinople*.)

Royal Archers: QUEENS: See **Scottish Archers**.

Royster-Doister, visiting the Castle of Perseverance: KINGS, III, 3: *Ralph Roister Doister* is the earliest surviving English comedy (in doggerel verse), written in 1553, by **Udall**. *The Castle of Perseverance*, from about 1400, is a late-medieval morality play, following the life of the main character from birth to Judgement.

Rudel, sicker than: KINGS, IV, 1: Jaufré or Geoffroi Rudel, twelfth-century trou-
badour from Blaye, Gironde. Tradition has it (probably falsely) that he fell in
love with the Countess of Tripoli, whom he had never seen, and that, having
fallen ill while on a crusade, landed in Tripoli and died in her arms.

Ruin señor cria ruin servidor: KINGS, I, 5: 'A bad master produces a bad servant'.

RUSTEM PASHA: PAWN: (d. 1560) Rustem's father was a poor peasant who
could not pay the sultan's *kharadi*, or alien tax, and offered his son as a page to
the Seraglio instead. Early acts of bravery earned him the attention of
Suleiman, and he was rapidly promoted. While he was Governor of Diarbekir,
Roxelana proposed marriage with her daughter Mihroumah Sultane, which
was agreed in 1539. He used his marriage and influence with the Sultan to his
best advantage, earning money for the Sultan whilst lining his own coffers.

Rustem Pasha was not particularly physically attractive, being small, with
an easily inflamed reddish face, described as always either sad or angry, with
little room for compassion. Although physically robust, there were rumours of
a secret illness. When he was Governor of Diarbekir his enemies claimed that
he had leprosy. A court doctor was sent to examine him, and found a flea on
his skin. This was seen as a sign of his perfect physical health, as parasites were
not considered able to live on the skin of the afflicted.

Rustem Pasha was in charge of all important negotiations and peace
treaties, especially with his 'allies' the French. Rustem was increasingly intol-
erant of Christians; he made no attempt to hide his distaste for the French
envoys, claiming one could never trust a Christian. He is said to have preferred peace to war, if only for the selfish reason that war would have disturbed
the status quo and may have ended his run of good luck and preferment at
court. He died in 1560, leaving behind a massive fortune including hundreds
of thousands of silver ducats, over a thousand farms and estates, a limitless
amount of gold and silver armour, several hundreds of thousands of slaves,
and a magnificent library of 5,000 manuscripts and 300 gem-encrusted copies
of the Koran. (Jean Chesnau, *Le Voyage de M. d'Aramon*, Paris, 1887.)

Sachetti: KNIGHTS, II, 7: A weapon of the **Janissaries**, these were fire grenades which burst, clinging to the armour of the **Knights of St John**. The unfortunate Knight would be roasted alive inside his armour unless he could immediately plunge into the barrels of water often placed on the ramparts of besieged cities. Incendiary devices had been popular with both Muslim and Christian forces since the days of the crusades; see also **Naphtha**. (Ernle Bradford, *The Great Siege*, London, 1961.)

Sacré chat d'Italie!: QUEENS, II, 1: Exclamation, equivalent to 'Holy cats!' literally 'of Italy'.

SAGRES: SCALES, 11: The promontory of Sagres and Cape St Vincent lie at the south-western corner of Europe, at 'finisterre', or the end of the world. The anchorage of Sagres, placed to the east of the Cape, provides a safe sanctuary protected from the north and north-westerly winds, and it was here, at the start of the fifteenth century, that Prince **Henry the Navigator** established his school of navigation. Today, on the probable site of his fortress and chapel, is a chapel dedicated to **St Catherine**, and on the ground, an ancient compass dial marked out in stones and a hundred feet in diameter. Cape St Vincent, two hundred feet above sea level, offers a view of ships passing to and from **Africa**, the Mediterranean and northern Europe. The cape was formerly called Promontorium Sacrum, from which Sagres is named. St Vincent of Saragossa (Zaragoza) in Spain was an early Christian martyr put to death in Valencia. According to legend, his body was then brought to the Cape by Christian followers in a boat guided by ravens. His beneficent ghost is still said to haunt the Cape, providing safe passage to mariners. St Vincent was a saint revered by **René, Duke of Anjou**, who had claims to the throne of Catalonia, and a mystery play on the subject of his martyrdom was performed in Angers in the last week of René's residence there in 1471.

ST ANDRÉ, Jacques d'Albon: QUEENS: (1505–1562) Marshal de St André, Marshal of France and Governor of Lyons after his father. Disliked by **Francis I**, but favoured by **Henri II** whilst he was still the Dauphin, St André saw military service at Boulogne and in Italy, and he did well at the battle of

Cerisoles. When Henri II acceded in 1547, St André was made a member of the Privy Coucil and Marshal of France within the same year, which caused jealous comment at being favoured so greatly at such a young age. Henri also made him First Gentleman of the King's Bedchamber, and Chevalier of the **Order of St Michael.** St André was considered a brave soldier, valiant but not cruel. When St Quentin fell to the Imperial forces of **Charles V** in 1557, St André was captured, still holding his bloody sword in his hand.

St André had a particular taste for expensive luxury goods, and used his position as one of the King's favourites to indulge his cravings. After the death of Henri II, St André allied himself with the **de Guises,** having made enemies of the Reformed Huguenots by his part in their suppression. The austere Protestants despised St André's taste for opulence, and his apparent sexual preference, calling him a *harquebuzier de ponant* (sodomite). They claimed his apparent lascivious conduct was justly punished by venereal disease, which troubled him all his life. He died in 1562 at the battle of Dreux.

His daughter, Catherine d'Albon was a *demoiselle d'honneur* to **Catherine de Médicis,** and was to become the bride of the Prince of **Condé.** Catherine, however, was poisoned and died at Longchamps monastery under somewhat mysterious circumstances. It is said that the poison was administered by her own mother, Marguerite de Lustrac, who had hopes of marrying Condé herself. Marguerite had certainly given Condé many of her former husband's estates in an attempt to woo him away from her daughter and towards herself.

Sakra-deva's diamond hand, washed in warm water by: QUEENS, II, 1: A tale from the Buddhist Scripture, the Dhammapada, in which Buddha humbly cleansed and treated a malodorous elderly mendicant, shunned by all others. (Samuel Beal, tr., *Texts from the Buddhist Canon, The Dhammapada,* London, 1902.)

Salon des singes: KNIGHTS, III, 15: 'Company of monkeys'.

Samoyèdes: CASTLE, I, 5: The pagan people of northern Lapland. One of their idols, Slata Baba, or the Golden Old Woman, was noted by **Herberstein** as a statue of a woman with a child in her lap, lately joined by another figure of a child, perhaps her grandson. Trumpets were placed around the idol which sounded as the wind blew through them.

Samson en perdit ses lunettes: QUEENS, IV, 4: 'Samson lost his spectacles [as a result of women]. Happy the man who has no dealings with them!' The ambiguous quote is from François Villon's (b. 1431) collection of verses based on the colourful experiences of his own life, *Le Grand Testament.* The Hebrew hero and enemy of the Philistines had his eyes put out by the Philistines when he was betrayed by Delilah (Judges, 13).

SANDILANDS, Sir James: KNIGHTS: Head of the Order of **Knights of St John** in Scotland, and Preceptor of Torphichen, formally installed in 1550. It appears that James had a brother called John James Sandilands, also a Knight of St John. In 1557 the brothers were involved in a brawl on Malta, for which John James was imprisoned for six months. He unsuccessfully tried to take the preceptory of Torphichen from his brother and from then on his behaviour became increasingly violent. In 1563 he was again caught fighting; this time in church over the outcome of a gambling game where the prize was a male black slave. John James fought with a senior officer of the English Langue on Malta and was subsequently deprived of his habit. In 1564, John James reappeared in the records of the Knights on Malta, this time accused of sacrilege and the theft of church plate from St Anthony's on Malta. He confessed under torture and was probably executed.

John James's illustrious brother was an angel in comparison, albeit an acquisitive self-seeking Reformed one. Sir James Sandilands had a seat in the Scots Parliament, and was on the Privy Council from 1546. James Sandilands and his father (also James) both supported the Reformation in Scotland (his father had invited **John Knox** to stay with him on Knox's return to Scotland in 1555). Sandilands joined the Reformed Lords of the Congregation in Scotland, and was appointed in 1559 as representative of the reformers to go to France and give the recently orphaned **Mary Queen of Scots** and the French monarchy an account of the abolition of popery in Scotland; a mission from which he was dismissed from France with no answer. Before 1563 he had married and in 1565 he resigned from the Order of St John, and handed the lands of Torphichen over to the crown. On payment of 10,000 crowns and an annual rent of 500 merks, the government granted Sandilands and his heirs the lands of the Order, now the temporal Lordship of Torphichen. On his death, the estate passed to his grand-nephew, James Sandilands of Calder. (Teulet, *Sir James Sandilands, Grand Prieur de l'Ordre de St Jean*; I. Cowan, P. Mackay & A. Macquarrie, eds, *The Knights of St John of Jerusalem in Scotland*, Edinburgh, 1983.)

Sanglier: QUEENS, IV, 2: See *Animal gregale.*

Sardanapalus: CHECKMATE, IV, 3: (d. 877 BC) Last King of the Assyrian empire of Nineveh. He spent the greater part of his reign in his palace, cross-dressing and surrounded by concubines. Eventually, the army under the high priest Arbaces rose up against him. At the first sign of trouble, Sardanapalus shed his women's clothing and showed himself to be a formidable warrior; defeating his enemies twice in battle. At the third conflict, he and his party were forced to retreat to Nineveh where they successfully withstood a siege of two years. At the end of the siege, Sardanapalus ordered that all his possessions (including his wives and concubines) be placed in a large pile in the centre of the city. Sardanapalus then set fire to the pile, destroying himself in the process.

Saturnalia: KINGS, I, 7: Roman festival held in late December in honour of the god Saturn; a time of relaxation, merriment and unbridled licence of all types. The festivities were transferred to New Year's Day in the fourth century AD, to become part of the traditional domestic celebrations of Christmas.

Sauveur's, St: RAM: The parish church of **Bruges**, first constructed in AD 961, and since 1834 the main cathedral of the city. The church was badly burned in 1116 and 1358, but its upper portions were later rebuilt. The nave and aisles date from the mid-fourteenth century whilst the chapels, ambulatory and apses date from between 1482 and 1527. The lower portions of the church tower are twelfth- and fourteenth-century, the upper portions were destroyed by fire in 1839 and subsequently rebuilt. (Malcolm Letts, *Bruges and its Past*, London, 1924.)

Schioppetti: RISING: See **Guns.**

Schwatzen horse, masked like a: PAWN, 10: According to contemporary sixteenth-century travellers in Imperial Germany, the horses carrying the wine of Schwatzen had their noses covered to prevent them from being overcome by the fumes of the alcohol. (Fynes Moryson, Gent., *An Itinerary*, 1617.)

Scott, Michael: KINGS, III, 3: (c. 1175–1235) Medieval translator and scholar, he was originally from Roxburgh and studied in Durham, Oxford, Paris and Palermo. Scott lived in Toledo for ten years, where he studied and translated various Arabic and Greek texts, returning to Palermo to take up residence as physician and court astronomer to the Emperor Frederick II. Amongst his medicinal specialities were after-dinner and headache pills, comprising a mixture of aloes, rhubarb, fruits and mixed flowers.

Legends of his magical powers and wizardry have displaced his scientific reputation, and it was this that earned him his place in Dante's *Inferno*. (John H. Comrie, *History of Scottish Medicine*; Wood Brown, *The Life and Legend of Michael Scott.*)

Scottish Archers: QUEENS: The Royal Guard of Scottish Archers made their first appearance in France in the fifteenth century. In 1417, Henry V of England invaded France and the Dauphin Charles asked for help from Scotland. A large auxiliary force of 150 men at arms and 300 archers arrived in France in August of 1419, followed by the Earl of Buchan who arrived with between seven and ten thousand men, all thoroughly trained and armed. The French denounced their unruly Scots allies as *sacs à vin, et mangeurs de mouton*, 'guzzlers of wine and eaters of sheep', but the Scottish forces rose to military prominence in the kingdom and by 1425 were employed specifically to guard the Kings of France, day and night. Charles VII had 124 Scots guarding his royal person and in 1474 **Louis XI** is recorded as having 100 Scots guardsmen.

The Scots soldiers were generally of good family, and many bore famous names. Louis XI owed his life to them. From 1513, Louis XII of France treated his Royal Archers as naturalised Frenchmen in terms of their property, inheritance and benefices. The guards were rewarded for their past services, and future loyalty was guaranteed by such royal favour. **Francis I**, maintaining the tradition of his forebears, had one hundred Scots Archers at his disposal. In addition to the Archers, there were also the men at arms, a separate Scottish force of well-born soldiers in France, also serving the monarchy. The Archers received the prerogative of bearing the royal coat of arms on their weapons, including their great bows. Their bows were 2 feet long, 8 inches wide in the centre, and an inch thick: formidable weapons. Until 1455 the guard also used crossbows. (William Forbes-Leith, *The Scots Men-At-Arms and Life Guards in France*, Edinburgh, 1882; Maitland Club, *Royal Guard of Scottish Archers in France*.)

Scylla: Circe changed Scylla into a hideous monster because the goddess was jealous of the love shown to Scylla by the fisherman Glaucus. On her transformation, Scylla threw herself into the ocean off Sicily and turned into a rock. See also **Charybdis**.

Seasickness: PAWN, 3, 11: Contemporary preventative measures include an unspecified amount of mixed hashish and opium; or failing that, wine and sagewater, to be drunk before the voyage. In large enough quantities, either solution would no doubt take the patient's mind off the expected difficulties of seatravel.

Another of the stranger remedies suggested to deter nausea is the combination of dried neates' tongues and marmalade. To avoid the disturbing odours present on long voyages, it is also recommended that one carries red roses, lemons and oranges in summer; and in winter the pungent combination of angelica, cloves, rosemary and rose petals. (Fynes Moryson, Gent., *An Itinerary*, 1617.)

Seek me in the broken hearts and by the crumbling tombs: CHECKMATE, IV, 9: A fragment of Ottoman poetry, preceded by the line 'The heart of the believer is the house of God': true faith is not based on great edifice, but on pain and suffering. (E.J.W. Gibb, *History of Ottoman Poetry*, Vol. I.)

Seid fröhlich, trinkt aus: PAWN, 1: 'Be Merry, Drink Up!' Travellers in Germany such as Fynes Moryson comment on the thick, evil-smelling beer, but do praise its 'medicinal' qualities. On one occasion his party were given dinner before they departed, consuming sixteen large pots of the brew between eight of them. The beer was so medicinal that they were obliged to travel by carriage, being too drunk to ride their horses. (Fynes Moryson, Gent., *An Itinerary*, 1617.)

Se'l ser un si, scrivero'n rima; Se'l ser un no amici come prima: KINGS, I, 2: An amicable proposition: 'If you give me a yes, I shall write you a verse, If you give me a no, then we're friends as before'.

Senchan Torpest: QUEENS, I, 2: Song of the ancient Irish bards reputed to rhyme rats to death; other venomous verse had the ability to blight crops, such as the *Aér;* or cause blisters to appear on the face of an enemy, to 'break out in bolga'. (P.W. Joyce, *Social History of Ancient Ireland.*)

Senchus Mor: QUEENS: Chapter Headings: Ancient Irish law tract, said to have been composed in the time of Laeghaire, Son of Niall, King of Erin, when Theodosius was Monarch of the World (Theodosius, [401–450] Emperor of the East from AD 408, later Emperor of the whole world). It was later written down by St Benignus, Bishop of Armagh, secretary and disciple to St Patrick. The Senchus Mor is one of the most important of the Brehon Law tracts (*Brehon* being the Gaelic term for judge). English law was introduced to Ireland by Henry II in the twelfth century, but mainly only in **The Pale.** Elsewhere, the Brehon Laws remained the main system of justice. From 1537, Anglo-Irish lords adopted the Brehon Laws, and kept Brehons in their service. The laws themselves remained in use till the reign of **Elizabeth I.** (*Ancient Laws and Institutes of Ireland;* P.W. Joyce, *Social History of Ancient Ireland.*)

Senex bis puer: KINGS, I, 7: 'Second childhood'. It was said that the process of advancing senility could be reversed by the **Philosopher's stone.**

Señora . . . señores . . . Estàn en el cuarto: KNIGHTS, III, 13: 'My lady . . . gentlemen . . . They are in the room'.

Sentiront que HENRY est leur fatal Jason: CHECKMATE, III, 2: A brief extract from the bombastic and disastrous masque performed for the heroes of Calais by **Jodelle.**

> They will feel that HENRY is their fateful Jason.
> If you know how to save in the course of such a journey
> All the people who travel with you,
> From monstrous, horrible, hungry Giants
> Incessantly yearning for the blood of little children . . .

Seraph: UNICORN, 37: See **Camelopard.**

SETON, George, Provost of Edinburgh: CHECKMATE: (c. 1530–1585) One of the Scots Commissioners sent to France to negotiate the marriage of **Mary Queen of Scots.** Seton had leanings towards the Reformed church and had attended services of the Scots Reformed kirk in 1558. Despite this, he protected the black and grey friars of Edinburgh and retained his own Roman Catholic beliefs. **Knox** lambasted him as 'a man without God, without honesty, and oftentimes without reason'.

Seton remained a Catholic under pressure to conform, and after the triumph of the Reformed Lords of the Congregation in 1560, briefly exiled himself in Paris. He claimed that he was being 'evilly used' by his Protestant enemies, but was determined to overcome their prejudice and return to Scotland to die. He became one of Mary's most loyal Scottish Catholic supporters and helped her to escape from the palace of Holyroodhouse after her husband and the Protestants had murdered her secretary and musician, David Riccio, in 1566.

Severus: CHECKMATE, I, 1: (AD 193–211) The Roman Emperor Lucius Septimus Severus. In 208, he and his sons Caracalla and Geta came to Britain to war against the rebellious Caledonians. He gave his name to the Severus wall which ran from Solway to the mouth of the Tyne.

Sew Tibet, knit Annot and spin Margerie: KINGS, IV, 1: Not a strange knitting or crochet instruction, but a quote from the early English play *Ralph Roister Doister* by **Udall** that refers to the comic complications caused by three of the characters featuring in the play.

SFORZA, Francesco, Duke of Milan: RISING: (1401–1466) Properly named Attendolo (Sforza meant either 'Stormer of Cities', or 'One of strong and fiery characteristics'), Francesco was a brilliant mercenary soldier like his father, who amassed lands and cities in the course of an illustrious fighting career, and like his older cousin Michelotto, whose exploits obtained him two knighthoods and a Venetian fief. The Attendoli appeared on the Italian scene at a time when the city-states were beginning to realise that the next best thing to creating your own army was to secure the services of a powerful mercenary force using your marriageable daughter as bait. Francesco I, the greatest soldier of his day and a ruler of quality, was born an illiterate and illegitimate member of a large, rough family in Cotignola, a small town between Ravenna and Bologna whose device was the quince, or *cotigna*. When, in time, his mother was diplomatically married off to the Fogliani of Ferrara, Francesco joined her there, and was educated with the children of Niccolò d'Este before joining his father in camp and adopting the career of a mercenary.

After the death of his father, such were Francesco's talents that all Italy competed for his services, and by 1425 he was commanding the armies of Filippo Maria Visconti, the then Duke of Milan, and served in several wars against **Venice** before detaching himself to follow new lines of profit. By 1434 he was Marquis of the March and commander of the papal armies; he later became Captain General of the league of Florence, Venice and the papacy against Milan, a campaign which gave him the lifelong support of **Cosimo de' Medici** and the chance to meet a frequent adversary, the *condottiere* Niccolò Piccinino, who was later to complain that the years spent in Visconti's service had not earned him sufficient land for his grave, and whose rivalry with Sforza was continued by Jacopo his son. Called in by Visconti in the end to make peace between Milan and Venice, Sforza did so at his own price — the long-awaited marriage between himself, now forty, and Visconti's seventeen-year-old daughter Bianca Maria, who had been promised to him since she was eight. The birth of the couple's first son, Galeazzo Maria, when the Visconti viper was quartered for the first time with the Sforza lion, foreshadowed the events of 1450, when Francesco became the first of the six Sforza Dukes of Milan, then the most powerful state in Italy.

The alliance between Milan, Venice and Florence was celebrated by an exchange of palaces: Sforza received a mansion in Venice, and in his turn gave to **Cosimo de' Medici** the building in Milan which became the Medici bank, run by Pigello and Accerito Portinari, the brothers of **Tommaso**. The uneasy situation caused by claims on Naples and Genoa continued. **René of Anjou** proved an unsatisfactory ally in an attempt to secure Angevin rule in Naples, and good relations with France suffered from the plotting of the Fregosi of Genoa who, in opposition to the King of Naples and their rivals the Adorni, offered the city to King **Charles VII** of France, only to combine later to drive the French out. When Charles was succeeded by his son, the new King **Louis XI** decided after some prevarication to invest in an alliance with Milan, and in 1463 promised to present Sforza with the fiefs of Genoa and Savona. Since the defeat of John of Calabria at Troya in 1462, the cause of Anjou in Naples seemed dead, and by 1464 René and his son left for France, while Sforza reaped the benefit of his eventual support for **Ferrante** of Aragon, and gained the friendship of Louis XI of France by sending troops to his aid.

Much of Sforza's foreign diplomacy devolved upon his famous secretary Cecco Simonetta, of whom he said, 'If I lose him I must have another Cecco in his place, even if I have to make him out of wax'. (Cecco was the bane of many foreigners, of whom **Prosper Camulio** was one.) At home, Francesco improved the waterways and built the great hospital of Milan, while maintaining good order as in camp, so that (unlike the days of the Visconti) 'a man could travel in safety though the country with gold in his hand'. The court lived simply at Milan or **Pavia**, with two other country houses at their disposal. Bianca had only four ladies-in-waiting in 1463: on one occasion an important visitor was asked to defer his entry 'for on that day the ladies will be washing their hair, and the troops have their work to do'. Although Francesco was no scholar, his eight children numbered Greek scholars, poets and humanists among their tutors, and were variously taught dancing, riding and fencing as well as classics and the art of government. When René of Anjou visited the court in 1453, the children entertained him with French songs specially learned for the occasion. Francesco was a concerned and affectionate father (as he was to his troops, winning the hearts of his soldiers by remembering the names of their horses).

The legacy he left Milan when he died in 1466, aged sixty-five, was less than he would have wished, since his heir Galeazzo Maria had early thrown off the good manners of childhood and at twenty-two was already displaying the violent temper and dissolute conduct which were to mar the magnificence of his court. Despite the apparent strength of the bond between Milan, Florence and Naples, the misrule of these years was to lead to the disruption of the alliance. When Galeazzo's murder in 1476 left only a child of seven to follow him, Pope **Sixtus IV** was prompted to remark 'the peace of Italy is dead'. In fact, the duchy was then controlled by the child's uncle Ludovico Sforza (Il Moro), the fourth son of Francesco, who eventually usurped the ducal throne and ruled until his death in 1508. (Cecilia M. Ady, *A History of Milan under the Sforza.*)

Shah Mahmút the Ghaznĕrides' elephants: CHECKMATE, I, 2: Tenth-century conqueror, with infamously fat and well-fed elephants.

Shawm: UNICORN, 18: Double-reeded instrument, the forerunner to the modern oboe. Shawms came in families, each with a different range from soprano to bass. The Shawms of Maidstone, Minstrels of Sandwich and the Waits of Dover were amongst the groups of musicians employed in the English royal court from 1492 to 1504 (QUEENS, II, 1). (Clement A. Harris & Mary Hargreave, *The Story of British Music*; CD Set, Musica Reservata, *The Instruments of the Middle Ages and Renaissance*, 1993, Vanguard Classics, 08 9060 72.)

Sheb-chiragh: PAWN, 15: A fabled gem, 'The Night Lamp'. On certain nights when the water bull would come up onto the land to graze, he brought this gem in his mouth and set it down on the ground. By the light of the rare jewel, the bull would be able to graze all night. (E.J.W. Gibb, *History of Ottoman Poetry*, Vol. I.)

Sheep: CASTLE: See **Cotswold lions; Cypriot sheep.**

Sherbet: PAWN: See **Rest to the soul, food to the spirit.**

Shore, Jane: CHECKMATE, IV, 4: (d. c. 1527) The London-born daughter of a mercer and wife to a goldsmith who, in about 1470, became the mistress of King **Edward IV**. Her husband subsequently abandoned her, but Jane continued to live a life of favour and luxury. On the death of Edward IV, Richard III reduced her to penury, and in penance for her adultery she was forced to walk through the streets of London dressed only in a kirtle.

Shoulder of Sagittarius: UNICORN, 25: See **Alfonso the Wise.**

Shred pie: SCALES, 34: Following is a Lombard recipe for chicken and bacon pastries. They can be served either hot or cold and are as easy to eat in a drinking house as on the road, and the perfect accompaniment to tall tales about giant ants who dig for gold. A shred pie is a general term for any type of meat in a 'coffin' of pastry as long as it has been finely sliced. It also makes the meat go further.

The recipe requires 12 oz shortcrust pastry, 2 beaten eggs, 2 tbsp freshly squeezed Seville orange juice or lemon juice, ⅛ tsp fresh ground black pepper, ½ tsp ground ginger, 1 lb chicken or turkey breast meat, thinly sliced (or shredded) and 3 large rashers of streaky or back bacon, sliced in half.

Roll out the pastry and cut into six large circles of 6½ inches. Preheat the oven to 425° F/220° C/Gas Mark 7. Mix the beaten egg with the fruit juice, fresh pepper and the ginger. Briefly marinade the meat in the liquid, then lay an equal amount of the meat in one half of each pastry circle. Lay a half-slice of the bacon over each pile of meat, and brush the edges of the pastry with the remaining egg and spice mixture. Fold the pastry over to make a half-circle, and flute the edges with a fork or fingers. Prick the surface of each pastry several times, and cook on a baking tray for fifteen minutes, then lower the temperature of the oven to 375° F/190° C/Gas Mark 5 and cook for a further 20 to 25 minutes. (Maggie Black, *The Medieval Cookbook*, British Museum Press, 1993.)

Si Dieu ne me veut ayder, le diable ne me peut manquer: CHECKMATE, I, 6: 'If God doesn't wish to help me, the devil won't fail me'.

Si la noche se hace oscura: QUEENS, I, 6: Anonymous Spanish song about the girl who awaits her beloved:

> *Si la noche se hace oscura*
> *y tan corto es el camino,*
> *cómo no venís, amigo?*
> *La media noche es pasada*
> *y él que me pena no viene,*
> *mi desdicha lo detiene,*
> *que nací tan desdichada.*
> *Hazeme vivir penada,*
> *y muéstraseme enemigo,*
> *cómo no venís, amigo?*

> Although the night grows darker,
> you have not far to come,
> Love, why are you so long?

And still my love tarries
though midnight's past and gone,
My bad luck keeps him from me
the luck I've always known.
How much I suffer for it.
Everything goes wrong.
Love why are you so long?

(LP: Victoria de Los Angeles & Ars Musica, *Spanish Songs of the Renaissance: 1440–1600*, 1961, HMV, ALP 1883.)

Si leonina pellis non satis est, assuenda vulpina: CHECKMATE, I, 6: 'If the lion's skin cannot, the fox's shall'; i.e. if brute force (skin of the lion) doesn't work, try cunning (that of the fox).

Si mundus vult decipi, decipiatur: KINGS, I, 1: 'If the world wants to be gulled, let it be gulled'.

Si non caste, tamen caute: KNIGHTS, III, 10: 'If not chastely, then at least cautiously'.

Si peccas, pecca fortiter: PAWN, 12 & 22: The sentiment of the phrase is roughly translated as 'You may as well be hanged for a sheep as a lamb'; if you are going to sin, sin heartily. Because drinking alcohol was considered as against the Koran, if you were going to break the law you might as well go to excess as you would be punished for it anyway. The anecdote of the old gentleman of Constantinople is mentioned in this context; before drinking, he shouted loudly to warn his soul to either stow itself in some part of his body, or leave it altogether, lest his spirit be defiled by the alcohol he was about to consume. (Roger B. Merriman, *Suleiman the Magnificent*, London, 1944.)

Sia maladetto: KNIGHTS, III, 16: 'Be damned'.

SIDNEY, Sir Henry: CASTLE: (1529–1586) Henry's boyhood was spent in the company of the young **Edward VI** who made him one of the four Gentlemen of the Privy Chamber, gave him his knighthood in 1550 and created him Chief Cupbearer for life. Henry's father William had also served the monarchy; Edward VI gave him the house of Penshurst.

Henry Sidney was to marry the eldest daughter of the **Earl of Warwick**, but after Edward VI had died in Henry's arms, he was one of the first to forsake his father-in-law's cause and support **Mary Tudor**, not the unfortunate Lady Jane Grey. He thus kept his position at court and his lands when Mary Tudor came to power. Mary's new husband **Philip II** acted as godfather to his namesake,

Henry's son Philip. The son was later to become one of the foremost poets of the Elizabethan court.

In 1556, Sidney was made Vice-Treasurer and Governor of the Crown's revenues in Ireland, and Member of the Irish Council. On the death of Mary Tudor, Sidney was appointed Lord President of the marches of Wales; a job which he seemed to find pleasurable and easy, claiming 'a better people to govern than the Welsh, Europe holdeth not'. In 1565 Sidney was appointed Lord Deputy of Ireland, and carried out an extensive survey of the country, including the collection of Irish records. He commissioned a new map of Ireland, completed by his secretary Emery Molyneux who was also responsible for the first English globe after a gap of twenty years. (E.G.R. Taylor, *Tudor Geography: 1485–1583*.)

Sigad id Din: KNIGHTS, II, 9: See **Gabriel.**

SIGISMOND OF AUSTRIA, Count of the Tyrol: UNICORN: (1426–1496) Cousin of the Emperor Frederick, Sigismond was a profligate and spendthrift ruler of a court which could not even attempt to rival that of Burgundy, however hard it tried. The capricious, fanciful and restless Count had little actual control over his widely spread territories. Many of his lands were so far from Innsbruck that they paid little or no heed to the whims of their territorial overlord, unless he chose to partition them off or involve them in outside conflict.

Such was the case after 1469. Sigismond was so desperate for money that he mortgaged much of his land to **Charles the Bold** of Burgundy. By the Treaty of St Omer, Charles was given lordship over the Upper Alsace, the county of Ferrete and many other towns, which secured the Duke a passage to the east of his Burgundian territories. Sigismond received 50,000 Rhenish florins, and the nickname 'Sigismond the Simple' because he had mortgaged his inheritance. The transaction has been described as unpleasantly necessary as that of a desperately needy student pawning his overcoat, and there was as much fond feeling between Sigismond and the Duke as there was between a usurer and his client.

Despite his costly debts, he kept a court of indolence and luxury, largely ruled by his wife Eleanor, sister of **James II** of Scotland. Like her father James I of Scotland, Eleanor had an interest in literature and the humanist scholars, whereas her husband showed a distinct preference for hunting and beautiful ladies. This was in spite of his tuition from Aeneas Piccolomini, later to become Pope **Pius II.** The youthful Sigismond tended to use Aeneas's scholarly learning to assist in the eloquent composition of love letters to impress his latest potential conquest. He and Eleanor produced no legitimate heirs, although he did have fourteen bastards to his credit, far exceeding the two illegitimate children of his tutor (one from Scotland, the other to an Englishwoman in Strassburg).

Sigismond was to fall foul of his youthful mentor after Pius exhibited strict moral tendencies on becoming Pope. The conflict began in 1450 with the appointment of the crusading reformer Nicholas of Cusa as Bishop of Brixen. Nicholas attempted to reform the corrupt Benedictine convent of Sonnenberg, a favourite retreat for the daughters of the Tyrolean nobility. Eventually, Nicholas excommunicated the Abbess Verena, and the 'chaste' sisters were expelled from their home by force of arms. They appealed to Sigismond and Nicholas fled the Tyrol in fear of his life. Pius was eventually obliged to intervene and decided against his profligate pupil, excommunicating him in 1460. The censure against Sigismond was only lifted in 1464.

His expensive tastes were not mitigated by his lack of hard cash; once he had no more territories to mortgage, Sigismond turned instead to the rich possibilities of mining for the silver and other minerals which lay underneath his lands. This encouraged his borrowing further; taking advance royalties and loans for the lease of mining rights. (Richard Vaughan, *Charles the Bold*; Ruth Putnam, *Charles the Bold*, London, 1908.)

Silent trade: SCALES, 19: As related by **Ca'da Mosto** and Herodotus before him, the African trade between the commodities of gold and salt had continued in the same manner for centuries. The exact location even of the point of trade was kept a close secret, and no amount of bribery or torture would reveal the source of the gold, especially to outsiders. Ca'da Mosto relates how the Emperor of Melli [Mali] had previously tried to find the trading place with the intention of capturing one of the traders in gold and forcing him to reveal the location of the mines. The captured man, perhaps one of the Lobi tribesmen, was described as very black, well formed and a span (nine inches) taller than his captors, his mouth attracting most interest:

> The lower lip, more than a span in width, hung down, huge and red, over the breast, displaying the inner part, glistening like blood. The upper lip was as small as their own. This form of the lips displayed the gums and teeth, the latter they said, being bigger than their own: they

had two large teeth on each side, and large black eyes. Their appearance is terrifying and the gums exude blood, as do the lips.

The physical appearance of the gold traders, due to tribal customs of ornamentation rather than genuine physical deformity, seemed to be accepted as their reason for remaining separate from the rest of the world. More importantly, their method of trading kept their monopoly over the gold trade and meant that no outsiders could learn its secret.

The tribesman captured by the King of Mali refused either to speak or eat and the source of the gold remained a secret. The gold traders were so incensed at the capture of one of their number that they refused to trade for the next three years; only returning to the barter system when their own survival was probably endangered due to the lack of salt. See also **Taghaza** and **Wangara**. (G.R. Crone, ed., *The Voyages of Cadamosto*, Hakluyt Society, 1937.)

Silenus: QUEENS, II, 6: The satyr who brought up and instructed the god Bacchus. Portrayed as a jovial old man, bald, blunt-nosed and as round as the wine bag continually at his side. It is said that he could never trust his own legs, being in a semi-permanent state of intoxication; thus he is represented as either riding on an ass or supported by other satyrs.

Silvanus: KINGS, IV, 3: Latin divinity of forests and fields, comparable to the Greek god **Pan**. He is represented as an old man, carrying a cypress tree.

Simonetta, Bella: QUEENS, IV, 4: Botticelli's (1447–1515) muse.

Sinai, Mount: UNICORN: *Gebel Musa*, where Moses communed with God and received the Ten Commandments, and an accepted religious site of significance for Jews, Muslims and Christians. From behind the monastery of **St Catherine**, founded in the sixth century by the Emperor Justinian, there are three thousand steps to the summit of Mount Sinai. Before reaching the summit, one would stop at the sixth-century gateway of St Stephanos, where the saint would hear the confession of the pilgrims and keep watch over the sanctity of the holy place (St Stephanos's preserved corpse has since been moved indoors, and now keeps watch at the ossuary of the monastery).

In the first half of the fifteenth century, all Christian pilgrims intending to proceed to Mount Sinai from Jerusalem would be registered by Muslim officials when they first arrived in the city. Their name, age, facial appearance, height and any distinguishing marks would be recorded, and a copy of the list sent to Cairo where many of the pilgrims would go after Mount Sinai. This was not an early form of visa or passport control, but was intended to protect the security of pilgrims as much as possible; if expected in Cairo, the pilgrim could not be kidnapped or substituted for another by the lawless tribes of desert nomads. (John

Galey, *Sinai and the Monastery of St Catherine*, Massada, 1979; Margaret Wade Labarge, *Medieval Travellers: The Rich and the Restless*, London, 1982.)

Sin-eaters: KINGS, III, 2: SCALES, 27: Better for the soul than hired mourners, sin-eaters were hired for funerals literally to consume the sins of the dead and take the guilt upon themselves. They would arrive at the house of the recently departed, and be offered food and drink. This they would accept, and in return for bodily sustenance and financial remuneration would successfully free the dead soul from time spent in Purgatory.

Sine lucro friget ludus: KINGS, IV, 4: 'It's a dull game with no stakes, or no promise of profit'.

Singing ut to Johannes: KINGS, IV, 1: Ut represents the first note of the musical scale, now called *doh*. The name of each keynote in the scale is taken from a hymn to St John the Baptist ascribed to Paulus Diaconus (d. 799) and used by Guido of Arezzo (d. c. 1050) for his solmization syllables ut, re, mi etc:

> Út queánt laxis resonáre fíbris
> Míra géstorúm   famulí tuórum
> Sólve pólluti   labíí reátum
> Sáncte Johánnes

(Willi Apel, *Gregorian Chant*.)

Sir Thomas ... his bowels burning before him: CASTLE, III, 2: The particularly gruesome fifteenth-century execution of Sir Thomas Blount, probably for treason. Firstly he was hanged, then cut down and made to speak. When revived, he was placed in front of an open fire, his hands tied as the executioner kneeled in front of him and cut open his stomach. His bowels were tied with whipcord, 'that the breath of the heart might not escape', and then they were cast into the fire, while still attached to him. He was then invited to drink, to which he replied, 'You have taken away the wherein to put it.' After his prolonged torture, Sir Thomas was then beheaded, quartered and the quarters were finally parboiled. (Edward, Second Duke of York, *The Master of Game*, 1413; tr. from Gaston III, 1904.)

Sir, what say ye? Sing on, let us see: KINGS, II, 2: From the popular early song 'Bon Jowre, Bon Jowre A Vous!' (Good Day, Good Day to You!) (extract):

> Sir, what say ye?
> Syng on, lett us see
> Now will it be
> This or another day?
> Bon Jowre.

Sisyphus: KINGS, IV, 1: Also known as Aeolides; King of Corinth and promoter of navigation and commerce, but an avaricious, deceitful and fraudulent man, who tried to trick even the gods. As a punishment, he had to spend eternity in Hades rolling a huge marble block uphill; a never-ending task, because as soon as it reached the peak, it would roll down again.

Sive Idolatra, sive Turca, sive Judaeus, sive Christianus: PAWN, 21: 'Whether Idolator or Turk, whether Jew or Christian'. The quote refers to the French naturalist Pierre Bellon's experience of Muslim hospitality to the traveller or stranger, regardless of their religious creed (see also *Loi, foi, nation que ce soit*). Bellon (or Belon, 1517–1564) travelled extensively in Arabia, Egypt and Asia Minor from 1546 to 1549, but was ironically attacked and murdered by bandits in Paris, whilst gathering herbs at the Bois du Boulogne.

SIXTUS IV: UNICORN: (1414–1484) Francesco della Rovere, the former Franciscan friar who was elected Pope in 1471 and initially brought methodical order to the administration of the church. He was obsessed with the possible reality of a crusade against the Ottoman Empire, although his Christian fleet eventually got no farther than Smyrna before falling apart in confusion. Like many other popes before and after, Sixtus made a point of promoting his ambitious relatives in church offices. Nepotism on such a large scale alienated non-family members with no chance of advancement. He also dragged the papal states into the long and complex wars of the Italian states.

Skanderbeg: SCALES: (c. 1405–1468) George Castriota, described by Pope **Calixtus III** as the 'athlete of Christendom'. When a child, Castriota was taken as a hostage from Upper Albania to Edirne, and obliged to renounce his Christianity and embrace Islam. On the death of his father in 1431, Castriota escaped to Albania, reconverted to Christianity and announced a Holy War against Turkish oppression. By the winter of 1443, he had 12,000 men under his control and had secured his country against Ottoman encroachment. He was elected Captain of Albania and began an offensive guerrilla war against the Turkish Empire which lasted for the next twenty-five years. With help from Venice, Naples and the papacy, Skanderbeg repulsed no less than thirteen invasions of Albania between 1444 and 1466, and is justly regarded as a national hero.

He died of a malignant fever in 1468, commending the safety of his countrymen to the republic of Venice, his 'loyal and powerful ally'. His body was buried in Alessio, and remained there until **Mehmet II** finally conquered the city of his greatest rival in 1478. The corpse was then publicly displayed, and it is said that many of Mehmet's troops took the bones and had them set in gold or silver as a talisman. They hoped that the possession of such a powerful relic might enable some of Skanderbeg's indefatigable bravery to rub off on them. (Franz Babinger, *Mehmet the Conqueror*, tr. Ralph Manheim, Princeton, 1978.)

Skelton: KINGS, III, 3: John Skelton (c. 1460–1529) English poet who was tutor to Prince Henry (later Henry VIII) and created 'poet-laureate' by both Oxford and Cambridge universities. He was ordained in 1498. See **Bob me on the noll.**

Slata Baba: CASTLE: See **Samoyedès.**

Slaves: See **Africa.**

Slieveen: QUEENS, I, 2: Gaelic for 'rogue' or 'churl'; not referring to one who comes from the mountainous district of the Slieve Bloom in Ireland.

So many buls do compass me: CASTLE, III, 10: Psalm 22, 12: The version used comes from the Geneva Psalms, printed by John Crespin, 1569 (extract):

> Then Lord depart not now from me,
> In this my present griefe:
> Since I have none to be my helpe,
> My succour and reliefe.
> So many Buls do compasse me,
> That be full strong of head:
> Yea, Buls so fat as though they had,
> In Basan fieldes bene fed.
>
> They gape upon me gredely,
> As though they would me slay:
> Much lyke a Lion roring out,
> And ramping for his pray.
> But I droope downe like water shed,
> My jointes in sunder breake:
> My hart doth in my body melt,
> Like waxe against the heate.

Socrates: KINGS, I, 2: (469–399 BC) Athenian philosopher despised by the state. He was impeached and found guilty of corrupting youth and condemned to death. Socrates espoused his fate by drinking hemlock, which he is said to have done with composure and cheerfulness.

Sohâib Rûmi: PAWN, 20: The Arabic patron saint of storytellers, who was employed by the Prophet Mohammed. Sohâib died at the age of one hundred and ten, and all future storytellers traced their lineage back to him. See also **Meddáh**. (Alexander Pallis, *In the Days of the Janissaries*.)

SOMERSET, Duke of: QUEENS, III, 4: (c. 1505–1552) Edward Seymour, first Duke of Somerset, Earl of Hertford and Protector of the Realm during the minority of **Edward VI**. Seymour rose to favour under Henry VIII, became a Knight of the **Order of the Garter**, and in 1542 was appointed Lord High Admiral and then Lord Great Chamberlain. He fought in Henry's campaigns in France, and notably against Scotland in 1544, 1545 and in 1547. With the demise of Henry VIII, he became Duke of Somerset and, with **Sir William Paget's** help, was virtually unchallenged by the Privy Council in his bid to become Protector. He pursued the reforms of the church set in motion by Henry VIII with a temperate hand. For example, no bishops were deprived of their see during his protectorate, nor were any Catholics executed for purely religious reasons. This leniency encouraged criticism, particularly after he allowed **Mary Tudor** a dispensation to hear Mass in her household. Enemies attacked the manner in which he enriched his own family from the spoils of ecclesiastical reform, but apparently he did his utmost to prevent others from profiting in similar style. His younger brother, Thomas Seymour, also did little to improve the family's reputation amongst jealous rivals. He married Catherine Parr, the Queen Dowager, and after her death, turned his attention to the Princess **Elizabeth**. He exerted great influence over the boy king, undermining the Protector. As if this were not enough to rouse hostility, he was involved in a serious swindle at the Bristol Mint, and was then accused of abusing his position as Lord High Admiral (a position he had taken over from **Warwick**) by making deals with known pirates, for which he was executed in 1549 (KINGS, I, 4).

Protector Somerset's fall from grace came partly as a result of his leniency and apparent fairness. In the summer of 1549 in Norfolk, 16,000 men rebelled against enclosures (an increasingly prevalent agrarian change of the period, where landowners enclosed common land and converted it from arable to pasture. Although larger farming tracts improved productivity, they also required less labour. The resultant unemployment caused increased poverty in a time of high inflation). The Privy Council expected Somerset to crush the rebels immediately, but instead he blamed the gentry for enclosing the land, and replied that he 'liked well the doing of the people'. He was even prepared to pardon the ringleaders if they would surrender. The rebellion was brutally crushed by October, but having lost the support of the landowners, the Privy Council divided against him. Somerset tried to flee to Windsor, fearing he would be overthrown if he stayed in London. He coerced the young king to come with him, and although Edward and the 'poor commons' of England undoubtedly saw him as a protector, the army would not now support him. He was arrested and sent to the Tower.

Although he was released in February 1550 with a full pardon, his troubles were not over. **Thomas Palmer**, having distinguished himself in the army under **Warwick**, was now looking for advancement at court. Warwick agreed to favour Palmer if he would confess to his involvement in a plot to reinstate Somerset as Protector and murder Warwick and his supporters. On these accusations, Somerset was once again arrested in October 1551 and found guilty of felonious intent, for which he was executed in January 1552. (William Seymour, 'Protector of the Realm', *History Today*, August, 1970; Penry Williams, *The Tudor Regime*, Oxford, 1983.)

Songhai: SCALES: A negroid north African race, whose capital was at Gao. The Empire of the Songhai flourished between 1468 and 1491, beginning with the conquest of **Timbuktu** by Sunni Ali who was unwisely invited to enter the city by its governor, who thought thus to get rid of a Tuareg commander. Es Sadi, the historian of the western Sudan, described Sunni Ali as 'master tyrant, libertine and scoundrel . . . one who glorified in the massacre of the learned and pious'.

After conquering Timbuktu, the Songhai then moved on to Jenne. Like Timbuktu, it was an *entrepôt* for the salt and gold trade, but was built to withstand attack, having successfully withstood ninety-nine assaults from the Kings of Mali. After a siege lasting several years, Jenne eventually fell in 1473. Sunni Ali then pursued his campaign of vengeance against Akil and the others from Timbuktu who had fled to Walata. Sunni Ali's barbarous reign over the Songhai ended only with his death in 1492. (Elias N. Saad, *Social History of Timbuktu*.)

Sordidi Dei: KINGS, I, 1: 'Base gods'. The original phrase has to do with a condemnation of animal oracles.

Sorghum: SCALES, 33: A millet-yielding grass, sorghum was grown in the old world for grain and forage, but one variety, sweet sorghum, which was common in Africa in the Sudan, was a source of **sugar**, though not as versatile as its rival, cane sugar.

Souillard, white, fleet children of: QUEENS, II, 2: The *bon chien* Souillard was the progenitor of the finest hunting hounds which held the field in France until the seventeenth century; a breed created by Anne, daughter of **Louis XI** of France, by crossing a gifted white Barbary hound (Souillard) with one of her fawn hounds. Souillard was much in demand as a breeding dog, and it is from this one dog and Anne's bitch that the famous white hounds of France originated. The white hounds were faster than the grey and more intelligent than the black, and were further improved by selective breeding in the reigns of **Francis I** and **Henri II** of France. (Lady Apsley, *Bridleways Through History*, 1936.)

Soul Vegetable, Soul Animal and Soul Sensible: PAWN, 13: From Ottoman psychology, these are the three degrees of soul. The first is concerned with growth, nourishment and reproduction; the second is in charge of sensation and movement; the third, Soul Sensible (or Reasonable), is in control of reason. The different kinds of soul are further subdivided into their virtues and motivation which govern all physical and moral conduct in their turn. When the soul reaches perfection, it returns to the Great Being, thus continuing the Circle of Existence. (E.J.W. Gibb, *History of Ottoman Poetry*, Vol. I.)

Soyez hardis, en joye mis: CHECKMATE, I, 1: From the song 'La Guerre' by Clément Jannequin (c. 1485–1558), celebrating the victory of **Francis I** over the forces of **Charles V** at the Battle of Marignon in 1515 (extract):

> *Avanturiers, bon compagnons*
> *Ensemble croisez vos bastons,*
> *Bendez soudain, gentilz Gascons,*
> *Nobles, sautez dens les arcons,*
> *La lance au poing hardiz et promptz*
> *Comme lyons!*
> *Harquebutiers, faictes voz sons!*
> *Armes bouclez, friques mignons,*
> *Donnez dedans!*
> *Frappez, criez*
> *Alarme, alarme.*
>
> *Soyez hardis, en joye mis,*
> *Chascun s'asaisonne,*
> *La fleur de lys,*
> *Fleur de hault pris*
> *Y est en personne.*
> *Suivez Françoys*
> *Suivez la couronne!*
> *Sonnez, trompettes et clarons,*
> *Pour resjouyr les coms, les coms, les compagnons . . .*

> Adventurers, good countrymen,
> together cross your staves,
> bend the bow, noble Gascons,
> noblemen, leap into the saddle,
> lance in and and ready
> as lions!
> Sackbut players, make your sound!
> Gird on your arms, gay squires,
> and lay on!

Strike and shout
the alarm!

Be bold and joyful,
Let each urge himself on,
the *fleur de lys*,
the noble flower,
is there in person.
Follow Francis
the French king,
follow the crown.
Resound, trumpets and clarions,
to gladden your count-, your count-, your countrymen . . .

(Tr. Frank Dobbins; LP: The King's Singers, *A French Collection*, 1973, EMI, CSD 3740.)

Spahis: KNIGHTS, II, 2: From the French spelling of the Persian word *sipahi*, meaning 'warrior', describing an archer on horseback. They were the fast and ruthless cavalry soldiers of the Ottoman army, who, because of their mounted status, were more prestigious than their colleagues in the infantry. It is also the general term used to describe the feudal, provincial fief-holding cavalry of the Empire.

There were an estimated 40,000 spahis in the fifteenth and sixteenth centuries, most of whom came from the provinces, but by the later part of the sixteenth century, this feudal cavalry was superceded by the *kapikulu* cavalry, based in Constantinople and of slave origin as opposed to the territorially based feudal cavalry.

This last remnant of mounted feudal archers could not compete with European infantry armed with muskets; Ottoman horsemen were eventually armed with the unchivalric pistol to move with the times.

Spectacles: SCALES, 5: Research suggests that reading glasses were invented in late–thirteenth-century Italy. Before 1285 there is evidence to prove that convex lenses were developed in Tuscany, to facilitate the correction of presbyopia, or long-sightedness, whilst concave lenses to correct myopia were manufactured in Florence by the middle of the fifteenth century, Florence then taking over from Venice as the source of the finest lenses. For example, in 1462 **Francesco Sforza**, Duke of Milan, asked his resident Ambassador in Florence for three dozen pairs of glasses, 'Because there are many who request of us eyeglasses that are made there in Florence, since it is reputed that they are made more perfectly [there] than in any other place in Italy'. The city was definitely geared up to the production and marketing of these precision items, as the Duke's order was ready and dispatched in only eleven days. Fine grinding of lenses allowed for a varied range of glasses; almost to the standard of modern optical prescriptions, but generally geared towards the age of the wearer, rather than an awareness of eye conditions.

Without doubt, spectacles did prove to be something of a fashion item amongst the rich and vain, but their development and popularity as a status symbol coincided with increased literacy in Italian urban society. They were also of vital importance to the artisan striving for meticulous accuracy in close-up detailed work. The ultimate discovery which came from the use of concave and convex lenses together was of course the telescope. (Vincent Ilardi, 'Eyeglasses and Concave Lenses in Fifteenth-Century Florence and Milan', *Renaissance Quarterly*, Autumn 1976; Wolf Winkler, *A Spectacle of Spectacles*, Museum Catalogue, National Museum of Scotland, Edinburgh, 1988–9.)

Spulzie: KNIGHTS, III, 10: Scots for 'plunder' or 'depredation'.

Squirrel, the little, full of business: KINGS, IV, 1: A quote from the poem, 'The Kingis Quair', attributed to James I of Scotland (1394–1437). See also **Hast thou no mind of love? Where is thy make?** (extract):

> The lion king and his fere [spouse] lioness,
> The panther like unto the smaragdyne [emerald],
> The little squirrel full of business,
> The slow ass, the drudger beast of pyne,
> The nice ape, the werely porpapyne [warlike porcupine],
> The piercing lynx, the lufare [loving] unicorn
> That voidis [voids, nullifies] venom with his ivory horn.

(J. Ross, ed., *The Book of Scottish Poems*, Edinburgh, 1878.)

STAFFORD, Sir Thomas: CASTLE: The English rebel who provided **Philip II** with his ultimate excuse to attack the French for undermining the English throne. Stafford, with French help, landed on the English coast and attempted to take control of the castle of Scarborough. According to Philip, France had been deliberately plotting against him by favouring such 'pirates and enemies of Christendom'. French citizens and merchants were henceforth given forty days to leave the country and Philip instructed his English subjects that they were to 'consider the King of France as a public enemy to ourselves and our nation, rather than suffer him to continue to deceive us under cover of friendship'. Stafford's promise to put Scarborough in French hands had been rumbled long before it represented a threat, but his treasonable activities did nothing to enhance the reputation of the French to Philip and the Empire of his father **Charles V.** (*English Calendar of State Papers*, June, 1557.)

Steen, the: RISING, 2: The town jail of Bruges, finally destroyed by fire in 1689, and now replaced by modern buildings. The prison rooms were on two separate floors, the upper floor reserved for prisoners who could pay their jailer for better food, bedding and even separate accommodation.

The lower floor was for common criminals, known as the 'Dark Chamber'. Prisoners were given the chance to collect alms from passersby via a long rod with a box which could be protruded from a grated window. An alms box was also passed round the town for the welfare of the prisoners in the lower dungeon. Every Friday the poorer prisoners were guaranteed bread, and on Twelfth Day, they would receive wine at the city's expense as a special treat. All prisoners (except small debtors) would be kept in irons, but this could be avoided if the prisoner would arrange for the payment of a small fine. (Wilfrid C. Robinson, *Bruges: An Historical Sketch*, Bruges, 1899.)

Stentor: KINGS, II, 1: Herald of the Greeks during the Trojan Wars. His voice was said to be as loud as that of fifty other men put together, and his name is proverbially used for anyone with a particularly loud voice.

STEWART, Alexander: UNICORN: See **Albany, Duke of.**

STEWART, Lord James: CHECKMATE: (1531–1570) Prior of St Andrews, Earl of Mar, and afterwards the Earl of Moray, James was the natural son of **James V** of Scotland and Lady Margaret Erskine, therefore he was an elder half-brother to **Mary Queen of Scots.** He had been appointed as Prior of St Andrews and of Mâçon in France whilst still a child, and accompanied the young Scots queen to France in 1548, returning to Scotland the following year to assist in repelling the English navy which was attacking the coast of Fife.

Lord James had sympathy with the aims of the Reformers, and was one of the signatories to the letter inviting **John Knox** to return to Scotland and advance the course of the nation's Protestant Reformation. In 1558 Stewart was appointed as one of the Commissioners to witness the marriage negotiations for Mary's wedding to the Dauphin. As he took leave of France, with several other Councillors he was afflicted with an illness; he was the first to claim that he and the other Commissioners had been deliberately poisoned. He survived, it is said, by flushing the poison out of his system by drinking sea water and hanging upside down by his heels. He suffered from a weak stomach for the rest of his life.

Whilst in France, he intimated to **Mary de Guise** that he would prefer to renounce the priories he held in Scotland and France in return for the Earldom of Moray. Mary neatly sidestepped his demand for preferment, saying she would rather he remained in the religious vocation into which his father the King had consecrated him. In pique at his frustrated ambitions, Stewart opposed the Queen Dowager on religious and political grounds, becoming leader of her powerful rivals, the Lords of the Protestant Congregation, in 1559.

When the Queen Dowager died, Stewart was sent to France in 1561 to win her daughter's confidence, 'to grope her mind' and assess her views on the Scots Reformation. He advised the young queen that she should be tolerant of her subjects' religious views, but received more favour from **Elizabeth I** than his own half-sister. After Mary's disastrous reign, Stewart was formally installed as Regent of Scotland in 1567, a position he retained until his assassination in 1570 by James Hamilton of Bothwellhaugh. (Maurice Lee, *James Stewart, Earl of Moray*, 1953.)

STEWART, Matthew: KINGS: See **LENNOX, Matthew.**

STEWART, Robin: QUEENS: See **Poison Plot.**

Still under the leavis green: PAWN, 29: First lines of the anonymous Scots poem, 'The Murning Maiden'. For the next verses, see **I love the love that loves not me.** (J. Ross, *The Book of Scottish Poems*, Edinburgh, 1878.)

Strabo, cross-eyed as: KINGS, IV, 3: A reference to the German monk and scholar Walafriedus Strabo (c. 808–849), 'Squinting Wilfrid'. He was the author of theological and liturgical works of note. See also *Glossa interlinearis.*

Strange birds cry in the air Today! Today!: CHECKMATE, IV, 2: From **Nostradamus**'s epistle to **Henri II** of France concerning the 'last epoch' of the world; interpreted by many to refer to the French Revolution; the 'strange birds' being imperial eagles (extract):

At this last epoch, all the kingdoms of Christianity, as well as of the infidel world, will be shaken during the space of twenty-five years, and the wars and battles will be most grievous . . . so many evils will be committed by means of Satan, the prince infernal, that nearly all the world will become undone and desolate. Before the events occur certain strange birds will cry in the air, 'Today! today!' and after a given time will disappear.

(Charles A. Ward, *Oracles of Nostradamus*, London, 1891.)

Strike on, strike on Glasgèrion: KINGS, IV, 1: From the anonymous ballad 'Glasgerion' (extract):

> Glasgèrion was a King's own son
> And a harper he was good:
> He harped in the King's chamber

Where cup and candle stood
And so did he in the Queen's chamber
The ladies waxèd wood [mad].

And then bespoke the King's daughter
And these words thus said she:
'There's never a stroke comes over this harp,
But it gladdens the heart of me.'

Said, 'Strike on, strike on, Glasgèrion,
Of thy striking do not blin [cease].
There's never a strike comes over thine harp
But it gladdens my heart within.'

'Fair might you fall, lady,' quoth he:
'Who taught you now to speak?
I have loved you, lady, seven year
My heart I durst ne'er break—'

'But come to my bower, my Glasgèrion,
When all men are at rest:
As I am a lady of my promise,
Thou shalt be a welcome guest.'

STROZZI, Alessandra di Filippo Macinghi: RAM: (c. 1404–1471) The Florentine widow of Matteo Strozzi (1397–1435), and mother of **Filippo** (1428–1491), **Lorenzo** (c. 1431–1479), Matteo (1436–1459), Caterina and Lessandra. Her husband Matteo had been a leading statesman, but was exiled to Pesaro in 1434 because **Cosimo de' Medici** considered him a threat to his reestablished control over Florentine politics. Matteo, a classical humanist scholar, was closely associated with Cosimo's rich and powerful enemy Palla Strozzi (d. 1434) as well as the Albizzi faction who had opposed Cosimo's return to Florence from political exile.

Within two years of his exile, Matteo and three of their children had died in an outbreak of plague, so Alessandra, her three remaining sons and two daughters returned to Florence. She devoted her life to advancing the prospects of her sons in their work, morals, marriage and career prospects, becoming a vociferous correspondent and adviser to them all, including her son-in-law, **Marco Parenti.**

On reaching adulthood, her sons Lorenzo and Filippo were also exiled from Florence, and Alessandra constantly petitioned the Medici for their return. She continued to live in Florence, on a small estate left to her by her husband. By 1459 she had sold nearly all of the property in order to release enough capital to ensure the success of her two surviving sons, keeping only her small town house of fewer than ten rooms, and a little farm at Pozzolatico. Finding good wives for her exiled sons was an onerous task for their formidable mother; despite their wealth and success in banking and commerce, a match would not be politically or diplomatically acceptable to many Florentine families wishing to remain in favour with the Medici family. The same was true of her struggle to find suitable husbands for her daughters. However, she did find a fortunate match for Caterina in the shape of Marco Parenti.

She lived to see her sons eventually reinstated to the Florentine hierarchy in 1466. Filippo returned permanently to Florence in 1470, but Lorenzo only did so for two years, before going back to Naples where he died. Alessandra died in 1471, poor but still amongst the élite of Florentine political and social life. In less than a generation the Florentine Strozzis were no longer just poor relations of their Neapolitan banking cousins. Her sons were to build a banking empire of their own, with branches in Naples, Rome and Florence, leaving a tangible indicator of their wealth in the Florentine palace which they began to build in 1489. (Mark Phillips, *The Memoir of Marco Parenti*, London, 1989.)

STROZZI, Filippo: CHECKMATE: (1488–1538) The youngest and favourite son of his father **Filippo di Mattco**'s second wife, Selvaggia di Bartolomeo (d. 1524). He was christened Giovan Battista, but renamed in honour of his father in 1491. His mother attempted to turn him into a literary genius with an intensive education from two grammarians, a singing master and Latin master. She also employed a master of Greek for her favourite, one Frate Zanobi Acciaiuoli. However, rather than fully utilising his humanistic education, Filippo was ultimately to follow in his father's footsteps as a successful merchant banker.

In 1508 he married Clarice de' Medici, the granddaughter of **Lorenzo the Magnificent**, thus uniting in one respect the families which had been rivals and enemies since the days of his grandfather. During this time, the Medici were not in power in Florence, as the city had proclaimed itself a Republic in 1494 and the Medici were exiled. The Strozzi had been traditional opponents to the Medici stranglehold over Florentine politics, but Filippo's marriage may have saved the family if the Medici were to regain power. In the meantime, the alliance served to alienate Filippo from the greater part of his family, and incurred the wrath of Florence's republican government. For marrying the daughter of an exile, Filippo's punishment was eventually reduced to a fine of 500 gold florins and a three-year exile in Naples, leaving his new wife in the Strozzi palace with his mother and brother. Incidentally, Clarice was described by Michelangelo as 'tall, good looking, well proportioned, and the rest is not bad either. Nor does she have an owl-like beak nose as was rumoured in Florence'. Filippo was summoned back to Florence in 1509 and given leave to remain in the city rather than return to Naples. In their time spent together, Clarice and Filippo had ten children, including **Piero** and **Leone.**

In 1512, the Republic of Florence came to an end with the return of the Medici from exile. Filippo and his immediate family did not take part in the revolution which accompanied the overthrow of the republic. Even though Filippo's marriage worked in his favour, as traditional enemies of the Medici, Filippo and Clarice were mistrusted by both sides. Filippo wisely remained neutral until the political situation stabilised, concentrating instead on his commercial and banking interests.

In 1513, when Clarice's uncle Giovanni de' Medici was elected as Pope **Leo X**, Filippo followed him to Rome, becoming Depositor General of the Apostolic Chamber. This post entailed the provision of banking services to the papacy, such as the advancement and depositing of funds and the issue and acceptance of bills of exchange. Using this honourable position, his own acumen and the family's considerable wealth, he began to build a banking empire which stretched from the Atlantic coast to Naples. The Florentine Pope was a stimulus and patron of his city's merchants and bankers, who consequently obtained lucrative posts under the Pope's new administration, overseeing the accounts of the papacy and lending vast sums of money to the curia. Leo's profligate spending led one contemporary to remark that it was just as impossible for the Pope to keep a thousand ducats together as it was for a stone to get up and fly.

When Leo X died in 1521, he was succeeded by the Flemish Pope Adrian VI. The Medici link between Florence and Rome was severed, and the new Pope was none too willing to patronise Florentine bankers as his predecessor had done; nor was he enthusiastic in honouring Leo X's debts to the Strozzi. Luckily for Filippo, Adrian was succeeded in 1523 by Filippo's friend Giulio de' Medici, as Pope **Clement VII.** Clement honoured his cousin Giovanni's debts, but ensured the Florentine bankers continued to pour large amounts into the ambitious Medici papacy's money pit. Filippo became increasingly dependent upon Clement and tied up a greater part of his capital on unsecured loans to the curia. The largest single loan to Clement was the provision of 130,000 scudi for the dowry of **Catherine de Médicis**, Filippo's wife's niece. Filippo escorted Catherine to France, paying all her expenses *en route*, a further drain on his capital funds. By overextending himself, Filippo faced potential ruin; if Clement were to die without repaying the dowry and his other unsecured loans, it would put severe financial strain upon him and his family.

In 1528 Filippo's wife Clarice died, cutting the marriage ties with the Medici and making him even more reliant upon the favour and patronage of the Pope. With Clement's death in 1534, there were riots in Rome against his favourites. Filippo's grain warehouses were sacked, and he was never to regain the unsecured loans he had made. The new pope, **Paul III,** patronised his own friends, just as the Medici had done, and Filippo found himself ousted from his lucrative positions.

Having personally suffered from the Medici's costly ambitions, Filippo gradually became the leader and financial supporter of Florentine exiles and enemies of the new duke Alessandro de' Medici, elected in 1532. The Strozzi once more became enemies of the Medici; Filippo's son Piero was accused of poisoning the Duke's favourite, Giuliano Salviati, in a dispute over Filippo's daughter Luisa (who died in mysterious cicumstances herself in 1534). Filippo sent his sons to different parts of Italy for safety, as the Duke's henchmen had retaliated in an assassination attempt on Filippo. Duke Alessandro declared him a rebel, and the Strozzi withdrew to the relative safety of Venice, but when Duke Alessandro was murdered in 1537 by Lorenzo di' Pierfrancesco de' Medici, the assassin fled to Filippo's house and he was once more implicated in the struggle to restore Florentine liberty.

Supported by the French King **Francis I**, Filippo and his sons launched an assault against the new leader of Florence, Duke **Cosimo de' Medici**. Cosimo's troops surprised the hopeful republicans at Montemurlo, near Prato, and Filippo was captured. He was taken to Florence, where he remained a prisoner for seventeen months before apparently taking his own life, possibly to avoid further torture. His death and suicide note were ultimately reliant upon his early classical education, and his self-image as defender of lost republican liberties, like Cato (d. 46 BC), who killed himself rather than admit defeat at the hands of a dictator. His last letter clearly marks the parallel:

> I commend my soul to God, who is the highest mercy, praying humbly that, if he can grant it no other gift, at least He will place it where Cato of Utica and other similar virtuous men have found their final end.

He concluded with his own epitaph, 'in dying for one's fatherland, any sort of death is sweet'. Filippo's exploitation by the Medici and his eventual death in captivity raised him to the status of republican martyr in the eyes of his sons and successive generations. It explains also the obsessive hatred of the Dukes of Florence sustained by his most famous sons, Piero and Leone Strozzi. (T. Adolphus Trollope, *Filippo Strozzi: A History of the Last Days of the Old Italian Liberty*, London, 1860; Melissa Meriam Bullard, *Filippo Strozzi and the Medici*, Cambridge, 1980.)

STROZZI, Filippo di Matteo: RISING (1428–1491) After his father's death and his brief return to Florence with his mother **Alessandra**, Filippo began his apprenticeship in banking with his father's friend and business colleague, Matteo Brandolini, in Florence. By 1446, he had moved to Spain and was working under his cousin in the family bank. The following year he moved to

Naples where he formed an association with the eldest of his three cousins, Niccolò di Leonardo, in the head office of the family's business.

Filippo rapidly established himself in Naples banking society, and by 1455 was listed as a correspondent of the **Medici** bank in Naples. He and his brother **Lorenzo** became increasingly powerful and prosperous; despite his exile from Florence, Filippo was made Consul of the Florentine nation. He was particularly favoured by King Ferdinand of Naples, who borrowed heavily from the Strozzi to fund his wars against his rebellious barons. In return Filippo was appointed as a councillor of the kingdom of Naples, in which position he was succeeded by his brother Lorenzo.

Filippo was married twice, firstly to Fiametta di Donato Adimari, then to Selvaggia di Bartolomeo Gianfigliazzi. By 1470 he had returned to Florence, opening and managing a branch of the family bank. By 1483, his personal wealth was estimated at 112,000 florins, four times the assets he had held twelve years before. When he died in 1491, his youngest son to his second wife was renamed Filippo in honour of his father. (Mark Phillips, *The Memoir of Marco Parenti*, London, 1989.)

STROZZI, Leone: KNIGHTS: (1515–1554) Son of **Filippo**, he joined the **Knights of St John** on Malta, and was made Prior of Capua, through the influence of their relative by marriage, Pope **Clement VII**. After the death of his father, Leone took service in France, and was given command of twenty galleys at first, then the entire Mediterranean fleet. Like his brother **Piero**, Leone was a brave fighter, but his bravado and risk-taking meant that his enemies in France had ample excuse to call for him to be replaced as commander of the Mediterranean fleet. He left the French court in 1551 and fled to Malta, after a supposed assassination attempt against him. **Juan de Homedes**, Grand Master of the Order, refused him a squadron of ships so he was forced to create his own, resorting to piracy and attacking Muslim and Christian alike in search of goods and munitions.

In 1554, France resumed war in Italy, and Strozzi was recalled to command the French galleys. He publicly proclaimed that he would repay all Christian merchants he had attacked in the Levantine seas. This done, he went to Porto Ecole to await the arrival of the French galleys, but was killed shortly thereafter at the siege of Scarlino, in the principality of Piombino.

STROZZI, Lorenzo di Matteo: RISING: (c. 1431–1479) Son of **Alessandra Strozzi** and brother of **Filippo di Matteo Strozzi**. In 1445, he entered the family's banking business at Valencia where he was followed by his younger brother Matteo. In 1450 they both joined the family branch at **Bruges** under their father's cousin Jacopo di Leonardo Strozzi. Matteo then moved to the bank's headquarters at Naples, where he remained until his death in 1459, leaving assets totalling only 500 florins. Lorenzo was concerned at his status in the bank as only the poor relation of the wealthier Strozzi and often wrote to his brother Filippo about their plans of raising enough capital to open a new office between them. With the death of Jacopo in 1461, Lorenzo headed to Naples to join his successful brother and also became a councillor to King Ferdinand. He remained in Naples until his death in 1479.

STROZZI, Piero: KNIGHTS: (1500–1558) Seigneur de Belleville, Count de Languillara; Marshal of France. A notable cynic, even perhaps an atheist, he trained first for the church, but abandoned it as a career when Pope **Clement VII** vacillated on his appointment as cardinal. Following his father **Filippo's** fall from grace with the **Medici**, Piero became a professional soldier, and went to France in 1536 as Colonel of the Italians serving at Piedmont. In 1537 he joined his father Filippo in his vain attempt to restore the Florentine Republic, but barely escaped with his life. On returning to France, and hearing of his father's death, he swore vengeance against the Medici and their allies. He devoted the rest of his life to fighting **Cosimo de' Medici** and **Charles V.** In 1544, he raised a corps of 7,000 men with his own money, and joined the French captain d'Enghien in Italy, but they were defeated. The following year with a corps of 8,000, he fought in Piedmont against Charles V.

In 1548, he was persuaded by **Montmorency** to go to Scotland, as Colonel in Charge of the Italian troops. Whilst on his way there, he successfully captured and burned several English merchant ships and fishing smacks off the east coast, at which he declared he could now properly call himself a Scotsman, adding antipathy for the English to his list of enemies. Preparing to besiege Haddington, he received the wounds which were to leave one leg permanently shorter than the other. Nine years later at Amiens, a hackbut ball in the mouth did no more damage than a few broken teeth.

His malicious sense of humour found a perfect outlet in **Henri II's** French court where he constantly goaded **Brusquet**, the king's fool. In his military career, Piero served the French army in its campaigns in Parmesan, Metz, Siena, Rome, Calais and Guines and finally died at the siege of **Thionville** in 1558. (*English Calendar of State Papers,* 1548ff.)

Stylites, Simeon: CASTLE, II, 3: (c. 390–459) Monk from the monastery of Eusebona, between Antioch and Aleppo. After several years as an anchorite, he took up residence on a low pillar, gradually increasing the height to forty cubits (nearly seventy feet). He became a major tourist attraction of his time, drawing pilgrims to marvel at the novelty of his worship and adoration. His innovative lifestyle greatly influenced the Christian and pagan world of his time, and he had many imitators. Not to be confused with his sixth-century namesake who ascended his pillar at Mons Admirabilis to the west of Antioch.

Stymphalian Bird: CASTLE, II, 10: Birds inhabiting the lake of Stymphalis in Arcadia. The huge birds, called Stymphalides, resembled storks or cranes; when they flew they discharged murderous feathers sharp as arrows, and fed upon human flesh whenever possible. They were finally destroyed by Hercules, aided by **Pallas-Athene**, as the sixth of his twelve labours.

Sub suave jugo Christi: PAWN, 5: 'Under the pleasant yoke of Christ'.

Sugar: SCORPIONS: The production of the addictively sweet end-product from cane sugar is both labour- and fuel-intensive. Sugar has been cultivated in the Mediterranean since the eighth century AD and was spread widely by the conquering Arabs. The sugar-cane plant itself takes between eight and twelve months to mature, and is planted in February or March with the expectation of harvesting the crop the following January. Cane-sugar plants require a great deal of water to sustain their rapid growth, hence the need for good irrigation. They are also dependent upon a steady hot climate and are particularly susceptible to frost, which can rapidly destroy nearly all growth.

When the plants are harvested, the priority is to extract as much juice as is possible from the cane of the plant. This is done by pounding or squeezing the plants between rollers, until the majority of the liquid has extruded from the fibrous mass of the stems. The liquid is then boiled and concentrated, and the impurities skimmed from the top. The early clarification process required two parts of alkaline lime to every part of sugar, and for every five tonnes of sugar, ninety eggs or two gallons of bullocks' blood were also required. The blood and egg whites act as coagulates, rendering the vegetable albumen and other foreign particles in the liquid sugar syrup insoluble. The liquid was further cleansed with the addition of **alum**, neutralised with further lime, removing all potential mould, bacteria and living organisms from the concentrated liquid.

At the point of crystallisation, the syrup is poured into earthenware cones in which it cools, crystallises and solidifies. The thick, brown molasses syrup drains through the crystals via a small aperture in the tip of the sugar cone. The resultant crystals in the cone can be dissolved in water and reboiled again and again, until the end product becomes purer and whiter; the molasses liquid also being reboiled until it yields more pure sugar crystals. This refining process was reliant upon the abundant availability of cheap fuel and local water supplies. The widely favoured Moroccan method of obtaining pure white crystals was to 'clay' the sugar cones. Waterlogged clay was placed over the top of the earthenware cones containing the crystallising sugar; the water would leach out the molasses from the sugar, turning the end product white by degrees. The whitest sugar would then be wrapped in blue paper, to disguise the fact that it still had a slight yellow hue. This method is still used in Morocco today, although the reason now given is that the blue paper has medicinal qualities. Thus a cosmetic device has become integral to the health-giving reputation of the product.

Generally speaking, the best sugar would be refined at its point of consumption because the crystals tended to coalesce on long, damp sea journeys.

By 1470, European importers were beginning to build their own sugar refineries in Venice, Bologna and then Antwerp, converting the rough sugar crystals into superior fine-grain sugar. Venice was eventually displaced by the West Indies, which supplied its product directly to the other cities of Europe.

As the taste for the expensive luxury grew, so too did its production. Portuguese settlers brought cane sugar to Madeira in the third decade of the fifteenth century, and rapidly exported the lucrative crop. By the second half of the century, cane sugar had replaced wheat as the principal export of the island. The Cypriot sugar industry was likewise flourishing in the fifteenth century; the Cornaro estate at Episkopi (see **Corner, Marco**) alone employed more than four hundred labourers.

Cane sugar was unknown in the New World until Columbus introduced it on his second voyage in 1493, but the Cypriot product was eventually displaced by cheaper Brazilian cane sugar. The travelling distance and expense of importing from Brazil was greater, but the climate was superior, and production became cheaper, although sugar retained its status as a luxury commodity. By the sixteenth century, white sugar, especially if displayed and served from a silver castor, was considered an ostentatious display of wealth and conspicuous consumption. (L.A.G. Strong, *The Story of Sugar*, London, 1954; J.H. Galloway, *The Sugar Cane Industry*, Cambridge, 1989.)

Suivez François: KINGS, III, 3: See *Soyez hardis, en joye mis.*

SULEIMAN the Magnificent: PAWN: (1494–1566) Sultan of the Ottoman Empire when the Empire was at its sixteenth-century zenith. (See **Osman.**) Also known as *El Kanuni,* 'The Lawgiver', Suleiman came to power at the age of twenty-six. In his twenties he was described as tall and lean, with a thin face and aquiline nose. His health was good throughout his life; old age was the only infirmity which slowed Suleiman down, and even that did not start to take effect until he was well into his late fifties.

In keeping with an inspiring, heroic portrait of the great conqueror by Titian, Suleiman was said to prefer reading about the conquests of Alexander the Great to love poetry or philosophy. He did attempt to foster the growth of a distinct Ottoman style of poetry rather than the reliance upon Persian models; Suleiman's favourite poets were allowed to criticise his regime, so long as they did so in fine verse.

His temperament is variously described as majestic, temperate, cold or melancholy, although his nature seems to have been warmer when it came to the inhabitants of his seraglio. His first favourite Sultana was the Montenegrin Gulbehar (Rose of Spring), mother of his eldest son **Mustapha.** By 1534 she had been displaced in his affections by **Roxelana.** She became Suleiman's wife by intrigue, and maintained her position in the same manner, supplanting all of his other concubines by becoming his wife; the first woman in one hundred and fifty years successfully to capture a sultan. His dependency upon her was criticised by contemporaries as bad for his empire, as in later years it encouraged him to stay at home with Roxelana rather than live with his soldiers and accompany them into battle.

Under Suleiman, the Ottoman Empire spread rapidly across the mainland and coast of Europe, destroying Hungarian independence and resulting in Turkish control over Genoese and Venetian trade in the Levant. With the conquest of Belgrade in 1521, the capitulation of the **Knights of St John** of Rhodes in 1522, and the defeat of the Hungarians at the battle of Mohacs in 1526, the powerful armies of Suleiman's empire seemed unstoppable, reaching the gates of Vienna by 1529. This was in addition to conquests in Persia, Georgia and Tunis and his alliance with France, formed with **Francis I.**

In addition to his reputation as conqueror, Suleiman was considered a great patron of architecture and of education, increasing the number of schools in Constantinople, and improving the standards of the eight mosque colleges, the eight paradises of knowledge'. He achieved his reputation as a law-giver from his revision of the penal code; making the law a little less severe than it had been under his predecessors. (Roger Merriman, *Suleiman the Magnificent*, London, 1944; Stanley Mayes, *An Organ for the Sultan*, London, 1956.)

Sultan of Cambaia: PAWN, 16: The account of the Sultan's feminine facial hair, tied up with a fillet, comes from a 1503 journal of travels in the Ottoman empire. It also confidently asserts that the Sultan had been trained to eat poison since childhood, to inure him to its taste and its effects. (Samuel Purchas, *Purchas, His Pilgrimes*, Hakluyt Society, 1905.)

Sweet Cicely: KINGS, III, 3: A plant attractive to bees. Beekeepers made use of its properties by rubbing empty hives with its leaves.

Sweet rose of virtue and of gentleness: KINGS, I, 1: From the poem by William Dunbar (c. 1460–1520), 'To A Lady':

> Sweet Rose of Virtue and of gentleness;
> Delightsome Lily of every lustiness,
> Richest in bounty, and in beauty clear,
> And every virtue that is held most dear,
> Except only that ye are merciless.
>
> Into your garthe [garden] this day I did pursue,
> There saw I flowris that fresh were of hue;
> Both white and red most lusty were to seen,
> And halesome herbis upon stalkis green;
> Yet leaf nor flower find could I none of rue.

I doubt [fear] that March, with his cauld blastis keen,
Has slain this gentle herb, that I of mean,
Whose piteous death does to my heart sic pain,
That I would make to plant his root again,
So comfort and his leavis unto me been.
(J. Ross, ed., *The Book of Scottish Poems*, Edinburgh, 1878.)

Sybarite: QUEENS, III, 7: Residents of the Greek city of Sybaris, founded in 720 BC. The city attained a remarkable degree of wealth and prosperity; its citizens regarded as such devotees of luxury and indolence that the term sybarite became a common term for any voluptuary. The city was eventually overcome by war and destroyed by flooding in 510 BC. See **Paestum.**

Syne Sweirness, at the secound bidding: CHECKMATE I, 6: The appearance of the character of Sloth in William Dunbar's (c. 1460–1520) 'The Dance of the Seven Deidly Sinnis' (extract):

Of Februar the fifteen night,
Full lang before the dais light,
I lay in till a trance,
And then I saw baith Heaven and Hell:
Me thought, among the fiendis fell,
Mahoun [Devil] gart cry ane Dance
Of shrews that were never shriven,
Agains the feast of Fastern's even,
To make their observance.
He bade gallants gae graith a gyse [prepare a mask],
And cast up gamountis [gambols] in the skies,
As varlets does in France . . .

Syne [next] Swearness [Sloth], at the secound bidding,
Come like a sow out of a midding [dungheap],
Full sleepy was his grunyie [grumble]:
Mony swear [much swearing] bumbard belly huddroun [glutton],
Mony slute [slothful] daw, and sleepy duddroun [sluggard],
Him servèd aye with sounyie [care];
He drew them forth in till a chain,
And Belial with a bridle rein,
Ever lashed them on the lunyie [loins]:
In dance they were so slow of feet,
They gave them in the fire a heat,
And made them quicker of cunyie [apprehension].
(J. Ross, ed., *The Book of Scottish Poems*, Edinburgh, 1878.)

Syphilis: KINGS, I, 1: Known from 1492 in Scotland, and also referred to as 'The Pox'. There was no definitive cure until this century. Taking a course of mercury as an antidote was popular from the sixteenth century onwards, of which one of the side effects was insanity. Hence the phrase 'A night in the arms of Venus and a month with [or a lifetime in the arms of] Mercury'; CASTLE: II, 2. (John D. Comrie, *History of Scottish Medicine to 1860*.)

Ta femme sera de la sorte: CHECKMATE, V, 4; UNICORN, 26: Fully quoted within the text of CHECKMATE, the poem is a paraphrase of Psalm 128:

Within the walls of thy house
Thy wife will be as a vine,
Bearing an abundance of good fruit
In season.

And thy sons set round the table,
Will be fresh and beautiful
As a grove of young olive trees.
(Tr. D.D. René de Bouillé, *Histoire des Ducs de Guise*, 1849.)

Ta sotte muse, avec ta rude Lyre!: QUEENS, III, 2: 'Your foolish Muse, with your rustic lyre!' From a fifteenth-century poem satirising the burlesque society 'L'Abbaye des Conards' in Rouen. (René Herval, *Histoire de Rouen*, Vol. II.)

Taghaza: SCALES: The principal source of salt required for the continuation of the **Silent trade** for **Wangara** gold. It is the home of a salt mine, where the salt deposits were, and still are, dug from the earth in slabs. Miners in the fifteenth century would probably have been slaves from the Mesufa tribe. Whoever controlled Taghaza controlled the gold trade. The Taghaza to **Timbuktu** camel route has always been a perilous one; as late as 1805 a caravan of 2,000 men and 1,800 camels all perished from thirst on their return from Timbuktu. (E.W. Bovill, *The Golden Trade of the Moors*, London, 1958.)

Tambour: SCALES, 30: Small shallow-framed drum, also known as the tabor, without the jingles associated with the tambourine. Tambours were often equipped with a snare, especially if they were used as military drums.

Tancred: CHECKMATE, II, 8: (c. 1075–1112) The great hero of the First Crusade against the Infidel, Tancred capitalised on the triumphs of the Christians regaining the Holy Land, becoming Prince of Galilee and Regent of Antioch.

TANI, Angelo di Jacopo: RISING: (1415–1492) From 1455 to 1465, Tani was the branch manager of the Medici bank in **Bruges**, and a thorn in the side of his junior **Tommaso Portinari**, who felt he was blocking his promotion. **Cosimo de' Medici**, wiser than his sons, made sure that the less gifted, cautious Angelo remained as a brake to the volatile impetuous Tommaso, even though he took the chance to chastise Angelo himself for risking bad debts with the Italian pawnbrokers in Bruges. In 1450, long before his office in Bruges, Angelo made an impression by his excellent handling of the great jubilee Indulgence at Malines, obliterating the mistakes of a few years before for which Cosimo had rebuked and demoted him. While based in Bruges, Angelo was required to visit the fairs of Antwerp and Bergen-ap-Zoom and make business trips to London, Calais and Middleburg, as well as the occasional visit to his headquarters in Florence. As with all Medici managers, he was not permitted to accept gifts over the value of one pound, or to gamble, or to entertain women in his quarters. With Tommaso, he shared in the frequent disputes with their masters in Florence over the selling of **alum** from Tolfa in the Papal States. In 1467 Angelo was at last removed from Bruges and sent back to London (where he had served in 1446) to try and obtain a settlement of the debts owed by King **Edward IV** to the London branch of the Medici. He was successful in arranging for a new loan to be paid for by wool, but stayed to see all his work come to nothing through a resurgence of the war between King Edward and his Lancastrian rivals. Angelo's removal from Bruges, which allowed Tommaso Portinari to lead the branch into extravagant debt, was probably the worst move the Medici could have made. Angelo remained a shareholder in the Bruges company even after leaving the town, but later adjusted matters with Tommaso before returning to Florence for good. Travelling through France in 1480, Angelo visited Tours at the request of King **Louis XI**, who offered him the post of Receiver General of Finance in France. Angelo refused, excusing himself on the grounds that he was too old, and unable to read and write French. He was married to Caterina Tanagli, probably the daughter of Jacopo Tanagli who managed the Medici silk manufacturing shop in Florence, and probably a kinsman of the brothers Tommaso and Andrea Tani who ran a wool company in Florence and later in Naples in the 1450s. He died in 1492 in the same month as **Lorenzo de' Medici**. (Raymond de Roover, *Money, Banking and Credit in Medieval Bruges*; Lauro Martines, *Social World of Florentine Humanists*; Curt S. Gutkind, *Cosimo de' Medici*; Raymond de Roover, *Medici Bank*; A. Grunzweig, *Correspondance de la Filiale de Bruges des Medicis.*)

Tanist heir: QUEENS, IV, 5: The ancient Irish term for the second to the king; next most likely to inherit and rule.

Tant de payis, tant' de Guises: CHECKMATE, III, 1: Common French proverb: 'As many different fashions as there are countries'. Used satirically in the novel, because of the optional capitalisation, to refer to the powerful and fecund **de Guise** family.

Tant que je vive: CHECKMATE, I, 6; UNICORN, 43: The poem appears in the poetry album of Marguerite of Austria (1480–1530), Regent of the Netherlands under Archduke Charles (later **Charles V**) from 1507 until her death. The original source of the poem is unclear; Marguerite may have written it herself, or copied down the verse from another source, echoing as it did her emotions after the death in 1504 of her second husband Philibert II le Beau, Duke of Savoy. She was never to marry again, despite an offer even from Henry VII of England. Marguerite saw herself as a victim of fate, and took as her motto *Fortune infortune fort une*; 'Fortune makes one very unfortunate'. After her death, the poetry and songbooks were inherited by her niece and successor to the regency, Mary of Hungary. The poem is reproduced from Marguerite's poetry album in its original form, from a woman to a man:

> *Tant que je vive, mon cueur ne changera*
> *Pour nul vivant, tant soit il bon ou saige,*
> *Fort et puissant, riche, de hault linaige:*
> *Mon chois est fait, aultre ne se fera.*

> *Il peult estre que l'on devisera;*
> *Mais ja pour ce ne meura mon couraige,*
> *Tant que je vive.*

> *Jamais mon cueur à l'encontre n'yra;*
> *D'ung franc vouloir l'en ay mis en oistaige;*
> *De l'en oster point ne suis si voulaige;*
> *Ou je l'ay mis a tousjours mais sera,*
> *Tant que je vive.*

> Long as I live, my heart will never change
> To no man else my love shall I consign
> However gallant, rich or proud his line
> My choice is made, and will not brook exchange.

> Let Fate conspire to thwart, to disarrange
> My spirit will not fail in its design
> Long as I live.

> Never will heart of mine seek pastures strange
> Its bright resolve, in bondage I'll confine
> Nor loose, from wanton fancy, what is mine

But hold it fast for ever in its cage
Long as I live.

(Tr. D.D. Marcel Françon, ed., *Albums Poétiques de Marguerite d'Autriche*, Paris, 1934; Martin Picker, *The Chanson Albums of Marguerite of Austria*, Los Angeles, 1965.)

Tant que je vivrai en âge fleurissant: KNIGHTS, III, 7: From the unascribed French poem:

Tant que je vivray en age florissant
Je serviray d'amour le dieu puissant
En faitz, en dictz, en chansons et acordz.

Par plusieurs jours m'a tenu languissant
Mais apres dueil m'a faict rejouissant
Car jay l'amour de la belle au gent corps.

Son aliance c'est ma fiance
Son cueur est mien, le mien est sien
Fi de tristesse vive liesse
Puis qu'en amours, Puis qu'en amours
A tant de biens.

So long as I live in the flower of my youth
I pay service to Love, the most powerful god
In deed, word and song
And in sweetest accord.

Languishing have I lain me these several days
But joy after sorrow is granted me now
With the love of my may [maiden]
With such grace at her brow.

In her dear love I place my trust
Her heart is mine, and mine her own
Sadness begone: let mirth arise
For in young love: For in young love
Such blessing lies.

(Tr. D.D.)

Tantum religio potuit suadere malorum: PAWN, 9: 'Superstition was able to encourage so much evil'; a moral maxim taken from Lucretius' *De Rerum Natura*.

Telemachus: KINGS, Gambit: Son of Odysseus and Penelope who assisted his father in the execution of Penelope's suitors. (Homer, *The Odyssey*, tr. Walter Shewring, Oxford, 1986.)

Temperantia, embracing his clock and his spectacles: CHECKMATE, V, 5: The reference is to one of the five statues which stood outside the Chambre des Comptes in Paris. The statue of Temperance had the Latin inscription under his feet, *Mihi spreta voluptas*. (De Breul, *Antiquité de Paris*, Paris, 1612.)

TENNANT, Mungo: KINGS: The character of Mungo is based on fact, although he was perhaps not the most law-abiding burgess that Edinburgh has ever bred. His name appears in the law records of Scotland in 1543 for the unlawful assembly of a group of armed men. Tennant, his son Francis and thirteen others were cautioned and fined between 500 and 1000 merks each for unlawful convocation, storming Edinburgh's court building the Tolbooth, for sedition and unlawfully bearing a standard or ensign called the 'Haly Gaist'. The charges are listed thus, in the presence of the Earl of **Arran**, then Governor of Scotland:

> For the contemptiounc done to the QUENIS grace autorité, in drawing of knyffis in the said Tolbuthe . . . in ane defensat [defence] Court, in presens of the PROVEST and BAILLIES of the said Burghe, sittand for the tyme in jugemement, invading and hurting ilkanc uthers [all the others present] for thare slachter [slaughter]: And for Seditioune, with Convocatioune [unlawful armed assembly] of our soverane lady the QUENYS leigis [subjects], maid within the said burcht [burgh], with ane displayit ansnzé [ensign] quhilk [which] thai call the HALY GAIST: And for the contemptioune of my lord GOVERNOURIS command and charge, he being thair present in propir persoune, gevin to thame be [by] Johne Cob, messinger, at my said lord GOVERNOURIS command.

(Robert Pitcairn, ed., *Criminal Trials in Scotland from* AD MCCCLXXXVIII *to* AD MDCXXIV, Edinburgh, 1883.)

Tes mains sont des nuages: PAWN, 17: 'Thy hands are as clouds'; an Arab proverb translated into French; it is intended as a compliment to the generosity of your host, literally dispensing a shower of gifts.

Tespi: PAWN, 24: Muslim prayer beads. Each of the ninety-nine beads corresponds to one of the different titles of God. It is said that Mohammed confided the hundredth name of God to his favourite camel Al Kaswa, who saved his life when the Prophet fled from Mecca. (James Dalloway, *Constantinople*, 1797; Albin Michel, *La Vie du Chameau*, Paris, 1938.)

Tetragrammaton: KINGS, IV, 2: Technical term for the Hebrew four-letter word for God (YHWH or JHVH). Owing to its sacred power, the word was not spoken and *Adonai* or Lord was used as a substitute. It is from the sum of the vowels and consonants of these two that the title 'Jehovah' originated.

Thady Boy: QUEENS: The name given to the rook, an Irish bard visiting the court of the papal peacock in Richard Holland's (d. 1482) poem the **Buke of the Howlat:** 'A bard out of Irland with Banachadee!' See **O Dermyne, O Donnall, O Dochardy droch.** (Priscilla Bawcutt & Felicity Riddy, eds, *Scottish Longer Poems*, Vol. I, Edinburgh, 1987.)

The baker's daughter is better in her gown than Queen Mary without her crown: CASTLE, I, 8: A scurrilous verse circulating in London following the marriage of **Mary Tudor** to **Philip II.** It is said that Philip preferred to sleep with common wenches rather than his new, pallid, flabby and rather mature bride. Rumours were rife by 1555 that Philip would get through three or four such poor whores a night while his wife no doubt lay in blissful ignorance of the unwholesome scandal surrounding his conduct. (Beatrice White, *Mary Tudor*, 1935.)

The country is stronger than the lord: QUEENS, II, 3: Translation of the Gaelic proverb *Is treise tuath ná tigheama.* (Gerard A. Hayes-McCoy, *Scots Mercenary Forces in Ireland.*)

The day . . . on which men shall be as scattered moths, and the mountains shall be as loosened wool: PAWN, 27: The day of Judgement according to the Holy Koran. As a point of comparison, the moth in Turkish poetry is a symbol of perfect love, perishing silently in its consuming love for the flame of the taper (PAWN, 21), rather than the nightingale which wails its lovelorn song to the rose. (E.J.W. Gibb, *History of Ottoman Poetry*, Vol. II.)

The foul yoke of sensual bondage: CHECKMATE, I, 1: From the song by **Sir Thomas Wyatt:**

> If thou wilt mighty be, flee from the rage
> Of cruel will; and see thou keep thee free
> From the foul yoke of sensual bondage:
> For though thine empire stretch to Indian sea
> And for thy fear trembleth the farthest Thule,
> If thy desire have over thee the power,
> Subject then art thou, and no governor.
>
> If to be noble and high thy mind be movèd,
> Consider well thy ground and thy beginning;

For he that hath each star in heaven fixèd,
And gives the moon her horns and her eclipsing,
Alike hath made thee noble in his working;
So that wretched no way may thou be,
Except foul lust and vice do conquer thee.

All were it so thou had a flood of gold
Unto thy thirst, yet should it not suffice;
And though with Indian stones, a thousandfold
More precious than can thyself devise,
Ychargèd were thy back, thy covetise
And busy biting yet should never let
Thy wretched life, ne do thy death profet.

(Gerald Bullett, ed., *Silver Poets of the Sixteenth Century*, London, 1970.)

The Frogge would a wooing ride: KINGS, I, 2: Old Scots rhyme and spinning song. The frog proposes marriage to the mouse, who accepts. They are married by the rat, followed by a wedding supper interrupted by **Gib** the cat, who catches the mouse. Dick the Drake carries off the frog and the rat manages to evade capture by escaping up the wall. Several versions exist, both as a song and a poem. (See also **It was the Frogge on the wall**, and **Where Dickie our Drake . . . takes the frog**).

It was a frogge in the well
Humble-dum, humble-dum
And the merry mouse in the mill
Tweedle, tweedle, twino

The frogge would a-wooing ride
Humble-dum, humble-dum
Sword and buckler by his side
Tweedle, tweedle, twino

When upon his high horse sat
Humble-dum, humble-dum
His boots they shone as black as jet
Tweedle, tweedle, twino

When he came to the merry mill pin
Humble-dum, humble-dum,
Lady Mouse, beene you within?
Tweedle, tweedle, twino

Then came out the dusty mouse
Humble-dum, humble-dum
I am the lady of this house
Tweedle, tweedle, twino

Hast thou any mind of me?
Humble-dum, humble-dum
I have e'en great mind of thee
Tweedle, tweedle, twino

Who shall this marriage make?
Humble-dum, humble-dum
Our lord, which is the rat
Tweedle, tweedle, twino

What shall we have to our supper?
Humble-dum, humble-dum
Three beans in a pound of butter
Tweedle, tweedle, twino

But, when the supper they were at
Humble-dum, humble-dum
The frogge, the mouse and e'en the rat
Tweedle, tweedle, twino

Then came in Gib, our cat
Humble-dum, humble-dum
And caught the mouse e'en by the back
Tweedle, tweedle, twino

Then did they separate
Humble-dum, humble-dum
The frogge leapt on the floor so flat
Tweedle, tweedle, twino

Then came in Dick, our drake
Humble-dum, humble-dum
And drew the frogge e'en to the lake
Tweedle, tweedle, twino

The rat he ran up the wall,
Humble-dum, humble-dum
And so the company parted all
Tweedle, tweedle, twino.

The fruit of all the service that I serve: CHECKMATE, IV, 4: The poem by **Sir Thomas Wyatt**, quoted within the text:

> The fruit of all the service that I serve
> Despair doth reap, such hapless hap have I.
> But though he have no power to make me swerve,
> Yet, by the fire, for cold I feel I die.
> In paradise, for hunger still I sterve [starve];
> And, in the flood, for thirst to death I dry.
> So Tantalus am I, and in worse pain
> Amids my help, and helpless doth remain.

The King of Spain is a foul paynim: KNIGHTS, III, 10: From the anonymous fifteenth-century ballad, 'King Estmere' (extract):

> Hearken to me, gentlemen,
> Come and you shall heare:
> Ile tell you of two of the boldest brether
> That ever borne were.
>
> The tone of them was Adler Yonge,
> The tother was King Estmere:
> They were as bolde men in their deeds
> As any were, farr and neare.
>
> 'You have a daughter,' sayd Adler Yonge,
> 'Men call her bright and sheene,
> My brother wold marrye her to his wiffe,
> Of Englande to be queene—'
>
> 'Yesterday was att my deere daughter
> Kyng Bremor his sonne of Spayn,
> And then she nickēd him of naye [refused]
> And I doubt sheele do you the same—'
>
> 'The King of Spayn is a foule paynim,
> and 'lieveth on Mahound,
> And pitye it were that fayre ladye
> Should marry a heathen hound.'

(D. Laing & W. Carew Hazlitt, *Early Popular Poetry of Scotland*, London, 1895.)

The Lion in Affrik and the Bear in Sarmatia: CASTLE, III, 9: **Richard Eden's** translation of Jacob Zeigler's travels in northern Europe, published in 1555.

He notes the 'mortifying quality of cold' that the visitor experiences in travelling far north and the empirical evidence that the aggressive character of animals is mollified when they are displaced from their natural climate.

The love of sweetmeats comes from the Faith: PAWN, 19: The Prophet Mohammed apparently had a sweet tooth; the liking for sugar relates also to the state of the soul; 'The Faithful are sweet and the wicked are sour'. In the sixteenth century, the finest confectioners in Constantinople were either Franks or Greeks from **Chios**, reputedly also experts in medicine. There were over five hundred of them resident in the Sublime Porte with sixty shops, displaying such fantasies as sugar trees covered with crystallised fruits. The highest aspiration of their trade would be to become Chief Confectioner to the Seraglio. (Alexander Pallis, *In the Days of the Janissaries.*)

The manifest fool is known by every ninth word: CASTLE, II, 6: Taken from the Brehon Laws of ancient Ireland, known as the **Senchus Mor.** The sentiment of the babbling fool is echoed in the Book of Proverbs: 'Wise men lay up knowledge; but the mouth of the foolish is near destruction' (10, 14); 'Go from the presence of a foolish man, when thou perceivest not in him the lips of knowledge' (14, 7); 'The tongue of the wise useth knowledge aright; but the mouth of fools poureth out foolishness' (15, 2).

The note called Coquetry and the note called True: CASTLE, II, 6: In the Oriental musical scale one of the notes is called *Shehnáz,* or 'Coquetry,' and another is called *Rást,* 'True'.

The Pillar pearisht is whearto I lent: CHECKMATE, IV, 1: The poem of **Sir Thomas Wyatt**, 'The Lover Laments the Death of his Love':

> The pillar perisht is wherto I lent,
> The strongest stay [support] of mine unquiet minde:
> The like of it no man again can finde:
> From east to west still seeking though he went.
> To mine unhappe for happe away hath rent,
> Of all my joy the very bark and rynde:
> And I (alas) by chance am thus assinde.
> Daily to moorne till death do it relent.
> But since that thus it is my desteny,
> What can I more but have a wofull hart,
> My penne, in plaint, my voyce in carefull crye:
> My minde in wo, my body full of smart.
> And I my self, my selfe alwayes to hate,
> Till dreadfull death do ease my dolefull state.

The prayer of Job upon the dunghill was as good as Paul's in the temple:
PAWN, 2: A typically Lutheran comment from William Tyndale (d. 1536), one of the early leaders of the English Reformation, and translator of the New Testament into vernacular English, for which heresy he was eventually strangled and burnt at the stake. (Henry Craik, ed., *English Prose Selections*, Vol. I.)

The Scot, the Frencheman, the Pope and heresie: KINGS, IV, 1: Quoted from **Roger Ascham** on Henry VIII's Protestant Reformation:

> The Scot, the Frencheman, the Pope and heresie
> Overcommed by Trothe [Truth], have had a fall:
> Sticke to the Trothe, and evermore thou shall
> Through Christ, King Henry, the Boke and the Bowe,
> All manner of enemies, quite overthrowe.

The sliding joy, the gladness short: KINGS, IV, 1: From the Scots poet William Dunbar's (c. 1460–1520) 'The World's Instability' (extract):

> This wavering world's wretchedness:
> The failing, fruitless business.
> The mis-spent time, the service vain:
> For to consider is a pain.
>
> The sliding joy, the gladness short:
> The feigned love, the false comfort:
> The sweet delayed, the flichtful train [changeful snare]:
> For to consider is a pain.
>
> The sugared mouths, with minds therefrae:
> The figured speech, with faces tway [two]:
> The pleasant tongues with hearts unplain:
> For to consider is a pain.

(H. Macaulay Fitzgibbon, ed., *Early English Poetry*.)

The smylere with the knyf under the cloke: CHECKMATE, III, 9: Treachery and treason afoot; taken from Geoffrey Chaucer, 'The Knight's Tale' (extract):

> Ther saugh [saw] I first the derke ymaginyng
> Of Felonye, and al the compassyng;
> The crueel Ire, reed as any gleede [live coal];
> The pykepurse [pickpocket], and eke the pale Drede;
> The smylere with the knyf under the cloke;
> The shepne [stable] brennynge [burning] with the blake smoke;
> The tresoun of the mordrynge [murdering] in the bedde;

The open werre, with woundes al bibledde;
Contek [conflict], with blody knyf and sharp menace.
Al ful of chirkyng [strident noises] was that sory place.
(F.N. Robinson, ed., *The Complete Works of Geoffrey Chaucer*, Oxford, 1974.)

The soul enters by the throat: PAWN, 21: An old Turcoman proverb, in hopeful expectation of an awaited feast. Cooking is seen in the Koran as a profession acceptable to Allah. Their patron was Adam, who apparently cooked soup known as *Babá Chorbasí*, or 'Daddy's Soup'. The Koran says of hospitality to hungry guests, 'They shall eat dinner for love of Him and unto you shall we give food for God's sake'. The Prophet's favourite food was tripe. (Alexander Pallis, *In the Days of the Janissaries*.)

Thekla, St: CASTLE, II, 13: Early Christian saint, from the first century AD, converted by St Paul at Iconium. She was then to achieve the dubious distinction of becoming the first female martyr of the Christian church.

There is a great difference between having discontented subjects and having desperate subjects: CHECKMATE, II, 7: Comment made by the Italian historian Francesco Guicciardini (1483–1540) with reference here to the danger of insurrection in sixteenth-century France if the rising number of Protestants were persecuted too harshly. Tolerance was necessary during periods of war, where internal conflict had to be kept to a manageable minimum in the interests of presenting a unified front to the enemy. This was particularly the case in 1558 when the Cardinal of Lorraine estimated that two-thirds of the country had already subscribed to the Lutheran heresy.

After the conclusion of peace with **Charles V**, France became a violent hotbed of religious dissent. Under **Henri II**, the Huguenots had become increasingly provocative. Henri swore that when peace was settled with Spain, he would make the streets run with the blood and heads of the 'infamous Lutheran rabble'. The repression of the Protestants continued under his successors, but the struggle turned into a pyrrhic victory for the zealous Catholics with the violent and costly Huguenot wars lasting until the end of the sixteenth century. (Jean Héritier, *Catherine de Medici*.)

There was an Ewe had three lambs: KINGS, IV, 4; UNICORN, 5: Scots nursery rhyme:

> There was an Ewe had three Lambs
> And one of them was black.
> There was a man had three sons
> Jeffery, James and Jack.
> The one was hanged, the other drowned
> The third was lost and never found.

Thevet, André: CASTLE, II, 9: (1517–1592) Royal Cosmographer to **Francis I, Henri II** of France and his successors, Thevet undertook an extensive voyage of research and discovery in the Levant. His studies, published in 1556, recount his travels from Venice to Jerusalem and are a practical mixture of geography, astronomy, history, ethnography, complete with his observations on the flora, fauna, morality and religious ethics of the societies he visited. On his return to France, **Catherine de Médicis** appointed the knowledgeable traveller as her almoner. (Frank Lestringant, ed., *Cosmographie de Levant*, Geneva, 1985.)

They caught thee on the mountain and bred thee: PAWN, 20: The song of Constantinople's gypsy bearkeepers, to make their animals perform for the crowd. The animal's trainer would lead the bear secured by a double chain; his tambourine in one hand and a cudgel in the other, just in case the music was not tempting enough on its own to induce the animal to dance. (Alexander Pallis, *In the Days of the Janissaries*.)

They made the whole world to hang in the air: CASTLE, III, 9; 14: **Richard Eden**'s comment on the first great Elizabethan explorers, like **Diccon Chancellor**. Eden's account of their journeys was first published in 1555.

They shall heap sorrow on their heads: QUEENS, II, 6: Psalm 16, 4, the most evocative verse being quoted within the text. The version comes from the Geneva Psalms, published in London by John Crespin in 1569.

They shall not hear therein vain or sinful discourse: PAWN, 11: According to the Koran, this is the vision of Paradise which will be experienced by the pure and devout believers.

Thionville: CHECKMATE, V, 3: The surrender of Thionville to the French in June 1558 was a decisive turning point in the war between **Henri II** and the Empire of **Charles V** and **Philip II**. The garrison of 1,500 troops and 4,000 inhabitants was taken at the cost of only four hundred French lives. Losses on the French side were thus relatively small, apart from the death of **Piero Strozzi**, possibly the only good news about the whole affair, according to the Duke of Florence's Ambassador in Brussels.

The town could have been taken sooner by the French, had not the troops been obliged to wait for the arrival of the **Duke de Guise.** The Governor of Metz was openly unhappy that the credit for the forthcoming victory would again go to the de Guise family rather than those who had prepared the entire attack. As the Master of Artillery, d'Estree said openly in the presence of the Duke de Guise that he need not have appeared at all; as it was, he would find it very easy to swallow down what had already been masticated. After sixteen days of the French siege, Thionville was forced to capitulate. Honour and all glories fell—as predicted—to the Duke de Guise.

As soon as the French had taken Thionville, they consolidated their position by repairing the fortifications, opening the possibility of an advance against the Empire in Luxembourg. It forced Philip II into an awkward position; not knowing whether he should continue to shore up Gravelines against a potential French attack or concentrate his efforts on the Luxembourg front. As it was, Calais and Gravelines soon fell to the French. (René de Bouillé, *Histoire des Ducs de Guise*, 1849.)

THIRLEBY, Thomas: CASTLE: (1506–1570) Bishop of Ely. Educated at Trinity Hall, Cambridge, Thirleby became a bachelor of both civil and canon law, and was used as an Ambassador to France and the Empire by both Henry VIII and **Mary Tudor**. Thirleby was apparently not as zealous in religious matters as his monarchs; under Mary Tudor, Thirleby did not make a concerted effort to persecute Protestants in his diocese; only three of his parishioners were made martyrs under the Queen.

This officer but doubt is callit Deid: KINGS, I, 1: A line from the anonymous Scots poem 'The Thrie Priests of Peblis' (Peebles) which forms the explanation of the third priest's moral tale (extract):

> This officer but [without] doubt is callit Deid [Death];
> Is nane [no one] his power agane may repleid [plead against]:
> Is nane sa [so] wicht [mighty], na [nor] wise, na of sic wit,
> Against his summons soothly [truly] that may sit.

Those who gather frankincense are dedicated unto divine honours: PAWN, 27: According to **Nicolas de Nicolay,** those entrusted with the duty of gathering the resin were called divine or holy and during the time of gathering abstained both from the carnal company of women, and attending burials. (*Harleian Collection of Voyages*, Vol. I, 1745.)

Though an Emperor in body is like all other men, yet in power he is like God: CASTLE, II, 3: A comment on the near omnipotence of rulers made by Deacon Agapetus in the sixth century AD. The sixteenth-century Russian view of monarchy credited even more power to their ruler. If any matter was uncertain, the standard response was 'God and the Grand Prince know'. (George Vernadsky & Michael Karpovich, *History of Russia*, Vol. IV.)

Three Estates, Ane Satire of the: KINGS, IV, 4: Sir David Lindsay's morality play, first performed in 1540 before King **James V** and his court at Linlithgow Palace, and last performed in Lindsay's lifetime at the Calton Hill Playfield in 1554. His bold, satirical play clearly exposes the corruption and excesses of the church and the moral laxity of the court at the time of its performance. In an extended version, the performance was said to have stretched to nine hours, including intervals. By 1558 such public expression of dissension was no longer acceptable in post-Reformation Scotland, and the play was burned by the public executioner. (Sir David Lindsay, *Ane Satyre of the Thrie Estaities*, acting text by Robert Kemp, Edinburgh, 1985.)

Three Queens and the Three Dead Men: QUEENS, IV, 1: The title of a medieval miracle play. (Reginald Nettel, *Seven Centuries of Popular Song*.)

Thy mother made thee unique in the world: KNIGHTS, III, 17: Stock phrase of Arabic poetry, *Jabatek ummek wahad f'il-dunya*.

Tibet: KINGS: IV, 1: See **Sew Tibet, knit Annot and spin Margerie.**

Tight in hardel: QUEENS, II, 2: A hunting term, referring to two or more hounds tied closely together, but ready to be unleashed for the chase. (C.E. Hare, *The Language of Field Sports*, Glasgow, 1949.)

Timbuktu: SCALES: On the threshold of the desert and close to the River Niger. There is an old Sudan proverb: Salt comes from the north, gold from the south and silver from the country of the white men, but the Word of God and the treasures of wisdom are only to be found in Timbuktu. From the eleventh century onwards the town became a meeting place and market for those travelling by both water and land to exchange goods; the main trade being an exchange of salt, dates and the merchandise of the Maghreb for the grain, kola nuts and gold dust of the Sudan. As a perfectly positioned *entrepôt* for trade, Timbuktu grew to become a great commercial centre for the powerful Kingdom of Mali, which controlled the city until 1433. It was also a long-established seat of learning, with a large body of accomplished scholars and valuable libraries, and had a strong local tradition of jurisprudence. The origin of Muslim learning in Timbuktu has been lost, but the noted Jedala scholars of the Sankhore mosque are mentioned in accounts of the fourteenth century. The Sankhore was a sister of the universities of Cairo, Cordoba, Fez and Damascus, and Muslim urban practices probably dictated the Timbuktu style of autonomous rule, which shared the administration between the *ulama* (the learned men) and the bourgeoisie of the city, with the judges ranking supreme in power under the Timbuktuy-Koy, or governor.

The inhabitants of Timbuktu were wholly reliant on peacetime trade, as the city produced no goods and had no natural defences. They were of mixed races and all colours. During the period after the withdrawal of Mali rule, when the administration fell for some decades under the control of the Maghsharen, the venerated scholars were mostly black, either Soninke or

Malinke or Sudanic men of learning from the south, while the highest positions of judgeship tended to be held by the races from further north.

The period of Maghsharen domination lasted until 1468, during which time the income from the Timbuktu taxes was divided beween Muhammed ben Idir, the Timbuktu-Koy, and the predatory **Tuareg** chief Akil ag Malwal, who provided a sporadic policing or garrison service, in between incursions on caravans and markets elsewhere. The uneasy relationship between the Tuareg chief and the Timbuktu-Koy developed into a quarrel over Akil's unruly attempts to enforce a higher tax profit for himself. Events were finally brought to a climax by the actions of Umar, the Koy's less politically adept son and successor who in 1468 decided to teach Akil a lesson by inviting into the city Sunni Ali, the able leader of the rising Songhai Empire based at Gao. The immediate results were tragic. Instead of merely replacing Akil, Sunni Ali took the chance to seize the city. Akil fled, and although many merchants and scholars succeeded in reaching Walata, many were killed, and the precious learning of the city dispersed.

Very little remains of ancient Timbuktu other than its romantic memory and the continual shortage of salt which still regulates much modern-day trade. (Elias N. Saad, *Social History of Timbuktu*; Georg Gerster, 'River of Sorrow, River of Hope', *National Geographic Magazine*, August, 1975.)

Timur the Lame: RAM, 19: (1336–1405) Also known as Tamburlaine; the conqueror of central Eurasia and the whole of the Near and Middle East. A leg wound caused his lameness, but in no way affected his abilities as a warrior, master opportunist and political manipulator. He campaigned against the Syrian **Mamelukes** and utterly destroyed Damascus in addition to his campaigns involving great carnage in India. He died whilst preparing for an assault on China. The empire of the world's greatest-ever steppe marauder did not long survive his death, based as it was on pillage, plunder and personal leadership. (Also referred to in CHECKMATE, III, 4: 'Time, le Boiteaux, the Lame One'.)

Tir-nan-óg: QUEENS, I, 4: Irish Gaelic and folklore; the land of everlasting youth and peace. (W.B. Yeats, ed., *Irish Fairy and Folk Tales*.)

Tir-Tairngiri: QUEENS, IV, 1: Irish Gaelic, similar to the above; the Land of Promise, 'Wherein there is nought save truth, and there is neither age nor decay, nor gloom, nor sadness, nor envy, nor jealousy, nor hatred, nor haughtiness'; a classless Paradise. (W.B. Yeats, ed., *Irish Fairy and Folk Tales*.)

Titans: PAWN, 1: The twelve sons of Uranus and **Gaea,** led by Cronus. They successfully deposed Uranus, but in time Cronus' own son Zeus rebelled against the Titans, causing the ten-year-long struggle between the gods known as the Titanomachia. Zeus deposed his father, and became the supreme god of the Greeks.

Tityus: QUEENS, IV, 1: Greek giant who attempted to injure Artemis. As punishment, Zeus flung him into Tartarus where he lay outstretched while two vultures eternally devoured his liver.

To kill up the clergy: KNIGHTS, III, 16: The words of **Sir Thomas More,** executed by Henry VIII for failing to accept that the King had authority over the Pope. The quote comes from More's *History of Richard III* and refers to More's opinion of the brutality of the regime, and the evil times that fell upon the nation, especially with reference to the treatment of the church. (Henry Craik, ed., *English Prose Selections,* Vol. I.)

To pass over grief . . . the Italian sleeps: PAWN, 5: See **National characteristics.**

To whomsoever of women we arrived: QUEENS, II, 4: Ancient Gaelic song quoted within the text. (*Ancient Laws and Institutes of Ireland,* Brehon Laws, Vol. III.)

Tonlieu: RISING: The Customs house of **Bruges,** later converted into the modern public library. The oldest part of the building is the porch, dating from the latter part of the fifteenth century. (Malcolm Letts, *Bruges and its Past,* London, 1924.)

Torquemada: KINGS, I, 1; CASTLE, III, 5: (1420–1498) Tomás de Torquemada, Spanish Dominican friar and Grand Inquisitor. In 1483 Queen Isabella entrusted him with the establishment of the Spanish Inquisition; he is infamous for the ruthlessness he displayed towards suspected or convicted heretics. Of 100,000 said to have been accused, about 2,000 were put to death.

Tout animal n'a pas toutes propriétés: KNIGHTS, III, 10: 'Not all animals have the same properties'.

Tout par raison, raison partout, partout raison: CASTLE, II, 2: 'All by reason, reason everywhere, everywhere reason'.

Toutes serez, êtes ou fûtes De fait on de volonté, putes: CHECKMATE, II, 7, 10: 'All will be, are or were In fact or fancy, whores'. Written by Jean de Meung, continuator of the *Roman de la Rose.*

Trebizond: RAM: From the time of the Roman Emperor Hadrian, Trebizond developed as a natural port to protect shipping from harsh winter storms of the Black Sea. It also provided a midpoint of communication between Rome and Persia. It soon grew to become one of the principal marketplaces for the produce of the East. After the fall of Constantinople to the Ottoman Empire in 1453, Trebizond remained as the last outpost of Christian Hellenism, although its survival was to be brief. Under Emperor John IV (1429–1458), the city was described as a marketplace for the whole world; **Bessarion** wrote his Encomium on the city in 1439, and described it as 'a secluded Paradise, rich with all the treasures of the earth', the promise of which had drawn the Genoese and Venetians from the fourteenth century.

Trebizond owed its survival to its geographical location and the diplomatic machinations of its rulers; guarded from behind by inhospitable mountains and from the front by the Euxine. The Emperors further strengthened their position by keeping neighbouring nations as vassals or allies. The renowned beauty of the Trapezuntine princesses proved an asset when it came to foreign marriages; courted by barbarians and Christians alike, they served to ally the Empire with potentially powerful foreign allies.

Sultan **Mehmet** ordered the Emperors of Trebizond to come to Constantinople (Stamboul) to pay tribute in person; following a direct attack on the city in 1456, it was reduced to the status of a tributory to the Ottoman Empire, at a cost of 2,000 gold pieces per annum. The tribute was raised two years later to 3,000 pieces per annum, but with **David Comnenos** potentially allying himself with both the West and **Uzum Hasan**, Mehmet moved fast to dispose of his troublesome tributory. In the late autumn of 1461, the Sultan launched his swift attack on the city. With no siege guns, little cavalry and limited supplies, Mehmet and his troops took eighteen days of fast marching to reach the city. The campaign had to be quick to succeed, as Mehmet's troops did not have an adequate train of supply to maintain a winter-long siege. Nor did his fleet carry siege artillery or make preparations to cast battering guns. Had the Emperor not given way so quickly, Mehmet's troops would probably have withdrawn until the following year, perhaps giving Trebizond the time it needed to call again for help from its European allies. As it was, Emperor David and his treacherous adviser **George Amiroutzes** surrendered almost immediately, and Trebizond fell to the Ottomans on August 15, 1461. (William Miller, *Trebizond, the Last Greek Empire*, London, 1926; George Finlay, *A History of Greece*, Vol. IV, Oxford, 1877.)

Tree of Error: QUEENS, IV, 2: The Roman Catholic Church and its doctrines, according to Henry VIII's Archbishop of Canterbury, Thomas Cranmer (1489–1556). In his sermons, Cranmer expostulated on the duty of every good Christian man to whet his tools of faith and destroy every root and branch of the papacy in sixteenth-century England. (Henry Craik, ed., *English Prose Selections*, Vol. I.)

Tres vidit et unum adoravit: QUEENS, IV, 5: 'He saw three and adored one'.

Triduana, St: KINGS, III, 2: Scottish saint, who perpetrated an act of self-mutilation similar to St Lucy in the preservation of her chastity. When a pagan suitor commented on the beauty of Triduana's eyes, she cut them out and presented them to him; hoping that he would cease to bother her now she had given him what he so admired. She was consequently held to be the patron saint of eye disorders, and had a popular shrine at Restalrig on the outskirts of Edinburgh, destroyed in 1560 and proclaimed as 'a monument of idolatry'. (Barbara Walker, *The Woman's Encyclopaedia of Myths and Secrets*, San Francisco, 1983.)

Tristram Trusty: CHECKMATE, I, 4: A character in **Udall's** play *Ralph Roister Doister*, a true and faithful friend. See also **Royster-Doister, visiting the Castle of Perseverance.**

Trois moines passoient: QUEENS, II, 2: A riddle which translates thus:

Three monks passed by
Three pears hanging down
Each one [*Chascun*] took one
Yet two still remained.

The punning solution is supplied in QUEENS, II, 6: 'One of the monks *was* called Chascun.'

Trumps: KNIGHTS, II, 2: A weapon used by the **Knights of St John.** A hollowed out tube of wood or metal was affixed to the end of a pole and filled with inflammable liquid, similar to **naphtha.** The pole could be shoved in the general direction of one's enemies, and would continue to splutter fire at them for a considerable time. An ingenious advancement on this technique was to use a mechanism whereby projectiles could be loaded into the tube. Just as the fire was about to go out, it would fire two small cylinders of iron or brass, also loaded with gunpowder. (Ernle Bradford, *The Great Siege*, London, 1961.)

Trussed it in black felt . . . as the Turks do: CHECKMATE, III, 3: Not really a Turkish speciality, but a preferred method of execution as performed by the ancient Mongols. Being particularly sensitive about the shedding of royal blood, they would swathe their noble captives in black velvet before kicking them to death. The Turks favoured trussing up their victim so expertly that when the package was dropped, almost every bone would be broken. (Stanley Mayes, *An Organ for the Sultan*, London, 1956; E.G. Brown, *Persian Literature in Modern Times.*)

Tu me verrois sécher sous le poids de mes fers: CHECKMATE, II, 7: 'You will watch me wither beneath the weight of my chains, As sheep ill-wished by the shepherd will pine'. Ronsard (1524–1585) referring to the traditional baleful eye of a shepherd, which can destroy a neighbour's sheep.

Tu ne fais pas miracles, mais merveilles: QUEENS, III, 6: 'You do not work miracles, but marvels'.

Tuareg: SCALES, 16: Nomadic Libyan tribesmen, also known, since the days of the Roman Empire, as the *Mulethemin* by the Arabs, meaning 'The Veiled People'. They were described as tall, long-faced and fair-skinned, with black wavy hair. The men distinctively covered their faces with a *litham*, or veil, from which their Arabic name derived. Although they were Muslim, the Arabs sometimes described them as 'The Christians of the Desert'. Perhaps briefly converted to Christianity in the sixth century, their favourite motif on weaponry was the cross. The Tuareg were the traditional camel drivers and herdsmen of the desert, maintaining the desert wells and controlling the Saharan trade routes. (E.W. Bovill, *The Golden Trade of the Moors*, London, 1958.)

Tulip: PAWN, 18: The bulbous colourful flower, prevalent in southern Russia and Turkey, from where two-thirds of the known species originate. First reports of the tulip reached Europe courtesy of Ogier Ghiselin de Busbecq, Imperial Ambassador to Constantinople in 1554. In Persian the tulip is called *lale*; a favourite flower in Persian love poetry, rhyming as it does with the word for wine cup, and it was an extremely popular girl's name. As for slave boys being called 'Tulip', this is probably from the traditional title of *Lala* as referring to any Turkish slave.

The flower is wrongly called 'tulip' from the Turkish *tulipam*, meaning turban, to which its shape had been compared by Busbecq's hosts. The first garden tulips to flourish in the West were described in 1559 in the garden of the wealthy bankers of Augsberg, the Fuggers. Crossbreeding and new varieties of tulip became a cult obsession in the Dutch Republic from the 1630s onwards. (Edward Seymour Foster, *The Turkish Letters of Ogier Ghiselin de Busbecq*, Oxford, 1927; Steven Usherwood, 'Tulipomania', *History Today*, May, 1970.)

Turbèh: PAWN, 18: Muslim sepulchural chapel.

Turcae non minus sunt insani quam nos circa aurifabrorum opera: PAWN, 25: 'The Turks are no less mad than we are about the work of goldsmiths'; from the French naturalist Pierre Bellon's point of view, the avarice of the Turk was rivalled by his Christian counterpart.

Turk's diabolical iron galley: CHECKMATE, V, 11: See **Galleys.**

Turpe est Doctori, cum culpa redurgit ipsum: PAWN, 28: Latin proverb, 'Base is the teacher who commits the same offence'.

Two Legs: PAWN, 3: Sixteenth-century children's riddle, the object of which is to identify correctly the provenance of the limbs:

> Two legs sat upon three legs
> With one leg in his lap.
> In comes four legs
> And runs away with one leg
> Up jumps two legs
> Catches up three legs
> Throws it after four legs
> And makes him bring back one leg

> That is, man, stool, beef, dog.

Tyrol: UNICORN: See **Sigismond of Austria, Count of the Tyrol.**

TZANI-BEY: SCORPIONS: Emir of the **Mameluke** troops sent from Egypt to help King **Zacco** of Cyprus in the struggle against his sister **Carlotta.** The first reference to Tzani-Bey (or Janibeg al-Ablak, or Jehan Pec as he is also called) comes when King Zacco returned to Cyprus from Cairo with two hundred Mamelukes and a further two hundred foot soldiers, given to him by the Egyptians. Perhaps a renegade, at best a troublemaker, the Emir was initially of help to the King, until Carlotta's supporters were finally defeated with the fall of Famagusta.

After Zacco had taken control of Famagusta, Tzani-Bey attempted to enter the city by night. Because the King was in residence, the Emir and his troops were forbidden entry. The next day, Tzani-Bey complained to Zacco about his treatment; although the King outwardly pacified the Emir, Zacco had been warned that there was a Mameluke plot afoot to murder him and seize control of the city. The Nicosian Franks and the Greeks murdered the Mamelukes that night.

On hearing of the execution of the Emir and his men, the Sultan was furious, as was Tzani-Bey's sister. She sent a hired assassin to Famagusta, disguised as a merchant. He attempted to stab the King in the neck, although Zacco fought off the attack and had the man murdered by his guards. (Sir George Hill, *A History of Cyprus*, Vol. III, Cambridge, 1948.)

Tzukanion: RAM, 34: Better known today as polo, the game is recorded as having been played in Persia in the sixth century BC, spreading to Asia, China and India in its brutally original form of two teams battling over the possession of an enemy's head. Over time, the severed human head was first replaced with the stuffed head of a sheep or goat, then with a ball made of willow root, or *pulu*. The Byzantine nobility of the fifteenth century still found the game popular, using a leather stuffed ball the size of an apple or pomegranate and thin bending sticks with a conical bowl at the end to catch and propel the ball.

A tablet at Gilgat in present-day Pakistan testifies to the endurance of the game over the centuries:

> Let other people play at other things
> The King of games is still the game of Kings.

(George Finlay, *A History of Greece*, Vol. IV, Oxford, 1877.)

Ubi tres medici, duo atheisti: CASTLE, IV, 8: Latin proverb; 'Where you find three doctors, you find two atheists'.

'Ud: UNICORN, 36: Turkish forerunner of the **lute.**

Udall, Nicholas: KINGS, IV, 3: (1505–1556) English dramatist and scholar; headmaster of Eton and Westminster colleges, and author of the earliest surviving English comedy, *Ralph Roister Doister*. See also **Royster-Doister** . . . and **Tristram Trusty.**

Un freet den Vogel fedderlos: KINGS, I, 1: The German version of the children's riddle; see **Volavit volucer sine plumis** for the solution.

> *Da köem en Vogel fedderlos*
> *Un sett sik op'n Boem blattlos*
> *Da köem de Jungfru mundelos*
> *Un freet den Vogel fedderlos*
> *Van den Boem blattlos.*

> There comes a bird without feathers
> And sits in a tree without leaves
> There comes a maiden without mouth
> And eats the bird without feathers
> In the tree without leaves.

Compare with an English version of the same type:

> White bird featherless
> Flew from Paradise
> Pitched on the castle wall.
> Along came Lord Landless
> Took it up handless
> And rode away horseless
> To the King's White Hall.

(Cassette: Steeleye Span, *Now We Are Six*, 1974, Chrysalis, ZCHR 1053.)

Un hidalgo no debe a otro que a Dios, y al Rei nada: KINGS, I, 5: 'A nobleman owes nothing to anyone other than God, and he owes the King nothing'.

Un myrte je dédierai: QUEENS, IV, 5: A love poem, which elevates the time-honoured barbaric practice of carving initials on a tree bark into a positive act of worship:

> I shall dedicate one myrtle tree
> On the banks of the Loire
> And on the bark I shall write
> These four lines to your glory.

Una miseria di speranza piena: CHECKMATE, II, 1: 'Misery full of hope'.

Uncivil clock, like the foolish tapping of a tipsy cobbler: PAWN, 29: From the fourteenth-century poem by Dafydd, 'Woe to the Black-Faced Clock' (extract):

> Woe to the black-faced clock on the ditch side which awoke me
> A curse on its head and tongue, its two ropes and its wheel
> Its weights, heavy balls, its yards and its hammer
> Its ducks which think it day and its unquiet mills
> Uncivil clock, like the foolish tapping of a tipsy cobbler
> A blasphemy on its face, a dark mill grinding the night.

(Carlo M. Cipolla, *Clocks and Culture: 1300–1700.*)

Unicorn: The mythical creature with a single horn, described as having the legs of a buck, the tail of a lion and the head and body of a small horse. The creature's body was white, with a reddish head and startling blue eyes. The horn itself is described as white at its root, black in the middle and red at its tip. It was impervious to capture unless its hunters happened to have a virgin in tow. The unwitting animal could only be killed when entranced by the virgin and caught lying in her lap.

The horn of the animal was also prized for its medicinal qualities; it could be used to detect and negate the presence of poison when dipped in the suspect food or liquid. The horn was also used for cutlery handles; a knife with a unicorn handle would sweat when it entered poisoned food. Poorer substitutes for the genuine horn included the long and twisted tusk of the narwhal, elephant ivory or rhino horn.

The seal of Scotland and the nation's coat of arms are both borne by the unicorn and the lion between them. King **James III** instituted the chivalric **Order of the Unicorn** in 1469, but the heraldic office of Unicorn Pursuivant was founded by his predecessor, James I of Scotland.

There are many biblical references to the unicorn (more likely to be the rhinoceros than the mythical creature); see **Canst thou bind the Unicorn with his band in the furrow?** and **And from the hornes . . . of Unicornes.**

Unlike the moon is to the sonne sheen: PAWN, 29: From 'The Kingis Quair', attributed to James I of Scotland (1394–1437). See also **Hast thou no mind of love? Where is thy make?** Extract:

And yet, considering the nakedness
Both of thy wit, thy person, and thy might,
It is no match of thine unworthiness
To her high birth, estate, and beauty bright;
As like ye been, as day is to the night,
Or sack-cloth is unto fine cremesye [cramoisie],
Or doken [dock] to the fresh daisye.

Unlike the moon is to the sonne sheen,
Eke January is unlike to May,
Unlike the cuckoo to the phylomene [nightingale];
Their tavartis [plumage] are not both made of aray,
Unlike the crow is to the papejay [parrot, papingo],
Unlike, in goldsmith's work, a fishes eye.
To purcress with pearl, or maked be so high.

(J. Ross, ed., *The Book of Scottish Poems*, Edinburgh, 1878.)

Upapa: UNICORN, 36: See **Hoopoe.**

URBINO, Federigo da Montefeltro, Duke of: RISING: (1422–1482) Nobleman and mercenary captain fighting for whichever ruler was prepared to hire him. He was successful both as a soldier and as a ruler, bringing political stability and wealth to the city and territories of Urbino. On the death of his half-brother in 1444, he was made Signore of the city and in 1474 became its duke. His military training had been taken under Niccolò Piccinino, father of Jacopo of Milan, another famous mercenary. Montefeltro fought for money rather than for political allies, but this in no way hindered his personal ambition to increase the size of his own territory, at the expense of **Malatesta** of Rimini. At the end of Montefeltro's reign, his duchy was three times the size that it had been under his half-brother.

In addition to enlarging his estates and palace and improving its furnishings, Montefeltro spent a great deal of time and money on his library of manuscripts. He was one of the greatest collectors of the written word in Italy (despising and rejecting printed volumes in favour of good calligraphy). By the time of his death, he owned over a thousand precious manuscripts. He was a passionate supporter of the humanists, as skilled with a quill as he was with a weapon of war: Justus of Ghent painted the battle-worn noble comfortably sitting in full armour, reading one of his many books. His son Guidobaldo followed in his father's footsteps as a patron of the arts, supporting both the painter Raphael and Baldassare Castiglione, author of *The Courtier*.

Urine glasses: The jordan or urine glass was virtually the symbol of the early physician, diagnostic theories being then based on the balance of the four humours (phlegm, blood, black bile and yellow bile) as shown through the urine or the pulse. Fifteenth-century medicine (in which Italy led the field) drew upon Latin versions of Arab manuscripts, based in turn on Greek medicine and especially the work of Galen. It also made use of the writings of the Salerno medical school and the work of living Italian surgeons, all of which stressed the diagnostic importance of urine. The basic interpretation of urine was held to depend largely on colour, and early charts presented up to twenty distinctive shades, ranging from *kyanos* (described as either blue or the colour of black wine) and *inopos* or wine-coloured/the colour of liver. A short list of common illnesses was attached to each colour. When the physician was too distant or too important to visit his patient, messengers brought him the glasses in a special small basket, plastic bags not yet having been invented. See also **Pisse-pot prophet.** (Peter Murray Jones, *Medieval Medical Miniatures*.)

Ut ameris Amabilis esto: PAWN, 6: Latin proverb, 'Be loving if you would be loved'.

UZUM HASAN: RAM: (c. 1408–1478) The Persian warlord Hasan (Uzum, meaning 'long' was a nickname referring to his height). Ruling vast territories in Eastern Anatolia, the land mass south of Constantinople, he shared Western Christendom's distrust of his neighbours the Ottoman Turks and, as the Turkish threat grew, found himself bombarded by Western diplomats from **Venice** and Rome (**Caterino Zeno, Ludovico de Severi da Bologna**) with promises of money, armies and **guns**, some of which occasionally arrived. Tailoring Western fears and promises with his own programme of aggrandisement, he manipulated it all with great skill, while engaging in a lifetime of hard fighting.

Uzum Hasan came from a line of politically shrewd Turcoman princes who had ruled Diarbakir in northern Mesopotamia from before the time of **Timur the Lame**, and had long learned how to use Western alliances and marriage for their own ends. Uzum Hasan had been chief of the tribe of the White Sheep (Ak-Koyunlu) since 1454, and consequently embarked on a successful career of conquest of states lying around his hereditary fief. He himself—tall, thin, handsome, with some Tartar in his features—was by blood more Christian than Muslim. His father Carailucas had been 'a friend of Christians, although not one himself'; his mother Sara Khatun was a Christian from Syria, and his grandmother had been a princess of **Trebizond**, that fragment of Byzantine Greek Empire which then lingered on the south shores of the Black Sea.

Trebizond, lying between Hasan and Constantinople, paid tribute to the Grand Turk but had powerful Christian friends. Uzum Hasan strengthened his family connection with the Trapezuntines by marrying in 1458 Theodora, the beautiful daughter of Emperor John IV of Trebizond and niece of John's successor the Emperor **David Comnenos**. By this union Uzum linked himself to Theodora's own nieces and their Venetian husbands, of whom Caterino Zeno and **Marco Corner** were two (see **Naxos**). Uzum's connection with the Emperor David also offered him a potential ally in the King of Georgia, the Emperor's son-in-law, and he was careful to foster alliances also with the Emirs of Sinope and Karamania.

Uzum Hasan was permitted several wives. His eldest son was by a Kurdish lady, and he had three more by another marriage. By Theodora, his only Christian wife, he had three daughters and one son who on Uzum's death was immediately strangled by a trio of step-brothers. As was usual in mixed marriages of the time (up to eleven princesses of Trebizond married Muslims) Theodora was allowed to keep her chaplain and to worship as she pleased both during Uzum's lifetime and after. Unusually, she was also given the title of Ulu Khatun, or Chief Wife. Although Western envoys saw her at Uzum's side and even in his bed, latterly Uzum arranged for her to maintain her own household at Kharput near Diarbakir, while her husband's court moved its lavish pavilions from place to place, settling briefly at Tabriz or Diarbakir or Erzerum. Kharput became the home of many Greeks, and Christians in the area were allowed to look upon Theodora as their protector. Her attempts after the fall of Trebizond to help the family of the Emperor David in 1463 ended in disaster, but she survived her husband to be buried in the Christian church in Diarbakir.

Uzum Hasan, who had become the leading Turcoman chieftain by conquering his rivals the Black Sheep, possessed an army reckoned to amount to 50,000 horse and 40,000 foot, led by skilled commanders. The fall of the Empire of Trebizond and the Black Sea coast towns about it in 1461 took place immediately after Uzum Hasan and the Emperor David had appealed to the Western powers for help through an embassy led by Ludovico da Bologna. Uzum, pledged by his wedding contract to support Trebizond, was forced by troubles at home and the threat of the forces of the Ottoman Empire to break his word.

In a gambit not uncommon for the times, his Christian mother Sara Khatun—described as one of the most influential figures in the Turcoman world—accompanied by a Kurdish bey and many Turcoman princes, set out with rich gifts to negotiate a peaceful compromise in the late summer of 1461. Received with honour (**Mehmet II** addressed Sara as 'mother' and the Sheikh as 'father') Sara managed to conclude a peace agreement between the Sultan and her son, but was unable to persuade Mehmet to cancel his attack on Trebizond, despite offering a graphic account of the geographical impossibilities of an assault. The Sultan did not believe her, and induced the Emperor's treacherous advisers (see **Amiroutzes, George**) to surrender by trapping him between his army and the Ottoman fleet in the Black Sea. The Sultan nevertheless continued to treat Uzum's mother with courtesy and presented her at the end of the campaign with rich jewels taken from the treasury of the Comneni.

In 1463 **Venice** finally declared war on Sultan Mehmet, and in 1464 welcomed letters from Uzum Hasan proposing an alliance. Checked by **Skanderbeg** in Albania, the Sultan shocked the Christian world by taking the key Venetian station of Negroponte in 1470. It seemed likely that an attack on Uzum's Anatolia might follow. Uzum sent envoys to the **Knights of St John** at Rhodes, and an alliance against the Turk was established between Cyprus, Uzum, Cairo and the ruler of Karamania. The Franciscan Ludovico da Bologna passed between Uzum and Rome, while Venetian envoys crossed to Persia to hear Uzum's price for a full-scale attack on the Turks—troops, arms, and an armada to provide diversionary raids on the coast. For a while, the military union of several powers of different religious persuasion took the place of the religious union of the two halves of the Christian church which did not succeed. But even that could only last as long as Uzum's life. (Kenneth M. Sutton, *The Papacy and the Levant*; Steven Runciman, *The Fall of Constantinople*; William Miller, *The Last Greek Empire*; Franz Babinger, *Mehmet the Conqueror and His Times*, tr. Ralph Manheim, Princeton, 1978.)

Va, va te cacher que le chat ne te voie: CHECKMATE, II, 2: 'Go and hide so that the cat cannot see you'.

VALETTE, LA, Jean Parisot de: KNIGHTS: See **La Valette, Jean Parisot de.**

Valley of Diamonds, there are snakes in the: PAWN, 18: From the legendary myths surrounding **Alexander the Great:** when presented with the problem of how to reach the diamonds without being bitten to death, his answer was to release a thousand starving eagles into the valley, and throw down meat for them. The diamonds would thus adhere to the food and could be collected as the birds flew back with their prize. (E.J.W. Gibb, *History of Ottoman Poetry.*)

Van Eyck, Ian: RISING, 17: (1390–1441) Born in Maaseik at the extreme east of present-day Belgium, the artist was employed as a painter in Holland by John of Bavaria (d. 1425), until Duke **Philip the Good** took control of John's territories and his artists. In 1425 Van Eyck moved to Lille where he became Valet to the Chamber and the official ducal painter to Philip the Good. He was entrusted with ambassadorial duties and artistic commissions, sometimes combined. In 1428 when Philip was considering marriage to Isabelle, daughter of King John of Portugal, Van Eyck was sent with the negotiators to paint her portrait from life. In 1431 he moved to **Bruges**, where he remained until his death, after which his wife continued to receive a ducal pension. He was buried in the cloisters of **St Donatiens** in Bruges, his body moved to rest near the font two years later.

Amongst his more famous works is the Ghent Altarpiece completed in 1432, probably begun by his brother Hubert Van Eyck (d. 1426) and the highly symbolic and allegorical 'Arnolfini's Marriage' from 1434, depicting the wedding of Giovanni Arnolfini (d. 1470) and Giovanna Cenami, both from wealthy Italian families resident in Bruges.

VANNES, Peter: CASTLE: (d. 1563) Dean of Salisbury and the English Ambassador to **Venice.** Born in Italy, he was the son of Stephen de Vannes of Lucca and a kinsman of Andrea Ammonio Vannes, Latin secretary to Henry VIII of England. In 1513, Andrea brought his relative to England to be his assistant, but Erasmus complained that he could find neither Ammonio's genius nor temper in Ammonio's young relative. After Ammonio's death Vannes himself became secretary to Cardinal Wolsey and the King.

In 1539, Vannes was made Dean of Salisbury; a post he was obliged to relinquish under **Edward VI**, although he did retain the secretaryship. In 1550 he was sent as English Ambassador to Venice. He was considered to be a little timid in his conduct with the Signoria, but continued in the position under **Mary Tudor**, until recalled in September 1556. See also **Courtenay, Sir Edward.**

Velut inter stellas luna minores: PAWN, 3: 'As shines the moon among the lesser stars'.

Venetian galleys: Venice first sought to establish regular trade links with western Europe as early as the thirteenth century, when Venetian merchants began a regular trading service to Provence. In the fourteenth century Venice and Genoa used great **galleys** to trade directly with northern Europe by sea rather than use the treacherous route across the Alps. Venice's goods could thus reach **Bruges** and the Low Countries in her own ships, and return laden with Flemish cloth and English wool. The galleys were the perfect vehicle to advertise and promulgate Venice's status as the greatest trading empire of the West, bringing exotic luxury goods to Bruges and England, much of which was dismissed as extravagant and nonessential fripperies, in 'The Libelle of Englyshe Polycye', published in 1436:

> The great galleys of Venice and Florence
> Be well laden with things of Complacence
> All spicery and other grocers' ware,
> With sweet wines, all manner of chaffare [merchandise]
> Apes and japes and marmosets tailed,
> Nifles, trifles that little have availed
> For much of this chaffare that is wastable
> Might be forborne as dear and disserviceable.

(Charles Singer, *The Earliest Chemical Industry*, London, 1948.)

Venice: Without doubt the Republic of Venice was the greatest Western trading empire and naval power in fifteenth-century Europe. The city considered itself to be the new Rome, making its money primarily from trade and freight, including the lucrative transfer of pilgrims to and from the Holy Land (the fifteenth-century cost of the basic round trip from Venice to the Holy Land, including admission prices to all the major holy places, was 50 ducats). Its prosperity is evident from the popularity and stability of the gold Venetian ducat which became the standard unit of currency and trade in the fifteenth century.

Venice's patriciate did not consider investment in trade as beneath their dignity; sons of the patriciate were encouraged to participate in the trading journeys of the state's galleys in their annual trips to the Low Countries and England: it was the best apprenticeship as sailor, merchant and state ambassador that the city could give to its next generation. The governing classes were the cornerstone of the Republic's mercantile wealth rather than just its rulers and arbiters. Through trade and its proximity to the waning Byzantine Empire, Venice became home to many cultured Greek exiles and scholars, with their manuscripts helping greatly in the dissemination of learning and literature that characterised the Renaissance. Printing, for example, had definitely become established in the city by 1471.

As the city's wealth grew, so did its population, estimated at 100,000 by the fifteenth century. As a cramped, overcrowded series of islands connected by canals, the city has never had a high reputation for the odour generated in long hot summers. A Spanish visitor to the city in 1438 noted the inhabitants burning aromatic spices in the street to lessen the stench from the canals. By 1485 the city had handed sanitation control over to the elected Board of Pub-

lic Health, which was also in charge of street cleaning, cisterns, vagabonds, prostitutes and burials.

The Venetian arsenal was the foundation of the city's wealth and security; acting as armoury, naval base and shipyard, it produced the fine galleys which were to trade the republic's wares abroad, and created the defences which safeguarded the republic's colonial acquisitions from the Turk. (D.S. Chambers, *The Imperial Age of Venice: 1380–1580*, London, 1970.)

Vennel: CHECKMATE, III, 3: From the French *venelle*, it signifies a narrow street.

Veramente, queste Rotisserie sono cosa stupenda: CHECKMATE, II, 2: 'Truly these roasted meats are stupendous'. A reference to the rotisserie at the Rue de la Huchette in Paris. It was a comment made by the Italian representative sent to Paris to negotiate the peace of Vervins. (Henri Saural, *Histoire et Recherches des Antiquités de la Ville de Paris*, 1724.)

Vernom-[venom]tongue of Loughbrickland [sic]: QUEENS, II, 1: The title Venom-tongue of Loughbrickland was given to the poet Bricriu Nemthenga, one of the Red Branch Knights of Ulster under Concobar MacNessa, King of Ulster, probably on account of the vitriolic content of his poetry; see **Senchan Torpest.** (P. W. Joyce, *Social History of Ancient Ireland*.)

Vice [voce] mea viva depello cuncta novica [nociva]: KINGS, IV, 3: 'By my living voice I banish all harm'. A common inscription on medieval bells. It refers with special meaning in the text to the bell of Hexham Abbey.

Vieille ridée, vieille édentée: QUEENS, II, 3: 'Wrinkled old woman, toothless old woman', Jean Voûtés' verse on **Diane de Poitiers.**

DE VILLEGAGNON, Nicholas Durand: KNIGHTS: (1510–1571) A member of the **Knights of St John** from 1531 and Vice-Admiral of Brittany. Nepotism to the fore, Villegagnon joined the Order when his uncle, Villiers de l'Isle-Adam, was Grand Master. His naval experience led Villegagnon to be entrusted with leadership of the French galleys which escorted **Mary Queen of Scots** to France in July 1548.

In 1551 he was warned by **Montmorency** that the Turks were planning to attack Malta. He returned to the Order in time to help fortify the headquarters but failed in his attempt to relieve Tripoli from the forces of Sultan **Suleiman.** Increasingly disillusioned with his own failure and that of the Order, Villegagnon was drawn towards the Reformed church. He proposed to Admiral **Coligny** that a French colony for Protestants should be founded in Brazil. In 1555 permission was given for Villegagnon to lead a colonising expedition of similarly disillusioned Calvinists, setting sail from Le Havre with two large ships and 10,000 livres. He took control of an island in the bay of Rio de Janeiro, and named the colonial outpost Fort Coligny, after his patron.

The experiment in religious toleration was dogged by leadership problems and doctrinal differences. The colony failed within three years; a theological dispute with his few remaining supporters led Villegagnon to be titled 'le Cain de l'Amérique' by the settlers. He returned to France to be further vilified by French Catholics as a heretic, and by Protestants as an apostate. He remained in France representing the Order until he retired in 1570, surviving to write opinionated accounts of his journeys, **Charles V** and his own controversial religious beliefs. (N. Barré, *Navigation de Villegagnon en Amérique*.)

Viol: QUEENS, II, 4: The predecessor of the violin. It had six or more strings; the back was always flat, the front often being the same. The bass viol was the medieval precursor to the violoncello. (C.A. Harris & M. Hargreave, *The Story of British Music*; *The Earlier French Musicians*.)

Virginals: QUEENS, III, 3: One of the three forms of **harpsichord**; a stringed keyboard instrument without legs, placed on a table or stand. (C.A. Harris & M. Hargreave, *The Story of British Music*; *The Earlier French Musicians*).

Vituperato sia chi mal pensa: CASTLE, III, 1: 'May he who thinks evil thoughts be reviled' (or *Honi soit qui mal y pense*, motto of the **Order of the Garter**).

Vitus, St: KINGS, I, 2: Perhaps dating from the third century AD, and associated with Sicily, although his bones have been venerated in Westphalia since the ninth century. He is said to have the power to cure many diseases; especially *chorea*, the so-called St Vitus' dance.

Vivit, et est vitae nescius ipse suae: QUEENS, I, 6: 'He lives, but doesn't know he is alive'.

Volavit volucer sine plumis: KINGS, I, 1: Children's riddle:

> *Volavit volucer sine plumis*
> *Sedit in arbore sine foliis*
> *Venit homo absque manibus*
> *Conscendit illum sine pedibus*
> *Assavit illum sine igne*
> *Comedit illum sine ore.*

> There flew a bird without wings
> Sat in a tree without leaves
> Came a man without hands

Brought it down without feet
Roasted it without fire
Ate it without mouth.

That is, a snowflake. Compare the German version of the riddle under *Un freet den Vogel fedderlos* and the English which is also given there.

Wadmoll mittens: CHECKMATE, I, 4: A thick Scottish knitted woollen cloth, used for mittens or stockings, particularly popular with sailors. (S.G.E. Lythe, *The Economy of Scotland: 1550–1625.*)

Wangara: SCALES, 20: Location of the **Silent trade**; the exchange of gold for desperately needed salt. Its location has been roughly located in the Bambuk-Bure area; the silent trade itself was first mentioned by Herodotus (c. 480–c. 425 BC) in his account of the women drawing up gold dust from the mines using birds' feathers smeared with pitch. The gold was then packed in quills and swapped for salt. Herodotus was incorrect in his assumption that the gold came from mines; in fact the supply was alluvial gold deposited and collected from the river mouths of the area. The unusual method of bartering the gold is described in the text. The invisible people of Wangara were supposed to have the heads and tails of dogs, according to the first reports to reach the dazzled Portuguese. This silent trade between gold and salt merchants continued well into the eighteenth century. Not only did it keep the location of the alluvial deposits secret, it enabled different peoples to trade without the need for a common language or any more complex and involved form of communication.

Wanton plough tail: QUEENS, IV, 3: Not to be confused with being whipped at a cart's arse for bawdry (CHECKMATE, III, 5), the reference is to the Irish habit of tying the plough directly to the horse's tail.

Wapenshaw: KINGS, I, 7: A count of arms and men, 'weapon-show', instituted by King **James IV** of Scotland in 1491. Each shire was to muster its potential contribution to the King's army and ensure that they were trained in archery. The gathering also doubled as the time when courts of law, or 'justice ayres' would be held and cases heard. In time it developed into an excuse for a fair; the influx of visitors of all classes providing a boost to the local economy as competitions and feats of strength replaced the genuine mustering of a potential militia.

War: In any analysis of the late medieval or early modern period, one must bear in mind that there are several different types and definitions of 'War'.

Codes of conduct and the treatment of captives depended upon what type of warfare was occurring, and the social status of potential captives.

The most brutal type of conflict was war to the death, or *guerre mortelle* in which the losers could expect no privilege or ransom; captives would either be slain or enslaved. The red banner unfurled at such conflict was indicative of the brutality which would follow. It was the type of warfare conducted against the Muslim armies during the crusades where the mortal enemy was given 'no quarter'. The unfurling of a banner was a declaration of combat as well as an indicator of the type of war waged. It declared war and the intention of its owner to fight in the same manner as a 'bellicose' war cry. To withdraw when your lord's banner was unfurled was seen as a damnable affront to his honour, worse than straightforward cowardice and more contemptible than treason.

The second type of war was public or open war, *bellum hostile*, and described the conflict and manner of warfare conducted between sovereign Christian princes. Soldiers could take spoil, and captured enemies would have the right to ransom themselves.

The third type, *guerre couverte*, is feudal or covered war; men could wound and kill their opponents without blame, but were forbidden from taking spoil or burning in their campaigns.

Siege warfare had a particular etiquette which began when a messenger was sent to the town or city in question with the summons to surrender. If the summons was refused, then the siege would formally commence, often accompanied by the firing of siege **cannon**. If and when the besieged city fell, the treatment of the captives was at the discretion of the victors. It often concluded in war to the death, including the massacre of women and children. Consequent pillage and spoilation of the territory was not against the rules of warfare, nor was it in itself an act of warfare; it was an act of justice against those who had refused to submit, thus making themselves 'fair game' for their victors. A besieged city was most definitely between a rock and a hard place when the first summons to surrender was announced. Depending on the intention of the attackers, they faced total carnage. If they were to surrender without the siege taking place, however, the commander or captain of the town in question would justifiably be charged with treason, if and when he was released.

One must also be aware that the chivalric treatment of ransomed captives only applied to the upper echelons of command, not the poor commons slaughtered in the brutal process of war; for them the fair-minded treatment of equals did not come into play. See also **Mercenaries.** (Maurice Keen, *The Laws of War in the Late Middle Ages*, London, 1965.)

Ware riot: CASTLE, III, 14: Hunting cry. It warns when hounds are chasing a rabbit instead of true game. (C.E. Hare, *The Language of Field Sports*.)

WARWICK, John Dudley, Earl of: KINGS: (c. 1502–1553) Also titled Duke of Northumberland, he was the son of Edward Dudley, Privy Councillor to

Henry VIII of England. His father was beheaded when John Dudley was a child, but John was restored to royal favour at the age of eleven and later taught the application of mathematics and warfare by **John Dee**. Dudley became a great military captain, and was renowned in the court for his daring. By 1547 he was High Chamberlain of England, and had been knighted and given his earldom. He was forced to resign as Lord High Admiral when the post was given to **Protector Somerset**'s brother.

As Lord Lieutenant of England he showed his brilliance in defeating the Scots at the battle of Pinkie in 1547, after which he was created Earl of Warwick, and two years later again campaigned against the Scots. He was diverted down south to crush the agrarian revolt in Norfolk in 1549, and with Somerset's fall from power he became one of **Edward VI**'s six lords in attendance, regaining the Admiralship. His greed and personal ambition were to be his downfall; he advocated that the two princesses **Elizabeth** and **Mary Tudor** be set aside as heirs in favour of the Duchess of Suffolk (niece of Henry VIII) or her daughter, Lady Jane Grey. Edward VI was very fond of Lady Jane and perfectly willing to disinherit his sisters in her favour. Warwick allied himself particularly closely to her cause, marrying his own son Guildford Dudley to Lady Jane in 1553. With the rapid collapse of her monarchy after only nine days, the Dudley family also fell from grace. Warwick was imprisoned and executed the same year. He died as a Catholic, having only followed the Reformation for his personal gain.

We are two pedants . . . guarding the moon from Wolves: QUEENS, IV, 5: The words of François Rabelais (c. 1494–1553), concerning himself and the French King **Francis I**. (Jehan d'Orliac, *Francis I*.)

Weights and measures: In trying to draw a comparison of weights and measures over time, let alone continents, there are insurmountable difficulties; in any form of measurement one faces a minefield of inadequate information. For example, there is apparently no such thing as a standard 'mile' in the sixteenth and early seventeenth century: 5 Italian = 3 French = 2½ English = 1 Dutch = 1 German = 1 Russian mile. And, 1½ Dutch miles = 1 Swiss, but 1 Italian mile also equals a Russian verst.

Official Scots weights are easier to differentiate: the Ell (linear), Pint (liquid), Stone (weight) and Firlot (dry weight). There are also Bolls, Pecks and Sleeks. A Boll of flour is 140 lbs, but of grain is 448 lbs. A Peck of pears would be 28 lbs in Edinburgh, but 42 lbs in Glasgow and a Sleek is equal to 18 *Scots* pints, which can be 40–50 lbs, depending on whether one was measuring a volume weight of apples or pears. To cap it all, twelve full eggshells (size not specified) equalled an Irish Imperial pint!

WHARTON, Thomas, First Baron: KINGS: (c. 1495–1568) Captain of Carlisle and Warden of the Middle Marches, he was in charge of the English attack against the Scots in 1542, when up to 20,000 Scots made a foray into England. With only a few hundred men at his command, Wharton harried the Scots, catching, killing and drowning as many Scots as his men could lay hands on.

Wharton and **Grey** of Wilton were not close, and apparently did not work well together, which explains why the English assault against Scotland in the winter of 1547–1548 failed. Because **Maxwell** changed his allegiance from the English side to the Scots, Wharton was obliged to withdraw and retaliated by hanging the men and boys Maxwell had left as his pledges at Carlisle. This was the start of the feud between the two men which was to dog their later years when Wharton was again Warden of the East and Middle Marches under **Mary Tudor** and Maxwell was his counterpart for the West Marches. His son, the second Baron Wharton, became one of Mary Tudor's trusted advisers, but was consequently suspect for his religious and political views when **Elizabeth** came to power in 1558.

Wheel-lock carbines: PAWN, 4: The Italian wheel-lock firearm first came to prominence early in the sixteenth century. The design produced sparks to ignite the gunpowder by friction between pyrites and a grooved steel wheel. Although costlier to produce than the mass-produced **match-lock** which relied on a lit fuse to ignite the powder, the wheel-lock method was more effective until it too was superceded in the seventeenth century by the cheaper and simpler flintlock. The flintlock remained as the standard means of ignition until the development of the percussive cap, reliant upon a chemical reaction rather than sparks.

When her loose gown from her shoulders did fall: CHECKMATE, IV, 1 & V, 12: Sir Thomas Wyatt, 'They Flee From Me':

> They flee from me, that sometime did me seek,
> With naked foot stalking in my chamber:
> I have seen them, gentle, tame, and meek,
> That now are wild, and do not remember
> That sometime they put themselves in danger
> To take bread at my hand; and now they range,
> Busily seeking with a continual change.
>
> Thanked be fortune it hath been otherwise,
> Twenty times better; but once in special,
> In thin array, after a pleasant guise,
> When her loose gown from her shoulders did fall,
> And she me caught in her arms long and small [slender],
> Therewith all sweetly did me kiss,
> And softly said, 'Dear heart, how like you this?'

It was no dream; I lay broad waking:
But all is turned, thorough my gentleness,
Into a strange fashion of forsaking;
And I have leave to go, of her goodness;
And she also to use newfangleness.
But since that I so kindely am servèd,
I would fain know what she hath deservèd.

(*Norton Anthology of English Literature*, Vol. I, fourth edn, 1979.)

Where Dickie our Drake . . . takes the frog: KINGS, IV, 2: A further reference to the song 'The Frogge would a wooing ride' (KINGS, I, 2).

Whereby all men of birth may discover a gentleman from a yeoman: CAS-TLE, II, 4: Sir Thomas Malory (d. 1471) on the language of venery and the delineation of class that its use indicates. In sixteenth-century France it was a criminal offence for those not of gentle blood to presume to hunt big game. For the first offence, the perpetrator would be fined twenty-five livres, or in default of payment, whipped until blood flowed. For a second offence, banishment was mandatory. Defiance would be met with the death penalty. (C.E. Hare, *The Language of Field Sports*.)

Whifflers: CASTLE, III, 9: Ushers or **heralds** who lead the way in a procession, rapidly swishing their wooden wands. They are mentioned by Machyn's diary for March 1555 at the Lady Day joust at Westminster, where King Philip's whifflers, footmen and armourers wore blue-trimmed yellow costumes and a company 'like Turks' rode in crimson satin. Whifflers are not, however, performers at a whiffle. (John Nicholl, *The Worshipful Company of Ironmongers*; Machyn's *Diary*, printed by the Camden Society.)

White Bear Society: RISING, 4: The ancient jousting society of **Bruges**, founded in honour of the old Foresters of Flanders, and revived in 1417. Their headquarters were in the **Poorterslogie** of Bruges, with a statue of their namesake on the outside of the building.

The Society would hold its annual tournament after Easter, awarding three prizes annually: a lance, a horn, and the carved figure of a bear. The tournaments ceased in 1487 when there was both a lack of funds and disinclination to continue with the chivalric posture.

Perhaps one origin for the name of the Society of Foresters comes in an old northern European folk tale. A prince went out hunting in the forest, and came across a magnificent white bear. He was about to shoot the bear when it said to him, 'Don't shoot me, kiss me!' The stunned prince obliged, and the bear miraculously turned into a beautiful princess; the hunter prince having rescued her from an evil enchantment. Of course the ending to the tale is a

happy one; the prince and princess were married and lived in connubial bliss
ever after.

White Company: SCORPIONS, 46: An amalgam of free veteran companies of
mercenaries, operating in the south of France in the mid-fourteenth century
under the control of the English captain **Sir John Hawkwood.** They variously
took service for Milan, the papacy and Florence. The English troops were
known as the White Company on account of the highly burnished plate
armour worn by their men at arms.

**Who sculptured Love and set him by the pool, Thinking with liquid such
a flame to cool:** UNICORN, 33, 35: A couplet ascribed to one of the early Librar-
ians of the Mouseion of Alexandria, and translated by R. A. Furness. (E. M.
Forster, *Alexandria.*)

Whoever lay by the rose has emphatically borne the flower away: KNIGHTS,
III, 13: A paraphrase of the following verse:

> All night by the Rose, Rose,
> All night by the Rose I lay.
> Dare I not the Rose stele,
> And yet I bare the flower away.

Whom have ye known die honestly without the help of a potecary?: PAWN,
29: From the play *The Four P's* by Thomas Heywood (c. 1497–c. 1578). The
mountebank explains to the other characters that his role in this life is without
equal; no one has ever reached Heaven without being dead first, and he has
helped so many people to die with his potions and cures, that he has provided
an invaluable service. (Karl J. Holzknecht, *Tudor and Stuart Plays in Outline*,
London, 1963.)

Whose nature, unlike the mastiff, is to be tenderly nosed: CHECKMATE, I, 3:
The comment of fourteenth-century hunting expert Gaston III, Count of
Foix, on the character of the mastiff: 'they are of a churlish nature and ugly
shape . . . their nature is not to be tenderly nosed'. Since they were not skilled
at picking up scent, mastiffs were used instead for wolf hunting. (Edward, Second Duke of York, *The Master of Game*, 1413, tr. from Gaston III, 1904.)

Whoso list to hunt, I know where is an hart: CHECKMATE, IV, 1: See **And
whoso list to hunt . . .**

Widdershins: KNIGHTS, III, 2: Scots for counterclockwise; often seen, like left-
handedness, as a 'sinister' sign of evil. One could conjure the devil by running
round a church widdershins.

Wildfire: See **Naphtha.**

Willoughby, Sir Hugh: CHECKMATE: (d. 1554) Capable military commander who had served in the English campaign against Scotland in 1544 and rose to favour under Protector **Somerset,** from whom he received his knighthood. Somerset's fall from power, followed by **Warwick**'s attempt to raise Lady Jane Grey to the monarchy, led Willoughby to turn his attentions from land to sea. He sailed aboard the *Confidentia* in company with **Chancellor**'s ship in the attempt to find the northeast passage to Cathay and India, but his absolute ignorance of all things nautical (including the lack of basic navigational skills) meant that his ship was doomed as soon as it became separated from Chancellor. Willoughby's ship drifted for a month as provisions dwindled, but they finally managed to winter at the harbour of Arzina, near to Kegor. Willoughby and his crew all perished in the Arctic winter; the ship itself was later discovered when Chancellor made his return voyage to Russia.

The English Calendar of State Papers relates how news of their death reached England in 1555. Chancellor's men found the *Confidentia* with many of the crew still on board, frozen like statues, 'as if they had been adjusted and placed there'; some in the act of writing, the pen still in their hand and the paper in front of them. The merchandise and personal effects of the crew were all returned intact to the men of the Muscovy company.

Wills, wives and wrecks: CASTLE, III, 2: See **Doctors' Commons.**

WILTON, Grey of: KINGS: See **Grey of Wilton, Sir William.**

Winchester, Bishop of, Organ: QUEENS, II, 4: The enormous instrument of Bishop Elpheges (AD 951), consisting of four hundred pipes. Seventy men were required to work the twenty-six pairs of bellows which provided the massive amount of pressure needed to work the organ. (C. A. Harris & Mary Hargreave, *The Story of British Music*.)

Wishart, George: KINGS, Gambit: (1513–1546) Scots Reformed cleric who studied in Germany and Switzerland and worked as an evangelist in England and Scotland. In 1545, his preaching came to the attention of Cardinal Beaton of St Andrews. In 1546, he was arrested and tried for heresy for the manner in which he espoused and publicised the heretical doctrines of the Reformers. He was found guilty of heresy, and sent to the stake in March 1546. Cardinal Beaton had the pleasure of watching Wishart burn, but his supremacy was to be short-lived. In May of the same year, a group of vengeful Protestant conspirators entered the castle of St Andrews and murdered the Cardinal; hanging his corpse from the ramparts. While they held control of the castle, they founded the first congregation of the Protestant Church in Scotland. The castle was eventually restored to its rightful rulers by the

French reinforcements of **Leone Strozzi**. Those involved in the rebellion were sentenced to death, or periods of service on the French galleys. Amongst those in the latter category was **John Knox**. (Charles Rogers, *Life of George Wishart*, Edinburgh, 1876.)

Witch ball: CASTLE, II, 5: A large glass ball, often lined with mercury to turn the sphere into a circular mirror. Rather like vampires, witches did not exhibit a reflection (as their soul was no longer intact). Tudor doctors would often hang a witch ball outside their shop, to prevent witches from entering. The fear of witches is one reason why broom was popularly used for hedges; witches were not able to cross its path. The same was the case with running water.

With Emeroides in the hinder parts: CHECKMATE, I, 6: Mainly quoted within the text, the verse is Psalm 78, 66. The version used is the Geneva Psalms, printed by John Crespin in London, 1569. Haemorrhoids are also known as *'le mal de St Fiacre'*, and caused the death of Henry V of England, as well as being the bane of King **Louis XI** of France.

Without pitie, hangèd to be: KINGS, I, 2: From the anonymous poem 'The Nut-Brown Maid'. An outlawed Knight laments that he must leave his beloved and flee to the greenwood; she (the Nut-Brown Maid) swears she will faithfully stand by him (extract):

> He:
> 'For an outlaw, this is the law
> That men him take and bind
> Without pitie, hangèd to be,
> And waver with the wind.
> If I had need, (as God forbede!)
> What rescues could ye find?
> Forsooth, I trow, you and your bow
> Should draw for fear behind.
> And no mervail: for little avail
> Were in your counsel than:
> Wherefore I to the wood will go,
> Alone, a banished man.'
>
> She:
> 'Full well know ye, that women be
> Full feeble for to fight:
> No womanhede it is indeed
> To be bold as a knight:
> Yet, in such fear if that ye were

Among enemies day and night,
I could withstand, with bow in hand,
To grieve them as I might,
And you to save, as women have
From death many a one:
For in my mind, of all mankind
I love but you alone.'
(H. Macauley Fitzgibbon, ed., *Early English Poetry*.)

Wooing o' Jock and Jenny: PAWN, 21: One of the most ancient Scots ballads still preserved, 'The Wowing of Jok and Jynny' relates the numerous goods which the prospective groom offers his bride if she will consent to the match. The poem is also known as 'The wooing of John and Joan', or 'Quoth John to Joan'; see **I can say naught but Hoy gee ho!** where the anglicised (and more modern) version is given. The extract below is taken from the Bannatyne manuscript of 1568:

Robeyns Jok come to wow [woo] our Jynny,
On our feist evin quhen we wer fow;
Scho brankit [hasted away] fast, and made hir bony,
And said, Jok, come ye for to wow?
Scho birneist hir baith breist and brow,
And maid hir cleir as ony clok [shining as a beetle];
Than spak hir deme [dame], and said, I trow,
Ye come to wow our Jynny, Jok.

Jock said, forsuth, I yern full fane,
To luk my heid, and sit doun by yow.
Thank spak hir modir, and said agane,
My bairne hes tocher-gud to ge yow.
Tee hec, quoth Jenny, keik, keik, I se yow;
Muder, yone man makis yow a mok.
O schro the, lyar! full leis me yow [Curse you for a liar, I love you heartily],
I come to wow our Jynny, quoth Jok.

My berne, scho sayis, hes of hir awin,
Ane guss [goose], ane gryce [pig], ane cok, ane hen,
Ane calf, ane hog, ane fute-braid sawin [corn to sow a foot's breadth],
Ane kirn [chum], ane pin, that ye weill ken,
Ane pig, ane pot, ane raip [rope] thair ben,
Ane fork, ane flaik [hurdle], ane reill, ane rok [distaff],
Dischis and dublaris [dishes with covers] nyne or ten;
Come ye to wow our Jynny, Jok? . . .

Ane furme [bench], ane furlet, ane pott, ane pek,
Ane tub, ane barrow, with ane quheilband,
Ane turs, ane troch, and ane meil-sek,
Ane spurtill braid and ane elwand [ell-measure].
Jock tuk Jynny be the hand,
And cryd, ane feist; and slew ane cok,
And maid a brydell up alland [was married up the country];
Now haif I gottin your Jynny, quoth Jok . . .

Words is but wind, but dunts is the devil: KINGS, I, 2: Traditional Scots proverb, 'dunts' being strokes or blows. Compare with the 'enlightened' version of the same saying as quoted by Allan Ramsay in 1750, 'Words are but wind, but dunts are out of season'. (Allan Ramsay, *Scots Proverbs*, Edinburgh, 1750.)

Worship the buttock-bone of Pentecost: CASTLE, I, 7: Some of the less savoury relics carried by the Pardoner in the sixteenth-century play *The Four Ps* by Thomas Heywood (c. 1497–c. 1578). The Pardoner also invites the complete suspension of disbelief by showing off the eye-tooth of the Great Turk, the bumble bees which stung Eve when she picked the forbidden fruit and the divine yeast which brewed Adam and Eve's wedding ale. (Karl J. Holzknecht, *Tudor and Stuart Plays in Outline*, London, 1963.)

Wyatt, Sir Thomas: CHECKMATE, IV, 1: (c. 1503–1542) The renowned English lyric poet, amongst the first to introduce the Italian sonnet form into England. Wyatt was both courtier and diplomat to Henry VIII's court, acting as Clerk of the King's jewels, and English Ambassador to the court of **Charles V.** Wyatt fell foul of Henry VIII's quixotic temper on a number of occasions; in 1535 he was arrested after a quarrel with the Duke of Suffolk, and in 1541 was sent to the Tower of London on a charge of treason. He was pardoned on both occasions by the King, and regained his property, but shortly after the treason charge decided that he could no longer continue to dissemble and flatter enough for life at court, retired to the country and died the following year. His son, also called Thomas (d. 1554) was involved in a conspiracy against **Mary Tudor**; see **Courtenay, Sir Edward.**

Wynd: KNIGHTS, III, 17: From the Anglo-Saxon *windan*, 'to turn'. In Scotland, it signified a lane running from a main street, wide enough to admit the passage of a cart.

Xenophon: RAM, 15, 17: (c. 430–356 BC) Born just outside the city of Athens at the start of the Peloponnesian war, Xenophon was a pupil of Socrates and a significant and likeable man of his time. Drawn by his own imagination and energy into the wars of young Cyrus of Persia, he made his reputation as a military commander in the famous Retreat of the Ten Thousand when, after the murder of Cyrus, Xenophon took command of the stranded Greek troops and led them back from the Tigris to the Black Sea, a journey of about 3,000 miles achieved in 215 days. They reached the sea at last at **Trebizond**, then a Hellenic colony of Sinope, and moved to Kerasous, where a count showed their numbers reduced to 8,600. Apart from war and privation, some of the deaths had occurred in the hills about Trebizond where, finding the villages full of beehives, the army gorged itself to such excess that it was rendered incapable as if drunk or drugged, and some died of it. In later years, Xenophon devoted his leisure to writing. His account of this expedition is famous, but he also produced many other works including histories, military manuals and work on hunting, all in the lucid prose taught by Socrates, about whom Xenophon also wrote. Out of all this, Xenophon's most lasting contribution to the future was probably his writing on horsemanship, the earliest work on the subject to survive. When, in Renaissance times, the revived interest in the classics led to a rediscovery of Xenophon's great work *The Art of Horsemanship*, some of the techniques of his period developed into the pirouettes and levades which the nobility employed in their spectacular carousels. His advice was less apposite in other directions: Greek horsemen of the time often rode without saddles, Xenophon holding that 'bare flesh on a sweated coat' gave the best purchase (he preferred roundbacked horses). Nor, unfortunately, did later disciples pay as much attention as Xenophon did to the need to understand and respect the horse.

Yâ Fattâh: PAWN, 22: Traditional Arabic beggar's cry, 'O thou the open handed'.

Ye leid, ye leid, ye filthy nurse: KINGS, IV, 1: From the anonymous 'Ballad of Child Maurice'. See also **My bird Willie, my boy Willie.** In a classic case of mistaken identity, Maurice's servant asks Lord Barnard's *wife* to meet Maurice in the woods instead of Barnard's *nurse*, who is Maurice's mother. Maurice is ultimately murdered by the jealous Lord Barnard (extract):

> The lady stamped wi her foot,
> And winked wi her eie:
> But a that she cold say or do
> Forbidden he wald nae be.
>
> 'It's surely to my bower-woman,
> It neir cold be to me.
> I brocht it to lord Barnards lady,
> I trow that ye be she.'
>
> Than up and spake the wylie nurse,
> (The bairn upon her knie)
> 'If it be come from Child Maurice
> It's deir welcum to me.'
>
> 'Ye lie, ye lie, ye filthy nurse,
> Sae loud as I heir ye lie:
> I brocht it to lord Barnards lady
> I trow ye bae nae shee.'

Ye shall be buxom and obedient to all justices: PAWN, 24: See **Leet oath.**

Yiğit Olanlar anilir: PAWN, 15: This fourteenth-century **Bektashi** poem and its translation (given within the text) expresses the simplistic theology of the peerless divinity of God. (John K. Birge, *The Bektashi Order of Dervishes*, London, 1937.)

You have no arm at all . . . unless England allows you a sleeve for it: CHECK-MATE, V, 9: A reference to the French name for the English Channel, 'La Manche' (sleeve). English mastery of the seas in the sixteenth century was significantly to limit the power of her potential aggressors.

You mee embraced; in bosom soft you mee: CHECKMATE, V, 13: From a Funeral Song by Nicholas Grimald (1519–1562) of Christ's College, Cambridge, addressed to his mother. It appeared in *Tottel's Miscellany* of poems, which he helped to compile:

> You mee embraced, in bosom soft you mee
> Cherished, as I your onely chylde had bee.
> Of yssue fayr with noombers were you blest·
> Yet I, the bestbeloved of all the rest.
> Good luck, certayn forereadyng moothers have,
> And you of mee a speciall iudgement gave.
> Then, when firm pase I fixèd on the ground:
> When toung gan cease to break the lispyng sound:
> You mee streightway did to the Muses send,
> Ne sufferend long a loyteryng lyfe to spend.

(A.C. Partridge, *The Language of Renaissance Poetry*, London, 1971)

You that in love find lucke and habundance: CHECKMATE, I, 2: The poem by Sir Thomas Wyatt, 'Ye that in love finde luck and swet abundance':

> Ye that in love finde luck and swet abundance,
> And lyve in lust of joyfull jolitie,
> Aryse for shame, do way your sluggards:
> Aryse I say, do May some observance:
> Let me in bed lye, dreamyng of mischance.
> Let me remember my missehappes unhappy,
> That me betide in May most commonly:
> As one whom love list little to advance.
> Stephan said true, that my nativitie
> Mischanced was with the rules of May,
> He gest (I prove) of that the veritie.
> In May my wealth, and eke my wittes, I say
> Have stand so oft in such perplexitie,
> Joye: let me dream of your felicitie.

Yúnus the Illiterate: PAWN, 2: A fourteenth-century Arabic poet who composed six hundred couplets in *mesneví* verse and a *divan* of over three hundred *gházels*. His illiteracy in no way stunted the beauty of his verse, indeed it left his imagination uncluttered by the complexity of the written language: 'The mirror of his heart was undulled by the turbidity of the lines and curves'. See also **Ottoman poetry.** (E.J.W. Gibb, *History of Ottoman Poetry.*)

ZACCO, King of Cyprus: SCORPIONS: (b. c. 1440) The Venetian pronunciation of the name of James II of Lusignan, King of Cyprus, one of the most picturesque of the contenders for the island which, over the centuries, has always been subject to strife because of its strategic importance in the eastern Mediterranean. The fall of Constantinople in 1453 and the consequent advances of Sultan **Mehmet II** caused Western Christendom to increase to fever pitch its normal violent interest in the ownership of Cyprus, a condition shared (to everyone's theological embarrassment) with those Muslim rulers of Egypt and Persia who also feared the power of the Ottoman Turks. When, accordingly, the death in 1458 of King John II left the island torn between the claims of a legitimate offspring (unfortunately female, **Carlotta**) and Zacco, a charming illegitimate son, an interested line of supporters immediately formed up behind each contestant. Behind Carlotta (child of a termagent Byzantine mother) were the **Knights of St John** at Rhodes, with whom she eventually stayed, to their sorrow, some considerable time; Pope **Pius II**, who financed her but found her over-talkative and excitable; and Genoa, which had a trading station it longed to keep in **Famagusta**. She also had the goodwill, if nothing more concrete, of Burgundy and France, and some grudging money from her husband's ruling family in Savoy.

The rest, not surprisingly, fell for Zacco. Wildly high-spirited, handsome, eloquent, he was the natural son of John of Lusignan (himself a descendant of the **Fairy Melusine**) and of a Greek girl, Marietta of Patras, who probably came to Cyprus in the train of the Queen, Helen Paleologa. Helen, less than amused by her husband's infatuation, retaliated by biting off the nose of her rival, a traditional form of punishment for adultery, although unorthodox in its execution, being more generally accomplished with a knife. From that time, Marietta was known as Commutene, or Cropnose, but nevertheless remained in **Nicosia** close to the King, employing her considerable matriarchal talents in the training and positioning of her son upon whom the King doted, appointing him Archbishop of Nicosia at the age of thirteen. Cropnose was to support her son throughout his reign, not to mention caring for his happy, carelessly loved brood of illegitimate children, engendered during the long years when policy dictated that would-be allies should vie with one another to provide him with a bride.

When it became apparent, on the death of King John, that Carlotta's strong party of adherents wished to see her crowned and also to exclude her half-brother from any position of power, Zacco promptly left the island for Cairo, where he made himself popular with the Mameluke Sultan Inal by acknowledging the Sultan's suzerainty over Cyprus ('If you cherish me, Cyprus will be as much yours as Egypt is'). Already sanctioned by his faith to place male claimants before female (a tendency lingering also in the Christian world), the Sultan had every reason, financial and political, to support Zacco as legal heir. In 1460 Zacco returned to Cyprus with a **Mameluke** army in a fleet of eighty ships under the Grand Devitdar—an act which the Knights of St John and the Throne of St Peter found hard to forgive at the time, although in later years Muslim aid would be fervently courted by both. In the war against Queen Carlotta (now crowned) which followed, Zacco employed his Mameluke army, reduced after the initial onslaught to a company under the troublesome Emir **Tzani-bey.** He also had the tacit support of **Venice,** which did not wish the Genoese or Naples or Milan or the Knights to control the island which they wanted to make their personal bastion, and where they already had a strong invested interest in the **sugar** crop through **Marco Corner.** Although immensely courageous, bludgeoning her court into action and relentlessly active in her own travels to raise money for her cause, Carlotta was forced to retire to the northern half of the island, allowing Zacco to re-enter and hold Nicosia. Fortified Kyrenia held out bravely for years but was at last conquered, and in due course the Genoese holding **Famagusta** were starved into surrendering after a desperate siege. Carlotta spent the rest of her life first in Rhodes and then in Rome, but her tireless efforts to raise troops and money were in vain.

Zacco now had no need of his Mameluke troops. A 'misunderstanding' resulted in the slaughter of the entire force and its commander, which caused a certain coolness with Cairo, but relations were resumed with a punitive increase in tribute. The island was now wholly under Zacco, but faced a period of hardship following the depradations of wartime, the increased taxes and imponderables such as plagues of locusts and lethal epidemics during which a large proportion of the population died. Intrigues and defections had always occurred at the Cypriot courts and these continued, exacerbated by the attempts of outside powers to infiltrate and control as the threat from the Turk became stronger. On the whole, Zacco's vigour and personality were sufficient to maintain his authority (with the help of his mother) but poisonings and stabbings were not uncommon. Zacco himself took a full share in the more precipitate episodes, such as when he had a musician, a certain Master Nicolas or Nicolino Constantino, flogged for playing badly. (The musician then attempted to stab the King with his own dagger.)

In 1468, now the recognised sovereign of Cyprus, Zacco yielded to Venetian pressure and allowed himself to be married by proxy to **Catherine Corner,** the daughter of the merchant Marco. For four further years he hedged his bets: while his young bride remained in Venice, Zacco continued to hold out hopes to all the rival claimants that he would cancel the unconsummated bond and marry someone else. But in the end, on the acrimonious insistence of Venice, and fearing the ill intentions of Milan against Famagusta, he gave in and had the girl shipped to him. Venice had won. (Sir George Hill, *A History of Cyprus*, Vol. II, Oxford, 1948; Sir Harry Luke, *Cyprus*; L. de Mas Latrie, *Histoire de l'Isle de Chypre*.)

Zara Ya'qob: SCALES: See **Prester John.**

ZENO, Caterino: SCORPIONS: Venetian merchant and husband of Violante, the granddaughter of Emperor John IV Comnenos of **Trebizond** (d. 1458). In 1471 he was sent as an envoy of the Republic of Venice to Persia, giving him the opportunity to improve his relationship with **Uzum Hasan.** The aunt of Zeno's wife had married the head of the White Sheep. (See also **Naxos.**)

Zenobia: KINGS, IV, 2: Celebrated Princess and ruler of Palmyra in Syria after the death of her husband in AD 266. In addition to stunning good looks, she was credited with a mind equally talented in jurisprudence, finance, languages, good government and successful warfare. In battle, she was continually on horseback to keep up with the rapid progress of her marching troops.

Although pure and moderate in her behaviour, Zenobia showed her equality by challenging her male Syrian and Persian rivals to drinking competitions, where she successfully drank them under the table. She was eventually defeated and her empire crushed by the Roman emperor Aurelian.

Ziraffe: PAWN, 10: See **Camelopard.**

Zoroaster: KINGS, Gambit: Also known as Zarathustra; the prophet of ancient Iran from the sixth century BC. His religion, Zoroastrianism, was eventually overtaken in the seventh century AD with the rise of Islam. Followers who exiled themselves in India later became the sect known as the Parsis. In addition to his religious and moral teachings, he is also credited as having certain magical powers. As a child, he was placed on a lit stake which immediately turned into a bed of roses, upon which he slept.

At the root of his religious philosophy is the inherent dualism of two warring spirits, Ahura Mazda (or Ormazd) representing good, and Anra Mainyu (or Ahriman) representing the impulse to evil.

ZORZI, Bartolomeo: SCORPIONS: As a Venetian, Bartolomeo gained control over the **alum** concession of Phocaea when it was seized by **Mehmet II** in 1455. The profitable concession, run by Zorzi and a partner, was to come to an end in 1463 when the Turk turned against the Venetian Empire. Zorzi was forced to flee, owing the Sultan 150,000 ducats. In 1469, he once more exploited his knowledge of alum by becoming the agent in Venice for papal alum coming from Tolfa. He was eventually supplanted in the role by the **Medici** family.

Zyf you know er you knyt, you mayst you Abate: CHECKMATE, I, 3: Fragment of poetry, to which the concluding line of the couplet is 'And yf you knyt er you knowe, Than yt ys to late'. The comment is fairly obvious: If you know the truth before you commit yourself to someone, then you can stop in time, but if you are tied before you realise fully the implications, it is obviously too late to retract.

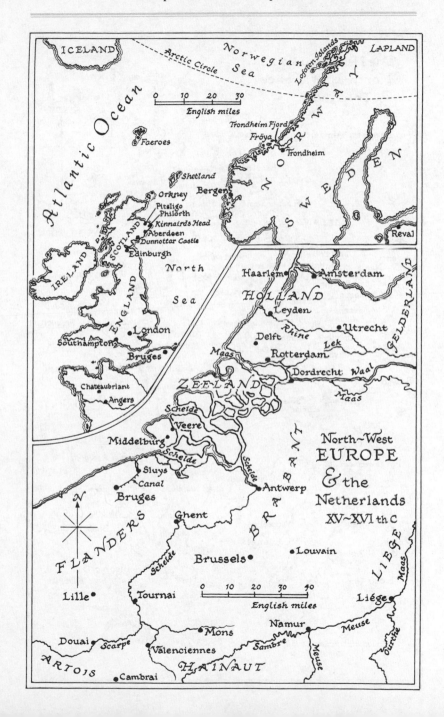

The Netherlands,
North~East France
& The Rhine
circa 1500

Bremen ~ underlining denotes
Imperial Free City

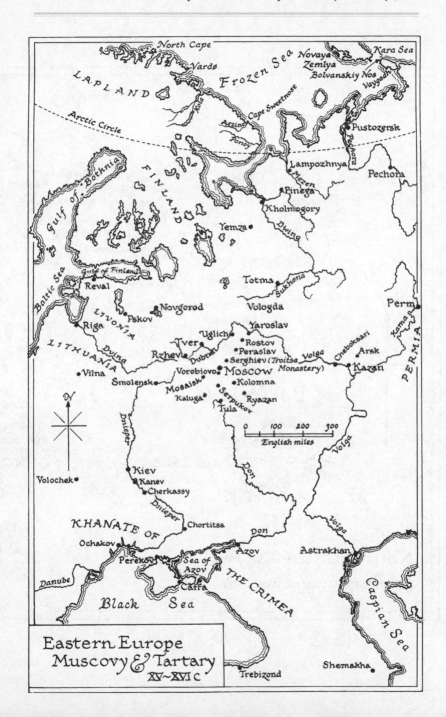

North Cape
Vardø
Kola
Frozen Sea
Novaya Zemlya
Kara Sea
Bolvanskiy Nos
Vaygach
LAPLAND
Arctic Circle
Arzina
Cape Sweetnose
Ponoy
Pustozersk
Pechora
Lampozhnya
Mezen
Pinega
Kholmogory
Dvina
PERMIA
Gulf of Bothnia
FINLAND
Yemza
Gulf of Finland
Reval
Totma
Sukhona
Vologda
Perm
Kama
Baltic Sea
Novgorod
LIVONIA
Pskov
Riga
Dvina
Yaroslav
Uglich
Rostov
Peraslav
Tver
Rzhev
Dubna
Serghiev (Troitsa Monastery)
Volga
Cheboksari
Arsk
LITHUANIA
Vilna
Smolensk
Vorobiovo
MOSCOW
Kolomna
Kazan
Mosaisk
Kaluga
Serpukov
Ryazan
Tula
0   100   200   300
English miles
Dnieper
Don
Volga
Kiev
Kanev
Cherkassy
Volochek
Dnieper
Chortitsa
Don
Volga
KHANATE OF
Ochakov
Perekov
Azov
Astrakhan
Danube
Sea of Azov
THE CRIMEA
Caffa
Caspian Sea
Black Sea
N

Eastern Europe
Muscovy & Tartary
XV–XVI C

Shemakha
Trebizond

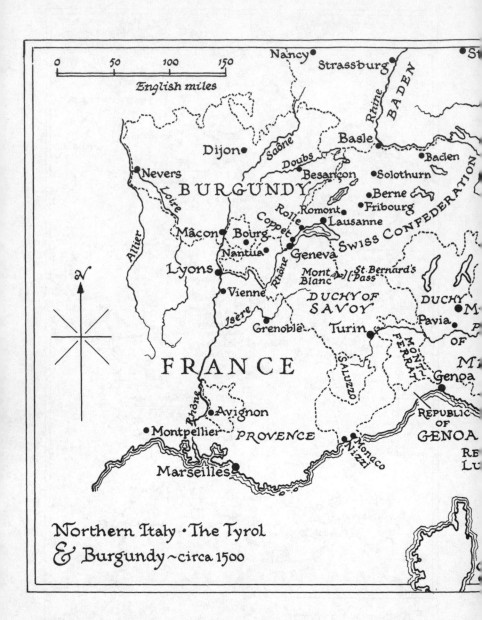

Northern Italy · The Tyrol & Burgundy ~circa 1500

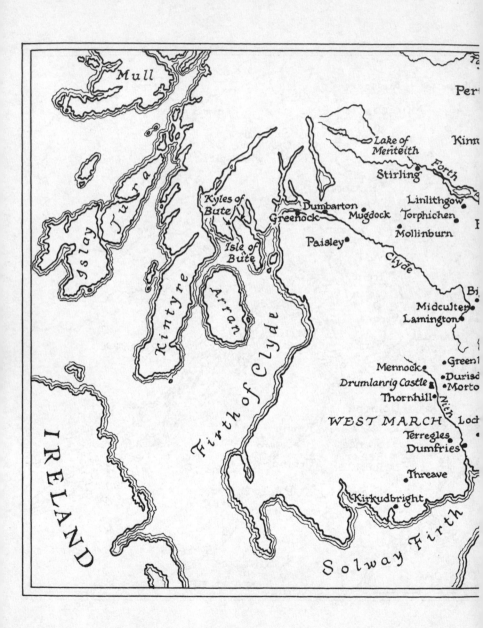

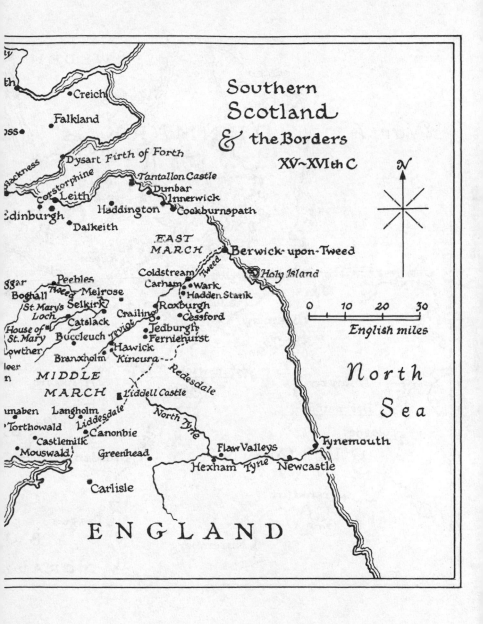

The Baltic Region
& Northern part of the
Holy Roman Empire

Danzig~ underlining denotes
cities of the Hansa

The Western Mediterranean XV~XVIth C

FRANC
Bordeaux

Atlantic Ocean

To

Porto
Tordesillas
(Valladolid)
Duero
Salamanca
Madrid
Saragossa
B

PORTUGAL

Lisbon
Tajo
Toledo

SPAIN
Valencia

Córdoba
Seville
Guadalquivir
Formen
Málaga
Granada

M

Cádiz
Alg
Tangier
Ceuta
Melilla
Tigz
Oran
Rabat
Tlemcen
Meknes
Fez
Oujda
Taza
BARBA

Marrakesh

Figuig

0   100   200   400

English miles

The
Eastern
Mediterranean
& The Levant
XV~XVI th C

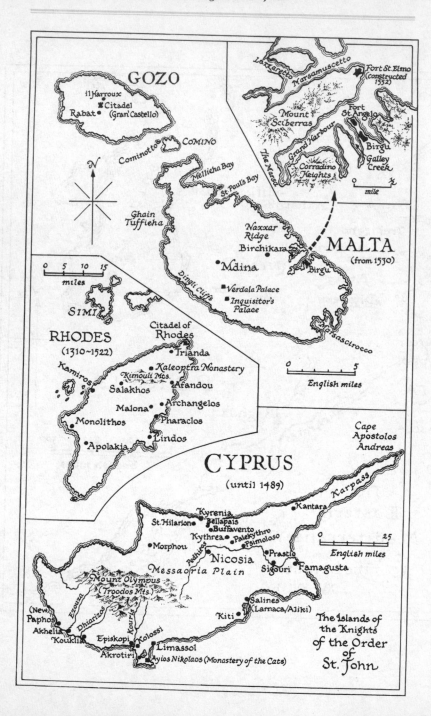

GOZO

il Harroux
✠ Citadel
Rabat • (Gran' Castello)

Cominotto COMINO

N

Mellieha Bay

St. Paul's Bay

Ghain
Tuffieha

Naxxar
Ridge
Birchikara

MALTA
(from 1530)

• Mdina

Birgu

■ Verdala Palace

■ Inquisitor's
Palace

Dingli Cliffs

Marsascirocco

Lazaretto
Marsamuscetto

Fort St. Elmo
(constructed
1552)

Mount
Sciberras

Fort
St. Angelo

Birgu
Galley
Creek

The Marsa

Grand Harbour

Corradino
Heights

½
mile

0   5   10   15
miles

SIMI

RHODES
(1310~1522)

Citadel of
Rhodes

Trianda

Kaleoptra Monastery

Kimouli Mts.

Kamiros

Salakhos

Afandou

Malona

Archangelos

Monolithos

Pharaclos

Apolakia

Lindos

0   5
English miles

Cape
Apostolos
Andreas

CYPRUS

(until 1489)

Karpass

Kyrenia

Kantara

St. Hilarion

Bellapais

Buffavento

Kythrea

Palekythro

Morphou

Psimoloso

Pedhios

Nicosia

Prastio

Messaoria Plain

Sigouri

Famagusta

0   25
English miles

Mount Olympus
(Troodos Mts.)

Salines
(Larnaca/Aliki)

(New)
Paphos

Kiti

Akhelia

Kouklia

Episkopi

Kolossi

Akrotiri

Limassol

Ayios Nikolaos (Monastery of the Cats)

Erouza

Dhiarizos

Kouris

The Islands of
the Knights
of the Order
of
St. John

KEY

1. Topkapi   2. St. Sophia
3. Hippodrome   4. Bazaar
5. Column of Constantine
6. Beyazit Mosque
7. Old Seraglio
8. Mosque of Suleiman
9. Aqueduct of Valens
10. Mosque of Mehmet II
11. Mosque of Selim
12. Edirne Gate
13. Christ Tower
14. Column of Arcadius
15. Golden Gate
16. Genoese Fort
17. Castle of the Seven Towers
18. Leander Tower

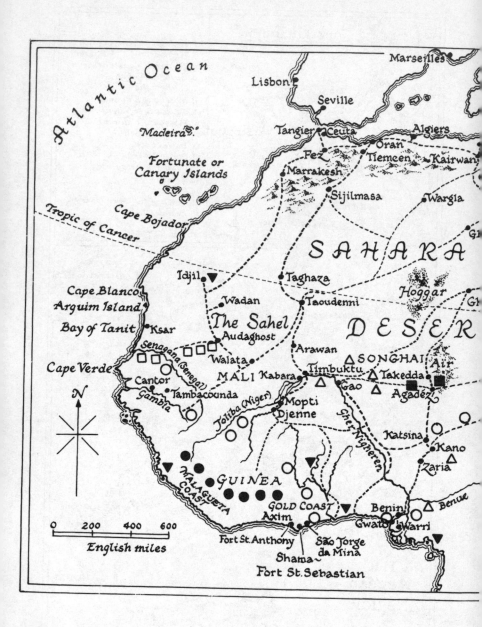

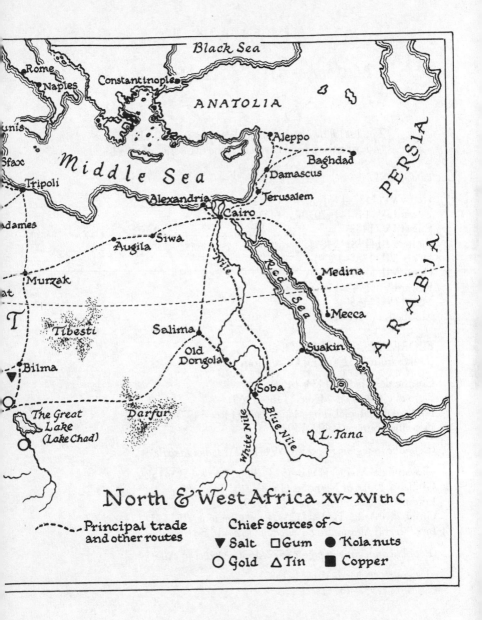

Black Sea

Rome
Naples
Constantinople
ANATOLIA

unis
Sfax
Tripoli
adames
Middle Sea
Alexandria
Aleppo
Baghdad
Damascus
Jerusalem
Cairo
PERSIA

Augila
Siwa
Murzak
at
Tibesti
Nile
Red Sea
Medina
Mecca
ARABIA

Salima
Old Dongola
Suakin

Bilma
Darfur
Soba

The Great
Lake
(Lake Chad)
White Nile
Blue Nile
L. Tana

North & West Africa XV~XVI th C

- - - - - Principal trade
and other routes

Chief sources of ~

▼ Salt   □ Gum   ● Kola nuts
○ Gold   △ Tin   ■ Copper

APPENDIX 1

MONARCHS AND RULERS

The list following shows the dates of reigns of rulers active during the period covered by the two series of novels:

ENGLAND

Henry VI (1422–1461, then 1470–1471)
Edward IV (1461–1470, then 1471–1483)
Edward V (1483)
Richard III (1483–1485)
Henry VII (1485–1509)
Henry VIII (1509–1547)
Edward VI (1547–1553)
Mary (1553–1558)
Elizabeth I (1558–1603)

FLORENCE, THE MEDICI OF
(Dukes from 1532, Grand Dukes from 1569)

Cosimo de' Medici (1434–1464)
Piero di Cosimo de' Medici (1464–1469)
Lorenzo de' Medici, The Magnificent (1469–1492)
Piero the Younger (1492–1494)

(*Republican regime in power 1494–1512, Medici in exile*)

Giovanni de' Medici (1512–1513) (Pope Leo X 1513–1521)
Giuliano, Duke of Nemours (1513)
Lorenzo, Duke of Urbino (1513–1519)
Giulio de' Medici (1519–1523) (Pope Clement VII 1523–1534)
Ippolito and Alessandro de' Medici (1523–1527)

(*Republican regime in power 1527–1530, Medici in exile*)

Alessandro de' Medici (1531–1537)
Cosimo I (1537–1574)

FRANCE

Charles VII (1422–1461)
Louis XI (1461–1483)
Charles VIII (1483–1498)
Louis XII (1498–1515)
Francis I (1515–1547)
Henri II (1547–1559)
Francis II (1559–1560)

MILAN, DUCHY OF

Francesco Sforza (1450–1466)
Galeazzo Maria Sforza (1466–1476)
Gian Galeazzo Sforza (1476–1494)
Lodovico (Il Moro) Sforza (1494–1499)
Louis XII of France (1499–1500)
Lodovico (Il Moro) Sforza (1500)
Louis XII of France (1500–1512)
Massimiliano Sforza (1512–1515)
Francis I of France (1515–1521)
Francesco II Sforza (1521–1524) (Puppet Duke 1524–1535)
Francis I of France (1525)
Charles V of Habsburg, Holy Roman Emperor (1525–1535)

(Followed by Imperial governors and occupied by Spanish troops)

NAPLES

Alfonso V of Aragon (1416–1458; King of Naples from 1442 and of Sicily from 1416)
Ferrante (Ferdinand I) of Aragon (1458–1494)
Alfonso II (1494–1495)
Ferdinand II (1495)
Charles VIII of France (1495)
Ferdinand II (1495–1496)
Federico (1496–1501)
Louis XII of France (1501–1503)

(Followed by Spanish governors from 1503 when it became a Viceroyalty of Spain)

OTTOMAN EMPIRE

Mehmet II (1451–1481)
Bayezid II (1481–1512)
Selim I (1512–1520)
Suleiman II, The Magnificent (1520–1566)

PAPACY

Calixtus III (1455–1458)
Pius II (1458–1464)
Paul II (1464–1471)
Sixtus IV (1471–1484)
Innocent VIII (1484–1492)
Alexander VI (1492–1503)
Pius III (1503)
Julius II (1503–1513)
Leo X (1513–1521)
Adrian VI (1522–1523)
Clement VII (1523–1534)
Paul III (1534–1549)
Julius III (1550–1555)
Marcellus II (1555)
Paul IV (1555–1559)
Pius IV (1559–1565)

HOLY ROMAN EMPIRE

Frederick III (c. 1440–1493)
Maximilian I (1493–1519)
Charles V (1519–1556)
Ferdinand I (1556–1564)

RUSSIA, GRAND DUCHY OF MOSCOW

Vasily II (1425–1462)
Ivan III, The Great (1462–1505)
Vasily III (1505–1533)
Ivan IV Grozny, The Terrible (1533–1584)

SCOTLAND

James II (1437–1460)
James III (1460–1488)
James IV (1488–1513)
James V (1513–1542)
Mary (1542–1567)

VENICE, DOGES OF THE REPUBLIC OF

Pasquale Malipiero (1457–1462)
Cristoforo Moro (1462–1471)
Niccolò Tron (1471–1473)
Niccolò Marcello (1473–1474)
Pietro Mocenigo (1474–1476)
Andrea Vendramin (1476–1478)
Giovanni Mocenigo (1478–1485)
Marco Barbarigo (1485–1486)
Agostino Barbarigo (1486–1501)
Leonardo Loredan (1501–1521)
Antonio Grimani (1521–1523)
Andrea Gritti (1523–1538)
Pietro Lando (1539–1545)
Francesco Donato (1545–1553)
Antonio Trevisan (1553–1554)
Francesco Venier (1554–1556)
Lorenzo Priuli (1556–1559)

PRONUNCIATION GUIDE

BELOW is a guide to pronouncing some of the names in the novels. It is obviously impossible to include every foreign name, so only those which are probably very unfamiliar to readers have been included. I have used a phonetic system of my own; the stress is denoted by capital letters. Spanish and Italian 'r's should be slightly rolled.

ACCIAJUOLI: Atch-eye-WOHL-ee
ALESSANDRA MACHINGHI NEGLI STROZZI: Aless-AN-dra ('an' as in 'can') Ma-CHING-ee NEL-yee STROT-see

BAIDA: BYE-da
BUCCLEUCH: Buck-CLOO (running the two syllables together)

CLAES VANDER POELE: Clarss vonder PULLer
CULTER: COOL-ter (or COO-ter, as in the Scots children's song 'Culter's Candy')

DINIZ: Din-EEJE (with the 'j' as in French 'je')
DIOGO GOMES: Deeyorgu Gomj (with the 'j' as in French 'je')
DRAGUT RAIS: Drah-GOOT Rye-EES

GELIS: GEH-lis (with a soft 'g' as in 'jealous')
GODSCALC: Godskalk (with a hard 'c')
GRUUTHUSE: GROOT-hoozer
GUZEL: Goo-ZEL (stress the last syllable, as in 'gazelle')

HOUGH ISA: Howff Eye-za, or How Eye-za ('how' as in 'cow')

JAIME: Jyme (with the 'j' as in French 'je' and rhyming with 'rhyme')
JOÃO VASQUEZ: Ju-ow (with the 'j' as in French 'je', 'ow' as in 'cow') Vashksh
JORGE DA SILVES: Jordj (with the 'j' as in French 'je', 'o' as in 'off') da Silvas
JUAN DE HOMEDES: Chwan (with the 'ch' as in Scottish 'loch') day Om-eh-DEZ ('o' as in 'off')

KATELINA: Kat-eh-LEEN-ner
KATELIJNE SERSANDERS: Kat-eh-LAY-ner Sair-SUN-ders
KHAIREDDIN: Char-ed-EEN (with the 'ch' as in Scottish 'loch', and run swiftly into the second syllable)

LAUDOMIA: Low-DOH-mee-a ('ow' as in 'cow', running the last two syllables together)
LEWISJE: Loh-WAY-zer
LOPEZ: Lopsh
LUADHAUS: LOOuhus (with a dental not a pallatal 'l' sound: try saying it with your mouth full)
LYMOND: LYE-mond

MEHMET: MECH-met (with the 'ch' as in Scottish 'loch')

OCHOA DE MARCHENA: Oh-CHOH-a day (Spanish and Italian 'de' is long, unlike the short French or Portuguese 'de') March-EH-na
OSEP NEPEJA: Osip Neeay-PEEAY-ya

QAYT BEY: Kayt Bay ('q' as a hard 'k' and the vowel a cross between 'kate' and 'kite')

THIBAULT: Teeb-oh
TRISTÃO: Trish-tow

WOLFAERT: Woll-fart ('woll' as in 'jolly')

ZORZI: Dzor-dzi

The Novels of Dorothy Dunnett

(Dates of first publication given in brackets)

The Lymond Chronicles

First published by Cassell & Company Ltd.
All now available in paperback from Vintage Books.

The Games of Kings (1962)

Queens' Play (1964)

The Disorderly Knights (1966)

Pawn in Frankincense (1969)

The Ringed Castle (1971)

Checkmate (1975)

The House of Niccolò

First published by Michael Joseph Ltd. in the UK and
by Alfred A. Knopf in the U.S.
All now available in paperback from Vintage Books. Only the first five
volumes are covered in *The Dorothy Dunnett Companion*.

Niccolò Rising (1986)

The Spring of the Ram (1987)

Race of Scorpions (1989)

Scales of Gold (1991)

The Unicorn Hunt (1993)

To Lie With Lions (1996)

Caprice and Rondo (1998)

Gemini (2000)

ELSPETH MORRISON

THE DOROTHY DUNNETT COMPANION

Elspeth Morrison was born and raised in Edinburgh where she still lives and works as a research historian. She has an MA from the University of Edinburgh, where she specialized in Renaissance history, and an MSc from the University of Strathclyde. She is currently at work on *The Dorothy Dunnett Companion II*.

ALSO BY ELSPETH MORRISON

THE DOROTHY DUNNETT COMPANION II

This sequel to *The Dorothy Dunnett Companion* is another encyclopedic resource, documenting the historical and literary riches in Dorothy Dunnett's beloved Lymond Chronicles and House of Niccolò novels. Once again, Elspeth Morrison illuminates the real figures and events as well as the cultural and literary allusions Dunnett weaves into her acclaimed works of historical fiction, covering for the first time the final three novels of the House of Niccolò and highlighting the links between the two now complete series. Together with the first volume, *The Dorothy Dunnett Companion II* will provide a comprehensive and essential guide to the worlds of Lymond and Niccolò.

Historical Fiction/0-375-72668-3

FORTHCOMING IN SPRING 2002